THE POPULAR SCHOOL

Advisory Editor: Alfred Harbage

The Popular School

A Survey and Bibliography of Recent Studies in English
Renaissance Drama

Edited by

Terence P. Logan and Denzell S. Smith

UNIVERSITY OF NEBRASKA PRESS • LINCOLN

Most recent printing shown by first digit below:
1   2   3   4   5   6   7   8   9   10

Library of Congress Cataloging in Publication Data

Logan, Terence P
The popular school.

Includes index.
1.   English drama—17th century—History and
criticism—Bibliography.   2.   English drama—Early
modern and Elizabethan, 1500-1600—History and
criticism—Bibliography.   I.   Smith, Denzell S.,
joint author.   II.   Title.
Z2014·D7L82   016.822'3'09   74-81364
ISBN 0-8032-0844-8

MANUFACTURED IN THE UNITED STATES OF AMERICA

CONTENTS

PREFACE

This volume is the second in Recent Studies in English Renaissance Drama, a series which in its entirety will provide a detailed account of both the historical development and current state of scholarship on playwrights and plays from 1580 to 1642, exclusive of Shakespeare. The first volume, *The Predecessors of Shakespeare* (1973), dealt with plays first performed between 1580 and 1593. This volume, *The Popular School*, and the next, *The New Intellectuals*, include discussions of dramatists who wrote most of their plays between 1593 and 1616 and of anonymous plays first performed in those years. *The Popular School* includes dramatists who wrote primarily for the open-air public theaters, and anonymous plays first performed in such theaters; *The New Intellectuals* will include dramatists who wrote primarily for private theaters or reflect their influence, and anonymous plays first performed in such theaters. The division was made principally by reference to Alfred Harbage, *Annals of English Drama*, revised by Samuel Schoenbaum (1964), to the *Supplements to the Revised Edition* (1966, 1970), and by consultation with Professor Harbage.

The publication dates of E. K. Chambers's *The Elizabethan Stage*, 4 vols. (1923), and of the initial volumes of G. E. Bentley's *The Jacobean and Caroline Stage*, 7 vols. (1941–68), provided appropriate starting points for the survey of scholarship and criticism in the series. Contributors used annual bibliographies published from 1923 through 1971 and were encouraged to include especially significant material published before and after those dates. (In the discussions of anonymous plays, only a few items published after 1967 have been included.) The chief sources for the items included in this volume were the author and title entries in twelve bibliographies and lists: *Essay and General Literature Index, International Index* (since 1965, *Social Sciences and Humanities Index), MLA International Bibliography, Modern Humanities Research Association Annual Bibliography of English Language and Literature, Readers' Guide to Periodical Literature, Research Opportunities in Renaissance Drama, Shakespeare Quarterly, Shakespeare Survey, Studies in Bibliography,*

Studies in Philology, Yearbook of Comparative and General Literature, and *The Year's Work in English Studies*. Those entries were supplemented by selected general studies of Elizabethan drama surveyed for discussions of individual playwrights, and by the additional research of individual contributors. Entries were restricted to published material except in the treatment of anonymous plays, where edition theses were included.

Each essay begins with a general section, including, when available, biographical material, general studies of the plays, and studies of the works at large. (It is assumed that later sections, particularly those dealing with individual plays, will be used in conjunction with this general section.) The next section discusses criticism of individual plays arranged in the order of their approximate critical importance, and concludes with a brief summary of the current state of criticism. The third section treats canon (including apocrypha), dates, and the state of the standard and other editions of the plays and nondramatic works. The arrangement of this section is chronological, following the preferred performance dates given in the *Annals of English Drama* and its *Supplements*; the play titles are cited as they appear in the *Annals* Index. At the contributor's discretion, items are either discussed in the commentary or listed in the See Also section. Contributors were free to modify these general guidelines to better accommodate the specific published material on a given author. Essays on the anonymous plays are organized independently according to the nature of the published studies; anonymous plays are discussed in the order of their performance date in the *Annals*. The section on minor named dramatists uses an annotated bibliography format arranged according to the date of publication of the criticism. Series titles are included only when they indicate the nature of the work or are useful as finding tools.

Since this series excludes Shakespeare, the most important dramatist of the popular school is not directly treated in this book. However, as the text and index indicate, he is very much present in the scholarship reviewed here. *The Popular School* includes many items dealing with Shakespeare's theater, his literary connections, and his apocrypha—as did *The Predecessors of Shakespeare*, and as will *The New Intellectuals*. It is hoped that one of the contributions of these volumes is a systematic review of scholarship ancillary to the study of Shakespeare.

The editors and contributors are especially grateful to the library staffs of their home institutions for assistance with the task of collecting and verifying the large number of items in this volume. The staffs of the Folger Shakespeare Library, Widener Library of Harvard

University, and the Library of Congress gave special help in locating rare items. Professors Alfred Harbage and Samuel Schoenbaum gave permission to use information from the revised *Annals of English Drama* and the *Supplements to the Revised Edition* and to follow those works as principles of organization. Permission to use the Master List and Table of Abbreviations of the *MLA International Bibliography* was granted by the Bibliographer of the Association, Harrison T. Meserole. Our list of journal and series abbreviations conforms to the MLA list except that we include several older titles not in the current MLA tables.

Ann Robinson, the University of Nebraska Press editor of the series, has contributed more than we had a right to expect to this volume and its predecessor. Professor Alfred Harbage's assistance as advisory editor has also gone beyond reasonable expectation. We are especially grateful for his authoritative resolution of questions affecting the organization and scope of this and other volumes in the series.

Terence P. Logan
Denzell S. Smith

LIST OF ABBREVIATIONS

AION-SG	Annali Istituto Universitario Orientale, Napoli, Sezione Germanica
AN&Q	American Notes and Queries
Archiv	Archiv für das Studium der Neueren Sprachen und Literaturen
ASNSP	Annali della Scuola Normale Superiore de Pisa
AUMLA	Journal of the Australasian Universities Language and Literature Association
AUR	Aberdeen University Review
BBr	Books at Brown
BFLS	Bulletin de la Faculté des Lettres de Strasbourg
BHR	Bibliothéque d'Humanisme et Renaissance
BJRL	Bulletin of the John Rylands Library
BLM	Bonniers Litterära Magasin
BNYPL	Bulletin of the New York Public Library
Boek	Het Boek
BRMMLA	Bulletin of the Rocky Mountain Modern Language Association
BUSE	Boston University Studies in English
CE	College English
CJ	Classical Journal
CL	Comparative Literature
CLAJ	College Language Association Journal
ClareQ	Claremont Quarterly
ColQ	Colorado Quarterly
CompD	Comparative Drama
CritQ	Critical Quarterly
CS	Cahiers du Sud
DA	Dissertation Abstracts
Drama	Drama: The Quarterly Theatre Review
DramS	Drama Survey
DUJ	Durham University Journal
EA	Etudes Anglaises
EDH	Essays by Divers Hands
EJ	English Journal

ELH	*Journal of English Literary History*
ELN	*English Language Notes*
EM	*English Miscellany*
E&S	*Essays and Studies by Members of the English Association*
ES	*English Studies*
ESA	*English Studies in Africa*
ESQ	*Emerson Society Quarterly*
ESRS	*Emporia State Research Studies*
ETJ	*Educational Theatre Journal*
Expl	*Explicator*
FK	*Filológiai Közlöny*
FurmS	*Furman Studies*
HAB	*Humanities Association Bulletin*
Hispano	*Hispanófila*
HLQ	*Huntington Library Quarterly*
HTR	*Harvard Theological Review*
IER	*Irish Ecclesiastical Record*
JEGP	*Journal of English and Germanic Philology*
JHI	*Journal of the History of Ideas*
JQ	*Journalism Quarterly*
JWCI	*Journal of the Warburg and Courtauld Institute*
KR	*Kenyon Review*
L&P	*Literature and Psychology*
LCrit	*Literary Criterion*
LHR	*Lock Haven Review*
Library	*The Library*
McNR	*McNeese Review*
MLN	*Modern Language Notes*
MLQ	*Modern Language Quarterly*
MLR	*Modern Language Review*
Month	*The Month*
MP	*Modern Philology*
MSpr	*Moderna Språk*
MuK	*Maske und Kothurn*
N&Q	*Notes and Queries*
Neophil	*Neophilologus*
NM	*Neuphilologische Mitteilungen*
NS	*Die Neueren Sprachen*
NSE	Norwegian Studies in English
NTg	*De Nieuwe Taalgids*

PBA	*Proceedings of the British Academy*
PBSA	*Papers of the Bibliographical Society of America*
PLPLS-LHS	*Proceedings of the Leeds Philosophic and Literary Society, Literary and Historical Section*
PMLA	*Publications of the Modern Language Association of America*
PP	*Philologica Pragensia*
PQ	*Philological Quarterly*
PTRSC	*Proceedings and Transactions of the Royal Society of Canada*
QQ	*Queen's Quarterly*
QR	*Quarterly Review*
QRL	*Quarterly Review of Literature*
RAA	*Revue Anglo-Américaine*
RBPH	*Revue Belge de Philologie et d'Histoire*
REL	*Review of English Literature*
RenD	*Renaissance Drama*
RenP	*Renaissance Papers*
RES	*Review of English Studies*
RIP	*Rice Institute Pamphlets*
RLC	*Revue de Littérature Comparée*
RLMC	*Rivista di Letterature Moderne e Comparate*
RLV	*Revue des Langues Vivantes*
RMS	*Renaissance and Modern Studies*
RN	*Renaissance News*
RORD	*Research Opportunities in Renaissance Drama*
RRDS	Regents Renaissance Drama Series
RS	*Research Studies*
SAB	*South Atlantic Bulletin*
SAQ	*South Atlantic Quarterly*
SB	*Studies in Bibliography: Papers of the Bibliographical Society of the University of Virginia*
ScS	*Scottish Studies*
SEL	*Studies in English Literature, 1500-1900*
SELit	*Studies in English Literature* (English Literary Society of Japan)
SFQ	*Southern Folklore Quarterly*
ShAB	*Shakespeare Association Bulletin*
ShakS	*Shakespeare Studies*
ShN	*Shakespeare Newsletter*

ShS	*Shakespeare Survey*
SJ	*Shakespeare-Jahrbuch*
SJH	*Shakespeare-Jahrbuch* (Heidelberg)
SJW	*Shakespeare-Jahrbuch* (Weimar)
SOF	*Sudöst-Forschungen*
SP	*Studies in Philology*
SQ	*Shakespeare Quarterly*
SR	*Sewanee Review*
SRen	*Studies in the Renaissance*
SSF	*Studies in Short Fiction*
SuAS	Stratford-upon-Avon Studies, ed. John Russell Brown and Bernard Harris
SzEP	Studien zur Englischen Philologie
TDR	*Tulane Drama Review* (since 1968, *The Drama Review*)
TEAS	Twayne's English Author Series
TFSB	*Tennessee Folklore Society Bulletin*
TLS	[London] *Times Literary Supplement*
TSE	*Tulane Studies in English*
TSL	*Tennessee Studies in Literature*
TSLL	*Texas Studies in Literature and Language*
UDR	*University of Dayton Review*
UFMH	University of Florida Monographs, Humanities Series
UMSE	*University of Mississippi Studies in English*
UTQ	*University of Toronto Quarterly*
VUSH	Vanderbilt University Studies in the Humanities
WF	*Western Folklore*
WSt	*Word Study*
WTW	Writers and Their Work
YWES	*Year's Work in English Studies*
ZAA	*Zeitschrift für Anglistik und Amerikanistik*

THE POPULAR SCHOOL

THOMAS DEKKER

M. L. Wine

The standard edition of the plays is Fredson Bowers's *The Dramatic Works of Thomas Dekker*, 4 vols. (1953–61). Ernest Rhys edited a selection for the Mermaid series (1887; rpt. 1949). *The Non-Dramatic Works of Thomas Dekker*, 5 vols. (1884–86; rpt. 1963) was edited by A. B. Grosart.

I. GENERAL

A. BIOGRAPHICAL

M. T. Jones-Davies's *Un peintre de la vie londonienne, Thomas Dekker (circa 1572–1632)*, 2 vols. (1958), is not only the complete biography of Dekker, complementing Bowers's edition of the dramatic works, but also virtually a compendium of Dekker scholarship and criticism of the past century. The volumes are documented with over 2900 footnotes and with 34 pages of bibliography. Volume 1 includes the first two parts of the study: (1) "Dekker: l'homme et son œuvre" and (2) "La peinture de Londres dans l'œuvre de Dekker." The third part—"Valeur esthetique de l'œuvre de Dekker" (including, of course, his nondramatic pieces)—comprises the second volume (see below, I,B). Objections have been raised to the length and operating principles of the second part, in which the author elaborately reconstructs Dekker's London from his writings and from supporting documents; but its justification lies in Jones-Davies's basic theme: Dekker is the poet of the city where he was born and raised, grew old and died; London is, in fact, the dramatist's collaborator, his symbol of life itself. A condensed one-volume English translation for the student and general reader would be welcome, especially if it still included one of the book's most attractive features—a pull-out map of the London of Dekker's day.

R. G. Howarth's "Dekker Not a Merchant Taylor," *N&Q* 1 (1954):52, confirms a point about Dekker's biography; and James E.

Ruoff's "Dekker's Dedication to *Match Me in London*," *N&Q* 4 (1957):8-9, and F. David Hoeniger's "Thomas Dekker, the Restoration of St. Paul's, and J. P. Collier, the Forger," *RN* 16 (1963):181-200, discuss the unsuccessful attempts by the playwright to court patronage in his later years. Jones-Davies also has an essay, "Thomas Dekker, écrivain élisabéthain, et la société de son temps," in *L'écrivain de langue anglais et la société de son temps* (Société des anglicistes de l'enseignement supérieur [1965], pp. 59-76).

B. GENERAL STUDIES OF THE PLAYS

In *Thomas Dekker, An Analysis of Dramatic Structure* (1969), James H. Conover discusses six plays definitely in the canon and not written in collaboration: "Each plot or action within a play is examined and evaluated in terms of exposition, articulation, the playwright's use of available materials, crisis, and climax." A final chapter considers the general characteristics of Dekker as a playwright. Suzanne Blow, *Rhetoric in the Plays of Thomas Dekker*, Salzburg Studies in English Literature: Jacobean Drama Studies, no. 3 (1972), analyzes, mainly in terms of Henry Peacham's rhetoric, seven plays "which most scholars agree Dekker wrote alone" and which "reflect purposeful and effective utilization of his rhetorical studies."

Dekker has always figured prominently, of course, in general studies of Elizabethan drama; but until fairly recently most of the commentary, like Algernon Charles Swinburne's "Thomas Dekker," *Nineteenth Century* 21 (1887):81-103 (rpt. in his *The Age of Shakespeare*, 1908), has tended to be impressionistic, to repeat clichés (valid though many of them may be), and to summarize plots. The most frequent consensus has been that Dekker was "Henslowe's hack," albeit a most engaging one; for example, John Gassner writes in *Masters of the Drama* (1940): "Perhaps the most talented, as he was certainly the most sunny, of the hacks was Thomas Dekker." Una Ellis-Fermor, in the chapter on Dekker in her *The Jacobean Drama* (1936; 4th ed. 1958; also rpt. in *Shakespeare's Contemporaries*, ed. Max Bluestone and Norman Rabkin [1961], pp. 157-65), considers Dekker "a poet of exceptional sweetness ... [who,] though he has apparently no artistic creed, has an intermittent moral code which seems to derive from a simple, but genuine, though unformulated, mysticism." Dekker's "gift of sympathy" is singled out for comment by Henri Fluchère in "Thomas Dekker et le Drame Bourgeois," *CS* 10 (1933):192-96; and Frederick

S. Boas's *An Introduction to Stuart Drama* (1946) makes the usual comments on Dekker's humanity and tolerance and summarizes the most familiar plays. As recently as 1960, David Daiches, in his *Critical History of English Literature* (vol. 1), concludes that Dekker has "a sentimentally optimistic view of human nature." The most devastating criticism, in some ways, is the general survey in M. C. Bradbrook's *The Growth and Structure of Elizabethan Comedy* (1955). Dekker, she writes, "could not achieve formal structure"; he was a "moral sloven"; and, as "the most traditional of Elizabethan writers," he "was by nature little of a dramatist and practised intermittently"; "the general effect [of his plays] is too often amorphous and blurred." In "Citizen Comedy and Domestic Drama," *Jacobean Theatre*, SuAS, vol. 1 (1960), pp. 66–83, Arthur Brown, comparing Dekker with Jonson and Heywood, finds that "Dekker is the least sophisticated of the three, his work the least complicated by adherence to literary, or even moral, theory"; but Brown's essay does make the needed point that the dramatist knew his theater and the audience for whom he was writing and that he served their needs well.

In view of this consistent line of interpretation, the books by Jones-Davies, Conover, and Blow, as well as George R. Price's *Thomas Dekker*, TEAS (1969), compliment the dramatist by examining his plays in greater detail. A change, too, is represented by Normand Berlin's "Thomas Dekker: A Partial Reappraisal," *SEL* 6 (1966): 263–77. Berlin finds that the commonly applied epithets of "gentle" and "cheery" describe only one side of Dekker's character and that "the condemnation of Dekker as a 'moral sloven,' although basically correct, needs discussion." The rogue pamphlets (see below, III,F), in which "the attitude is more condemnatory than any of his contemporaries," reveal the writer as "essentially a stern moralist," as does *The Honest Whore*, in which the playwright not only makes Bellafront pay for her sins but also subjects her, even after she is converted, to continuous trials. Berlin concludes that under "specific theatrical conditions"—as in the collaboration with Webster in the *Ho* plays and with Middleton in *The Roaring Girl*, where a romanticized view of the underworld is portrayed—"Dekker's basically stern morality could be compromised." This study is expanded by Berlin in the chapter on Dekker in his *The Base String: The Underworld in Elizabethan Drama* (1968).

Elizabeth Holmes, *Aspects of Elizabethan Imagery* (1929), and Caroline F. E. Spurgeon, *Shakespeare's Imagery and What It Tells Us* (1935), discuss the imagery of Dekker's plays. Gamaliel Bradford's

"The Women of Dekker," *SR* 33 (1925): 284–90 (rpt. in his *Elizabethan Women* [1936], pp. 104–13), might be compared with Ellis-Fermor's less exalted view of the subject expressed in *The Jacobean Drama*. Constance Spender offers an impressionistic general review in "The Plays of Thomas Dekker," *Contemporary Review* 130 (1926):332–39. J. W. Ashton discusses the playwright's integration of "learned" and "popular" literature in three plays in "Dekker's Use of Folklore in *Old Fortunatus, If This Be Not a Good Play*, and *The Witch of Edmonton*," *PQ* 41 (1962):240–48. Paul de Reul's *Présentation du théâtre jacobéen de Marston à Beaumont et Fletcher (1600–1625)* (1946) contains many appreciative remarks on Dekker; but the discussion consists mainly of plot summaries of *Old Fortunatus, The Shoemakers' Holiday*, the two parts of *The Honest Whore*, and *The Witch of Edmonton*. Aldo Maugeri's *Studi su Thomas Dekker* (1958), after a general introductory review, devotes a chapter each to *Old Fortunatus, The Shoemakers' Holiday*, and *Patient Grissil*—the "trilogy of Fortune," as the author describes them. The plays are discussed in terms of sources, plot summaries, and, to a small extent, editorial problems. Brian Gibbons discusses *Satiromastix* and the *Ho* plays in *Jacobean City Comedy* (1968).

C. THE WORKS AT LARGE

The third part (vol. 2), "Valeur esthetique de l'œuvre de Dekker," of M. T. Jones-Davies's *Un peintre de la vie londonienne* (above, I,A) is the first comprehensive study of the plays and of Dekker's work at large since Mary Leland Hunt's *Thomas Dekker* (1911). Jones-Davies covers such topics as Dekker the "realist," "romantic," "master of humor," "satirist," and "moralist"; the characteristics of the pamphlets and the plays; language and style; Dekker and his contemporaries; his influence and reputation. Despite this wide-ranging and informative treatment, one misses a rigorous evaluation or assessment of the works, as well as a discussion of the stage-worthiness of the plays. Much of the value of the study lies in the genuine enthusiasm that the author conveys for the works and for her subject generally.

A briefer study is George R. Price's *Thomas Dekker* (I,B). Price covers the salient facts of Dekker's biography, analyzes eight of his "independent" plays, four of the collaborations, the nondramatic work, and Dekker's religious and social thought. A final chapter discusses Dekker's achievement. A "Selected Bibliography" lists Dekker's canonical and apocryphal works.

A. H. Bullen devotes a chapter to Dekker's plays and pamphlets in *Elizabethans* (1924). Harold Child, "Thomas Dekker and the Underdog: The Compassionate Realist," *TLS*, 31 May 1941, pp. 262-64 (rpt. in *Essays and Reflections*, ed. S. C. Roberts [1948], pp. 95-104), dismisses Dekker the dramatist but judges his prose "a manifold joy" and his lyric verse "among the best of its period." In "Puritanism in the Plays and Pamphlets of Thomas Dekker," *Studies in English* (Univ. of Texas) 19 (1939):86-113, Mary G. M. Adkins finds Dekker's attitude towards Puritanism inconsistent; his temperament did not sustain the "harshness of invective."

Kate L. Gregg, "Thomas Dekker: A Study in Economic and Social Backgrounds," *Univ. of Washington Publications: Language and Literature* 2 (1924):55-112, observes that "by birth and environment [Dekker] had the ethics and beliefs of the Puritan middle class; by alliance with the stage, he assumed allegiance to ethics, principles, and a program of life more or less opposed thereto." As the footnotes indicate, George E. Thornton's "The Social and Moral Philosophy of Thomas Dekker," *ESRS* 4 (1955):1-36, does not supersede Gregg's study although an interesting feature is his relating the two parts of *The Honest Whore* to this larger background: these plays "are experiments in the negative presentation of moral virtue, in which are depicted various levels of morality, or the lack of it, which exist in mankind from the lowest state of society to the highest." L. C. Knights's chapter on Dekker and "citizen morality" in his *Drama and Society in the Age of Jonson* (1937) maintains that "Dekker accepts the traditional social ethic, but his Protestant Christianity is that of the seventeenth-century middle class," and, as a result, his satire "does not penetrate far below the surface." David G. Hale, "Dekker and the Body Politic," *NM* 67 (1966): 132-37, writes on the new use that the playwright-pamphleteer makes of the common analogy of the political entity to the human body: it is "no longer a part of the political argument; this is implicit testimony that the analogy is losing its traditional validity and is becoming simply an ornament of rhetoric."

No full-length study of Dekker's nondramatic works exists, but informative discussions are to be found in the introductions to A. V. Judges's *The Elizabethan Underworld* and E. D. Pendry's edition of selected pamphlets (see below, III,F). Hugh Walker has a general discussion of the satirical pamphlets in *English Satire and Satirists* (1925), and E. A. Baker discusses the journalistic qualities of Dekker's prose in *The History of the English Novel* (1924-39), vol.

2, *The Elizabethan Age and After* (1929). Phillip Shaw's "The Position of Thomas Dekker in Jacobean Prison Literature," *PMLA* 62 (1947):366–91, points out that Dekker was the "earliest principal writer" of a genre which "first flourished in the Jacobean period" and that he practiced all the types from rogue exposures to reformatory essays and "characters." Edwin Haviland Miller, "Thomas Dekker, Hack Writer," *N&Q* 2 (1955):145–50, is more critical of the pamphleteer; he describes *The Bellman of London* (1608) and *Lantern and Candlelight* (1609) as "hack works" for the market place, with much of their contents copied from other contemporary rogue literature. In "Samuel Rid's Borrowings from Robert Greene," *N&Q* 1 (1954):236–38, Miller notes that Samuel Rid, in *Martin Mark-All, Beadle of Bridewell* (1610), upbraids Dekker for the latter's pilferings from Thomas Harmon in *The Bellman of London*. In contrast to Miller's additional commentary in *The Profession of Writer in Elizabethan England* (1959) on Dekker's "flagrant" borrowings in his underworld tracts, Maria Ijobzowska, "Conventional and Original Elements in Thomas Dekker's Non-Dramatic Prose Satire," *Kwartalnik Neofilologiczny* 13 (1966):171–81, points out the "original elements in Dekker's pamphlets, connected precisely with his analysis of conditions and his search for their cause": "Dekker is one of the first pamphlet-writers to see and to understand the social unrest caused by the changing environment and existence of country people looking for work in towns, as well as by the aspirations of the 'nouveaux riches.' "

F. P. Wilson discusses the originality of Dekker's *The Raven's Almanack* (1609) in "Some English Mock-Prognostications," *Library* 19 (1938):6–43. Herbert G. Wright, "Some Sixteenth and Seventeenth Century Writers on the Plague," *E&S* 6 (1953):41–55, argues that Dekker, who witnessed the epidemics of 1603, 1625, and 1630, deals with the subject of the plague "more extensively than any other Elizabethan writer." The early pamphlets, Wright observes, are sensational in nature; but in later ones "the journalist is lost in the humanitarian and the prophet." Benjamin Boyce examines Dekker's "characters" in *The Theophrastan Character in England to 1642* (1947); and W. J. Paylor in his edition of *The Overburian Characters* (1936) and in "Thomas Dekker and the 'Overburian' Characters," *MLR* 31 (1936):155–60, attributes to Dekker the six "characters" dealing with a debtor's life in the early part of the seventeenth century that appeared for the first time in the ninth impression of the *Overburian Collection*. In "News from Hell," *PMLA* 58

(1943):402–37, which traces "satiric communications with the nether world" in Renaissance English literature. Boyce observes that, "although an acknowledged imitator of Lucian, Dekker could catch the spirit of this pagan model only for a moment." An examination of the names that Dekker applies to the devils in his *News from Hell* (1606) is the subject of Kelsie B. Harder's "The Names of Thomas Dekker's Devils," *Names* 3 (1955):210–18: "Dekker uses some twenty-seven names for the *devil,* applying them to the various manifestations of the dark prince's multi-faceted personality to illustrate the aspects of contemporary religious, political, and social life." Earlier discussions of Dekker the pamphleteer that are of value are F. W. Chandler's *The Literature of Roguery,* 2 vols. (1907) and F. Aydelott's *Elizabethan Rogues and Vagabonds* (1913).

Thomas Dekker (A Concise Bibliography) by Samuel A. Tannenbaum was published in 1939, followed by a supplement, compiled with Dorothy R. Tannenbaum, in 1945; both are reprinted in *Elizabethan Bibliographies,* vol. 2 (1967). In 1967 Dennis Donovan issued a chronological listing from 1945 to 1965 in vol. 2 of *Elizabethan Bibliographies Supplements,* ed. C. A. Pennel. Irving Ribner's *Tudor and Stuart Drama,* Goldentree Bibliographies (1966), provides a selective list of titles. *Thomas Dekker c. 1572–1632, a Bibliographical Catalogue of the Early Editions (to the End of the 17th Century)* was compiled in 1972 by A. F. Allison for the Pall Mall Bibliographies. W. P. Barrett and F. P. Wilson compiled the listing for Dekker in the *Cambridge Bibliography of English Literature,* ed. F. W. Bateson (1941), vol. 1, *600–1660,* pp. 619–22; a supplementary fifth volume of the *CBEL,* edited in 1957 by George Watson, has an additional listing on pp. 300-301 by J. F. Kermode; see the listing in the *New CBEL,* vol. 1, cols. 1673-82.

II. CRITICISM OF INDIVIDUAL PLAYS AND STATE OF SCHOLARSHIP

A. INDIVIDUAL PLAYS

The Shoemakers' Holiday, or The Gentle Craft

Harold E. Toliver, "*The Shoemaker's Holiday:* Theme and Image," *BUSE* 5 (1961):208–18, explores the full significance of the title and examines two clichés of Dekker criticism: his realism and his romanticism. In the lives of the shoemakers, Toliver finds, "a holiday atmosphere of irresponsible festivity and the crude necessities of life stand opposed .... But the conflict between life as it is and life as the romantic spirit would have it be is nevertheless intimately involved in the differences between social and economic levels" (as Jane, for instance, discovers). The two songs in the play are discussed in relation to the theme.

In "Virtue's Holiday: Thomas Dekker and Simon Eyre," *RenD* 2 (1969):103–22, Joel H. Kaplan observes that the holiday atmosphere created mainly by Eyre's rhetoric revitalizes "a disreputable society that seems to melt away in his presence." The play, in fact, enlarges his "influence until an entire country is seized with his genial madness." The mood of the play is "saturnalian and festive rather than proscriptively moral."

Patricia Thomson, "The Old Way and the New Way in Dekker and Massinger," *MLR* 51 (1956):168–78, compares *The Shoemakers' Holiday* (1599) with *A New Way to Pay Old Debts* (dated 1621–26), two plays that approximately coincide with the beginning and end of the reign of James I (1603–25). Although their plots have much in common (the ambitions of men humbly born; "the project of marriage between two people of unequal birth"), "the experience of the reign of James I lies solidly" between them. Only the later play is concerned with class whereas the earlier reverts to Elizabethan social theory to create a feudal world "safe from the touch of time." Dekker, unlike Massinger, does not deal seriously with the "laws of society." Price (above, I,B) thinks that to find in the play "any deep social truth or vision of Elizabethan society is ... to see both the play and the society in a sentimental mood."

Price, Conover (I,B), and Michael Manheim, "The Construction of *The Shoemakers' Holiday*," *SEL* 10 (1970):315–23, all praise Dekker's craftsmanship, the seeming ease with which he unifies the play. (See also Harbage, "The Mystery of *Perkin Warbeck*," II,B, below.) For Manheim, the play "is constructed about the irony implicit in Simon Eyre's middle-class attack on courtiers in III.3"; but Frederick M. Burelbach, Jr., "War and Peace in *The Shoemakers' Holiday*," *TSL* 13 (1968):99–107, finds that the war with France unites the three plots while solving the problems of plotting.

David Novarr, "Dekker's Gentle Craft and the Lord Mayor of London," *MP* 57 (1960):233–39, examines details that make "the contemporaneity of Dekker's play" so evident. Particularly interesting is the example of Sir John ("Rich") Spencer, Lord Mayor of London for the year starting 25 October 1594; the playwright may well have had him in mind as the prototype of Sir Roger Oatley. Like Rose

Oatley in the play, Sir John's daughter Elizabeth was in love with a nobleman, William, the second Lord Compton; and the lovers were married only after much opposition from her father. Spencer was even sent to Fleet prison for a time for hiding and mistreating his daughter. W. K. Chandler, "The Topography of Dekker's *The Shoemaker's Holiday*," *SP* 26 (1929):499–504, discusses the "thirty-five landmarks" of London referred to in the play; and in "The Sources of the Characters in *The Shoemaker's Holiday*," *MP* 27 (1929): 175-82, Chandler observes that "Dekker exercised reasonable historical accuracy in naming his characters"—much more so than Deloney in *The Gentle Craft*, the source of the play. In "The King in Dekker's *The Shoemakers Holiday*," *N&Q* 4 (1957):432–33, L. M. Manheim supports Alexis F. Lange's original contention (Introduction to the play in *Representative English Comedies*, ed. C. M. Gayley, vol. 3 [1914]) that Dekker's king is Henry V. Chandler ("Sources of the Characters"), Jones-Davies, and Burelbach identify the king as Henry VI. Robert Adger Law, "*The Shoemaker's Holiday* and *Romeo and Juliet*," *SP* 21 (1924):356–61, argues that the last three acts of Dekker's play are indebted to Shakespeare—a comparison which Paul C. Davies finds "strained" (in the introduction to his edition of the play; see below, III,E).

1 The Honest Whore (with Middleton) and *2 The Honest Whore*

In "Patient Madman and Honest Whore: The Middleton-Dekker Oxymoron," *E&S* 19 (1966):18–40, Peter Ure argues that the presence of the "more radically witty" talent of Middleton in the first part unifies that play in a way that Dekker could not see when he came to write the second part alone. Convinced that the Candido of the earlier play is Middleton's creation, Ure suggests that as "the patient madman" he "makes an honest point" whereas Dekker's Candido in the later play "makes none at all" in his new role as "the patient thief." Ure feels that in the sequel Dekker "botches" Middleton's idea by "collapsing" Candido's patient character (a role that Bellafront now takes over): the man who would threaten to beat his wife is not the same character. The "fairy-godfather presence of Friscobaldo" in the second part, furthermore, "draws attention away from the honest study of Bellafront's dilemma." Ure concludes that "the coupling of [Dekker's] name with Middleton's is the last oxymoron, and perhaps the most fascinating." Evidence of authorship in the first play on more solid bibliographical grounds (see III,A, below) would give greater weight to Ure's criticism.

In contrast to Ure, Michael Manheim, who, in "The Thematic Structure of Dekker's *2 Honest Whore*," *SEL* 5 (1965):363–81, calls the subplot of *1 Honest Whore* "little more than a comic reversal of the Matheo-Bellafront action," argues that it "lacks the unity of the subplot, or Candido plot, of *2 Honest Whore*." The testing of Bellafront, Matheo, and Hippolito ("the whore converter" become "the whore monger") in the sequel explains the unifying presence of Friscobaldo; and in the Bridewell scene at the end—which Ure feels does not properly balance the Bedlam ending of the first play—the three tests are concluded. So, too, Larry S. Champion, "From Melodrama to Comedy: A Study of the Dramatic Perspective in Dekker's *The Honest Whore*, Parts I and II," *SP* 69 (1972):192–209, believes that there is "significant structural evidence to support the generalized assumptions that Part II is [Dekker's] greatest work." The presence of Friscobaldo as "the comic pointer or comic controller" in the later play clarifies the comic perspective, which was blurred in the earlier play. *2 Honest Whore* is a "comic vision of the transforming power of human love." Conover (I,B) also believes that the subplot of the second play "is justified by its contribution and relevance to the main action" and, like Champion, compares the play to *Measure for Measure*. Price (I,B) feels that the "moral worlds of the romance and the morality plots are not assimilated" in the first part, that "Part II is much better unified in this respect."

In "Dekker's *Whore* and Marston's *Courtesan*," *ELN* 4 (1967): 261–66, Harry Keyishian agrees with T. M. Parrott's contention (in *The Plays and Poems of George Chapman*, vol. 2 [1914], p. 841) that Marston's *The Dutch Courtesan* is an "intentional retort" to *1 Honest Whore*: Marston "questioned Dekker's oversimplified, oversentimental presentation of human nature"—a view that M. L. Wine questions in the introduction to his edition of *The Dutch Courtesan*, RRDS (1965).

Old Fortunatus

Price (I,B) finds that, "without question, *Old Fortunatus*, as we have it, was written by Dekker as a parable for the moral instruction of the audience at Queen Elizabeth's court"; however, the playwright's "genuine earnestness . . . is partly frustrated by his employment of conventional elements and spectacle." Price also qualifies C. H. Herford's study of the play's source (the German *Volksbuch* "Of Fortunatus and His Purse and Wishing-Hat") in the latter's *Studies in the Literary Relations of England and Germany in the Sixteenth*

Century (1886). Although Price believes that "it is likely that the Elizabethan audience saw little or no inconsistency" in the Fortune–Virtue relation, Conover (I,B) finds that because of this relation the play is finally structurally defective: "there is no relationship between the action of the plot and its outcome"—a view that also opposes Jones-Davies's conviction that the play has a linear construction. Kaplan ("Virtue's Holiday" above, under *Shoemaker*), like Price, finds that the "theatrical effect remains at odds with the didactic nature of a genre that demands strict judgment"; and, like Conover, he finds "the resulting denouement . . . less a metamorphosis than a trick." In *"Doctor Faustus*, Dekker's *Old Fortunatus*, and the Morality Plays," *MLQ* 26 (1965):497–505, Sidney R. Homan, Jr., notes the source of Dekker's play in Marlowe's, as well as the greater influence of the moralities in the former: Fortunatus is a "lower level" Faustus, embracing riches rather than wisdom.

Satiromastix, or The Untrussing of the Humorous Poet

Almost every standard history of Elizabethan drama and satire, as well as almost every biographical study of Shakespeare, Jonson, and Marston, refers to *Satiromastix* and Dekker's role in the so-called "War of the Theaters" or Poetomachia. Robert Boies Sharpe, *The Real War of the Theaters* (1935), saw the "war" as a rivalry between the two leading companies, the Admiral's and the Lord Chamberlain's, culminating after a decade in victory for the latter; but W. L. Halstead has asked, "What 'War of the Theatres'?" *CE* 9 (1948): 424–26. Drawing his argument from the preface to the published text of *Satiromastix*, Halstead doubts that Dekker satirizes any dramatist other than Jonson, whom actually he always respected; instead, Jonson, Marston, and Dekker planned the quarrel to advertize each other as literary figures and for profit. Commenting on Halstead's article, Robert Withington, *CE* 10 (1948):163–64, agrees that "the quarrel does not seem to have led to bitterness at the time"; but he emphasizes the importance of the concept of the "war" for undergraduates because it reveals "the interest of at least some of the audience in critical debates and the growth of Jonson's art" (from classical to realistic satire). John J. Enck's "The Peace of the Poetomachia," *PMLA* 77 (1962):386–96, although mainly concerned with Shakespeare's *Troilus and Cressida* and Jonson's *Poetaster*, is important for its emphasis on the literary nature of the entire matter: "The Poetomachia, as a struggle about correctness based generally but not wholly on rivalries, explains more than any other conjecture why a school of talented professional writers should all, inside two years, experiment with a style which forcefully yokes lightness and intensity, and then abandons it."

Price (I,B) finds *Satiromastix* "good theater" although the serious and comic plots "seem to be devoid of thematic relation to each other" and "incongruities of tone or dramatic method . . . vitiate the play." Albert H. Marckwardt, referring to the phrase "in one's element," in "A Fashionable Expression: Its Status in *Poetaster* and *Satiromastix*," *MLN* 44 (1929):93–96, does not find that Dekker is mocking Jonson; and Alvin Kernan, *The Cankered Muse: Satire of the English Renaissance* (1959), comments on the traditional role of the satirist in the play: "Dekker simply presents Jonson under the figure of Horace as a living example of the standard satiric character." Gibbons (I,B) concludes that "if Dekker has no skill in Comical Satyre, he has a positive talent for creating situation comedy, straightforward and broad, with the minimum of dependence on verbal richness and subtlety." In " 'These Pretty Devices,' A Study of Masques in Plays," in *A Book of Masques*, ed. T. J. B. Spencer and S. W. Wells (1967), pp. 405–48, Inga-Stina Ewbank discusses the marriage masque in *Satiromastix*.

Patient Grissil

Price (I,B) says of this play, written by Dekker in collaboration with Chettle and Haughton: "Despite its very familiar story, *Patient Grissil* must have delighted its audience at the Fortune," for "it reaches the deepest idealism of its wide audience"—not only in terms of Christian reassurance but also of social mobility "in an era when children of wealthy merchants were beginning to marry more frequently into the nobility." Both Price and Harold Jenkins, *The Life and Work of Henry Chettle* (1934), praise the play for its constructive skill and humor. In *Multiple Plots in English Renaissance Drama* (1971), Richard Levin argues, however, that "the comedy of the subplot actually works at cross-purposes with the idealization of the main-plot heroine." Enid Welsford discusses the character of Babulo in *The Fool: His Social and Literary History* (1935).

The Witch of Edmonton

Leonora Leet Brodwin, "The Domestic Tragedy of Frank Thorney in *The Witch of Edmonton*," *SEL* 7 (1967):311–28, judges this play, written by Dekker with Ford and W. Rowley, "probably the most sophisticated treatment of domestic tragedy in the whole of Elizabethan-Jacobean drama." She demonstrates that Frank Thorney is a study of "erotic irresponsibility," a man "too weak to bear a life of truth, and it is only the fact of imminent death which gives him the necessary strength." In "The Significance of *The Witch of Edmonton*," *Criterion* 17 (1937):23–32, Edward Sackville West also praises the dramatization of Frank Thorney's "intensity of conflict within him." Price (I,B) admires Thorney's characterization but finds the two plots (Thorney's and Mother Sawyer's) not strongly unified. Katherine M. Briggs, *Pale Hecate's Team: An Examination of the Beliefs in Witchcraft and Magic among Shakespeare's Contemporaries and His Immediate Successors* (1962), and Robert Rentoul Reed, Jr., *The Occult on the Tudor and Stuart Stage* (1965), discuss the play in terms of its contemporary ideas of witchcraft. For Reed, "there is little doubt that the witchcraft of which it treats was believed by its authors."

The Roaring Girl, or Moll Cutpurse

In "A Note on Moll Cutpurse—'The Roaring Girl,'" *RES* 10 (1934):67–71, Margaret Dowling affirms, from the evidence of a contemporary lawsuit, that "Moll appears to be very much the kind of woman described by Dekker and Middleton" in this collaborative play.

The Virgin Martyr

Louise George Clubb, "*The Virgin Martyr* and the *Tragedia Sacra*," *RenD* 7 (1964):103–26, defines the genre of this play, written jointly by Dekker and Massinger, as a Counter-Reformation saint's play or *tragedia sacra* imported from the Continent. In England the plot had allegorical possibilities because "only in a Protestant country could the representation of a struggle between a saint and the state religion suggest to a Roman Catholic mind the actual conflict of religious right and wrong; the Catholic in England was in the position of Dorothea in Rome-governed Caesaria." Price (I,B) observes that dramatic records confirm the play's popularity, but he judges it "sincere but shallow in its conceptions, and therefore not very moving."

If It Be Not Good, the Devil Is in It

Conover (I,B) considers *If It Be Not Good* "a typically Dekkerian play, with an abundance of incidents, attention to a complete society, sensational theatrical devices, and fundamentally good humored tone." Furthermore, Dekker is skillful in creating "a critical and satirical objectivity." Price, on the other hand, judges that "an unresolved tension between the expectations raised by the ironic situation and by Dekker's failure to satisfy them is the weakness of the play." The popularity of the devil figure in the theater during this period is noted by Russell Potter, "The Jacobean Devil Plays," *SP* 28 (1931):730–36.

Match Me in London

Both Jones-Davies and Price comment on the Fletcherian influence on the play, and Bradbrook (I,B) compares the plot to that of Middleton's *Women Beware Women*, with Dekker's play having "a happy instead of a tragic" ending. Price, too, observes that Dekker "has modified many elements of his Jacobean play in an Elizabethan fashion." Whereas Price, despite strong reservations about the play, finds that Dekker here nevertheless "displays his mastery of stage-craft," Conover (I,B) finds that the major plot "dwindles out in an ineffective final scene" and that the secondary plot is "arbitrary."

The Whore of Babylon

Irving Ribner, *The English History Play in the Age of Shakespeare* (1957; rev. ed. 1965), notes that "Dekker's one extant serious attempt to portray actual British history and to do so for political purposes is *The Whore of Babylon*"; the play's failure comes from casting the work "into an elaborate allegory based obviously upon Spenser's *Faerie Queene*." Price observes that "despite [its] timely patriotic fervor . . . and its eloquent verse, the audience may have found its dramaturgy too old-fashioned"; Conover argues "that much of the action is not clear for the modern reader," but he praises "the way in which Dekker shapes his materials toward a concentration at the end of the play." In "Source du Latin scolastique dans *The Whore of Babylon* de Thomas Dekker," *EA* 6 (1953):142–43, M. T. Jones-Davies points out Dekker's indebtedness to the 1587 edition of Holinshed. C. van der Spek, *The Church and the Churchman in English Dramatic Literature before 1642* (1930), dismisses the play as a "worthless product."

Westward Ho

Northward Ho

Gibbons (I,B) notes: "Both plays [by Dekker and Webster] articulate complex plots and the audience is directed simply to the intrigue and the cleverness with which it is worked out: of course neither play has an intrigue of sufficient intelligence or witty design to reward the audience's closest attention."

The Sun's Darling

M. Joan Sargeaunt, *John Ford* (1935), judges this collaborative work "considered either as a masque or a play . . . a failure"; but Price calls it "perhaps the best of the small group of plays called 'theater masques.' " Price notes that "in one aspect . . . [it] presents us the traditional Prodigal Son theme once again, but with a more humanistic and wittier rendering." H. K. Russell, "Tudor and Stuart Dramatizations of the Doctrines of Natural and Moral Philosophy," *SP* 31 (1934):1-27, observes that *The Sun's Darling* combines the form of the morality and the masque—"not carelessly thrown together."

The Magnificent Entertainment Given to King James

The major point of Glynne Wickham's "Contribution de Ben Jonson et de Dekker aux fêtes du couronnement de Jacques 1er," *Les fêtes de la Renaissance*, ed. Jean Jacquot, vol. 1 (1956), pp. 279-83, is that these tableaux, of which Dekker was author of the fourth, represented by the above title, and apparently director of all, indicate a taste for elaborate settings and that, consequently, they may lead us to revise our conception of the interior of the Globe theater. In "Harrison, Jonson and Dekker, *The Magnificent Entertainment for King James (1604)*," *JWCI* 31 (1968):445-48, David M. Bergeron notes "a number of discrepancies" between the pictorial record of Stephen Harrison, the artificer, in *Arches of Triumph* (1604), "and the printed texts of Jonson and Dekker."

Troia Nova Triumphans

Britannia's Honour

London's Tempe, or The Field of Happiness

David M. Bergeron, *English Civic Pageantry, 1558-1642* (1972), argues that "Dekker's most significant contribution to mayoral pageantry is doubtless his effort to impose on the somewhat nebulous form of the show a morality play structure." The structure of *Troia Nova Triumphans* "closely resembles the dramatic development of a typical medieval morality play, following the comic pattern from encounter with evil to victory." In *Britannia's Honor*, "instructive value there is in abundance, but theatrical interest is minimal." *London's Tempe* "on the whole . . . suffers from its lack of unity, either thematic or dramatic."

The Book of Sir Thomas More, Dekker's Addition

In "*The Book of Sir Thomas More*: A Theatrical View," *MP* 68 (1970):10–24, Scott McMillin attempts to "place *The Book of Sir Thomas More* in its proper position as a manuscript intended for real theatrical use," arguing that "even Dekker's thirty-one line conclusion to Addition IV adds a dramatic point in showing that Faulkner remains unrepentant despite More's attempts at education."

B. OVER-ALL STATE OF CRITICISM

Reviewing Jones-Davies's two-volume study of Dekker, M. A. Shaaber, *MP* 57 (1960):202–4, observed that with this compendious monograph and with Bowers's edition of the dramatic works "our generation might be thought to have made handsome amends to a writer whose own treated him rather shabbily." With a major "life and works" now completed and with an outstanding critical old-spelling edition available, criticism is beginning to focus more closely on the actual craftsmanship of the plays than it has in the past. Dekker's political, moral, and social philosophies present no over-whelming problems; and Jones-Davies's work places the playwright in his milieu. Until very recently, however, few critics have come to terms, either to elaborate or to disparage, with the assessment made as early as 1936 by Una Ellis-Fermor (I,B): "We seldom or never find miscalculation of a stage effect: everything that [Dekker] wrote could be played, I believe; most of it better than it can be read." A good start has been made, but more profitable work may well be done along the lines suggested by Alfred Harbage in "The Mystery of *Perkin Warbeck*," in *Studies in the English Renaissance Drama in Memory of Karl Julius Holzknecht*, ed. J. W. Bennett, et al. (1959), pp. 125–41, where, in setting forth reasons for considering Dekker as a collaborator in a play always attributed solely to Ford, he comments on the former's splendid technical facility and sense of staging in the opening scene of *The Shoemakers' Holiday*: in 200 lines Dekker introduces and differentiates "ten major and minor characters," "establishes immediate interest, sets a situation, provides for future development, creates and qualifies our sense of social antagonisms, writes language of great vitality . . . and rounds the action off with a parade of Londoners to the French wars in a way that is at once stirring, comical, and touching—and all with such an appearance of ease as to make the unwary reader say, 'Why, this is nothing at all.' "

For Harbage, "to watch Dekker getting under way is a lesson in craftsmanship." Dekker himself hints at the approach to his plays, as we can see from George F. Reynolds's "Aims of a Popular Elizabethan Dramatist," *PQ* 20 (1941): 340–44. Reynolds observes that Dekker's Prologue to *If It Be Not Good, the Devil Is in It* is the only statement of the aims of a playwright of popular Elizabethan romantic plays that can be set against Jonson's pseudo-classical theories. In it Dekker asks the playwright to quickly create vivid audience responses, to "give the actor a good opportunity to display strong emotions," to arrange these emotions so as to provide a pattern of striking contrasts, and to "tye" the ears of the auditors "(with golden chaines) to his Melody."

The difficulty of establishing Dekker's canon (see III,A, B below) has always been the stumbling block for full-length criticism. As Una Ellis-Fermor (I,B) writes, "It is hard to form any clear opinion on Dekker's structural capacity when we know so little of the shares of the collaborators in his plays." As editions of Dekker's fellow playwrights comparable to Bowers's appear, many—certainly not all—problems of canon should be cleared up; in the meantime, a goodly portion of the canon is sufficiently established to invite further criticism along the lines reflected in Price, Conover, and recent essayists.

III. CANON

A. PLAYS IN CHRONOLOGICAL ORDER

The source for the type of play, the acting date (in italics preceding semicolon), and the original date of publication, as well as information on lost plays, is Alfred Harbage, *Annals of English Drama, 975–1700*, rev. S. Schoenbaum (1964). Readers are directed to Bowers's textual introductions, to the descriptions of the original quartos in W. W. Greg, *A Bibliography of the English Printed Drama to the Restoration*, 4 vols. (1939–59), and in Wilfred T. Jewkes, *Act Division in Elizabethan and Jacobean Plays, 1583–1616* (1958), and to the discussions of canon in E. K. Chambers, *The Elizabethan Stage* (1923), vol. 3, in G. E. Bentley, *The Jacobean and Caroline Stage*, vol. 3 (1956), and in Price (I,B).

The Jew of Venice, comedy? (*1594?;* lost)

Entered to Humphrey Moseley in the Stationers' Register for 9 September 1653 as a play "by Tho: Decker,' *The Jew of Venice* has been identified conjecturally with two anonymous plays acted by the Admiral's company in 1594: *The Venetian Comedy* (lost) and *The French Doctor* (lost). Bentley, vol. 3, however, concludes: "The plain facts are that there is no reason to connect *The Jew of Venice* which Moseley owned in 1653 with any other play at all." The play is not formally entered in the *Annals*.

Disguises, or Love in Disguise, a Petticoat Voyage, comedy? (*1595;* lost)

Attributed to Dekker in a manuscript listing of a late seventeenth-century bookseller's stock found among Abraham Hill's papers (see Joseph Quincy Adams, "Hill's List of Early Plays in Manuscript," *Library* 20 [1939]: 71–99), the play has been identified conjecturally with *The Disguises*, an anonymous play newly performed by the Admiral's company on 2 October 1595, although no evidence exists for the identification.

Additions to *The Book of Sir Thomas More*, with Munday, Chettle, Heywood (?), and Shakespeare (?); history (ca. *1593–ca. 1601*; MS— revision of a play originally composed ca. 1590–93)

W. W. Greg, "The Handwritings of the Manuscript," in *Shakespeare's Hand in the Play of Sir Thomas More*, papers by Alfred W. Pollard, et al. (1923), pp. 41–56, identifies Hand E as Dekker's. In *William Shakespeare* (1930), vol. 1, E. K. Chambers concludes that "the date, or dates, must remain undetermined"; and R. C. Bald, "*The Booke of Sir Thomas More* and Its Problems," *ShS* 2 (1949): 44–61, believes that the work "was begun in the latter part of 1600" and abandoned because of contemporary political events. P. W. M. Blayney, however, in *"The Booke of Sir Thomas Moore* Re-Examined," *SP* 69 (1972):167–91, dates the history of the manuscript from early 1592 to early 1593. Samuel A. Tannenbaum, *The Book of "Sir Thomas Moore": A Bibliotic Study* (1927), argues that Dekker had nothing to do with the original composition of the play.

Phaeton, classical legend (*1598;* lost)

The Triangle (or *Triplicity) of Cuckolds*, comedy (*1598;* lost)

The Famous Wars of Henry I and the Prince of Wales, with Chettle and Drayton; history (*1598;* lost)

1 and *2 Earl Godwin and His Three Sons*, with Chettle, Drayton, and Wilson; history (*1598;* lost)

Pierce of Exton, with Chettle, Drayton, and Wilson; history (*1598;* lost—not completed?)

1 Black Bateman of the North, with Chettle, Drayton, and Wilson; tragedy? (*1598;* lost)

The Madman's Morris, with Drayton and Wilson; comedy? (*1598;* lost)

1 Hannibal and Hermes, with Drayton and Wilson; unknown (*1598;* lost)

See *Annals* and Chambers, vol. 3, for identification with the next listing.

Worse Afeard than Hurt, with Drayton; unknown (*1598;* lost)

Pierce of Winchester, with Drayton and Wilson; unknown (*1598;* lost)

1, 2, and *3 The Civil Wars of France*, with Drayton; foreign history (*1598;* lost)

Connan, Prince of Cornwall, with Drayton; history (*1598;* lost)

The First Introduction of the Civil Wars of France, history (*1599;* lost)

Troilus and Cressida, with Chettle; classical legend (*1599;* MS "plot" fragment)

Agamemnon, with Chettle; classical legend (*1599;* lost)

The Shoemakers' Holiday, or The Gentle Craft, comedy (*1599;* 1600)

   In "Thomas Dekker, Robert Wilson, and *The Shoemakers Holiday*," *MLN* 64 (1949):517-19, Fredson Bowers proves that the theory of Robert Wilson's having collaborated with Dekker on the play (see Chambers, vol. 3) rests solely on a signed copy of the 1600 first quarto forged by J. P. Collier and now in Harvard's Houghton Library.

The Stepmother's Tragedy, with Chettle (*1599;* lost)

Bear a Brain, comedy (*1599;* lost?)

   The title of this play was altered from *Better Late than Never*.

Page of Plymouth, with Jonson; tragedy (*1599;* lost)

Robert II, King of Scots, with Jonson, Chettle, "& other Jentellman" (so Henslowe), possibly Marston; history (*1599;* lost)

Old Fortunatus, comedy (*1599;* 1600)

   W. L. Halstead, "Note on Dekker's *Old Fortunatus*," *MLN* 54 (1939):351-52, argues that Dekker revised for performance at Court an earlier (ca. 1580-96; lost) version of the play which had not met with public success. In "Surviving Original Materials in Dekker's *Old Fortunatus*," *N&Q* 182 (1942):30-31, Halstead also argues that the euphuistic passages in the later (printed) version survive from the earlier lost version. Heinz Thieme, *Zur Verfasserfrage des Dekkerschen Stückes "The Pleasant Comedy of Old Fortunatus"* (1934), attributes the play to Greene, working under the influence of Marlowe and Kyd; but, as Tucker Brooke points out in a review in *JEGP* 35 (1936): 289-90, "the evidence is frail." Albert Feuillerat, *The Composition of Shakespeare's Plays* (1953), cites *Old Fortunatus* as an example of an altered play which Dekker was paid a "high price" to transform.

Patient Grissil, with Chettle and Haughton; comedy (*1600;* 1603)

Confirming the earlier "tentative" attribution by W. L. Halstead of the Welsh roles of Sir Owen ap Meredith and his "querulous bride" to Haughton ("Collaboration on *The Patient Grissill*," *PQ* 18 [1939]: 381-94), David Mason Greene, "The Welsh Characters in *Patient Grissil*," *BUSE* 4 (1960):171-80, finds that the Welsh "impresses one as a serious attempt either to imitate fairly exactly a real spoken dialect, or to create a synthetic one on sound linguistic principles." H. D. Sykes, "The Dramatic Work of Henry Chettle," *N&Q* 143 (1923):345-47, 365-66, attempts specific attribution of acts and scenes on the basis of parallel passages and characteristic habits of speech of the individual playwrights. Harold Jenkins (II,A), however, refutes the argument that any "elaborate division of the play among the three collaborators can be satisfactorily made": "It is against the weight of evidence to give almost all the play to Dekker." Jenkins considers Chettle the "originator of the comedy," and he questions the usual attribution of the play's three songs to Dekker.

Truth's Supplication to Candlelight, allegorical history? (*1600;* lost)

The Spanish Moor's Tragedy, with Day and Haughton (*1600;* lost?)

See *Lust's Dominion* (III,B).

The Seven Wise Masters, with Chettle, Day, and Haughton; tragicomedy? (*1600;* lost)

Cupid and Psyche, with Day and Chettle; classical legend (*1600;* lost)

1 Fair Constance of Rome, with Drayton, Hathway, Munday, and Wilson; classical history? (*1600;* lost)

The Fortewn Tenes (Fortune's Tennis?) unknown (*1600;* lost)

Satiromastix, or The Untrussing of the Humorous Poet, comedy (*1601;* 1602)

Chambers, vol. 3, cites the "generally held" view that "Marston helped Dekker with the play, in spite of the single name on the title-page." The evidence is not totally convincing.

Sebastian, King of Portugal, with Chettle; foreign history (*1601;* lost)

Prologue and Epilogue to *Pontius Pilate*, 1602

Henslowe records payment to Dekker for the Prologue and Epilogue to this anonymous play in January, 1602 (new style dating; the *Annals* records old style dating of 1601). The *Annals* queries whether Dekker might be the author of this lost play of biblical history which is dated ca. 1597–1601.

Revision of *Tasso's Melancholy*, 1602

Henslowe records payment to Dekker in 1602 for alterations to this lost anonymous play (tragedy?) which was newly performed in 1594.

Jephthah, with Munday; biblical history (*1602;* lost)

Caesar's Fall, with Drayton, Middleton, Munday, and Webster; tragedy (*1602;* lost)

A Medicine for a Curst Wife, comedy (*1602*; lost)

Additions to *Sir John Oldcastle*, 1602

Price (I,B) notes that "if these additions were to Part II [*1600;* lost], as seems likely, they have been lost." Part I was performed in 1599 and published in 1600. Both history plays were written by Drayton, Hathway, Munday, and Wilson.

1 Lady Jane, with Chettle, Heywood, W. Smith, and Webster; history (*1602;* lost?)

See next two entries.

2 Lady Jane (with others?), history (*1602;* lost—not completed?)

See next entry.

Sir Thomas Wyatt, with Webster (and possibly Chettle, Heywood, and W. Smith?); history (*1602–7;* 1607)

In *"Sir Thomas Wyat* and the Scenario of *Lady Jane,"* *MLQ* 13 (1952):227–38, Phillip Shaw casts doubt on the title page's exclusive attribution of this play to Dekker and Webster. Finding in it four different sources, he believes that the play as it now stands represents all the sources of the lost *Lady Jane* play for which Henslowe paid Chettle, Dekker, Heywood, W. Smith, and Webster in 1602; and thus "it also represents the shares of all the original authors." Mary Foster Martin, *"If You Know Not Me You Know Nobodie,* and *The Famous Historie of Sir Thomas Wyat,"* *Library* 13 (1932):272–81, also argues that parts of *Wyatt* are the work of Heywood. And in "Note on the Text of *The Famous History of Sir Thomas Wyatt,"* *MLN* 54 (1939):585–89, W. L. Halstead concludes: "The possibilities and probabilities seem very great that *The Famous History of Sir Thomas Wyatt,* 1607, was printed from an actors' built version of the Wyatt– Lady Jane plot shortened for performance in the Provinces. The title-page ascription to Dekker and Webster went back to the remembered work of these two dramatists in the original version, or versions, of 1602." Bowers, vol. 1, suggests that "the text is too corrupt to determine Dekker's or Webster's share with any certainty."

Christmas Comes But Once a Year, with Chettle, Heywood, and Webster; comedy? (*1602;* lost)

The Magnificent Entertainment Given to King James, coronation entertainment (*1604;* 1604)

Although Jonson was also a contributor to the complete coronation entertainment, this title represents only Dekker's share, which incorporates Middleton's speech for Zeal (lines 1409–1468 in Bowers's edition); Jonson published his contribution, *The Coronation Triumph,* separately. Bowers, vol. 2, believes that the first quarto of *The Magnificent Entertainment* represents "that printed edition nearest in descent to Dekker's holograph manuscript, a document which there is every reason to suppose stands directly behind the printed version."

1 The Honest Whore, with Middleton; comedy (*1604;* 1604)

Matthew Baird, "The Early Editions of Thomas Dekker's *The Converted Courtesan* or *The Honest Whore,* Part I," *Library* 10 (1929):52–60, argues that the title of the corrected second edition of the play, *The Converted Courtesan,* represents the true title—a point with which W. W. Greg, *"The Honest Whore* or *The Converted Courtesan,"* *Library* 15 (1934):54–60, agrees. Bowers, vol. 2, bases his edition on the first quarto and argues for the present title (*The Honest Whore*) as the one originally intended. See next entry.

2 *The Honest Whore*, comedy (*1604–*ca. *1605;* 1630)

Henslowe records a payment to Dekker and Middleton in 1604 for Part 1. In "Middleton's Share in *The Honest Whore,* Parts I and II," *N&Q* 197 (1952):3–4, S. Schoenbaum finds that Middleton's share in Part 1 is negligible, in Part 2 "nothing at all": "In diction and in characterization, in manner and in sentiment, *The Honest Whore* is entirely in Dekker's hand"—a view substantiated by Richard H. Barker, *Thomas Middleton* (1958). Schoenbaum also observes that "efforts to find Middleton characteristics in the play have proved fruitless." But Peter Ure, in "Patient Madman and Honest Whore" (II,A), remains "unpersuaded by Schoenbaum's assertions." Ure makes out a "very strong *prima facie* case for Middleton's creation of Candido of Part I" on the basis of the sequence from the character of Quieto in Middleton's *The Phoenix* (1602–4) to that of Candido in the first part of *The Honest Whore* to that of Water Chamlet in Middleton's *Anything for a Quiet Life* (1621); he then argues that "when we take into account the Henslowe payment to Dekker and Middleton for *1 Honest Whore*—an entry that can hardly be regarded except as clear evidence that the text we have contains work by Middleton—and the absence of any evidence for Middleton's participation in *2 Honest Whore*—, it looks as though Dekker in the second part must have been botching the continuation of what was originally a Middleton idea." The question is open to further investigation.

Westward Ho, with Webster; comedy (*1604;* 1607)

See next entry.

Northward Ho, with Webster; comedy (*1605;* 1607)

Bowers, vol. 2, states that Webster's share in these plays is small, but he gives no explanation. In "The Collaboration of Dekker and Webster in *Northward Ho* and *Westward Ho,"* *PBSA* 56 (1962): 482–86, Peter B. Murray studies the colloquial contractions to conclude that "Webster wrote more of these plays than we have thought, and they give us a clearer picture of the method of his collaboration with Dekker than we have had before." His findings lead him to determine that Webster wrote about forty per cent of each play: I, III, and IV.i of *Westward Ho* and I.i, II.ii, III, and V (to somewhere between lines 263 and 359) of *Northward Ho* Frederick Erastus Pierce's *The Collaboration of Webster and Dekker* (1909), which applies elaborate tests to these two plays, as well as to *Sir Thomas Wyatt*, is generally questioned (see S. Schoenbaum, *Internal Evidence and Elizabethan Dramatic Authorship*, 1966). F. L. Lucas has an Appendix, "Webster's Early Collaboration with Dekker," in his edition of *The Complete Works of John Webster* (1927), vol. 4; his conclusion is that "Webster's contribution is of minor importance."

The Roaring Girl, or Moll Cutpurse, with Middleton; comedy (*1604–10;* 1611)

Using tests based on versification, diction, preferred themes, characterization, and constructive skill, George R. Price, "The Shares of Middleton and Dekker in a Collaborated Play," *Papers of the Michigan Academy of Science, Arts, and Letters* 30 (1945, for 1944): 601–15, finds that Dekker composed about two-fifths of the play, concluding the realistic plot which Middleton began. Price also credits Middleton with having finished the romantic plot and with creating the play's "most memorable character," Moll Cutpurse. In "Double, Double," *N&Q* 6 (1959):4–8, William Power, thinking it unlikely that the same dramatist would create two characters with the same name (Mary [Moll] Fitzallard of the main plot, Moll [Mary] Cutpurse of the subplot), also attributes Moll Cutpurse to Middleton. Price also has written to support the view that the printer's manuscript was in Dekker's own hand ("The Manuscript and the Quarto of *The Roaring Girl*," *Library* 11 [1956]:180–86)—a view that Bowers, vol. 3, supports "even though we may differ about the circumstances and the source of transcription." Richard H. Barker, *Thomas Middleton* (1958) believes that "during the greater part" of the play Middleton "was apparently content to fill in the outlines of Dekker's plan"; but David M. Holmes, *The Art of Thomas Middleton* (1970), believes that "the plot, characters, and themes bear Middleton's mark," just as "the over-all plan was clearly his." Holmes attributes the canting scene (V.i)—a scene which "has little connection with the rest of the play"—mainly to Dekker. Norman A. Brittin, *Thomas Middleton, TEAS* (1972), believes that the "shares of the two authors are nearly even. . . . it is possible that each man added some touches to scenes by the other."

The Whore of Babylon, allegorical history (ca. *1606–7;* 1607)

W. L. Halstead, "Dating and Holograph Evidence in *The Whore of Babylon*," *N&Q* 180 (1941):38–40, provides evidence that the play, "printed from Dekker's holograph," is not a rewrite of an older lost play, *Truth's Supplication to Candlelight*, as W. W. Greg thought (in "A Fragment from Henslowe's Diary," *Library* 19 [1938]:180–84). Daniel B. Dodson, "Allusions to the Gunpowder Plot in Dekker's *The Whore of Babylon*," *N&Q* 6 (1959):257, indicates that the date for final revisions cannot be more accurately determined than 1606, following the apprehension on 30 January of that year of a couple of the conspirators in the Gunpowder Plot who are alluded to in the play.

If It Be Not Good, the Devil Is in It (with Daborne?), comedy (*1611–12;* 1612)

In the epistle to his play *A Christian Turned Turk* (*1609–12;* 1612), Robert Daborne seems to be claiming a share in this play; but no further evidence has come to light. Only Dekker's name appears on the title page. Arthur Freeman, "The Date of Dekker's *If This Be Not a Good Play, the Devil Is in It*," *PQ* 44 (1965): 122–24, points out that the play cannot be dated earlier than mid-January, 1611, when the report of the death of the Dutch pirate Dantziker, who figures in the play, would have reached England.

Troia Nova Triumphans, civic pageant (*1612;* 1612)

Match Me in London, tragicomedy (ca. *1611–*ca. *1613;* 1631)

The Life and Death of Guy of Warwick, with Day; tragedy? (*1620 Stationers' Register;* lost)

Bentley, vol. 3, doubts the identification of this play with *The Tragical History of Guy of Warwick*, published in 1661. The *Annals* queries whether the play is a revision of a 1593 *Guy of Warwick*.

The Virgin Martyr, with Massinger; tragedy (*licensed 6 October 1620;* 1622)

H. D. Sykes, "Massinger and Dekker's *The Virgin Martyr*," *N&Q* 142 (1922):61–65, 83–88, allocates scenes between the two drama-tists on the basis of "characteristic words, phrases, allusions and tricks of speech"; Bowers, vol. 3, does so on bibliographical evidence. Bentley, vol. 3, concludes: "Various attempts have been made to separate the work of Dekker and of Massinger in the play—none seems very convincing to me." Louise George Clubb (II,A) believes that the subject probably originated with Massinger, whose name has been linked with popery.

The Witch of Edmonton, with Ford and W. Rowley; tragicomedy (*1621;* 1658)

Leonora Leet Brodwin (II,A) argues, contrary to many, that Dekker conceived the character of Frank Thorney "and contributed to the Frank Thorney portion of the play," for "nowhere in the work of Ford do we find an important character even partially motivated by a clear perception of economic necessity" whereas the reverse is true of Dekker's work. H. D. Sykes, "The Authorship of *The Witch of Edmonton,*" *N&Q* 151 (1926):435–38, 453–57, attributes, on the basis of parallel passages, the greater portion to Ford, the Mother Sawyer (witch) plot "almost entirely" to Dekker. M. Joan Sargeaunt, *John Ford* (1935), states that "there can be . . . no serious question as to Dekker's authorship of the sturdy yeoman family." Bentley, vol. 3, however, finds all the attempts at attribution "largely impressionistic." Authorship on the 1658 title-page is atrributed to "divers well-esteemed Poets' William Rowley, Thomas Dekker, John Ford, &c."; and Bentley suggests that "the possibility that Webster," who collaborated with the other three dramatists years later on another play, "also contributed to *The Witch of Edmonton* might repay investigation."

The Noble Spanish Soldier, foreign pseudo-history (*1622?–31;* 1634)

The title page of the 1634 quarto ascribes the play to "S.R.," generally taken to stand for Samuel Rowley; but previous entries in the Stationers' Register in 1631 and in 1633 ascribe the play definitely to Dekker, and no one has taken seriously Rowley's authorship. (See Bentley, vol. 3, on the accuracy of Sir Henry Herbert's licensing records.) William Peery, "*The Noble Soldier* and *The Parliament of Bees,*" *SP* 48 (1951):219–33, argues for John Day as a collaborator because of parallels between Characters IV and V of Day's *Parliament of Bees* (1641) and II.i and III.ii of the play (as well as with some scenes in *The Wonder of a Kingdom*, below). Bentley, vol. 3, and Bowers, vol. 4, however, accept the interpretation of S. R. Golding, *"The Parliament of Bees,"* *RES* 3 (1927): 280–304, that Day seems to have "lifted almost bodily—in some cases with only slight modification—from *The Noble Soldier* and *The Wonder of a Kingdom* . . . . Where the quarto of the *Bees* corresponds to passages in these plays, Dekker's craftsmanship is nearly always distinguishable; where it deviates, Day's hand is equally well marked." Bertram Lloyd, *"The Noble Soldier* and *The Welsh Embassador,"* *RES* 3 (1927):304–7, suggests a "downward limit for *The Noble Soldier* at least ten years earlier than its published date of 1634."

The Bellman of Paris, with Day; tragedy (*licensed 30 July 1623;* lost)

The Wonder of a Kingdom (with Day?), comedy (*1623–31;* 1636)

The assumption has been that the play is the same as *Come See a Wonder*, perhaps with revisions, which Sir Henry Herbert records was written by John Day and licensed in 1623. Furthermore, Day's *Parliament of Bees*, published in 1641, reproduces, at times verbatim, dialogue from I.iii, III.i, IV.i, and IV.ii of *The Wonder*. Bentley, vol. 3, suggests that the "plausible conclusion seems . . . that Day simply appropriated suitable material where he found it" and that it is best "to accept Dekker's authorship, which is asserted not only twice in the Stationers' Register but on the title-page of the only contemporary edition as well." Bentley also finds no evidence of dating before the entry in the Stationers' Register on 16 May 1631. Bowers, vol. 3, supports Bentley's conclusion with bibliographical evidence.

The Welsh Ambassador, or A Comedy in Disguises, possibly with Ford; pseudo-history (ca. *1623?;* MS)

The ascription to Dekker of this play in manuscript, edited by H. Littledale and W. W. Greg for the Malone Society (1920), was first found in a late seventeenth-century list (1677–1703) representing some bookseller's stock found among the papers of Abraham Hill (see Joseph Quincy Adams, "Hill's List of Early Plays," above, *Disguises*). W. W. Greg describes the manuscript and discusses its history in *Dramatic Documents from the Elizabethan Playhouses* (1931), vol. 2, pp. 279–82. Significant parallels in dialogue, plot, and characterization led Bertram Lloyd (above, *The Noble Spanish Soldier*) to conclude that *The Welsh Ambassador* was a reworking of *The Noble Soldier*. In a later article, "The Authorship of *The Welsh Embassador,"* *RES* 21 (1945):192–201, Lloyd claims for Dekker, on the basis of stylistic similarities, "the chief plot of the play"; he also thinks that he detects "more than a touch of characteristic Fordian pathos and seriousness in the verse" of III.iii and V.i. The play is included in vol. 4 of Bowers's edition.

The Sun's Darling, with Ford; moral masque (*licensed 3 March 1624 and revised 1638–39;* 1656)

Both Bentley, who reviews the scholarship in vol. 3, and Bowers, vol. 4, agree with W. L. Halstead (in "Dekker's *Phaeton,*" *N&Q* 175 [1938]:380–85) that no evidence exists to support the once commonly held position that *The Sun's Darling* represents a revision by Ford of Dekker's lost *Phaeton* (above). Albert Feuillerat, *The Composition of Shakespeare's Plays* (1953), upholds the earlier view. A performance at Court during the Christmas season of 1638–39 may possibly account for later revisions. W. J. Lawrence, *Pre-Restoration Stage Studies* (1927), believes that "there is absolutely no warrant for the belief that it was originally a court masque." Lawrence, "The Problem of Lyly's Songs," *TLS,* 20 Dec. 1923, p. 894, also writes that "the nightingale song was added considerably after the appearance of Blount's 'Lyly' [1623]"; but John Robert Moore, "The Songs in Lyly's Plays," *PMLA* 42 (1927): 623–40, argues that "the song would surely belong to the original work."

The Fairy Knight, with Ford; masque? (*licensed 11 June 1624;* lost)

The Late Murder in Whitechapel, or Keep the Widow Waking, with Ford, W. Rowley, and Webster; comedy and tragedy (*licensed September 1624;* lost)

The attribution of this play and the historical circumstances inspiring its composition are recorded in C. J. Sisson, *Lost Plays of Shakespeare's Age,* 1936 (which includes a revision of his article, "*Keep the Widow Waking,* a Lost Play by Dekker," *Library* 8 [1927]:39–57, 233–59). Sisson writes that "it seems probable that Dekker, who wrote the first act and so introduced the stories and the characters, who reserved for himself the outstanding opportunity offered by the murder plot, and who alone appeared before the Court [of the Star Chamber], was the principal agent in the making of the play and was entrusted with its execution." G. B. Harrison's "Keep the Widow Waking," *Library* 11 (1930):97–101, is not a discussion of the play but of the proverbial phrase and its popularity "at least thirty years before" the play was written.

The Bristow Merchant, with Ford; comedy? (*licensed 22 October 1624;* lost)

The *Annals* queries whether this play is the same as Ford's *The London Merchant*, comedy (*1624?;* lost).

A City Show on the Lord Mayor's Day (?), civic pageant (*1627?;* lost?)

This item, not included in the *Annals*, appears in Abraham Hill's list of manuscript plays (see Joseph Quincy Adams, above, *Disguises*); and Bentley, vol. 3, observes that it may refer to one of Dekker's three extant Lord Mayor's shows "which may have survived in manuscript as well as in print" or that it may indeed be a fourth civic pageant. Price (I,B) points out that "Dekker in his epistle of *Wars, Wars, Wars,* 1628, sigs. $A_2{}^v$, A_3," mentions a now lost Lord Mayor's show for the inauguration of Sir Hugh Hamersley the preceding year.

Britannia's Honour, civic pageant (*1628;* 1628)

London's Tempe, or The Field of Happiness, civic pageant (*1629;* 1629)

Believe It Is So and 'Tis So, unknown (ca. *1594–*ca. *1629;* lost)

This play is attributed to Dekker in Abraham Hill's list of manuscript plays. Robert Davenport employed the title-page motto of *Crede Quod Habes et Habes*, but Joseph Quincy Adams, "Hill's List of Early Plays" (above, *Disguises*), sees no connection here; the motto is proverbial. Alfred Harbage, "The Mystery of *Perkin Warbeck*" (II,B), suggests possible identification with *Perkin Warbeck*, jointly authored by Ford and Dekker.

The White Moor, tragicomedy? (ca. *1594–*ca. *1629;* lost?)

A play by this title is attributed to Dekker in Abraham Hill's list of manuscript plays. Adams (see entry above) says that "nothing is known of a play with this title" but observes that Elizabethan dramatists were familiar with the story of the black Ethiopian queen's white daughter in Heliodorus's *Æthiopica*. Bentley, vol. 3, rejects as Dekker's the anonymous play manuscript, *The White Ethiopian,* at the British Museum.

Gustavus, King of Sweden, history (*1630?–32;* lost)

A play by this title was entered to Humphrey Moseley as by Dekker in the Stationers' Register on 29 June 1660, and the same ascription appears on "Warburton's famous list of manuscript plays allegedly burned by his cook" (Bentley, vol. 3; W. W. Greg, "The Bakings of Betsy," *Library* 2 [1911]:225–59, comments on this list). Bentley, vol. 3, in dating the play, observes: "A play by Dekker on the great Gustavus Adolphus could have been written between the time of his emergence as an English hero in 1630 and Dekker's death in August 1632."

Joconda and Astols[f?]o, comedy (*before 1632;* lost)

A play by this title was entered to Humphrey Moseley as by Dekker in the Stationers' Register on 29 June 1660, and the same ascription appears on Warburton's list (see entry above). Bentley, vol. 3, takes the spelling "to be a misreading, or perhaps a perversion, of Jocundo and Astolpho, the principal characters of Canto 28 of Ariosto's *Orlando Furioso*." Bentley also conjectures a date of ca. 1630–32(?), but Price (I,B) lists the play under 1626.

B. UNCERTAIN ASCRIPTIONS; APOCRYPHA

Antony and Vallia, romance? (ca. *1590?–95;* lost)

Chambers, vol. 3, discusses the conjectural ascription to Dekker.

The Bloody Banquet, tragedy (*1639;* 1639)

The title page of the 1639 edition reads: "By T. D." Bentley, vol. 3, and S. Schoenbaum, ed., *The Bloody Banquet* (for the Malone Society, 1962) find no evidence for attribution to Dekker. E. H. C. Oliphant, "*The Bloodie Banquet*, A Dekker-Middleton Play," *TLS*, 17 Dec. 1925, p. 882, assigns the play to Dekker and Middleton "on both external and internal grounds." In *Middleton's Tragedies* (1955), S. Schoenbaum concludes that the authorship question "is still an open one."

Blurt, Master Constable, or The Spaniard's Night Walk, comedy (*1601–2;* 1602 and MS fragment)

The play was published anonymously. W. J. Lawrence, "Thomas Dekker's Theatrical Allusiveness," *TLS*, 30 Jan. 1937, p. 72 (rpt. in his *Speeding up Shakespeare* [1937]) argues for Dekker's authorship on the basis of allusions to other plays; and Daniel B. Dodson, *"Blurt, Master Constable,"* *N&Q* 6 (1959):61-65, concludes, also on the basis of "legitimate parallel passages," that the play is Dekker's. In "The Stage Quarrel in *Wily Beguiled,"* *N&Q* 3 (1956); 380-83, Matthew P. McDiarmid suggests that the allusions to "Tom Shoo-maker" and to "Constable oth towne" in scene xiii of the anonymous *Wily Beguiled* (probably acted around 1602) refer to Thomas Dekker, author of the recently successful *Shoemakers' Holiday* and apparently of *Blurt, Master Constable*—a view supported by Samuel Schoenbaum in *"Blurt, Master Constable*: A Possible Author-ship Clue," *RN* 12 (1960):7-9, as well as by Price (I,B) and Holmes and Barker (III,A, *The Roaring Girl*). Bowers, vol. 4, believes "that there is fairly good evidence for seeing Dekker's hand in some scenes"; but he does not include the play in his edition.

Captain Thomas Stukeley, history (*1596;* 1605)

Neither Henslowe nor the title page of 1605 indicates authorship. See the essay on this play in the Anonymous Plays section of this volume.

Chance Medley, comedy (*1598;* lost)

Attributed to Dekker in Chambers, vol. 3; but, as Price (I,B) points out, "A better reading of the *Diary* [Henslowe's], however, shows that Henslowe erred in regard to the authors, who were Robert Wilson, Henry Chettle, Michael Drayton, and Anthony Munday."

Charlemagne, or The Distracted Emperor, tragedy (*1584*-ca. *1605;* MS)

See Chambers, vol. 4, for the conjectural ascription to Dekker, and the essay on this play in the Anonymous Plays section of this volume.

Diocletian, classical history? (*1594;* lost)

Chambers, vol. 3, discusses, though he himself doubts, the conjec-ture that this anonymous play is Dekker's and that it was revised as *The Virgin Martyr* (III,A) by Massinger.

The Additions to Marlowe's *Doctor Faustus*, 1602

W. W. Greg, *Marlowe's "Doctor Faustus," 1604–1616* (1950), finds no evidence of Dekker's hand in the additions.

The Fairy Knight, or Oberon the Second, comedy (*1637?–58?*; MS)

Bentley, vol. 3, believes that the "recently discovered manuscript" of this anonymous play is not likely to be *The Fairy Knight* (III,A), on which Dekker collaborated with Ford in 1624.

The Family of Love, comedy (ca. *1602–7*; 1608)

In "Dekker's Part in *The Familie of Love*," *Joseph Quincy Adams Memorial Studies*, ed. J. G. McManaway, et al., (1948), pp. 723–38, Gerald J. Eberle argues that this anonymously published play reveals "several strata of composition": "I believe that *The Familie of Love*, as we know it, is a revision by Dekker and Middleton of an early play written by Middleton with considerable help from Dekker." S. Schoenbaum, *Internal Evidence and Elizabethan Dramatic Authorship* (1966), observes that many of Eberle's "parallels, or 'touchstones,' as he calls them," are in fact "not parallel" and that "the entire essay is, indeed, a fine illustration of the inadequacy of good intentions alone." Norman A. Brittin, *Thomas Middleton* (1972), concludes: "Even if Dekker wrote parts of the play, the firm plotting is evidently Middleton's."

The London Prodigal, comedy (*1603–5*; 1605)

Baldwin Maxwell, "Conjectures on *The London Prodigal*," *Studies in Honor of T. W. Baldwin*, ed. Don Cameron Allen (1958), pp. 171–84, suggests that if a date closer to 1601, when Dekker was briefly associated with the Globe Company, is accepted for this Shakespeare Apocrypha play, then "Dekker's authorship would not be difficult to accept.... Presumably, he could have written it at no other date." Price (I,B) offers reasons why Dekker is an unlikely candidate. Also see the essay on this play in the Anonymous Plays section of this volume.

Look About You, comedy (ca. *1598–1600*; 1600)

This play is sometimes conjectured to be Dekker's *Bear a Brain* (III,A): see Chambers, vol. 3; *Annals*; and the essay in the Anonymous Plays section of this volume.

Love's Cure, or The Martial Maid, comedy (*1625?*; 1647)

H. Dugdale Sykes, *Sidelights on Elizabethan Drama* (1924), claims for Dekker a share in this play; but E. H. C. Oliphant, *The Plays of Beaumont and Fletcher* (1927), finds that the play does not at all "impress" him as Dekker's. The play has been attributed to Beaumont and Fletcher, revised by Massinger. See Bentley, vol. 3, who notes: "Nearly everything about the play is in a state of confusion."

Lust's Dominion, or The Lascivious Queen, tragedy (*1600?*; 1657)

The second issue of the 1657 quarto ascribes the play to "*Christofer Marloe*, Gent." S. R. Golding, "The Authorship of *Lust's Dominion*," *N&Q* 155 (1928):399–402, takes issue with the general identification of the play with *The Spanish Moor's Tragedy* (III,A) for which Henslowe "layd out" three pounds to Dekker, Haughton, and Day. J. Le Gay Brereton, in the introduction to his edition of the play for *Materials for the Study of the Old English Drama*, ed. Henry de Vocht, vol. 5 (1931), argues that "the general structure is Dekker's"; and H. Dugdale Sykes (above, *Love's Cure*) takes issue with M. L. Hunt's rejection of Dekker as a collaborator (*Thomas Dekker*, 1911). In "The Authorship of *Lust's Dominion*," *SP* 55 (1958):39–61, K. Gustav Cross writes that it "may be accepted as proven that *Lust's Dominion* is the play called *The Spanish Moor's Tragedy*" and then offers "evidence" for Marston's being the first to rewrite or to revise a work "which was further revised by Dekker, Haughton, and Day." Cross offers further "evidence" for Marston's involvement in "The Vocabulary of *Lust's Dominion*," *NM* 59 (1958):41–48. Philip J. Ayres, "The Revision of *Lust's Dominion*," *N&Q* 17 (1970):212–13, believes that "the play was first written in 1600 and revised subsequently [after 1610]." Bowers includes the play in vol. 4 of his edition. Also see the discussion of this play in the Anonymous Plays section of this volume.

The Mack, comedy? (*1595*; lost)

See Chambers, vol. 3, for the conjecture that this play was the original of *The Wonder of a Kingdom* (III,A).

The Merry Devil of Edmonton, comedy (*1599–1604*; 1608)

Published anonymously, the play belongs to the Shakespeare Apocrypha. In 1942 William Amos Abrams edited the play with introduction and notes, and he cautiously advanced the claim for Dekker's authorship—a claim which, the editor admitted, depends "upon internal evidence [vocabulary, figures of speech, images; style, characterization, and plot], and such conclusions, thus arrived at, can never be absolutely final." Bowers rejects the play for his edition, claiming that he has "no faith in the evidence so far offered" (see his letter to the editor, *Library* 10 [1955]:130–33). Also see the essay on this play in the Anonymous Plays section of this volume.

The "gulling scenes" of Middleton's *Michaelmas Term*, comedy (*1604-6;* 1607)

In "The Dekker-Middleton Problem in *Michaelmas Term,*" *Studies in English* (Univ. of Texas) [26] (1947):49-58, Lucetta J. Teagarden notes "a definite relationship between certain of the gulling scenes of Middleton's *Michaelmas Term* and Dekker's pamphlet of the London scene called *Lanthorne and Candlelight* [1608]." Although the play was published a year before the pamphlet, this study questions whether Dekker could have written the cheating scenes in the play; the author offers alternatives.

Perkin Warbeck by John Ford; history (ca. *1629-34;* 1634 and MS)

In "The Mystery of *Perkin Warbeck*" (II,B), Alfred Harbage queries whether "the presence of so individual a writer as Dekker" can be detected in a play so untypically Fordian. Although he admits that his belief "that Dekker wrote part of *Perkin Warbeck* and shaped the play as a whole" is frankly "impressionistic," Harbage does "scrutinize the association of Dekker and Ford" and cites a number of external reasons to support a view that warrants further investigation. Sidney R. Homan, Jr., "Dekker as Collaborator in Ford's *Perkin Warbeck,*" *ELN* 3 (1965): 104-6, establishes parallels between this play and *The Witch of Edmonton*, their known collaborative effort, and suggests that the character of Huntley (whom Homan compares with Old Thorney in *The Witch*) is Dekker's. Homan also suggests an earlier date for the play (ca. 1621-24) when the two dramatists were known to be collaborating. Price (I,B) sees "nothing of Dekker" in this play.

Philipo and Hippolito, tragicomedy? (*1594;* lost)

Chambers, vol. 3, cites the inference that this work was revised as *Philenzo and Hypollita* (lost), entered in the Stationers' Register on

29 June 1660 as by Massinger, "who revised other early work of Dekker." Price observes that "Dekker's connection with *Philipo* is a weak inference."

The Set at Maw, comedy? *(1594;* lost)

See Chambers, vol. 3, for the conjecture that this anonymous play was the original of *Match Me in London* (III,A).

The Spanish Fig, unknown *(6 Jan. 1602, bought;* lost)

Chambers, vol. 3, discusses the conjecture that this anonymous play can be identified with *The Noble Spanish Soldier* (III,A). Bentley, vol. 3, writes: "There is no evidence whatever of any connexion between the two plays."

The Spanish Gypsy by Middleton and W. Rowley; tragicomedy *(licensed 9 July 1623;* 1653)

The play was assigned to Thomas Middleton and William Rowley in 1653, but H. Dugdale Sykes (above, *Love's Cure*) favored the attribution to Ford. E. H. C. Oliphant, *Shakespeare and His Fellow Dramatists* (1929), vol. 2, found "a few uncertain signs of Middleton" but thought the play to be "in the main . . . from the workshop of Ford and Dekker." Brittin (above, *Family of Love*) observes: "If Dekker's name had been attached to it, one would be hard put to it to prove that Dekker had no hand in its composition."

The Additions to Kyd's *The Spanish Tragedy*, 1602

In a series of notes and replies to *N&Q* (164 [1933]: 147-49; 166 [1934]:246; 167 [1934]:88; and 180 [1941]:8-9), H. W. Crundell and R. G. Howarth offer examples of "common idiom and common imagery" from Dekker's works to support his authorship of these additions. No editor has taken this ascription seriously.

Prologue to Marlowe's *Tamburlaine (1587-88;* 1590)

Chambers, vol. 3, observes that this conjecture "rests on a forged entry in Henslowe's Diary for 20 Dec. 1597."

The Telltale, tragicomedy *(1605-*ca. *1640;* MS, Act IV incomplete)

Arthur Freeman, "The Authorship of *The Tell-Tale*," *JEGP* 62

(1963):288–92, challenges the suggestion of "multiple authorship" by the editors of the Malone Society Reprint (R. A. Foakes and J. C. Gibson, 1959–60). Freeman conjectures on "entirely internal" evidence ("resemblances of plots and incidentals" that are close to Dekker's surviving last plays) that the play "is chiefly, if not entirely, the work of Thomas Dekker"—a position held also by Price (I,B). W. W. Greg, *Dramatic Documents from the Elizabethan Playhouses*, vol. 2 (1931), attributes the "literary hand" of this anonymous Dulwich College manuscript to a scribe of about 1630–40(?) and finds no evidence of performance. Bentley, vol. 5, queries whether this play "could be the lost unnamed comedy by John Nichols or Nicholas . . . that was performed at Trinity College, Cambridge, in 1639 or 1640."

The Weakest Goeth to the Wall, pseudo-history (ca. *1599–1600;* 1600)

M. L. Hunt (I,C) argues in favor of Dekker's share in this anonymous play, as does H. Dugdale Sykes (above, *Love's Cure*). Price (I,B) rejects the attribution. See the essay on this play in the Anonymous Plays section of this volume.

C. CRITIQUE OF THE STANDARD EDITION

Fredson Bowers's four-volume *The Dramatic Works of Thomas Dekker* (1953–61) is the standard edition that replaces the Pearson reprint (ed. R. H. Shepherd, 4 vols., 1873). In "Old-Spelling Editions of Dramatic Texts," *Studies in Honor of T. W. Baldwin*, ed. Don Cameron Allen (1958), pp. 9–15, Bowers states the rationale for a "critical old-spelling edition": "to establish the text and thereby become a definitive edition," that is, one that "has recovered what appears to be the most authoritative form of the dramatic text." His Cambridge edition of Dekker illustrates this standard. The introduction to the first volume sets forth the principles upon which the entire edition is based—namely, the use of first editions ("the only ones set from manuscript") for the copy-text except (as in two cases) where later editions show authorial revision or correction; the collation of all seventeenth-century editions and of the known multiple copies of the copy-text edition; the consideration of proof-corrected variants on their own merits, with preference given to uncorrected readings over "printing-house sophistications"; and the retention of the old-spelling "accidentals" of the copy-text.

The minimum of editorial interference on each page of the text makes the plays easily accessible to the reader; a few notes "list all substantive departures in the present edition from the early edition chosen as the copy-text." Appended to each text are notes explaining "the more important emendations or examples of refusals to emend" and lists of "the press-variant formes in authoritative editions," "of the readings in the accidentals altered from the copy-text," and of the "historical collation of the substantive and semi-substantive variants in editions other than the copy-text before 1700." Introductions to each work discuss the nature of the printer's copy, the printing-house procedure, the copies collated, and "the method by which the critical text has been derived." The fourth volume contains notes and corrections to earlier volumes and also includes "three plays from the list that at one time or another has been attributed to" Dekker (III,B).

Bowers's edition has provoked the criticism of being unduly "austere," "very conservative," and of reflecting an "extreme bibliographical approach." Most reviewers miss the discussion of such non-textual matters as the nature of Dekker's collaborative efforts, his sources, dates, language, and allusions. The editor is very careful, however, to define his own particular role: the Foreword to the last volume begins, "With this fourth volume the textual editor's assignment is completed." Two volumes of *Introductions and Commentary* by Cyrus Hoy are scheduled for publication in 1974 to complete the Cambridge Dekker.

D. TEXTUAL STUDIES

The separate introductions to each play in the four-volume Cambridge Dekker by Fredson Bowers provide, as noted above, complete textual studies. Most other textual studies attempt to determine Dekker's share in his known collaborative efforts or to affirm or deny his authorship or partial authorship of anonymous plays.

E. SINGLE-WORK EDITIONS

Of the canonical works, only *The Shoemakers' Holiday* continues to be edited in single-work editions, just as it also remains the work most frequently anthologized. A banner year was 1927 when it was edited by W. J. Halliday, G. B. Harrison (the Fortune Playbooks), G. N. Pocock, and W. T. Williams. The Bankside Playbook edition appeared in 1924. J. R. Sutherland edited the play in 1928 in a volume that also included Wilfrid J. Halliday's edition of *The First Part of Deloney's "The Gentle Craft."* The Nelson Playbook edition (no. 117) came out in 1932. Informative introductions and notes are provided in the recent editions by J. B. Steane (1965), Merritt Lawlis (1966), and Paul C. Davies (Fountainwell Drama Texts, 1968). The Scolar Press facsimile of the 1600 quarto was published in 1971.

F. EDITIONS OF NONDRAMATIC WORKS

No edition of the nondramatic works comparable to Bowers's edition of the plays exists although the late F. P. Wilson reported in *RORD* 6 (1963):63, that his "work on the text of the pamphlets—three volumes—has been completed, as has the commentary on the earliest of the pamphlets" and that "Clarendon Press will publish the edition." Arthur Brown is preparing the edition for press. Until that appears, the standard work is A. B. Grosart's *The Non-Dramatic Works of Thomas Dekker*, 5 vols. (1884–86). Wilson edited six of the pamphlets with introduction and notes in *The Plague Pamphlets of Thomas Dekker* (1925), as well as *Four Birds of Noah's Ark* (1924). Wilson has also edited (1929) *The Batchelars Banquet*—an Elizabethan translation of *Les quinze joyes de mariage*, but he "suspects" that Dekker had no share in it; he favors the attribution to Robert Tofte. A. V. Judges included portions of *The Bellman of London, Lantern and Candlelight*, and *O per se O* in *The Elizabethan Underworld* (1930). In the introduction to his edition (1943) of *The Owles Almanacke*, Don Cameron Allen argues against J. P. Collier's attribution of the work to Dekker. G. B. Harrison edited the plague pamphlet of *The Wonderful Year, 1603* for the Bodley Head quartos (1924), and G. R. Hibbard includes it in *Three Elizabethan Pamphlets* (1951). Most recently, E. D. Pendry, in *Thomas Dekker*, has edited, with introduction, illustrations, and notes on sources and texts, a substantial portion of Dekker's prose as vol. 4 of the Stratford-upon-Avon Library (1968).

IV. SEE ALSO

A. GENERAL

Adams, Henry Hitch. *English Domestic or, Homiletic Tragedy, 1575–1642.* 1943.

Adams, Joseph Quincy. *A Life of William Shakespeare.* 1923.

Aksenov, I. A. *Gamlet i drugie opyty v sodeistvie otechestvennoi Shekspirologii* [*"Hamlet" and other experiments contributing to native Shakespeare scholarship*]. 1930.

42   The Popular School

Albright, Evelyn May. *Dramatic Publication in England, 1580-1640: A Study of Conditions Affecting Content and Form of Drama.* 1927.

Allen, Don Cameron. *The Star-Crossed Renaissance.* 1941.

Allen, Morse S. *The Satire of John Marston.* 1920.

Aronstein, Philipp. *Das englische Renaissancedrama.* 1929.

Atkins, J. W. H. *English Literary Criticism: The Renascence.* 1947.

Axelrad, A. José. *Un malcontent élizabéthain: John Marston (1576-1634).* 1955.

Babb, Lawrence. *The Elizabethan Malady: A Study of Melancholia in English Literature from 1580-1642.* 1951.

Bakeless, John. *The Tragicall History of Christopher Marlowe.* 2 vols. 1942.

Barber, C. L. *The Idea of Honour in the English Drama 1591-1700.* 1957.

Barish, Jonas A. *Ben Jonson and the Language of Prose Comedy.* 1960.

Baskervill, Charles Read. *The Elizabethan Jig and Related Song Drama.* 1929.

Bentley, Gerald Eades. *Shakespeare and Jonson: Their Reputations in the Seventeenth Century Compared.* 2 vols. 1945.

———. *The Profession of Dramatist in Shakespeare's Time, 1590-1642.* 1971.

Berringer, Ralph W. "Jonson's *Cynthia's Revels* and the War of the Theatres." *PQ* 22 (1942):1-22.

Bevington, David. *Tudor Drama and Politics: A Critical Approach to Topical Meaning.* 1968.

Black, A. Bruce, and Robert Metcalf Smith. *Shakespeare Allusions and Parallels.* 1931.

Boas, F. S. "Charles Lamb and the Elizabethan Dramatists." *E&S 1943* 29 (1944):62-81.

Bolte, Johannes. "Das Echo in Volksglaube und Dichtung." *Forschungen und Fortschritte* 11 (1935):320-21.

Bowden, William R. *The English Dramatic Lyric, 1603-42.* 1951.

Bowers, Fredson Thayer. *Elizabethan Revenge Tragedy, 1587-1642.* 1940.

Boyce, Benjamin. "A Restoration 'Improvement' of Thomas Dekker." *MLN* 50 (1935):460-61.

Bradbrook, M. C. *Themes and Conventions of Elizabethan Tragedy.* 1935.

———. *Shakespeare and Elizabethan Poetry: A Study of His Earlier Work in Relation to the Poetry of the Time.* 1951.

———. *The Rise of the Common Player.* 1962.

Bridges-Adams, W. *The Irresistible Theatre.* Vol. 1, *From the Conquest to the Commonwealth.* 1957.

Busby, Olive Mary. *Studies in the Development of the Fool in the Elizabethan Drama.* 1923.

Bush, Douglas. *English Literature in the Earlier Seventeenth Century, 1600-1660.* 1945; 2nd ed. 1962.

Camden, Carroll. *The Elizabethan Woman.* 1952.

Camp, Charles W. *The Artisan in English Literature.* 1924.

Campbell, Oscar James. *Comicall Satyre and Shakespeare's "Troilus and Cressida."* 1938.

Caputi, Anthony. *John Marston, Satirist.* 1961.

Carrère, Felix. *Le théâtre de Thomas Kyd.* 1951.

Cawley, Robert R. *The Voyagers and Elizabethan Drama.* 1938.

———. *Unpathed Waters.* 1940.

Cazamian, Louis. *The Development of English Humor.* 1952.

Chambers, E. K., ed. *The Shakspere Allusion-Book.* 1932.

Chew, Samuel C. *Swinburne.* 1929.

———. *The Crescent and the Rose: Islam and England during the Renaissance.* 1937.

Clark, Arthur Melville. *Thomas Heywood, Playwright and Miscellanist.* 1931.

Clarkson, P. S., and C. T. Warren. *The Law of Property in Shakespeare and Elizabethan Drama.* 1942.

Cookman, A. V. "Shakespeare's Contemporaries on the Modern English Stage." *SJ* 94 (1958):37-38.

Courthope, W. J. *A History of English Poetry.* Vol. 5. 1903.

Craig, Hardin. *The Enchanted Glass: The Elizabethan Mind in Literature.* 1936.

Cromwell, Otelia. *Thomas Heywood: A Study in the Elizabethan Drama of Everyday Life.* 1928.

Cunningham, John E. *Elizabethan and Early Stuart Drama.* 1965.

Curry, John V. *Deception in Elizabethan Comedy.* 1955.

Davril, Robert. *Le drame de John Ford.* 1954.

De Luna, B. N. *Jonson's Romish Plot.* 1967.

Doran, Madeleine. *Endeavors of Art: A Study of Form in Elizabethan Drama.* 1954.

Downer, Alan S. *The British Drama.* 1950.

Dunn, Esther Cloudman. *Ben Jonson's Art.* 1925.

Eccles, Mark. "Thomas Dekker: Burial-Place." *N&Q* 177 (1939):157.

Eckhardt, Eduard. *Das englische Drama der Spätrenaissance (Shakespeares Nachfolger).* 1929.

Enck, John J. *Jonson and the Comic Truth.* 1957.

Evans, Ifor. *A Short History of English Drama.* 1948; rev. ed., 1965.

Farnham, Willard. *The Medieval Heritage of Elizabethan Tragedy.* 1936.

Finkelpearl, Philip J. *John Marston of the Middle Temple.* 1969.

Forsythe, Robert S. "Comic Effects in Elizabethan Drama." *Quarterly Journal of the Univ. of North Dakota* 17 (1927):266-92.

Freeman, Arthur. *Thomas Kyd: Facts and Problems.* 1967.

Frost, David L. *The School of Shakespeare.* 1968.

Granville-Barker, Harley, and G. B. Harrison, ed. *A Companion to Shakespeare Studies.* 1934.

Gray, Arthur. *How Shakespeare "Purged" Jonson: A Problem Solved.* 1928.

Grupenhoff, Richard L. "The Lord Mayors' Shows: From Their Origins to 1640." *Theatre Studies* 18 (1971/72):13-22.

Gurr, Andrew. *The Shakespearean Stage, 1574-1642.* 1970.

Halstead, W. L. "Dekker's Arrest by the Chamberlain's Men." *N&Q* 176 (1939): 41-42.

Harbage, Alfred. "A Contemporary Attack upon Shakspere?" *ShAB* 16 (1941): 42-49.

———. *Shakespeare's Audience.* 1941.

———. *Shakespeare and the Rival Traditions.* 1952.

Harrison, G. B. *Shakespeare's Fellows; Being a Brief Chronicle of the Shakespearean Age.* 1923.

———. *Shakespeare at Work, 1592-1603.* 1933.

———. *The Elizabethan Journals; Being a record of Those Things Most Talked of during the Years 1591-1603.* 1939.

————. *Elizabethan Plays and Players.* 1940.

Hartnoll, Phyllis. *The Oxford Companion to the Theatre.* 1951; 3rd ed. 1967.

Herford, C. H., and Percy and Evelyn Simpson, ed. *Ben Jonson.* 11 vols. 1925-52.

Herrick, M. T. *Tragicomedy: Its Origins and Development in Italy, France, and England.* 1955.

Höhna, H. *Der Physiologus in der elisabethan Literatur.* 1930.

Holzknecht, Karl J. *Outlines of Tudor and Stuart Plays, 1497-1642.* 1947.

————. *The Backgrounds of Shakespeare's Plays.* 1950.

Howarth, R. G. *Literature of the Theatre: Marlowe to Shirley.* 1953.

————. "John Webster, Property-owner?" *N&Q* 12 (1965):236-37.

Hoy, Cyrus. *The Hyacinth Room: An Investigation into the Nature of Comedy, Tragedy, and Tragicomedy.* 1964.

Hyde, Mary Crapo. *Playwriting for Elizabethans, 1600-1605.* 1949.

Jacquot, Jean, et al. *La lieu théâtral à la renaissance.* 1964.

Jones-Davies, M. T. "Thomas Dekker et les Marchands-Tailleurs." *EA* 6 (1953): 50-53.

Joseph, B. L. *Elizabethan Acting.* 1951; 2nd ed., 1964.

Kimbrough, Robert. *Shakespeare's "Troilus and Cressida" and Its Setting.* 1964.

Kitchin, George. *A Survey of Burlesque and Parody in English.* 1931.

Klein, David. *The Elizabethan Dramatists as Critics.* 1963.

Knight, G. Wilson. *The Golden Labyrinth: A Study of the British Drama.* 1962.

Knoll, Robert E. *Ben Jonson's Plays.* 1964.

Koskenniemi, Inna. *Studies in the Vocabulary of English Drama, 1550-1660, Excluding Shakespeare and Ben Jonson.* 1962.

Lawrence, W. J. *Shakespeare's Workshop.* 1928.

————. *Old Theatre Days and Ways.* 1935.

LeComte, Edward S. *Endymion in England.* 1944.

Leech, Clifford. *John Webster.* 1951.

————. *John Ford and the Drama of His Time.* 1957.

Leishman, J. B., ed. *The Three Parnassus Plays (1598-1601).* 1949.

Levin, Richard. "Elizabethan 'Clown' Subplots." *Essays in Criticism* 16 (1966):84-91.

Lindabury, R. V. *A Study of Patriotism in the Elizabethan Drama.* 1931.

Linthicum, M. Channing. *Costume in the Drama of Shakespeare and His Contemporaries.* 1936.

Ļobzowska, Maria. "Two English Translations of the XVth Century French Satire 'Les quinze joyes de mariage.' " *Kwartalnik Neofilologiczny* 10 (1963):17-32.

Looten, Chanoine C. *Shakespeare et la religion.* 1924.

McDonald, Charles Osborne. *The Rhetoric of Tragedy.* 1966.

McGinn, Donald Joseph. *Shakespeare's Influence on the Drama of His Age Studied in "Hamlet."* 1938.

Mehl, Dieter. *The Elizabethan Dumb Show: The History of a Dramatic Convention.* 1966; German ed. 1964.

————. "Emblems in English Renaissance Drama." *RenD* 2 (1969):39-57.

Mezger, Fritz. *Der Ire in der englischen Literatur bis zum Anfang des 19. Jahrhunderts.* 1929.

Michelson, Hijman. *The Jew in Early English Literature.* 1926.

Miller, Henry Knight. "The Paradoxical Encomium with Special Reference to Its Vogue in England, 1600-1800." *MP* 53 (1956):145-78.

Millett, Fred B., and Gerald Eades Bentley. *The Art of the Drama.* 1935.

Mohl, Ruth. *The Three Estates in Medieval and Renaissance Literature.* 1962.

Moore, John B. *The Comic and the Realistic in English Drama.* 1925.

Moore, John Robert. "The Songs of the Public Theaters in the Time of Shakespeare." *JEGP* 28 (1929):166-202.

Morris, Helen. *Elizabethan Literature.* 1957.

Muir, Kenneth, and S. Schoenbaum, ed. *A New Companion to Shakespeare Studies.* 1971.

Mullett, Charles F. "The Plague of 1603 in England." *Annals of Medical History* 9 (1937):230-47.

Myers, Aaron Michael. *Representation and Misrepresentation of the Puritan in Elizabethan Drama.* 1931.

Nicoll, Allardyce. *British Drama: An Historical Survey from the Beginnings to the Present Time.* 1925; rev. ed. 1963.

Niemeyer, Paul. *Das bürgerliche Drama in England im zeitalter Shakespeares.* 1930.

Oliver, H. J. *The Problem of John Ford.* 1955.

Oras, Ants. *Pause Patterns in Elizabethan and Jacobean Drama: An Experiment in Prosody.* UFMH, no. 3 (1960).

Palmer, John. *Ben Jonson.* 1934.

Parrott, Thomas Marc, and Robert Hamilton Ball. *A Short View of Elizabethan Drama.* 1943.

Passman, Hans. *Der Typus der Kurtisane im elisabethanischen Drama.* 1926.

Peter, John. *Complaint and Satire in Early English Literature.* 1956.

Pietzker, Annemarie. *Der Kaufman in der elisabethanischen Literatur.* 1931.

Pinto, V. de Sola. *The English Renaissance, 1510-1688.* 1938.

Rabkin, Norman. "The Double Plot: Notes on the History of a Convention." *RenD* 7 (1964):55-69.

Rébora, Piero. *L'Italia nel dramma inglese (1558-1642).* 1925.

Reed, Robert Rentoul, Jr. *Bedlam on the Jacobean Stage.* 1952.

Reese, Gertrude C. "The Question of the Succession in Elizabethan Drama." *Studies in English* (Univ. of Texas) 22 (1942):59-85.

Reynolds, George Fullmer. *The Staging of Elizabethan Plays at the Red Bull Theater, 1605-1625.* 1940.

Ricci, Seymour de. *Census of Medieval and Renaissance Manuscripts in the United States and Canada.* Vol. 1. 1935.

Schelling, Felix E. *Foreign Influences in Elizabethan Plays.* 1923.

———. *Elizabethan Playwrights: A Short History of the English Drama from Medieval Times to the Closing of the Theatres in 1642.* 1925.

Scherer, Bernhard. *Vers und Prosa bei den jüngeren dramatischen zeitgenossen Shakespeares.* 1932.

Schirmer, Walter F. *Geschichte der englischer und amerikanischen Literatur von den anfängen bis zur Gegenwart.* 2 vols. 1954.

Schoenbaum, S. *Shakespeare's Lives.* 1970.

Seronsy, Cecil C. "Dekker and Falstaff." *SQ* 4 (1953):365-66.

Shakespeare Association, Members of the. *A Series of Papers on Shakespeare and the Theatre.* 1927.

Shapiro, Michael. "Toward a Reappraisal of the Children's Troupes." *Theater Survey* 13 (1972):1-19.

Shaw, Phillip. "Richard Vennar and *The Double PP." PBSA* 43 (1949):199-202.
Sibley, G. M. *The Lost Plays and Masques.* 1933.
Silvette, Herbert. *The Doctor on the Stage.* 1967.
Sisson, Charles J. *Le goût public et le théâtre élisabéthain jusqu'à la mort de Shakespeare.* 1922.
Smet, Robert de [Romain Sanvic]. *Le théâtre élisabéthain. 1955.*
Spencer, Theodore. *Death and Elizabethan Tragedy: A Study of Convention and Opinion in the Elizabethan Drama.* 1936.
Spens, Janet. *Elizabethan Drama.* 1922.
Squire, J. C. "Dekker on the Plague." *The Observer* (London), 13 June 1926, p. 6.
Stavig, Mark. *John Ford and the Traditional Moral Order.* 1968.
Stroup, Thomas B. *Microcosmos: The Shape of the Elizabethan Play.* 1965.
Sugden, E. H. *A Topographical Dictionary to the Works of Shakespeare and His Fellow Dramatists.* 1925.
Talbert, Ernest W. *Elizabethan Drama and Shakespeare's Early Plays: An Essay in Historical Criticism.* 1963.
Thaler, Alwin. *Shakspere to Sheridan.* 1922.
Thorndike, Ashley. *English Comedy.* 1929.
Thorp, Willard. *The Triumph of Realism in Elizabethan Drama, 1558-1612.* 1928.
Tiegs, Alexander. *Zum Zusammenarbeit englischer Berufsdramatiker unmittelbar ver, neben und nach Shakespeare.* 1933.
Tilley, Morris Palmer. *A Dictionary of the Proverbs in England in the Sixteenth and Seventeenth Centuries.* 1950.
Tillyard, E. M. W., ed. *Lamb's Criticism.* 1923.
Turner [Wright], Julia Celeste. *Anthony Mundy: An Elizabethan Man of Letters.* 1928.
Venezky, Alice S. *Pageantry on the Shakespearean Stage.* 1951. (Also issued under Alice V. Griffin.)
Wells, Henry W. *Elizabethan and Jacobean Playwrights.* 1939.
———. *A Chronological List of Extant Plays Produced in or about London, 1581-1642.* 1940.
West, Robert Hunter. *The Invisible World: A Study of Pneumatology in Elizabethan Drama.* 1939.
White, Harold Ogden. *Plagiarism and Imitation during the English Renaissance.* 1935.
Wickham, Glynne. *Early English Stages, 1300-1660.* 2 vols. 1959-72.
Wilson, Elkin Calhoun. *England's Eliza.* 1939.
Wilson, F. P. *Elizabethan and Jacobean.* 1945.
———. "Dekker, Segar, and Some Others." *HLQ* 18 (1955):297-300.
Yearsley, Macleod. *Doctors in Elizabethan Drama.* 1933.

B. INDIVIDUAL PLAYS

Bartley, J. O. "The Development of a Stock Character: The Stage Scotsman and Welshman." *MLR* 38 (1943): 279-88. [*Patient Grissil*]
Benham, Allen R. "Notes on Plays." *MLN* 38 (1923):252. [*The Shoemakers' Holiday*, I.i.68]

Bergeron, David M. "The Emblematic Nature of English Civic Pageantry." *RenD* 1 (1968):167–98.

———. "The Elizabethan Lord Mayor's Show." *SEL* 10 (1970):269–85.

Blake, H. M. *Classic Myth in the Poetic Drama of the Age of Elizabeth.* [n.d.] [*The Sun's Darling*]

Bolte, Johannes. "Zwei Fortunatus-dramen aus dem jahre 1643." *Euphorion* 31 (1930):21–30.

Bowers, Fredson. "Dekker and Jonson." *TLS,* 12 Sept. 1936, p. 729. [*Satiromastix*]

———. "The Pictures in *Hamlet* III.iv: A Possible Contemporary Reference." *SQ* 3 (1952):280–81. [*Satiromastix*]

Brown, John Mason. *Two on the Aisle.* 1938. [*The Shoemakers' Holiday*]

Chambers, E. K. "Elizabethan Stage Gleanings." *RES* 1 (1925):75–78, 182–86. [*The Roaring Girl*]

Cope, Jackson I. *The Theater and the Dream: From Metaphor to Form in Renaissance Drama.* 1973. [*The Sun's Darling*]

Davenport, A. "Dekker's *Westward Hoe* and Hall's *Virgidemiæ.*" *N&Q* 192 (1947):143–44.

Dent, Alan. *Preludes and Studies.* 1942. [*The Shoemakers' Holiday*]

Evans, G. Blakemore. "Dryden's *Mac Flecknoe* and Dekker's *Satiromastix.*" *MLN* 76 (1961):598–600.

Halstead, W. L. "New Source Influence on *The Shoemaker's Holiday.*" *MLN* 56 (1941):127–29.

———. "Dekker's *Cupid and Psyche* and Thomas Heywood." *ELH* 11 (1944): 182–91.

Homan, Sidney R., Jr. "*A Looking-Glass for London and England:* The Source for Dekker's *If It Be Not A Good Play, the Devil Is in It.*" *N&Q* 13 (1966):301–2.

———. "Shakespeare and Dekker as Keys to Ford's *'Tis Pity She's a Whore.*" *SEL* 7 (1967):269–76. [Influence of Dekker's collaboration in *The Witch of Edmonton*]

Jorgensen, Paul A. "The Courtship Scene in *Henry V.*" *MLQ* 11 (1950):180–88. [*Old Fortunatus*]

Kolin, Philip C. "A Shakespearian Echo in Dekker's *Old Fortunatus.*" *N&Q* 19 (1972):125.

Lawlis, Merritt E. "Another Look at Simon Eyre's Will." *N&Q* 1 (1954):13–16.

McNeir, Waldo F. "The Source of Simon Eyre's Catch-Phrase." *MLN* 53 (1938): 275–76.

Martin, Mary Foster. "An Early Use of the Feminine Form of the Word *Heir* [in *Sir Thomas Wyatt,* I.iii]." *MLN* 71 (1956):270–71.

———. "Stow's *Annals* and *The Famous Historie of Sir Thomas Wyat.*" *MLR* 53 (1958):75–77.

Nathan, Norman. "*Julius Caesar* and *The Shoemakers' Holiday.*" *MLR* 48 (1953):178–79.

Nicoll, Allardyce. "The Dramatic Portrait of George Chapman." *PQ* 41 (1962):215–28. [*Northward Ho!*]

Pineas, Rainer. "Dekker's *The Whore of Babylon* and Milton's *Paradise Lost.*" *ELN* 2 (1965):257–60.

Pocock, Guy N. "A Shoemaker's Holiday." In his *The Little Room* (1926), pp. 218-31.

Rhodes, Ernest L. "Me thinks this stage shews like a Tennis Court." *RenP*, 1968, pp. 21-28. [*Lust's Dominion*]

Weeks, J. R. "A Masticke Patch and Masticke Jaws." *N&Q* 15 (1968):140-41. [*Westward Ho!*]

Williams, Gwyn. "The Cuckoo, the Welsh Ambassador." *MLR* 51 (1956):223-25.

Williams, Sheila. "Two Seventeenth Century Semi-Dramatic Allegories of Truth the Daughter of Time." *The Guildhall Miscellany* 2 (1963):207-20. [*The Magnificent Entertainment; Troia Nova Triumphans*]

Wilson, Edward M. "Family Honour in the Plays of Shakespeare's Predecessors and Contemporaries." *E&S* 6 (1953):19-40. [*The Honest Whore*]

C. TEXTUAL STUDIES

Acheson, Arthur. *Shakespeare, Chapman, and "Sir Thomas More."* 1931.

Bowers, Fredson. "Bibliographical Problems in Dekker's *Magnificent Entertainment.*" *Library* 17 (1936):333-39.

———. "Thomas Dekker: Two Textual Notes." *Library* 18 (1937):338-41. [*The Roaring Girl* and *The Honest Whore*]

———. "Notes on Running-Titles as Bibliographical Evidence." *Library* 19 (1938): 315-38.

———. "Notes on Standing Type in Elizabethan Printing." *PBSA* 40 (1946): 205-24. [*The Magnificent Entertainment* and *The Honest Whore*]

———. *Principles of Bibliographical Description.* 1949.

———. "A Late Appearance of 'Cornwall' for 'Cornhill.' " *N&Q* 195 (1950): 97-98.

———. "Essex's Rebellion and Dekker's *Old Fortunatus.*" *RES* 3 (1952):365-66.

———. *On Editing Shakespeare and the Elizabethan Dramatists.* 1955.

———. *Textual and Literary Criticism.* 1959.

———. "Established Texts and Definitive Editions." *PQ* 41 (1962):1-17. [*Match Me in London*]

———. *Bibliography and Textual Criticism.* 1964.

Brown, Arthur. "The Rationale of Old-Spelling Editions of the Plays of Shakespeare and His Contemporaries: A Rejoinder." *SB* 13 (1960):69-76.

Brown, John Russell. "The Rationale of Old-Spelling Editions of the Plays of Shakespeare and His Contemporaries." *SB* 13 (1960):49-67.

Cole, George Watson. "*The Bloody Banquet.*" *TLS*, 25 Feb. 1926, p. 142.

Erdman, David V., and Ephim G. Fogel, ed. *Evidence for Authorship.* 1966. [Includes R. C. Bald, "*The Booke of Sir Thomas More* and Its Problems," and S. Schoenbaum, "Internal Evidence and Attribution of Elizabethan Plays"]

Ferguson, W. Craig. "The Compositors of *Henry IV, Part 2, Much Ado about Nothing, The Shoemakers' Holiday,* and *The First Part of the Contention.*" *SB* 13 (1960):19-29.

Freeman, Arthur. "An Emendation to Dekker." *N&Q* 9 (1962):334. [*If It Be Not Good, the Devil Is in It*]

George, J. "Four Notes on the Text of Dekker's *Shoemaker's Holiday.*" *N&Q* 194 (1949):192.

———. "*The Dramatic Works of Thomas Dekker*, ed. Fredson Bowers, Vol. III." *AUR* 38 (1959):161-63.

Gerrard, Ernest A. *Elizabethan Drama and Dramatists, 1583–1603.* 1928.

Greg, W. W. "More Massinger Corrections." *Library* 5 (1924):59–91. [*The Virgin Martyr*]

———. *English Literary Autographs.* 4 vols. 1925–32.

———. "Bibliographical Problems in *The Magnificent Entertainment.*" *Library* 17 (1937):476–78.

———. "Entrance in the Stationers' Register: Some Statistics." *Library* 25 (1944): 1–7.

Henslowe, Philip. *Henslowe's Diary,* ed. R. A. Foakes and R. T. Rickert. 1961.

Hinman, Charlton. "Principles Governing the Use of Variant Spellings as Evidence of Alternate Settings by Two Compositors." *Library* 21 (1940):78–94. [*The Sun's Darling*]

Jackson, MacD. P. "Dekker's Back-Door'd Italian." *N&Q* 11 (1964):37. [*1 Honest Whore*]

Jenkins, Harold. "Chettle and Dekker." *TLS,* 25 Oct. 1941, p. 531.

Jones, Frederic LaFayette. "An Experiment with Massinger's Verse." *PMLA* 47 (1932):727–40.

Levin, Richard. "Dekker's Back-Door'd Italian and Middleton's Hebrew Pen." *N&Q* 10 (1963):338–40, 428–29.

McManaway, J. G. "Thomas Dekker: Further Textual Notes." *Library* 19 (1938): 176–79.

Marcham, Frank. "The Early Editions of Thomas Dekker's *The Converted Courtesan* or *The Honest Whore,* Part 1." *Library* 10 (1929):339.

Ovaa, W. A. "Dekker and *The Virgin Martyr.*" *ES* 4 (1922): 167–68.

Partridge, A. C.: *Orthography in Shakespeare and Elizabethan Drama.* 1964.

Schoenbaum, Samuel. "John Day and Elizabethan Drama." *Boston Public Library Quarterly* 5 (1953):140–52.

Spencer, Hazelton. "The Undated Quarto of *1 Honest Whore.*" *Library* 16 (1935):241–42.

Stratman, Carl J. *Bibliography of English Printed Tragedy, 1565–1900.* 1966.

Turner, Robert K., Jr. "Dekker's 'Back-Door'd Italian': *1 Honest Whore,* II.i.355." *N&Q* 7 (1960):25–26.

D. EDITIONS

Single-Work Editions

Koszul, A., ed. and trans. *Thomas Dekker, "Fête chez le cordonnier."* Collection du théâtre anglais de la renaissance. 1955.

Loisseau, J., ed. and trans. *Thomas Dekker, "Le jour de fête des cordonniers"* ("*The Shoemakers Holiday*") suivi de "*L'abécédaire des bénets*" ("*The Guls Hornbook*"). 1957.

Sanza, Vittoria, ed. *The Shoemaker's Holiday, or The Gentle Craft.* Biblioteca Italiana di testi Inglesi. 1968.

Anthologies

Bald, R. C., ed. *Six Elizabethan Plays.* 1963. [*The Shoemakers' Holiday*]

Baskervill, C. R., V. G. Heltzel, and A. H. Nethercot, ed. *Elizabethan and Stuart Plays.* 1934. [*The Shoemakers' Holiday* and *1 Honest Whore,* both rpt. in *Elizabethan Plays,* 1971]

Brooke, C. F. T., and N. B. Paradise, ed. *English Drama, 1580–1642.* 1933. [*The Shoemakers' Holiday*]

Coffman, G. R., ed. *Five Significant English Plays.* 1930. [*The Shoemakers' Holiday*]

Dunn, E. C., ed. *Eight Famous Elizabethan Plays.* 1932. [*The Shoemakers' Holiday*]

Gassner, J., ed. *Four Great Elizabethan Plays.* 1960. [*The Shoemakers' Holiday*]

———. *Elizabethan Drama.* 1967. [*The Shoemakers' Holiday*]

Howard, E. J., ed. *Ten Elizabethan Plays.* 1931. [*The Shoemakers' Holiday*]

McIlwraith, A. K., ed. *Five Elizabethan Comedies.* 1934. [*The Shoemakers' Holiday*]

Messiaen, Pierre, ed. *Théâtre anglais, moyen-age et XVIe siècle: Anonymes, Marlowe, Dekker, Heywood, Ben Jonson, Webster, Tourneur, etc. Nouvelle traduction française avec remarques et notes.* 1948. [*The Shoemakers' Holiday;* extracts from *The Honest Whore*]

Oliphant, E. H. C., ed. *Shakespeare and His Fellow Dramatists.* 1929. Vol. 1. [*2 Honest Whore*]

———. *Elizabethan Dramatists Other than Shakespeare.* 1931. [*2 Honest Whore*]

Ornstein, R., and H. Spencer, ed. *Elizabethan and Jacobean Comedy.* 1964. [*The Shoemakers' Holiday*]

Parks, E. W., and R. C. Beatty, ed. *The English Drama.* 1935. [*The Shoemakers' Holiday*]

Rhys, Ernest, ed. *The Best Plays of Thomas Dekker.* 1949 (rpt. of 1887 Mermaid edition). [*The Shoemakers' Holiday, Old Fortunatus, 1* and *2 Honest Whore,* and *The Witch of Edmonton*]

Rubinstein, H. F., ed. *Great English Plays.* 1928. [*The Shoemakers' Holiday*]

Schelling, F. E., and M. W. Black, ed. *Typical Elizabethan Plays.* Rev. and enl., 1931. [*Old Fortunatus* and *The Shoemakers' Holiday*]

Schweikert, H. C., ed. *Early English Plays.* 1928. [*The Shoemakers' Holiday*]

Spencer, Hazelton, ed. *Elizabethan Plays.* 1933. [*The Shoemakers' Holiday* and *1* and *2 Honest Whore*]

Vallance, R., adaptor. "Shoemakers' Progress." In *Little Plays from the English Drama.* 1935.

Walley, H. R., and J. H. Wilson, ed. *Early Seventeenth-Century Plays, 1600–1642.* 1930. [*1 Honest Whore*]

Wine, M. L., ed. *Drama of the English Renaissance.* 1969. [*The Shoemakers' Holiday*]

Wright, L. B., and V. A. LaMar, ed. *Four Famous Tudor and Stuart Plays.* 1963. [*The Shoemakers' Holiday*]

Woods, G. B., H. A. Watt, and G. K. Anderson. *The Literature of England.* 1936. [*The Shoemakers' Holiday*]

THOMAS MIDDLETON

John B. Brooks

The standard edition is *The Works of Thomas Middleton*, ed. A. H. Bullen, 8 vols. (1885-86). A Yale edition of the plays by George R. Price and S. Schoenbaum is in progress.

I. GENERAL

A. BIOGRAPHICAL

Much of our present knowledge of Middleton's life comes from the research of Mark Eccles, whose findings first appeared in "Middleton's Birth and Education," *RES* 7 (1931):431-41. Eccles established that the playwright was born in 1580, not about 1570, as had been previously believed; that he was matriculated at Queen's College, Oxford, in April, 1598; and that he could not have been one of the three Thomas Middletons who were admitted in Gray's Inn between 1593 and 1596. Supplementing Eccles are the following articles, each of which throws new light on Middleton's life: Harold N. Hillebrand, "Thomas Middleton's *The Viper's Brood*," *MLN* 42 (1927):35-38; Mildred G. Christian, "An Autobiographical Note by Thomas Middleton," *N&Q* 175 (1938):259-60, "Middleton's Residence at Oxford," *MLN* 61 (1946):90-91, and "A Sidelight on the Family History of Thomas Middleton," *SP* 44 (1947):490-96; P. G. Phialas, "Middleton's Early Contact with the Law," *SP* 52 (1955):186-94; S. Schoenbaum, "A New Middleton Record," *MLR* 55 (1960):82-84; and David George, "Thomas Middleton at Oxford," *MLR* 65 (1970): 734-36. Most of the information presented in these articles comes from legal documents: the will of the playwright's father, William Middleton; the various lawsuits brought by Thomas's mother Anne and his stepfather Thomas Harvey against each other for control of William's property; and a suit brought against Thomas by the manager of the Queen's Revels Company, Robert Keysar, for non-payment of a debt (which Middleton claimed he had repaid with the manuscript of a tragedy, since lost, called *The Viper and Her Brood*). Eccles sums up most of the pre-1957 information in "Thomas Middleton A Poett," *SP* 54 (1957):516–36, and presents new evidence as well for an "as yet unwritten biography." He concludes that "Middleton wrote his best comedies about the life he knew best, that of London citizens and of young gentlemen who lived by their wits. . . . He learned about law, not by studying at Gray's Inn, but from experience, for before he came of age he had been sued in the courts of Chancery and Requests, and had helped his mother in her lawsuits."

Evelyn May Albright, *Dramatic Publication in England, 1580–1640: A Study of Conditions Affecting Content and Form of Drama* (1927), deduces from preface and title page evidence that Middleton was one of the Jacobean authors who oversaw the publication of some of his plays; and, according to his preface to *The Roaring Girl*, he wrote for readers as well as the audience at the theater. Richard H. Barker's *Thomas Middleton* (1958) gives the most complete available biographical sketch of Middleton.

B. GENERAL STUDIES OF THE PLAYS

Barker's *Middleton* is the only comprehensive study of the author's complete works, and it suffers, as Irving Ribner points out in his review in *RN* 12 (1959):178–81, from being outdated and too much concerned with unsolvable authorship problems. Nevertheless, it remains the handiest single book on Middleton. The biographical sketch is especially valuable, as is the comprehensive treatment of all the works, dramatic and nondramatic, in chronological order. A useful appendix examines the canon in three categories: "Works," "Lost Works," and "Works Attributed to Middleton." Barker convincingly disputes the influential opinions of T. S. Eliot in *For Lancelot Andrewes* (1928) (rpt. in *Le théâtre elizabéthain: Études et traductions de Joseph Aynard*, et al. [1933] and in Eliot's *Selected Essays, 1917–1932* [1932] and *Essays on Elizabethan Drama* [1956]) that Middleton "has no point of view" and that "his greatest tragedies and his greatest comedies are as if written by two different men" by showing that the playwright's characteristic realism, irony, and "highly developed sense of sin" are the red threads that run throughout his plays, comedy, tragicomedy, and tragedy alike. Agreeing with Barker is Arthur C. Kirsch, *Jacobean Dramatic Perspectives*

(1972), who finds Middleton's dramatic point of view highly individualistic and powerfully expressed.

Also stressing the unity of Middleton's dramatic work, Una Ellis-Fermor's *The Jacobean Drama* (1936; 4th ed., 1958) sees a consistent line of development: "In comedy he early developed the ironic detachment which only a potential tragic sense can give, and into tragedy he carried the habit of clear, singleminded observation learnt during almost a lifetime's practice in naturalistic comedy." Similarly, G. Wilson Knight's *The Golden Labyrinth: A Study of British Drama* (1962) finds Middleton's "efficient and emotionally uninvolved sense of moral corruption" in his comedies reaching an intensity in his tragedies.

Critics of Middleton's comedies disagree as to their worth. Generally unfavorable commentaries are made by Frederick S. Boas in *An Introduction to Stuart Drama* (1946), M. C. Bradbrook in *The Rise of the Common Player* (1962), and Alfred Harbage in *Shakespeare and the Rival Traditions* (1952). Boas thinks Middleton has an "obsession . . . with abnormal sexual complications," Bradbrook finds him reaching "new depths of cynicism," and Harbage alludes extensively to his comedies for the Paul's Boys as prime examples of the typically "lewd" and "perverse" fare purveyed by the private theaters of the early seventeenth century. In *Endeavors of Art: A Study of Form in Elizabethan Drama* (1954), Madeleine Doran finds "a certain amount of conventional moralizing" in Middleton's comedies, but "little feeling of genuine reproof." In his best comedies she finds "the spirit of Plautus in his most bawdy farcical moods and of the Italians who were Plautus's successors." W. D. Dunkel, *The Dramatic Technique of Thomas Middleton in His Comedies of London Life* (1925), finds "no apparent moralistic purpose" in the City comedies; rather, the playwright uses satire based on popular opinion for comic effects. However, A. P. Rossiter's *English Drama from Early Times to the Elizabethans* (1959) points out definite links in plot structure and characterization between Middleton's "social-moralist" comedies and the medieval morality tradition. Bradbrook, in *The Growth and Structure of Elizabethan Comedy* (1955), finds similar links, but much weaker ones, for she feels that in Middleton's early satiric comedies the "endorsement of popular morality has ceased."

The related questions of Middleton's "realism" and "morality," mainly as these terms apply to his comedies, are discussed by Helene B. Bullock in "Thomas Middleton and the Fashion in Playmaking,"

PMLA 42 (1927):766-76, and by L. C. Knights in *Drama and Society in the Age of Jonson* (1937). Bullock observes that, rather than assuming a moral stance, Middleton "watched the audience and gave it what it wanted"; Knights finds it necessary to "sharply discriminate" between Middleton as part author of *The Changeling*, which he feels deserves the epithet "great," and as author of a number of comedies, which he feels do not. Middleton's "realism," says Knights, was overrated by critics such as F. E. Schelling, Kathleen Lynch, and Eliot; compared to Jonson or Dryden, Middleton lags far behind as realist, moralist, satirist, or social commentator. In *Growth and Structure*, Bradbrook agrees with Knights, finding Middleton's comedies "journalistic"—yellow journalism, at that—but, strangely, largely devoid of the details of London life. Leonard Goldstein labels Middleton a caricaturist rather than a realist in "On the Transition from Formal to Naturalistic Acting in the Elizabethan and Post-Elizabethan Theater," *BNYPL* 62 (1958): 330-49; Middleton attempted to "present to a sophisticated Court audience the concrete businessman with all his shoddy morals," but without any understanding of the general process which had created such "concrete manifestations." Charles A. Hallett's "Middleton's Overreachers and the Ironic Ending," *TSL* 16 (1971):1-13, finds three basic weaknesses in Middleton's comedies: he places too much reliance on irony, his overreachers are "little men," and his characters are not developed by the action.

But other critics have found Middleton to be superior even to Jonson, Chapman, and Marston in portraying contemporary manners. Felix Schelling, *Elizabethan Playwrights* (1925), observes that "Middleton's plots run easily, encumbered neither by the fine phrases of Chapman's moralizing nor by the wealth of satirical comment with which Jonson embroiders even ordinary converse." In *The Development of English Humor* (1952), Louis Cazamian finds that Middleton "handles the brush more lightly and naturally" than Jonson and creates characters that are "more finely shaded and freer from the suspicion of caricature." Brian Gibbons, *Jacobean City Comedy* (1968), points out the contributions that Middleton made to the development of London comedy and finds him in some respects superior to Marston—comparable, in fact, to Bertolt Brecht. L. B. Wallis's *Fletcher, Beaumont and Company* (1947) finds that Middleton's London comedies significantly influenced the plot construction, characterization, and dialogue of the tragicomedies of Beaumont and Fletcher.

Two outstanding articles on Middleton's City comedy show how the playwright progressively developed his talents as a dramatist of social and moral issues: Schoenbaum's "*A Chaste Maid in Cheapside* and Middleton's City Comedy," in *Studies in the English Renaissance Drama in Memory of Karl Julius Holzknecht*, ed. J. W. Bennett, et al. (1959), pp. 287-309; and R. B. Parker's "Middleton's Experiments with Comedy and Judgement," in *Jacobean Theatre*, SuAS, vol. 1 (1960), pp. 179-99. Schoenbaum asserts that Middleton "created, almost singlehandedly, a repertory of original and distinctive plays" for the Paul's Boys, and crowned his achievement in realistic comedy with *A Chaste Maid*. Middleton saw clearly the "breakdown or corruption of traditional values in the wake of the new materialistic order" and was particularly concerned in his comedies with "the effects of the competitive struggle on family relationships—on ties of blood or marriage." At the heart of Middleton's "very personal comic style," Parker finds a "tension between skill in the presentation of manners and a desire to denounce immorality," or between "a completely amoral vitalism and a more than Calvinistically determined scheme of retribution." Middleton's "greatest" tragedy, *Women Beware Women*, is a natural development from his earlier experiments in comedy, and the bloody conclusion to the play is "a return to the grotesque humour into which Middleton retreats in his later comedies" from the "problem of punishment." John V. Curry's *Deception in Elizabethan Comedy* (1955) treats Middleton's use in his comedies of disguise and deception, often for the purpose of exposing vice.

In "Middleton's Tragicomedies," *MP* 54 (1956):7-19, Schoenbaum revalues the neglected tragicomedies of the playwright's middle period and shows how they form a natural transition from his earlier intrigue comedy to the psychological tragedies of his later years. A more typical reaction to these plays may be found in Marvin T. Herrick's *Tragicomedy: Its Origin and Development in Italy, France, and England* (1955), where Middleton's tragicomedies are said to have seldom surpassed such crude Elizabethan "tragical comedies" as *Damon and Pithias*, *Cambises*, and *Promos and Cassandra*.

On Middleton's two tragedies, *The Changeling* and *Women Beware Women*, the critics are agreed: they are among the best, if not the best, of the later Jacobean period. To these are sometimes added *Hengist, King of Kent* as well as two plays of disputed authorship, *The Revenger's Tragedy* and *The Second Maiden's Tragedy*. The single most important study of the tragedies is Schoenbaum's

Middleton's Tragedies (1955). Middleton is a true innovator in tragedy who attempted to create a "psychological and realistic" drama that was "essentially different from the romantic and heroic drama of his contemporaries." More than any other playwright of his time, Middleton employs rhetorical and dramatic irony to expose the self-destructive impulses of his tragic protagonists who find themselves "entangled . . . in a web of sin." Like Parker, Irving Ribner, in *Jacobean Tragedy: The Quest for Moral Order* (1962), sees a "Calvinist strain" in Middleton and "moral categories [that] are clear and precise." Middleton's constant theme, says Ribner, is "man's slow awareness of his own damnation, which he is able to portray with a psychological realism unique in his age." Fredson Bowers, *Elizabethan Revenge Tragedy, 1587-1642* (1940), agrees that Middleton was psychologically acute, and he finds *Women Beware Women* and especially *The Changeling* to be significant advances in the art of revenge tragedy.

Robert Ornstein's *The Moral Vision of Jacobean Tragedy* (1960) dissents from the usual view, finding Middleton "unique among the tragedians not so much for his 'clinical detachment' as for his total indifference to the ideal in human nature." Yet Ornstein finds an "astringent virtue" in Middleton's "pitilessness" and irony, especially as compared to the "speciosity" of his contemporary, John Fletcher. G. R. Hibbard goes even farther than Ornstein in condemning Middleton's tragedies as "decadent," in "The Tragedies of Thomas Middleton and the Decadence of the Drama," *RMS* 1 (1957):35-64. Hibbard finds Middleton's tragic heroes and heroines unheroic, his dramatic construction and characterizations sometimes faulty, and his tragic vision inhibited by the tastes of his "gentlemanly" audience.

An attempt to pinpoint Middleton's differences from his fellow dramatists is made by John D. Jump's "Middleton's Tragedies," in *The Age of Shakespeare* (1955; vol. 2 of *The Pelican Guide to English Literature*, ed. Boris Ford), pp. 355-68; unlike Webster, Tourneur, or Shakespeare, says Jump, Middleton does not rely for his tragic effects on "patterns of poetic imagery." Instead, his tragedies depend almost entirely upon the more specifically dramatic attributes of "significant, often ironical, juxtapositions of characters, speeches, and events and his lucid, flexible, highly dramatic but always unobtrusive verse." Jump may have taken his cue from Bradbrook's influential *Themes and Conventions of Elizabethan Tragedy* (1935); however, while Bradbrook concludes that "the stress which should fall upon imagery is much lighter in Middleton's plays than in those of most of his contemporaries," she still finds "certain dominating images in the Shakespearean manner" in the two major tragedies which give them a "distinct tone." Bradbrook praises the "pregnant simplicity" of Middleton's blank verse, as does F. P. Wilson's *Elizabethan and Jacobean* (1945), which rates Middleton next to Shakespeare as "the writer who . . . gets the profoundest effects of tragedy with the utmost plainness of speech."

Among the more important recent general studies of Middleton are a number of mainly analytical works. Wilfred T. Jewkes's *Act Division in Elizabethan and Jacobean Plays, 1583-1616* (1958) and Henry L. Snuggs's *Shakespeare and Five Acts* (1960) both conclude, from examinations of Middleton's plays among others, that, at least until about 1607-1610, act division was much more common in plays written for the private theaters than in those written for the public stage. Snuggs also finds inter-act music a regular practice in private theater plays, such as Middleton's *The Phoenix*, but extremely rare in public theater plays. Jewkes adds the information that Middleton's stage directions are typically brief and infrequent. In *The Elizabethan Dumb Show: The History of a Dramatic Convention* (1966; German ed. 1964), Dieter Mehl asserts that Middleton is the Jacobean dramatist who has the most in common with Shakespeare in dramatic style and character portrayal: "Like Shakespeare, Middleton often does not seem to take sides, but to throw light on situations from different angles, without committing himself to a final judgment." Mehl finds Middleton's plays "especially rich in elements that betray the strong influence of the pageants and masques in which he showed great interest": i.e., such elements as pantomimes, masques, and dumb shows. In "Forms and Functions of the Play within a Play," *RenD* 8 (1965): 41-61, Mehl makes a similar analysis of Middleton's use of the play within a play. Mary Crapo Hyde's *Playwriting for Elizabethans, 1600-1605* (1949) discusses conventional characters and plot situations in *Blurt, Master Constable, The Family of Love, The Phoenix,* and *Michaelmas Term*. And in *The Multiple Plot in English Renaissance Drama* (1971), Richard Levin accords Middleton's plays special prominence, since Levin finds him "one of the most inventive and effective architects of multiple plots in the period, and one of the most neglected." Levin gives a whole chapter to *A Chaste Maid in Cheapside* and Jonson's *Bartholomew Fair*, which "realize . . . the full potentialities inherent in the convention of the multiple plot."

Bertil Johansson's *Religion and Superstition in the Plays of Ben*

Jonson and Thomas Middleton (1950) shows how contemporary religious beliefs and superstitions are reflected in Jonson's and Middleton's plays. Unlike Donne and possibly Jonson, Middleton apparently accepted the old Ptolemaic view of the universe with relative equanimity, according to Johansson, and his plays generally reflect popular ideas and attitudes of the time concerning magic, witches, Puritanism, and Roman Catholicism. In *The Elizabethan Dramatists as Critics* (1963), David Klein quotes comments from the plays, prologues, epilogues, and prefaces of Middleton that can, sometimes loosely, be called "literary criticism." And David George's "Thomas Middleton's Sources: A Survey," *N&Q* 18 (1971):17-24, gives all the known sources for Middleton's plays, including collaborations.

C. THE WORKS AT LARGE

Barker's *Middleton* recognizes the close relationship of early City comedies such as *The Family of Love, The Phoenix*, and *Your Five Gallants* to Middleton's rogue pamphlets, *The Ant and the Nightingale* and *The Black Book*, which were written at about the same time. The three poems that were apparently Middleton's earliest literary works, *The Wisdom of Solomon Paraphrased, Micro-Cynicon*, and *The Ghost of Lucrece*, are regarded by Barker as illustrations of Middleton's early attempts to free himself from Elizabethan romantic conventions and to find his true métier, realistic comedy. J. Q. Adams, in his edition of *The Ghost of Lucrece* (1937), suggests that the story in the second edition of *The Ant and the Nightingale: or Father Hubburds Tales* (1604) of the poor young scholar from London who went up to Oxford and began writing poetry there in vain hopes of finding a patron is at least partly autobiographical. Adams finds a gradual maturing in style, from the "distinctly amateurish" *Wisdom*, through the mechanically superior *Ghost*, to the, in part, "extremely well written" *Micro-Cynicon*. G. R. Price's "The Early Editions of *The Ant and the Nightingale*," *PBSA* 43 (1949):179-90, gives bibliographical descriptions of the two 1604 editions of the pamphlet, and M. A. Shaaber's "*The Ant and the Nightingale* and *Father Hubburds Tales*," *University of Pennsylvania Library Chronicle* 14 (1947):13-16, points out the differences between the two editions. Richard Levin finds a possible allusion to Middleton's great contemporary in *Micro-Cynicon* ("A New Shakespearean Allusion in Middleton?" *AN&Q* 2 [1964]:100-103). Rhodes

Dunlap's "James I, Bacon, Middleton, and the Making of *The Peace-Maker*," in *Studies in the English Renaissance Drama in Memory of Karl Julius Holzknecht*, ed. J. W. Bennett, et al. (1959), pp. 82–94, describes his conception of how his quarto pamphlet came to be written and published: King James apparently took a personal interest in the pamphlet, and arranged for its licensing on terms favorable to both Middleton and his printer, William Alley. Dunlap notes that, throughout his writing career (*A Game at Chess* to the contrary notwithstanding), Middleton "repeatedly stresses the blessings of peace, which he associates with foreign trade and the flow of wealth to the city." R. C. Bald, "Middleton's Civic Employments," *MP* 31 (1933):65–78, summarizes the author's considerable contributions to London pageants, celebrations, and entertainments, contributions that were officially recognized by his appointment as City Chronologer in 1620 and by a number of additional awards and grants.

Samuel A. Tannenbaum's *Concise Bibliography* appeared in 1940 and is reprinted in *Elizabethan Bibliographies*, vol. 5 (1967). *Elizabethan Bibliographies Supplements* I, compiled by Dennis Donovan, brought Tannenbaum up to date as of 1967. Irving Ribner's selective list appears in *Tudor and Stuart Drama*, Goldentree Bibliographies (1966).

II. CRITICISM OF INDIVIDUAL PLAYS AND STATE OF SCHOLARSHIP

A. INDIVIDUAL PLAYS

The Changeling

The main critical controversy involves the two plots and whether or not they are artistically unified. William Empson in *Some Versions of Pastoral* (1935) first suggested that they are, and pointed to the significance of the title, which may refer not only to Antonio and Lollio of the comic subplot, but, more importantly, to De Flores and Beatrice of the main plot: each, in his or her own way, is a "changeling." Empson's suggestion has been considerably developed by other writers, notably by Bradbrook in *Themes and Conventions*; by Karl J. Holzknecht in "The Dramatic Structure of *The Changeling*," *RenP*, 1954, pp. 77-87, rpt. in *Shakespeare's Contemporaries*, ed. Max Bluestone and Norman Rabkin (1961), pp. 263-72; 2nd ed.

(1970), pp. 367–77; and by N. W. Bawcutt in the introduction to his edition of the play (1961). Barker, Schoenbaum (*Middleton's Tragedies*), and Doran (*Endeavors of Art*), among many others, represent the opposing view that the subplot, in Doran's words, is "silly and only fortuitously connected" to the main action.

In "Milton's 'Satan' and the Theme of Damnation in Elizabethan Tragedy," *E&S* 1 (1948):46–66, Helen Gardner finds striking similarities between the tragic protagonists of Marlowe, Shakespeare, and Middleton: "Middleton is usually praised and praised rightly for the intense realism of his characterization, and particularly for the two studies of Beatrice-Joanna and De Flores; but there is more than realism here. What Mephistophilis is to Faustus, what the 'supernatural solicitings' and the horror of the deed are to MacBeth, De Flores is to Beatrice-Joanna." Edward Engelberg's "Tragic Blindness in *The Changeling* and *Women Beware Women*," *MLQ* 23 (1962): 20–28, finds Middleton's "central perception of human nature" in his two famous tragedies to be "embodied in the dominant metaphor of sight—or the lack of it." In "The Murdered Substitute Tale," *MLQ* 6 (1945):187–95, Ernst G. Mathews surveys the various seventeenth-century occurrences, in legends and folk-tales, of the substitute bride episode in *The Changeling*. Robert R. Reed, Jr., in *Bedlam on the Jacobean Stage* (1952) and "A Factual Interpretation of *The Changeling*'s Madhouse Scenes," *N&Q* 195 (1950):247–48, interprets Alibius's madhouse as a satire on Bethlehem Hospital and its keeper, the notorious Dr. Hilkish Crooke; however, Bawcutt, in the introduction to his edition, remains unconvinced that a specific, topical satire of "Bedlam" was intended by Middleton and Rowley.

Women Beware Women

Although generally regarded as a lesser play than *The Changeling* (see for example Schoenbaum, *Middleton's Tragedies*, and Jump, "Middleton's Tragedies"), several critics have recently declared that, in Barker's words, "it is as a whole a far more perfect specimen of Middleton's art and deserves to rank as the masterpiece of his later years." Debate centers on the problem of the bloody and violent masque that concludes the play. Schoenbaum and Jump, among others, find it gratuitous—a "ridiculous holocaust," says Jump. Barker, on the other hand, regards the ending as fantastic symbolism, comparable to *The Revenger's Tragedy* (which he believes is also Middleton's); R. B. Parker states that the ending, though "not a success," is a result of "an over-intensification of the very elements which distinguish Middleton from his fellow dramatists." Mehl, *Elizabethan Dumb Show*, finds the ending dramatically justified: "No dramatist before Middleton achieved such a grotesque juxtaposition of reality and play within a play. The general confusion at the end is surely not a sign of the dramatist's incompetence, but a deliberate device."

The character in the play attracting most attention recently has been the bawd, Livia. Barker finds Livia "fully deserving her reputation as one of Middleton's most memorable characters." Daniel B. Dodson agrees, and adds that, among her other colorful vices, Livia may have an incestuous attraction to her brother Hippolito ("Middleton's Livia," *PQ* 27 [1948]:376–81). Christopher Ricks, in "Word-Play in *Women Beware Women*," *RES* 12 (1961):238–50, agrees with Eliot that Middleton in this play shows his interest—greater than that of any of his punning contemporaries—in "innuendo and double meanings," especially those of a sexual nature. However, Middleton's word-play is "certainly not a concession to bawdy groundlings" for it has a "serious relevance to the moral analysis in the play, and Middleton creates a pattern which encourages one phrase to influence another." In *"The Tenant of Wildfell Hall* and *Women Beware Women*," *N&Q* 10 (1963):449–50, Inga-Stina Ekeblad finds a close resemblance between Anne Bronte's symbolic use of a chess game and Middleton's.

A Chaste Maid in Cheapside

In "*A Chaste Maid* . . . and Middleton's City Comedy," Schoenbaum declares that this play is "the richest, most impressive of Middleton's comedies, the culmination of a decade of creative experimentation and growth." *Chaste Maid* has attracted more critical attention in recent years than any other Middleton comedy. In her analysis of the thematic and stylistic patterns of the play, "Theme, Imagery, and Unity in *A Chaste Maid in Cheapside*," *RenD* 8 (1965): 105–26, Ruby Chatterji discerns "a fundamental design" that reveals Middleton's "splendid . . . architectonic abilities." The play combines the realism of Middleton's "social comedies" with the fancifulness of his "domestic-intrigue comedies" in "a rare synthesis of poetic sensibility and intellectual energy." Richard Levin, "The Four Plots of *A Chaste Maid in Cheapside*," *RES* 16 (1965):14–24, agrees that the play is neatly unified, at least on the level of plot. He sees the four plots as being arranged in order of decreasing importance and serious-ness: "the first action is serious-sympathetic comedy, the second serious-unsympathetic, the third farcical but sympathetic, and the last farcical-unsympathetic." Bradbrook's *Growth and Structure* finds the christening scene (III.ii) "amongst the rankest in all Elizabethan drama." However, Barker dissents from her view and that of others (he refers specifically to Ellis-Fermor's *Jacobean Drama* and Knights's *Drama and Society*) who see in this scene, and the play as a whole, a hardening of Middleton's attitude toward human nature, "as though he had suddenly realized for the first time that he was dealing with a repulsive world . . . . To me at least this harshness is never very clearly reflected in the text."

Michaelmas Term

Ephestian Quomodo, the social-climbing woollen-draper of this comedy, has fascinated critics, from Kathleen M. Lynch, *The Social Mode of Restoration Comedy* (1926), to Eliot to Barker: invariably Quomodo's lyrical speeches on the acquisition of land in the country are quoted as prime examples of Middleton's satire of the Jacobean businessman, who would presumably do anything, legal or not, to advance himself socially. Bald's "The Sources of Middleton's City Comedies," *JEGP* 33 (1934):373–87, finds personal satire of a merchant named Howe (Quomodo may be a Latin pun on his name) who was convicted in 1596 for a swindle similar to Quomodo's. In his edition for RRDS (1966), Richard Levin disputes the findings of sources for Quomodo's tricks in pamphlets by Greene and Dekker; more likely "the common gossip of the city" served as Middleton's source.

A Trick to Catch the Old One

Robert de Smet [Romain Sanvic], in *Le théâtre élisabéthain* (1955), praises this intrigue comedy as "une de ses plus allègres comédies . . . . Tout s'arrange à la fin, après de nombreux quiproquos. Middleton a de la verve. Ses décasyllabes sont souples. Il ne craint pas les précisions physiologiques. C'est un homme de théâtre né." The three Dampit scenes, particularly, have attracted close critical scru-tiny. Reed's *Bedlam* sees Dampit as "perhaps the most profanely alive characterization of the Jacobean drama"; and he adds that "as a pathological study of an alcoholic, Dampit is one of the most modern examples of theatricalism in Jacobean drama." He favorably compares

Middleton's more concrete realism, as illustrated in the Dampit scenes, to Jonson's method, which is "dependent too precisely upon humour theory." In "The Dampit Scenes in *A Trick to Catch the Old One*," *MLQ* 25 (1964):140–52, Levin finds that these scenes "add up to . . . a kind of Hogarthian 'Usurer's Progress.' " They are significantly, though not perfectly, related to the main action of the play; Dampit, like Pecunius Lucre and Walkadine Hoard of the main plot, is an "old one," but he is more specifically "devilish" and is thus a more serious commentary on usury than they.

A Mad World, My Masters

Christian's "Middleton's Acquaintance with the *Merrie Conceited Jests of George Peele*," *PMLA* 50 (1935):753–60, points out similarities between the play and the pamphlet, which may have been one of Middleton's sources. Dunkel, *Dramatic Technique*, thinks that *Mad World* has the most skillfully constructed plot of any of Middleton's London comedies. Barker finds *Mad World* "even more hilarious" than *A Trick to Catch the Old One*, and a superior example of the liveliness of Middleton's comic plots and dialogue. Both Barker and Standish Henning, in his introduction to the RRDS edition (1965), think it important to qualify the usual comments concerning Middleton's "realism" when applied to this play: as Henning says, "the sense of realism imparted to us depends principally upon the details of local color"; the characters and action of the play are often "fantastic."

The Roaring Girl

Eliot regarded this as the "one comedy which more than any Elizabethan comedy realizes a free and noble womanhood." Other critics, however, have been less favorable. In Middleton's signed epistle to the play, which according to the first quarto title page was performed at the Fortune, Alfred Harbage finds "the cynic of Paul's" unconvincingly transformed into "the idealist of the Fortune" (*Shakespeare and the Rival Traditions*). And Bradbrook's *Growth and Structure* implies that Moll's appeal, in her masculine disguise, was intended by Middleton to be at least partly homosexual.

A Game At Chess

The most popular of Middleton's plays in his own lifetime, *Game* was a political *cause célèbre* which may have resulted in his brief imprisonment; J. R. Moore, "The Contemporary Significance of Middleton's *Game at Chesse*," *PMLA* 50 (1935):761–68, points out that the play was licensed in June 1624 but was not produced until August when the Court was away from London on a progress; this fact suggests that perhaps someone highly placed, such as Buckingham, was trying to stir up the Londoners against the former Spanish ambassador, Gondomar, and the Spanish party in England. The numerous contemporary allusions to *Game* are quoted by B. M. Wagner, "New Allusions to *A Game at Chesse*," *PMLA* 44 (1929): 827–34; by Bald in his edition (1929); by G. E. Bentley, *The Jacobean and Caroline Stage*, vol. 4 (1956); and by Geoffrey Bullough, "The *Game at Chesse*: How It Struck a Contemporary," *MLR* 49 (1954):156–63.

Hengist, King of Kent

Since the appearance in 1938 of Bald's edition, with its comprehensive introduction, critical interest in this "sophisticated chronicle play" (to use Barker's phrase) has sharply increased. Barker finds in *Hengist*, along with "obvious" faults, a "dark grandeur that is not easy to parallel elsewhere in Middleton's serious work, not even in *The Changeling* and *Women Beware Women*." Schoenbaum's *Middleton's Tragedies* finds a particularly close relationship between treatment of material and the audience for which it was intended. Middleton, writing for a Blackfriars audience that had "little taste for history," de-emphasized the political aspects of this story out of Holinshed of legendary British history, and greatly magnified the sexual aspects: "Middleton's preoccupation is so great that he is always intruding irrelevant allusions to chastity and infidelity, lust and ravishment." Yet Schoenbaum denies that the playwright pandered to his audience; rather, he created "genuine characters that appear at times to possess what a psychologist might describe as unconscious minds." Although the play is generally referred to by its original manuscript subtitle, Bentley, in *Jacobean and Caroline Stage*, vol. 4 (1956), wants to retain the traditional quarto title, *The Mayor of Queenborough*, which refers to the comic subplot, on grounds that it is "more confusing than helpful to try to alter now the misguided preference of three centuries."

The Phoenix

In *"A Chaste Maid in Cheapside* and Middleton's City Comedy," Schoenbaum describes this early comedy as "an odd mixture of allegory, harsh satire, and goodhumored farce" and adds that in it, for the first time, Middleton used "the ironic method that stamps all his characteristic later writing." Alan C. Dessen finds a strong influence of the morality-play tradition in "Middleton's *The Phoenix* and the Allegorical Tradition," *SEL* 6 (1966):291-308; Clifford Davidson also stresses the play's moralistic elements in *"The Phoenix*: Middleton's Didactic Comedy," *Papers on Language and Literature* 4 (1968):121-30, and he finds that the didacticism of this "remarkable apprentice piece" provides a useful background for the study of Middleton's mature work. In "Middleton's Stepfather and the Captain of *The Phoenix,"* *N&Q* 8 (1961):382-84, J. B. Brooks points out parallels between the career of Middleton's ne'er-do-well step-father, Thomas Harvey, and that of the sea-captain in this play which, along with other considerations, suggest that Middleton drew this character from life.

The Family of Love

Barker regards this as "apparently the earliest of Middleton's sur-viving plays," a "confused and unsatisfactory" transitional work between the Elizabethan romanticism of *The Ghost of Lucrece* and the later realistic and satirical City comedies. Levin's "The Family of Lust and *The Family of Love,"* *SEL* 6 (1966):309-22, finds the play more coherent than is generally supposed, an example of Middleton's early handling of the multiple plot which helps in understanding his later, more successful, attempts to integrate main plots with subplots. Bald's "The Sources of Middleton's City Comedies" points out possible borrowings from the rogue pamphlets of Greene.

A Fair Quarrel

Fredson Bowers, "Middleton's 'Fair Quarrel' and the Duelling Code," *JEGP* 36 (1937):40-65, shows how the play is related to attempts by the Jacobean authorities to curb duelling as well as to contemporary concepts of gentlemanly honor. Levin's "The Three Quarrels of *A Fair Quarrel,"* *SP* 61 (1964):219-31, points out connections and relationships between the main plot (by Middleton) of his tragicomedy and the subplots (by Rowley). The main connection: "Each plot leads to a 'quarrel' of the same sort—a threatened duel over a woman's honor that fails to come off."

The Witch

The Witch has attracted attention for two main reasons: its uncertain relationship to *Macbeth* and its extensive use of Elizabethan ideas of witchcraft and the occult. At least two songs in the play are thought to have been interpolated into the First Folio text of *Macbeth*, according to G. E. Bentley's *Jacobean and Caroline Stage*, vol. 4 (1956). Johansson, *Religion and Supersitition*, shows the extent of Middleton's indebtedness for his witch lore to Reginald Scot's *The Discovery of Witchcraft* (1584). Robert Reed's *The Occult on the Tudor and Stuart Stage* (1965) finds *The Witch* to be the "most informative play of the period on the topic of contemporary witchcraft . . . . Whereas Shakespeare in *Macbeth* uses witches only to the extent that they contribute to the mood and the plot, Middleton introduces many episodes for the sole purpose of illustrating popular notions of the occult."

No Wit, No Help Like a Woman's

D. J. Gordon finds the source of Middleton's subplot in Giambattista della Porta's *La Sorella*, in "Middleton's *No Wit, No Help Like a Woman's* and della Porta's *La Sorella*," *RES* 17 (1941):400- 414.

The Inner-Temple Masque

In "Some Jacobean Catch-Phrases and Some Light on Thomas Bretnor," in *Elizabethan and Jacobean Studies*, ed. Herbert Davis and Helen Gardner (1949), pp. 250-78, John Crow indicates the indebtedness of Middleton in this masque to Bretnor's 1618 almanac.

B. STATE OF SCHOLARSHIP

In spite of the amount of attention the playwright has received in recent years, two basic deficiencies remain: there has been no comprehensive and definitive critical reassessment of Middleton's works comparable to Anthony Caputi's *John Marston, Satirist*, or M. T. Jones-Davies's recent two-volume study of Dekker; and there is as yet no modern edition of the complete works, though Middleton scholars await the planned *Complete Dramatic Works*, ed. George R. Price and S. Schoenbaum (as described in *RenD Supplement* 7 [1964]:27).

III. CANON

A. PLAYS IN CHRONOLOGICAL ORDER (INCLUDING
MASQUES, PAGEANTS, AND ENTERTAINMENTS)

The chronology and dates are those of Alfred Harbage, *Annals of English Drama, 975-1700* (1940; rev. S. Schoenbaum, 1964). The dates in parentheses following the title of each entry are those of first performance (in italics) and first edition. If there was no seventeenth-century edition, and the play remained in manuscript throughout the period, this is indicated by "MS" followed, in brackets, by the date of the first printed edition. Important variant dates and works in which these are discussed are given under individual plays. The Middleton canon is discussed in E. K. Chamoers, *The Elizabethan Stage*, vol. 3 (1923); in Bentley's *Jacobean and Caroline Stage*, vol. 4 (1956); in Barker's *Middleton*; and in Schoenbaum's *Internal Evidence and Elizabethan Dramatic Authorship* (1966). W. W. Greg's *A Bibliography of the English Printed Drama to the Restoration*, 4 vols. (1939-62), describes the editions of the plays published before 1660.

The Family of Love, with Dekker (?), comedy (ca. *1602-7;* 1608)

Authorship and date are discussed by Barker and by Schoenbaum (*Internal Evidence*); Gerald J. Eberle makes a case for Dekker's collaboration in "Dekker's Part in *The Familie of Love*," in *Joseph Quincy Adams Memorial Studies*, ed. James G. McManaway et al. (1948), pp. 723-38. Barker dates the play in 1602-3, with possible revisions "several years after its original production"; Baldwin Maxwell argues for a date later than 1605 in "A Note on the Date of Middleton's *The Family of Love* with a Query on the Porters Hall Theatre," in *Elizabethan Studies and Other Essays in Honor of George F. Reynolds*, Univ. of Colorado Studies, Ser. B, Studies in the Humanities, vol. 2, no. 4 (1945), pp. 195-200.

The Phoenix, comedy (*1603-4;* 1607)

R. C. Bald's "The Chronology of Middleton's Plays," *MLR* 32 (1937):33-43, argues that "the most likely date" for the composition of *The Phoenix* is 1602. Maxwell, "Middleton's *The Phoenix*," in *Joseph Quincy Adams Memorial Studies*, ed. James G. McManaway et al. (1948), pp. 743-53, dates it between June and December of

1603, on grounds of style and several topical allusions. In "Middleton's *The Phoenix* as a Royal Play," *N&Q* 3 (1956):287–88, Bawcutt also speculates on possible topical allusions which were perhaps a result of its being specifically written for a court performance on February 20, 1603/4 (Chambers's date in *Elizabethan Stage*, vol. 3).

The Magnificent Entertainment Given to King James, with Dekker, coronation entertainment (*1604;* 1604)

Most of this work is by Dekker, and was published as his, but after Zeal's speech, Dekker made the following note: "If there be any glory to be won by writing these lines, I do freely bestow it, as his due, on Tho. Middleton, in whose brain they were begotten, though they were delivered here: *quae nos non fecimus ipsi, vix ea nostra voco.*" In spite of Dekker's note, Kate L. Gregg's *Thomas Dekker: A Study in Economic and Social Backgrounds* (1924) ascribes Zeal's speech to Dekker on the grounds that "its spirit and language . . . agree with Dekker's own sentiments in many another passage."

1 The Honest Whore, with the Humours of the Patient Man and the Longing Wife, with Dekker, comedy (*1604;* 1604)

See M. L. Wine's Dekker essay in this volume.

A Trick to Catch the Old One, comedy (*1604–7;* 1608)

Your Five Gallants, comedy (*1604–7;* ca. 1608)

A Mad World, My Masters, comedy (*1604–7;* 1608)

Michaelmas Term, comedy (*1604–6;* 1607)

Baldwin Maxwell, in "Middleton's *Michaelmas Term*," *PQ* 22 (1943):29–35, discusses several topical allusions which indicate a date of 1605 or 1606. Lucetta J. Teagarden, in "The Dekker-Middleton Problem in *Michaelmas Term*," *Studies in English* (Univ. of Texas) 26 (1947): 49–58, suggests that Dekker may have had a hand in the play.

The Roaring Girl, or Moll Cutpurse, with Dekker, comedy (*1604–10;* 1611)

Barker's *Middleton* thoroughly surveys the writings concerning the authorship of this comedy, which is generally accepted as a Middleton-Dekker collaboration. He also attempts to assign acts, scenes, and even lines to either Dekker or Middleton. For further information, see M. L. Wine's Dekker essay in this volume.

No Wit No Help Like a Woman's, comedy (ca. *1612;* 1657)

In "Weather-Wise's Almanac and the Date of Middleton's *No Wit No Help Like a Woman's*," *N&Q* 13 (1966):297–301, David George points out that Weatherwise in the play continually refers to actual almanacs of the year 1611, indicating that was the date of the play's composition. George's evidence is accepted by Schoenbaum in his first supplement (1966) to the revised *Annals*, and Schoenbaum establishes a probable performance date of 1612.

A Chaste Maid in Cheapside, comedy (*1613;* 1630)

The performance date is as given in Schoenbaum's second supplement (1970) to the revised edition of the *Annals*.

The Entertainment at the Opening of the New River, civic entertainment (*1613;* 1613)

The Triumphs of Truth, civic pageant (*1613;* 1613)

More Dissemblers Besides Women, comedy (ca. *1615?;* 1657)

The Witch, tragicomedy (ca. *1609*–ca. *1616;* MS [1945])

Frank Sullivan, in "*Macbeth*, Middleton's *Witch*, and *Macbeth* Again," *Los Angeles Tidings*, 24 Sept. 1948, p. 6, dates *The Witch* in 1609; however, David George, "The Problem of Middleton's *The Witch* and Its Sources," *N&Q* 14 (1967):209–11, discovers new allusions and borrowings in the play which suggest a more likely date of 1614.

Civitatis Amor, civic pageant (*1616;* 1616)

A work for which Middleton was apparently only partly responsible, according to Barker.

The Widow, with Jonson and Fletcher?, comedy (ca. *1615–17;* 1652)

According to the title page of the 1652 edition, this was a

collaboration with Ben Jonson and John Fletcher. However, Barker points out that "in one copy the first names [i.e., Jonson's and Fletcher's] have been struck out in an old hand and the word *alone* has been written after the name of Middleton . . . . Archer attributes the play to Middleton alone, Kirkman to Middleton and Rowley." Although he finds no internal evidence of Jonson's hand, Barker thinks Fletcher may have been concerned with the play, even though it appears in neither of the Beaumont and Fletcher folios.

The Triumphs of Honour and Industry, civic pageant (*1617;* 1617)

A Fair Quarrel, with W. Rowley, tragicomedy (ca. *1616–17;* 1617)

Concerning this Middleton-Rowley collaboration, Edward Engelberg, "A Middleton-Rowley Dispute," *N&Q* 198 (1953):330–32, argues that part of III.ii, usually assigned to Rowley, is in fact by Middleton.

Hengist, King of Kent, or The Mayor of Queenborough, with W. Rowley?, tragedy (ca. *1615–20;* 1661)

For the slim evidence concerning attribution of a few passages in this play to Rowley, see Schoenbaum's *Middleton's Tragedies*, and Bentley, vol. 4.

The Old Law, or A New Way to Please You, with Massinger and W. Rowley, comedy (ca. *1615–18;* 1656)

In "The Authorship and the Manuscript of *The Old Law*," *HLQ* 16 (1953):117–39, George R. Price, on the basis of bibliographical evidence, assigns scenes of this play to the three dramatists named on the quarto title page: Massinger, Middleton, and Rowley. Middleton he finds "primarily responsible" for the serious scenes concerning Cleanthes, Hippolita, Leonides, and Eugenia; Rowley for the farcical Gnotho episodes; and Massinger for later (ca. 1626) revisions.

The Inner-Temple Mask, or Mask of Heroes, mask (*1619;* 1619)

The Triumphs of Love and Antiquity, civic pageant (*1619;* 1619)

The World Tossed at Tennis, with W. Rowley, mask (*1620;* 1620)

See Barker's *Middleton* for speculation on the contributions of each author.

Anything For a Quiet Life, with Webster?, comedy (ca. *1620-21;* 1662)

Barker suggests that Webster wrote the main plot and Middleton the subplot; but Bentley, vol. 4, maintains that the title page ascription to Middleton should be sufficient to establish the play's authorship, in the absence of contradictory external evidence. Dunkel's "The Authorship of *Anything for a Quiet Life,*" *PMLA* 43 (1928):793-99, cites internal evidence supporting the view that the play is entirely Middleton's.

Honourable Entertainments, collection of ten entertainments (*1620-21;* 1621)

The Sun in Aries, with Munday?, civic pageant (*1621;* 1621)

Bentley, vol. 4, suspects collaboration with Anthony Munday.

Women Beware Women, tragedy (ca. *1620-27;* 1657)

Dating this play has proved difficult. Baldwin Maxwell, "The Date of Middleton's *Women Beware Women,*" *PQ* 22 (1943):338-42, argues for a date of "late 1620 or 1621"; however, Elizabeth R. Jacobs, in her unpublished Ph.D. dissertation for the University of Wisconsin, "A Critical Edition of Thomas Middleton's *Women Beware Women*" (1942), as noted in Barker's *Middleton*, points out that Maxwell's topical allusions are undependable as evidence of the play's date of composition. The earliest date proposed is that of Jackson I. Cope, who argues, from parallels to Middleton's masque *The Triumphs of Truth*, for 1613 or 1614; Cope's "The Date of Middleton's *Women Beware Women,*" *MLN* 76 (1961):295-300, also provides a useful review of scholarship on the dating of the play. Since as yet no external evidence and no clear references in the text to contemporary events have been found, the date of this tragedy remains, in Bentley's words, "highly speculative."

An Invention for the Service of the Right Honourable Edward Barkham, Lord Mayor, dinner entertainment (*1622;* MS [1885])

The Triumphs of Honour and Virtue, civic pageant (*1622;* 1622)

The Changeling, with W. Rowley, tragedy (*1622;* 1653)

Those who have studied the collaboration of Middleton and

Rowley on this tragedy agree almost entirely on the allocation of the individual scenes: see Schoenbaum, *Internal Evidence*, and Bawcutt's edition. One exception is C. L. Barber's "A Rare Use of 'Honour' as a Criterion of Middleton's Authorship," *ES* 38 (1957):161–68; using Middleton's characteristic and rather rare usage of *honor* ("a bow or curtsey") as a criterion, Barber finds Middleton's hand in a scene (IV.iii) usually assigned to Rowley.

The Triumphs of Integrity, civic pageant (*1623;* 1623)

The Spanish Gypsy, with W. Rowley, and Ford?, tragicomedy (*1623;* 1653)

Barker surveys the scholarship concerned with the authorship of this tragicomedy, most of which regards it as a Middleton-Rowley collaboration. However, Barker finds H. Dugdale Sykes's evidence, in *Sidelights on Elizabethan Drama* (1924), for Ford's authorship convincing; and Schoenbaum's *Middleton's Tragedies* agrees that it "may very well have been the unaided work of Ford."

A Game at Chess, political satire (*1624;* 1625?)

The Triumphs of Health and Prosperity, civic pageant (*1626;* 1626)

B. UNCERTAIN ASCRIPTIONS AND APOCRYPHA

Blurt, Master Constable, or The Spaniard's Night Walk, comedy (*1601–2;* 1602)

Both Chambers and Bentley accept this play, one of Francis Kirkman's late seventeenth-century attributions, in the Middleton canon. However, a strong case on grounds of both style and external evidence has recently been made for Dekker's authorship: see Barker, and M. L. Wine's essay on Dekker in this volume.

The Puritan, or The Widow of Watling Street, comedy (*1606;* 1607)

Mainly on the basis of similarities in dramatic structure and satirical point of view to his known plays, W. D. Dunkel, "Authorship of *The Puritan*," *PMLA* 45 (1930): 804–8, favors Middleton as the author of this comedy in the Shakespeare Apocrypha. Baldwin Maxwell, *Studies in the Shakespeare Apocrypha* (1956), agrees;

although he cannot find conclusive evidence that the play is Middleton's, he knows of "no author to whose plays *The Puritan* shows greater likeness." Barker, after surveying the scholarship, concludes that "a reasonable doubt must remain. It may not be Middleton's after all."

The Revenger's Tragedy, tragedy *(1606- 7;* 1607- 8)

The main Middleton authorship problem dealt with by Schoenbaum in *Internal Evidence* concerns this play; after reviewing the extensive scholarship, he concludes that the scanty external evidence favors Tourneur as author and the internal evidence Middleton, with the balance between these two candidates being about even. In *"The Revenger's Tragedy* and the Virtue of Anonymity," in *Essays on Shakespeare and Elizabethan Drama in Honor of Hardin Craig,* ed. Richard Hosley (1962), pp. 309- 16, Allardyce Nicoll argues that excessive attention has been devoted to the authorship problem, some of which might well have been spent in examining the more specifically literary and historical aspects of the play. The same point is made, more forcefully, by Irving Ribner in "Criticism of Elizabethan and Jacobean Drama," *RenD* 6 (1963):7- 13.

Wit at Several Weapons, comedy (ca. *1609- 20;* 1647)

After reviewing the scholarship, which is about equally divided on the question of Middleton's hand in this comedy, Barker concludes that he is "reasonably sure" Middleton had "something to do with it." However, he admits the external evidence is not conducive to this conclusion: "The play was published in the first folio of their [Beaumont and Fletcher's] work and later entered as theirs in the S.R. It is ascribed to them in Archer's play list. In the folio text the epilogue, written 'at the reviving of this Play,' mentions Fletcher as one of the authors."

The Second Maiden's Tragedy, tragedy *(1611;* MS [1909])

In "The Authorship of the *Second Maiden's Tragedy* and *The Revenger's Tragedy,"* *ShAB* 20 (1945):51- 62, 121- 33, Barker finds stylistic similarities between this play, *The Revenger's Tragedy,* and Middleton's known work, as does Schoenbaum in *Middleton's Tragedies.* But Schoenbaum qualifies his position in *Internal Evidence,* where he discusses the implications of revisions made to the scribally written manuscript: "I have (I now feel) attached insufficient weight to their presence. The hand responsible for these corrections does not belong to Middleton." In *Pause Patterns in Elizabethan and Jacobean Drama* (1960), Ants Oras finds support for the theory of Middleton's authorship in the *Second Maiden's* "line-split design"—the pattern of pauses within lines of verse—which resembles closely the pause patterns of plays in the Middleton canon written at about the same time, particularly *The Witch*. But Leonora Leet Brodwin, "Authorship of *The Second Maiden's Tragedy:* A Reconsideration of the Manuscript Attribution to Chapman," *SP* 63 (1966):51-77, points out that simialrities of style and stage technique, as well as a manuscript notation, indicate George Chapman's authorship.

The Nice Valour, or The Passionate Madmun, comedy (ca. *1615-25;* 1647)

Barker discusses the weak stylistic evidence for Middleton's hand in this play, which was probably mainly the work of Fletcher.

A Match at Midnight, comedy (*1621-23;* 1633)

Pauline G. Wiggin, *An Inquiry into the Authorship of the Middleton-Rowley Plays* (1897), found evidence of Middleton's authorship; however, both Chambers and Bentley put the play in the Rowley canon.

The Bloody Banquet, tragedy (*1639;* 1639)

E. H. C. Oliphant, "A Dekker-Middleton Play, *The Bloodie Banquet*," *TLS*, 17 Dec. 1925, p. 882, found evidence of collaboration by the two dramatists on this play of unknown composition date; however, Schoenbaum, *Middleton's Tragedies*, and Barker dismiss Oliphant's evidence as too subjective. The *Annals* listing assigns the play, with a question mark, to Thomas Drue, evidently mainly on the basis of the phrase "By T. D." which appears on the title page of the 1639 quarto.

C. CRITIQUE OF THE STANDARD EDITION

There is as yet no complete modern edition of Middleton's works. Bullen's edition (8 vols.; 1885-86), which in the main merely reprints that of Alexander Dyce (5 vols.; 1840) with a new introduction and additional notes, is sparsely and sometimes misleadingly annotated, as a comparison with the full and accurate notes to such modern editions of single plays as Bawcutt's of *The Changeling*, Harper's of *A Game at Chess*, or Henning's of *A Mad World, My Masters* will indicate. Bullen sometimes misinterprets seventeenth-century spellings and punctuations, mislineates verse as prose or prose as verse, omits or misplaces stage directions, and assigns speeches to the wrong characters: see Kenneth Muir, "Swinburne on Middleton," *TLS*, 24 Feb. 1945, p. 91, on an emendation to the Bullen text of *The Phoenix*, and the bibliographical and textual studies of George R. Price listed below.

D. TEXTUAL STUDIES

George R. Price has provided bibliographical and textual information on Middleton's plays in: "The First Edition of *A Faire Quarrell*," *Library* 4 (1949):137–41; "Compositors' Methods with Two Quartos Reprinted by Augustine Mathewes," *PBSA* 44 (1950): 269–74 (on *A Fair Quarrel*); "The First Editions of *Your Five Gallants* and of *Michaelmas Term*," *Library* 8 (1953):23–29; "The Huntington MS of *A Game at Chesse*," *HLQ* 17 (1953): 83–88; "The Quartos of *The Spanish Gypsy* and Their Relation to *The Changeling*," *PBSA* 52 (1958):111–25; "The Authorship and the Bibliography of *The Revenger's Tragedy*," *Library* 15 (1960):262–77 (which supports Middleton's authorship by reference to his characteristic abbreviations, speech prefixes, spellings, and punctuations as found in his other plays, and especially the autograph copies of *A Game at Chess*); "The Latin Oration in *A Game at Chesse*," *HLQ* 23 (1960):389–93; "Setting by Formes in the First Edition of *The Phoenix*," *PBSA* 56 (1962):414–27 (gives new evidence of the casting-off of copy and setting by formes rather than consecutive pages in the first edition of a Jacobean play); "Dividing the Copy for *Michaelmas Term*," *PBSA* 60 (1966):327–36.

R. C. Bald, in "An Early Version of Middleton's *Game at Chesse*," *MLR* 38 (1943):177–80, describes a new manuscript (the sixth) of *Game* which had recently come to light. It shows signs of revision by the author and is probably the earliest of the remarkable number of surviving manuscripts. J. W. Harper gives additional information on this and the other early texts of the play in his edition (1966). In addition to Price's "The First Editions of *Your Five Gallants* and of *Michaelmas Term*" (above), Bald in "The Foul Papers of a Revision," *Library* 1 (1945):37–50, and Maxwell in "Thomas Middleton's *Your Five Gallants*," *PQ* 30 (1951):30–39, find considerable bibliographical and textual evidence that *Gallants* was printed from Middleton's foul papers, rather than from prompt copy—probably the foul papers of a revision by Middleton. Gerald J. Eberle reaches a similar conclusion concerning another Middleton City comedy in "The Composition and Printing of Middleton's *A Mad World, My Masters,*" *SB* 3 (1950): 246–52. Robert G. Lawrence's "A Bibliographical Study of Middleton and Rowley's *The Changeling,*" *Library* 16 (1961):37–43, concludes that "the text of *The Changeling* did not suffer seriously at the hands of its first printer."

E. SINGLE-WORK EDITIONS OF THE PLAYS

The largest number of modern editions are of *The Changeling.* The Revels edition, by N. W. Bawcutt (1958; rev. ed. 1961), is the most thoroughly annotated; in an appendix, Bawcutt includes lengthy selections from two plot sources, Reynold's *The Triumphs of God's Revenge against . . . Murther* and Digges's *Gerardo the Unfortunate Spaniard.* Other recent editions are Patricia Thomson's for the New Mermaids (1964), Matthew W. Black's (1966), and George W. Williams's RRDS edition (1966).

A Chaste Maid in Cheapside is the next most frequently edited play, including A. Brissenden's New Mermaids edition (1968), R. B. Parker's Revels Plays edition (1969), and Charles Barber's for Fountainwell Drama Texts (1969). *A Game at Chess* has been edited twice, by R. C. Bald (1929) and by J. W. Harper for the New Mermaids (1966). Other Middleton plays appearing in two modern editions are: *A Trick to Catch the Old One,* by Charles Barber for Fountainwell (1968) and by G. J. Watson for New Mermaids (1969); and *The Witch,* by L. Drees and H. De Vocht (1945) and by W. W. Greg and F. P. Wilson for the Malone Society (1948).

Single editions have appeared of the following: *Hengist, King of Kent,* by R. C. Bald (1938); *A Mad World, My Masters,* by Standish Henning for RRDS (1965); *Michaelmas Term,* by Richard Levin for RRDS (1966); and *Women Beware Women,* by Roma Gill for the New Mermaids (1968).

F. EDITIONS OF NONDRAMATIC WORKS

The only modern edition of Middleton's nondramatic works is *The Ghost of Lucrece,* ed. J. Q. Adams (1937). Of the numerous masques, entertainments, and pageants, the one modern edition is *Honorable Entertainments by Thomas Middleton,* ed. R. C. Bald for the Malone Society (1953).

IV. SEE ALSO

A. GENERAL

Adams, John C. *The Globe Playhouse.* 1942.

Akrigg, G. P. V. "Middleton: An Allusion to the Shakespeare First Folio?" *ShAB* 21 (1946):25-26.

Appleton, William W. *Beaumont and Fletcher: A Critical Study.* 1956.

Aronstein, Philipp. *Das englische Renaissancedrama.* 1929.

Bakeless, John. *The Tragicall History of Christopher Marlowe.* 2 vols. 1942.

Balch, Marston. "Thomas Middleton, Three Hundred Years After." *Theatre Arts Monthly* 11 (1927):911-16.

Barber, C. L. *The Idea of Honour in the English Drama, 1591-1700.* 1957.

Bowden, William R. *The English Dramatic Lyric, 1603-42.* 1951.

Bowers, R. H. " 'The Masque of the Four Seasons' (Egerton MS 2623)." *N&Q* 197 (1952):96-97.

Bowers, Fredson. *On Editing Shakespeare and the Elizabethan Dramatists.* 1955.

———. *Bibliography and Textual Criticism.* 1964.

Bradbrook, M. C. "Lucrece and Othello." *TLS,* 27 Oct. 1950, p. 677.

Briggs, K. M. *Pale Hecate's Team.* 1962.

Brown, Arthur. "The Play within a Play: An Elizabethan Dramatic Device." *E&S* 13 (1960):36-48.

Cawley, Robert R. *The Voyagers and Elizabethan Drama.* 1938.

Christian, Mildred G. *Non-Dramatic Sources for the Rogues in Middleton's Plays.* 1936.

Churchill, R. C. *Shakespeare and His Betters.* 1958.

Clarkson, Paul S., and Clyde T. Warren. *The Law of Property in Shakespeare and the Elizabethan Drama.* 1942.

Craig, Hardin. "Textual Degeneration of Elizabethan and Stuart Plays: An Examination of Plays in Manuscript." *RIP* 46 (1960):71-84.

Cutts, John P. "Who Wrote the Hecate-Scene?" *SJ* 194 (1958):200-202.

Davril, Robert. *Le drame de John Ford.* 1954.

Downer, Alan S. *The British Drama.* 1950.

Dunkel, W. D. "Did Not Rowley Merely Revise Middleton?" *PMLA* 48 (1933): 799-805.

Fisher, Margery. "Notes on the Sources of Some Incidents in Middleton's London Plays." *RES* 15 (1939):283-93.

Flatter, Richard. "Who Wrote the Hecate-Scene?" *SJ* 193 (1957):196-210.

Grivelet, Michel. *Thomas Heywood et le drame domestique élisabéthain.* 1957.

Holmes, David M. *The Art of Thomas Middleton: A Critical Study.* 1970.

Howarth, R. G. *Literature of the Theatre: Marlowe to Shirley.* 1953.

Hoy, Cyrus H. "The Shares of Fletcher and his Collaborators in the Beaumont and Fletcher Canon (V)." *SB* 13 (1960):77-108.

———. *The Hyacinth Room: An Investigation into the Nature of Comedy, Tragedy, and Tragicomedy.* 1964.

Hunter, G. K."The Marking of Sententiae." *Library* 6 (1951):171-88.

Jacquot, Jean, ed. *La lieu théâtral à la Renaissance.* Vol. 1, 1964.

Jones-Davies, M. T. *Un peintre de la vie Londonienne: Thomas Dekker.* 2 vols. 1958.

Kernan, Alvin. *The Cankered Muse: Satire of the English Renaissance.* 1959.

Knoll, Robert E. *Ben Jonson's Plays: An Introduction.* 1964.

Kreutz, I. "Three Collector's Items." *ETJ* 14 (1962): 141-47.

Krzyzanowski, Juliusz. "Conjectural Remarks on Elizabethan Dramatists." *N&Q* 195 (1950):400-402.

Larsen, T. "Swinburne on Middleton." *TLS*, 17 June 1939, pp. 357-58.

Lawrence, William J. *Pre-Restoration Stage Studies.* 1927.

Leech, Clifford. *Shakespeare's Tragedies and Other Studies in Seventeenth Century Drama.* 1950.

———. *The John Fletcher Plays.* 1962.

Levin, Richard. "The Lady and Her Horsekeeper: Middleton or Rowley?" *N&Q* 10 (1963):303-6.

———. "Dekker's Back-Door'd Italian and Middleton's Hebrew Pen." *N&Q* 10 (1963):338-40.

———. "Proverbial Phrases in the Titles of Thomas Middleton's Plays." *SFQ* 28 (1964):142-45.

———. " 'The Ass in Compound': A Lost Pun in Middleton, Ford, and Jonson." *ELN* 4 (1966):12-15.

———. "Mistress Quickly's Case." *N&Q* 13 (1966):293.

———. " 'Nuns' and 'Nunnery' in Elizabethan Drama." *N&Q* 15 (1968):248-49.

———. "The Elizabethan 'Three-Level' Play." *RenD* 2 (1969):23-37.

Levine, Robert T. "Rare Use of 'Since' in Middleton's *The Widow* and *A Chaste Maid in Cheapside.*" *N&Q* 18 (1971):457-58.

McCullen, Joseph T., Jr. "The Use of Parlor and Tavern Games in Elizabethan and Early Stuart Drama." *MLQ* 14 (1953):7-14.

McManaway, James G. "Fortune's Wheel." *TLS*, 16 April 1938, p. 264.

———. "Latin Title-Page Mottoes as a Clue to Dramatic Authorship." *Library* 26 (1945):28-36.

Manifold, J. S. *The Music in English Drama: From Shakespeare to Purcell.* 1956.

Maugeri, Aldo. *Studi su Thomas Dekker.* 1958.

Nicoll, Allardyce. *British Drama: An Historical Survey from the Beginnings to the Present Time.* 1925.

Parrott, Thomas Marc, and Robert Hamilton Ball. *A Short View of Elizabethan Drama.* 1943.

Partridge, A. C. *Orthography in Shakespeare and Elizabethan Drama: A Study of Colloquial Contractions, Elision, Prosody, and Punctuation.* 1964.

Peter, John. *Complaint and Satire in Early English Literature.* 1956.

Phialas, Peter G. "Middleton and Munday." *TLS*, 23 Nov. 1956, p. 697.

Power, William. "Thomas Middleton vs. King James I." *N&Q* 4 (1957):526-34.

———. "Double, Double." *N&Q* 6 (1959):4-8.

———. "Middleton's Way with Names." *N&Q* 7 (1960):26-29, 56-60, 95-98, 136-40, 175-79.

Rabkin, Norman. "The Double Plot: Notes on the History of a Convention." *RenD* 7 (1964):55-69.

Reeves, John D. "Thomas Middleton and Lily's Grammar: Some Parallels." *N&Q* 197 (1952):75-76.

Schelling, Felix E. *Foreign Influences in Elizabethan Plays.* 1923.

Schoenbaum, S. "Internal Evidence and the Attribution of Elizabethan Plays." *BNYPL* 65 (1961):102-24.

Scott-Kilvert, Ian. "Thomas Middleton." *Nine* 5 (1950):315-27.
Sewall, Richard B. *The Vision of Tragedy*. 1959.
Smith, Hallett. *Elizabethan Poetry: A Study in Conventions, Meaning and Expression*. 1952.
Spencer, Theodore. *Death and Elizabethan Tragedy: A Study of Convention and Opinion in the Elizabethan Drama*. 1936.
Spens, Janet. *Elizabethan Drama*. 1922.
Stagg, Louis C. *An Index to the Figurative Language of Thomas Middleton's Tragedies*. 1970.
Stoll, Elmer E. "Heroes and Villains: Shakespeare, Middleton, Byron, Dickens." *RES* 17 (1942):257-69.
Stroup, Thomas B. *Microcosmos: The Shape of the Elizabethan Play*. 1965.
Sykes, H. Dugdale. "Thomas Middleton's Early Non-Dramatic Work." *N&Q* 148 (1925):435-38.
Szenczi, N. I. "The Tragi-Comedies of Middleton and Rowley." In *Studies in English Philology: Essays Presented ... to Prof. A. B. Yolland. Dept. of English, Royal Hungarian Pázmány Péter University of Sciences*, vol. 2, 1937.
Tannenbaum, S. A. "A Middleton Forgery." *PQ* 12 (1933):33-36.
Taylor, Archer. "Proverbs and Proverbial Phrases in the Plays of Thomas Middleton." *SFQ* 23 (1959):79-89.
Thaler, Alwin. *Shakespeare to Sheridan*. 1922.
"Thomas Middleton." *TLS*, 30 June 1927, pp. 445-46.
Tomlinson, T. B. *A Study of Elizabethan and Jacobean Tragedy*. 1964.
Waith, Eugene M. *The Pattern of Tragicomedy in Beaumont and Fletcher*. 1952.
Watson, Harold F. *The Sailor in English Fiction and Drama, 1550-1800*. 1931.
Wedgwood, C. V. *Seventeenth-Century English Literature*. 1950.
Wells, Henry W. *Elizabethan and Jacobean Playwrights*. 1939.
West, Robert H. *The Invisible World: A Study of Pneumatology in Elizabethan Drama*. 1939.
Wickham, Glynne. *Early English Stages, 1300-1660*. Vol. 2, 1963.
Williams, Gordon. "A Sample of Elizabethan Sexual Periphrasis." *Trivium* 3 (1968):94-100.
Williams, Gwyn. "The Cuckoo, the Welsh Ambassador." *MLR* 51 (1956):223-24.

B. INDIVIDUAL PLAYS

Blurt, Master Constable

Bains, Yashdip Singh. "Thomas Middleton's *Blurt, Master Constable* as a Burlesque on Love." In *Essays Presented to Amy G. Stock, Professor of English, Rajasthan University, 1961-65*, ed. R. K. Kaul (1965), pp. 41-57.
Dodson, Daniel B. *"Blurt, Master Constable." N&Q* 6 (1959):61-65.
Holmes, David M. "Thomas Middleton's *Blurt Master Constable, or The Spaniard's Night-Walk." MLR* 64 (1969):1-10.
Sabol, Andrew J. "Two Songs for an Elizabethan Play." *SRen* 5 (1958):145-59.
Williamson, Marilyn L. *"Blurt, Master Constable, III, iii, and The Batchelar's Banquet." N&Q* 4 (1957):519-21.

The Family of Love

Baker, Donald C. "Metaphors in Swift's *A Tale of a Tub* and Middleton's *The Family of Love.*" *N&Q* 5 (1958):107-8.

Davidson, Clifford. "Middleton and the Family of Love." *EM* 20 (1969):81-92.

Levin, Richard. "Name Puns in *The Family of Love.*" *N&Q* 12 (1965):340-42.

Marotti, Arthur F. "The Purgations of Middleton's *The Family of Love.*" *Papers on Language and Literature* 6 (1971):80-84.

Maxwell, Baldwin. " 'Twenty Good-Nights'—*The Knight of the Burning Pestle*, and Middleton's *Family of Love.*" *MLN* 63 (1948):233-37.

Olive, W. J. "Imitation of Shakespeare in Middleton's *The Family of Love.*" *PQ* 29 (1950):75-78.

———. " 'Twenty Good Nights'—*The Knight of the Burning Pestle, The Family of Love* and *Romeo and Juliet.*" *SP* 47 (1950):182-89.

The Phoenix

Dodson, Daniel B. "King James and *The Phoenix*—Again." *N&Q* 5 (1958): 434-37.

Jackson, MacD. P. "A Non-Shakespearian Parallel to the Comic Mispronunciation of 'Ergo' in Hand D." *N&Q* 18 (1971):139.

Knight, G. Wilson. *The Mutual Flame: On Shakespeare's Sonnets and "The Phoenix and the Turtle."* 1955.

Lascelles, Mary. *Shakespeare's "Measure for Measure."* 1953.

Power, William L. *"The Phoenix*: Ralegh, and King James," *N&Q* 5 (1958):434-37.

Williamson, Marilyn L. *"The Phoenix*: Middleton's Comedy *de Regimine Principum. RN* 10 (1957):183-87.

A Trick to Catch the Old One

Falk, Signi. "Plautus' *Persa* and Middleton's *A Trick to Catch the Old One.*" *MLN* 66 (1951):19-21.

Sabol, Andrew J. "Ravenscroft's *Melismata* and the Children of Pauls." *RN* 12 (1959):3-9.

Your Five Gallants

Gross, Alan G. "Middleton's *Your Five Gallants:* The Fifth Act." *PQ* 44 (1965): 124-29.

Hoole, William S. "Thomas Middleton's Use of *Imprese* in *Your Five Gallants.*" *SP* 31 (1934):215-23.

A Mad World, My Masters

Hallett, Charles A. *"Volpone* as the Source of the Sickroom Scene in Middleton's *Mad World.*" *N&Q* 18 (1971):24-26.

Marotti, Arthur F. "The Method in the Madness of *A Mad World, My Masters.*" *TSL* 15 (1970):99-108.

Slights, William W. E. "The Trickster-Hero and Middleton's *A Mad World, My Masters.*" *CompD* 3 (1969):87-98.

Taylor, Michael. "Realism and Morality in Middleton's *A Mad World, My Masters." L&P* 18 (1968):166–78.

Michaelmas Term

Chatterji, Ruby. "Unity and Disparity in *Michaelmas Term." SEL* 8 (1968):349–63.
Levin, Richard. "*Littera Canina* in *Romeo and Juliet* and *Michaelmas Term.*" *N&Q* 9 (1962):333–34.
Maxwell, J. C. " 'Desperate Debts.' " *N&Q* 14 (1967):141.

The Puritan

Williamson, Marilyn L. "Middleton's Workmanship and the Authorship of *The Puritan." N&Q* 4 (1957):50–51.

The Revenger's Tragedy

Dunkel, W. D. "The Authorship of *The Revenger's Tragedy." PMLA* 46 (1931): 781–85.
Ekeblad, Inga-Stina. "A Note on *The Revenger's Tragedy." N&Q* 2 (1955): 98–99.
———. "An Approach to Tourneur's Imagery." *MLR* 54 (1959): 489–98.
———. "The Authorship of *The Revenger's Tragedy." ES* 41 (1960):225–40.
Foakes, R. A. "On the Authorship of *The Revenger's Tragedy." MLR* 48 (1953):129–38.
Jewkes, W. T. "The Nightmares of Internal Evidence in Jacobean Drama." *Seventeenth Century News* 24 (1966):4–8.
Lake, D. J. "*The Revenger's Tragedy:* Internal Evidence for Tourneur's Authorship Negated." *N&Q* 18 (1971):455–56.
Mincoff, Marco K. "The Authorship of *The Revenger's Tragedy.*" *Studia Historico-Philologica-Serdicensia* 2 (1940):1–87.
Ornstein, Robert. "The Ethical Design of *The Revenger's Tragedy." ELH* 21 (1954):81–93.
Salinger, L. G. "*The Revenger's Tragedy*: Some Possible Sources." *MLR* 60 (1965):3–12.
Schoenbaum, S. "*The Revenger's Tragedy*: A Neglected Source." *N&Q* 195 (1950):338.
———. "*The Revenger's Tragedy* and Middleton's Moral Outlook." *N&Q* 196 (1951):8–10.
———. "*The Revenger's Tragedy:* Jacobean Dance of Death." *MLQ* 15 (1954): 201–7.
Wadsworth, Frank W. "*The Revenger's Tragedy." MLR* 50 (1955):307.
Waith, Eugene M. "The Ascription of Speeches in *The Revenger's Tragedy.*" *MLN* 57 (1942):119–21.

The Roaring Girl

Dowling, M. "A Note on Moll Cutpurse—'The Roaring Girl.' " *RES* 10 (1934): 67–71.
Price, George R. "The Shares of Middleton and Dekker in a Collaborated Play." *Papers of the Michigan Academy of Science, Arts, and Letters* 30 (1944): 601–15.

———. "The Manuscript and the Quarto of *The Roaring Girl.*" *Library* 11 (1956):180–86.

A Chaste Maid in Cheapside

Buckingham, E. L. "Campion's *Art of English Poesie* and Middleton's *Chaste Maid in Cheapside.*" *PMLA* 43 (1928):784–92.

Gilbert, A. H. "The Prosperous Wittol in Giovanni Battista Modio and Thomas Middleton." *SP* 41 (1944):235–37.

Hallett, Charles A. "Middleton's Allwit: The Urban Cynic." *MLQ* 30 (1969): 498–507.

Levin, Richard. "Middleton's Way with Names in *A Chaste Maid in Cheapside.*" *N&Q* 12 (1965):102–3.

Marotti, Arthur F. "Fertility and Comic Form in *A Chaste Maid in Cheapside.*" *CompD* 3 (1969):65–74.

Williams, Robert I. "Machiavelli's *Mandragola*, Touchwood Senior, and the Comedy of Middleton's *A Chaste Maid in Cheapside.*" *SEL* 10 (1970):385–96.

The Witch

Cutts, John P. "The Original Music to Middleton's *The Witch.*" *SQ* 7 (1956): 203–9.

Greg, W. W. "Some Notes on Crane's Manuscript of *The Witch*. Now Malone MS 12 in the Bodleian." *Library* 22 (1942):208–22.

A Fair Quarrel

Fisher, Margery. " 'Bronstrops.' A Note on *A Faire Quarrell.*" *MLR* 35 (1940): 59–62.

Holdsworth, R. V. "Middleton and Rowley's *A Fair Quarrel*: An Unnoticed Borrowing." *N&Q* 18 (1971):25–27.

Johnson, Gerald D. "Trollope's Note on Middleton and Rowley's *A Fair Quarrel.*" *N&Q* 18 (1971):27.

Price, George R. "Medical Men in *A Faire Quarrell.*" *Bulletin of the History of Medicine* 24 (1950):38–42.

Hengist, King of Kent

Ribner, Irving. *The English History Play in the Age of Shakespeare*. 1957; rev. ed. 1965.

Schoenbaum, S. "*Hengist, King of Kent* and Sexual Preoccupation in Jacobean Drama." *PQ* 29 (1950):182–98.

Anything For a Quiet Life

Forker, Charles R. "Shakespearean Imitation in Act V of *Anything for a Quiet Life.*" *Papers on Language and Literature* 7 (1971):75–80.

Linthicum, M. Channing. "Gingerline." *PQ* 9 (1930):212–13.

Soens, Adolph L. "Lawyers, Collusions and Cudgels: Middleton's *Anything for a Quiet Life*, I.i.220–221." *ELN* 7 (1970):248–54.

Women Beware Women

Aggeler, Geoffrey. "Irony and Honour in Jacobean Tragedy." *HAB* 18 (1967): 8-19.

Core, George. "The Canker and the Muse: Imagery in *Women Beware Women*." *RenP*, 1968, pp. 65-76.

Johnson, Jeffrey L. "The Spoils of Love and Vengeance: A Study of Jacobean Revenge Tragedy Motivated by Lust." *Xavier Univ. Studies* 7 (1968):31-43.

Krook, Dorothea. "Tragedy and Satire: Middleton's *Women Beware Women*." *SEL* 53 (1966):96-120.

Ribner, Irving. "Middleton's *Women Beware Women*: Poetic Imagery and the Moral Vision." *TSE* 9 (1959):19-33.

Simpson, Percy. "Thomas Middleton's *Women Beware Women*." *MLR* 33 (1938): 45-46.

The Changelings

Bawcutt, N. W. "*The Changeling*: A Source for the Subplot." *N&Q* 2 (1955):233.

Berger, Thomas L. "The Petrarchan Fortress of *The Changeling*." *RenP*, 1969, pp. 37-46.

Berlin, Normand. "The Finger Image and Relationship of Character in *The Changeling*." *ESA* 12 (1969):162-66.

Brustein, Robert. "We Are Two Cultural Nations." *New Republic* 151 (1964): 25-26, 28.

Burelbach, F. M., Jr. "Middleton and Rowley's *The Changeling*, I.i.52-56." *Expl* 26 (1968):item 60.

Ekeblad, Inga-Stina. "A Textual Note on *The Changeling*." *N&Q* 2 (1955):156-57.

Farr, Dorothy M. "*The Changeling*." *MLR* 62 (1967):586-97.

Feldman, A. Bronson. "The Yellow Malady: Short Studies of Five Tragedies of Jealousy." *L&P* 6 (1957):38-52.

Hébert, Catherine A. "A Note on the Significance of the Title of Middleton's *The Changeling*." *CLAJ* 12 (1968):66-69.

Helton, Tinsley. "Middleton and Rowley's *The Changeling*, V.iii. 175-177." *Expl* 21 (1963):item 74.

Hewes, Henry. "The Teenageling." *Saturday Review*, 21 Nov. 1964, p. 35.

Kehler, Dorothea. "Rings and Jewels in *The Changeling*." *ELN* 5 (1967):15-17.

———. "Middleton and Rowley's *The Changeling*, V.iii.175-177." *Expl* 26 (1968):item 41.

Lloyd, Bertram. "A Minor Source of *The Changeling*." *MLR* 19 (1924):101-2.

McCarten, John. "Kindergarten in the Village." *New Yorker*, 7 Nov. 1964, p. 99.

Ricks, Christopher. "The Moral and Poetical Structure of *The Changeling*." *Essays in Criticism* 10 (1960):290-306.

Stafford, T. J. "Middleton's Debt to Chaucer in *The Changeling*." *BRMMLA* 22 (1968):208-13.

Tomlinson, T. B. "Poetic Naturalism—*The Changeling*." *JEGP* 63 (1964):648-59.

The Spanish Gypsy

Burelbach, F. M., Jr. "Theme and Structure in *The Spanish Gipsy*." *HAB* 19 (1968):37-41.

Huddlestone, Eugene L. "*The Spanish Gypsy* and *La Gitanilla:* An Unnoticed Borrowing." *N&Q* 12 (1965):103-4.

A Game at Chess

Bald, R. C. "*A Game at Chesse.*" *TLS*, 17 May 1928, p. 379.

———. "A New Manuscript of Middleton's *Game at Chesse.*" *MLR* 25 (1930): 474-78.

Kaplan, Joel H. "The Feast Day of Middleton's Loyola." *N&Q* 18 (1971):27-28.

Phialas, Peter G. "An Unpublished Letter about *A Game at Chess.*" *MLN* 69 (1954):398-99.

Pineas, Rainer. "A Missing Source-Book for Middleton's *A Game at Chesse.*" *N&Q* 12 (1965):353-54.

Sargent, Roussel. "Theme and Structure in Middleton's *A Game at Chesse.*" *MLR* 66 (1971):721-30.

Southall, R. "A Missing Source-Book for Middleton's *A Game at Chesse.*" *N&Q* 9 (1962):145-46.

Wilson, Edward M., and Olga Turner. "The Spanish Protest against *A Game at Chesse.*" *MLR* 44 (1949):476-82.

Wright, Louis B. "*A Game at Chess.*" *TLS*, 16 Feb. 1928, p. 112.

JOHN WEBSTER

Don D. Moore

The standard edition is F. L. Lucas's *The Complete Works of John Webster*, 4 vols. (1927; American ed. 1937). Lucas re-edited *The White Devil* and *The Duchess of Malfi* in 1958; the *Complete Works* was reprinted in 1967.

I. GENERAL

A. BIOGRAPHICAL

The best biographical and general introductory essay is that by F. L. Lucas in volume one of the *Complete Works*; chapter one in Peter B. Murray's *A Study of John Webster* (1969) is a useful brief summary. Aside from Webster's own statement that he was "born free" of the Merchant Taylors' Company in the preface to *Monuments of Honour* (1624) and the existence of a "Johannes Webster" on the Middle Temple Records, we know nothing of his earlier life and education. R. G. Howarth, in "Two Notes on John Webster," *MLR* 63 (1968):785–89, considers Webster's parentage and his connection with the Merchant Taylors' Company. The earliest records of Webster as a working dramatist are found in Henslowe's diary in 1602 when Webster and several other playwrights, including Middleton, Dekker, and Heywood, received payment for plays which have not survived. The period 1612–14 brought *The White Devil* and *The Duchess of Malfi*; after that until his death in the 1630s Webster generally collaborated with other dramatists.

B. GENERAL STUDIES OF THE PLAYS

Peter B. Murray's *A Study of John Webster* (1969) defines the themes and structure of the plays and relates them to the ideas and patterns of Webster's cultural traditions. Murray considers Webster's relation to medieval literature and Christian thought and finds Webster's vision more tragic than moral, "a Christian compromise between Stoicism and the ideas of Montaigne." With his stress on the futility of man's efforts in the world, Webster is close to the theater of the absurd, especially the world of Samuel Beckett (see below, II, B); however Murray notes Webster's positive emphasis on an ultimately greater order and meaning which lie beyond appearances: "The creation of symbolic and other formal patterns that is so typical of his writing becomes itself a testament of faith in order, in the idea that there is meaning in things, though one must look closely for it, deeper than surface appearances." Murray's useful study includes chapters on *The Devil's Law Case*, *A Cure For a Cuckold*, and *Appius and Virginia*.

Travis Bogard's *The Tragic Satire of John Webster* (1955) is an account of Webster's use of the techniques of Marston and Chapman in an endeavor to show man both as he might be and as he is. The theme of social evil is strong in *The White Devil* and is further emphasized in *The Duchess of Malfi*, the latter play bringing into focus "all the terrors of a dying universe"; yet always the satiric voice is coequal with the tragic. Bogard's account of the stubborn consistency of Webster's characters—their determination to be only what they are—is of interest. Clifford Leech takes a more general view in *John Webster: A Critical Study* (1951). The overall theme reflects T. S. Eliot's earlier impression of a "genius directed toward chaos" (*Elizabethan Essays*, 1934), although some of Leech's judgments are qualified in his later study, *Webster: "The Duchess of Malfi"* (1963). There exists a world of gray negation in Webster, and though he has excelled in the moving exploration of the human mind, there is no total design in either of the two great tragedies; *The Duchess of Malfi*, particularly, for all its impressive scenes, is "blurred in its total meaning." In Leech's opinion, Webster may not have fully realized the significance of his work.

Ian Scott-Kilvert considers Webster's conception of tragedy in *John Webster* (WTW, 1964; rev. ed. 1970). He theorizes that instead of presenting a meeting of character and fate, Webster defies convention by gaining admiration for amoral characters. There is no moral center in *The White Devil*, yet Webster makes a moral point by focusing attention not on a hero, but on the social setting, the corruption of which is held up as a warning. Yet he also feels that "in its general design, the plot lacks the unifying power of a single dominant motive." *The Duchess of Malfi* is more world-weary, more melancholy, but in the Duchess and Bosola Webster creates characters capable of self-judgment; there is the possibility that "the spiritual chaos of the early seventeenth century is not eternity."

The chapters on Webster in two earlier studies, M. C. Bradbrook's *Themes and Conventions of Elizabethan Tragedy* (1935) and Una Ellis-Fermor's *The Jacobean Drama* (1936; 4th ed., 1958) remain influential. Bradbrook finds Webster concerned with perfection of detail rather than general design, and one who confused his conventions: the attitudes in *The White Devil* are meant to be naturalistic, but the characters are not. Ellis-Fermor cites Webster as the dramatist who most clearly perceived the chaos and conflict in which his age was caught. His plays—particularly *The Duchess of Malfi*—are structured like certain paintings, with a form which grows out of the mass. She states that ultimately, Webster can find only a misty world, empty and meaningless, in which the sole virtue is courage; the moral system is superimposed through the *sententiae* of the plays and does not correspond with the author's instinctive affections.

Robert Ornstein reflects Ellis-Fermor's views in *The Moral Vision of Jacobean Tragedy* (1960): *The White Devil* lacks the moral emphasis and focus which unite the similarly episodic *King Lear;* guilt and innocence seem equally irrelevant. In *The Duchess of Malfi*, a more mature play, the Duchess triumphs over adversity, and some form of moral awareness comes to all the characters; yet this awareness seems only an intuition of a realm of values, obscured by corruption. However, Irving Ribner in *Jacobean Tragedy: The Quest for Moral Order* (1962) sees *The Duchess of Malfi* as the exploration of a value—integrity of life—first postulated in *The White Devil*, which in the second play cleanses the social order and reaffirms the permanence of the human spirit. Ribner interprets the characters symbolically, with ethical and allegorical dimensions, following the thinking of, among others, F. P. Wilson in *Elizabethan and Jacobean* (1945). Dominic Baker-Smith, "Religion and John Webster," in *John Webster*, Mermaid Critical Commentaries, ed. Brian Morris (1970), pp. 207-28, considers the two major plays against the background of a "pessimism generated by a Calvinistic view of man." With his disregard of moral choice and emphasis on determinism, Webster is responding "to the spiritual temper of his particular age."

The most negative assessment of Webster comes in Ian Jack's "The Case of John Webster," *Scrutiny* 16 (1949):38-43. Jack finds no steady moral vision and regards Webster as a second-rank writer. Great tragedy can be written only by one who has achieved a balanced and profound insight into life; Webster achieved no such depth: "There is, in fact, something a trifle ridiculous about Webster."

R. W. Dent studies Webster's methods of composition in *John Webster's Borrowing* (1960) and notes eight major points which he feels governed Webster's selection of others' phrases. J. R. Mulryne, in "*The White Devil* and *The Duchess of Malfi,*" *Jacobean Theatre*, SuAS, vol. 1 (1960), pp. 201–25, calls attention to the breathless blank verse which overrides the metric pattern to tremendous effect; Mulryne however can find little sense of order in *The White Devil*, and while there is a coherence and moral norm in *The Duchess of Malfi*, there remain many moments in which the dramatic movement is stifled by extraneous material. In "Webster and the Uses of Tragicomedy," *John Webster*, ed. Morris (above), pp. 133–55, Mulryne examines Webster's dramatic practices and the dramaturgy of modern absurdist experiments in tragicomic form. The comic and the tragic coexist; this precarious tension "defines the 'unstable equilibrium' of modern tragicomedy; and under some such rubric Webster's major plays might . . . be read." T. B. Tomlinson's chapter on Webster in *A Study of Elizabethan and Jacobean Drama* (1964) marked an earlier step toward this approach.

T. S. Eliot's *Elizabethan Essays* (1934) and the *Selected Essays* (1932) contain several references to Webster. Rupert Brooke's *John Webster and the Elizabethan Drama* (1916) has moments of interest (Brooke was one of the first to note a concept of emotional unity in Webster's work, as opposed to "logical content"); E. E. Stoll's *John Webster* (1905) is occasionally rewarding in its close examination of the influence of Marston, Tourneur, and Shakespeare on Webster. Ralph Berry's *The Art of John Webster* was published in 1972.

C. THE WORKS AT LARGE

The studies by Murray, Leech, and Scott-Kilvert survey the full canon. Scott-Kilvert observes that "character" writing was clearly congenial to Webster; Charles R. Forker's useful study "Wit's Descant: The Prose Characters of John Webster," *MLQ* 30 (1969): 33–52, compares the prose style of the characters to Webster's dramatic characters. Forker concludes that certain passages "entitle Webster to a place with Sir Thomas Browne among the great prose writers of the period." See also Benjamin Boyce, *The Theophrastan Character in England to 1642* (1947). Douglas Bush, *English Litera-*

ture in the Earlier Seventeenth Century (1945; 2nd ed. 1962), provides a general look at the character writing of the Overbury group.

The *Concise Bibliography* by Samuel A. Tannenbaum was published in 1941 and reprinted in vol. 10 of *Elizabethan Bibliographies* (1967); a continuation compiled by Dennis Donovan, *Elizabethan Bibliographies Supplements I,* appeared in 1967. A selected list appears in Irving Ribner, *Tudor and Stuart Drama,* Goldentree Bibliographies (1966).

II. CRITICISM OF INDIVIDUAL PLAYS AND STATE OF SCHOLARSHIP

A. INDIVIDUAL PLAYS

The Duchess of Malfi

The most comprehensive study is Gunnar Boklund's *"The Duchess of Malfi": Sources, Themes, Characters* (1962). The first half surveys important sources and notes Webster's own contributions; the modern view of Ferdinand as a victim of incestuous passion is considered improbable since Webster was simply following passages in Painter. The Duchess and Antonio reflect Webster's interest in the distinction between nature and custom; Bosola remains an enigma. Boklund accounts for the much maligned horrors of Act IV, artistically and thematically; in his concluding chapter he considers the play as a Jacobean tragedy. Although moral integrity is accepted as a guiding principle of man's life, the pattern of *The Duchess of Malfi* "is not a moral one"; what governs the events "is nothing but chance," which operates independently of good and evil. Evil can be self-destructive, Boklund suggests, but the dark mood of the play cannot be dispelled. M. C. Bradbrook, "Two Notes upon Webster," *MLR* 42 (1947): 281-92 (rpt. in *Shakespeare's Contemporaries,* ed. Max Bluestone and Norman Rabkin [1961], pp. 210-22), had previously considered fate and chance in the play, noting that the horror of the events "depends upon a powerful sense of the supernatural combined with a skepticism far deeper than that of professed rebels like Marlowe"; the uncertainty of the power of fate as opposed to the power of chance centers the play in a heart of darkness.

Clifford Leech's discussion of the play in *Webster: "The Duchess of Malfi"* (1963) surveys each act and offers a brief but close analysis. Act V suggests the presence of the dead Duchess haunting those who had lived along with her; Leech sees her in earlier acts as a vital human being, not as a pale and pathetic sufferer. William Empson's essay-review of Leech's study, "Mine Eyes Dazzle," *Essays in Criticism* 14 (1964):80–86, is of interest, particularly regarding the controversy over Ferdinand's possible incestuous motivations. A positive view of the moral implications is taken by Alexander W. Allison in "Ethical Themes in *The Duchess of Malfi*," *SEL* 4 (1964): 263–73, which considers how good and evil may enter into a diversity of relationships with human psychic traits. Ultimately, the principle of virtue has an autonomy and permanence which evil lacks. Yet Jane Marie Luecke, "*The Duchess of Malfi*: Comic and Satiric Confusion in Tragedy," *SEL* 4 (1964):275–90, refutes this and Bogard's earlier thesis (I,B), noting that a latent confusion in the play rises from the injudicious mixing of comic and satiric elements. P. F. Vernon, "The Duchess of Malfi's Guilt," *N&Q* 10 (1963):335–38, concludes that the Duchess and Antonio, violators of Machiavellian norms, grow in stature by learning to suffer for "what is just."

James L. Calderwood, "*The Duchess of Malfi*: Styles of Ceremony," *Essays in Criticism* 12 (1962):133–47 (rpt. in *Shakespeare's Contemporaries*, ed. Bluestone and Rabkin, 2nd ed. [1970], pp. 278–91), treats the relation between individual impulse and societal norms, finding Webster greatly concerned with the doctrine of degree and employing ritual for the evaluation of private action. Elizabeth M. Brennan considers the psychopathic personalities involved in the play in "The Relationship between Brother and Sister in the Plays of John Webster," *MLR* 58 (1963):488–94: brothers are overly concerned with their sisters' honor; and Ferdinand's actions resemble a husband's revenge for his wife's adultery. However, James P. Driscoll, "Integrity of Life in *The Duchess of Malfi*," *DramS* 6 (1967):42–53, maintains that the theme of the play—integrity of life—explains the actions and motivations of the characters: "Each man is the keeper of his own integrity; he is a responsible value center in an irresponsible and valueless universe." Ferdinand is thus motivated not by incestuous desire, but by the threat to his pride the Duchess represents. Inga-Stina Ekeblad in "The 'Impure Art' of John Webster," *RES* 9(1958): 253–67 (rpt. in *Elizabethan Drama: Modern Essays in Criticism*, ed. Ralph J. Kaufmann [1961] pp. 250–67), rejects the view that Webster uses conventional dramatic devices for show value when his poetry fails. The masque of madmen is part of a larger masque developed on the framework of realistic dramatic representation: the madmen serve as an anti-masque, acting as an ideograph of disunity and incoherence. In a later article, "A Cunning Piece Wrought Perspective," in *John Webster*, ed. Morris (I,B), pp. 159–78, (Ekeblad) Ewbank considers Webster's "realism" further, noting that the method of Webster's art "is much akin to that of the perspective." In the same volume, Nigel Alexander, "Intelligence in *The Duchess of Malfi*," pp. 93–112, interprets the play as a study of "one woman's psychology which is misinterpreted, religiously, socially, and psychologically in terms of the masculine ideology of her brothers"; and D. C. Gunby, "*The Duchess of Malfi*: A Theological Approach," pp. 181–204, discusses the play in the light of the views of the Jacobean Church of England, concluding that Webster's view is not skeptical, "but fideistic."

The White Devil

Gunnar Boklund's *The Sources of "The White Devil"* (1957) distinguishes between the historical facts of the action and the variant sources Webster may have used. But "no document which would immediately and completely solve the problem of the origin of the play has been identified." Boklund presents a corpus of the facts Webster had at hand and his use of those facts, noting that though irony becomes a unifying factor, the play involves a detrimental shifting of focus. Hereward T. Price's interesting study "The Function of Imagery in Webster," *PMLA* 70 (1955):717–39 (rpt. in *Elizabethan Drama*, ed. Kaufmann [1961] pp. 225–49), demonstrates how the imagery of poison, pandarism, and infection is linked with the theme of appearance and reality in the play. James R. Hurt further notes three parodies of religious ritual introduced in the play, related to lost souls, in "Inverted Rituals in Webster's *The White Devil*," *JEGP* 61 (1962): 42–47.

Several articles on the play appeared during 1965–66. George Sensabaugh, "Tragic Effect in Webster's *The White Devil*," *SEL* 5 (1965):345–61, considers once again the satiric and tragic coexistence in the play, finding a perplexing mixture of elements. Roma Gill, however, in " 'Quaintly Done': A Reading of *The White Devil*," *E&S* 19 (1966):41–59, finds that Webster's mixture of the characteristics of tragedy, satire, revenge plots, and psychological studies produces a play with a vigorous, nervous daring. E. B. Benjamin, "Patterns of Morality in *The White Devil*," *ES* 46 (1965):1–15, maintains that ethically, Webster is a conservative: Vittoria, Flamineo, and Lodovico are responsible moral agents who have a choice in their own destinies; Webster is far more subtle than earlier playwrights in considering the operation of moral law.

In "The White Devil or Vittoria Corombona?", *RenD* 9 (1966): 179-204, R. W. Dent finds Vittoria an ambiguous character, given the lack of any explanatory conventions: she exists as a theatrical character rather than a tragic figure. B. J. Layman's "The Equilibrium of Opposites in *The White Devil*," *PMLA* 74 (1959):336-47, is a close analysis of the relationship between Vittoria and Flamineo: Vittoria achieves a sort of nobility by assuming a Yeatsian mask of virtue and goodness, thereby balancing the outright evil of Flamineo.

Two essays in *John Webster*, ed. Morris (I,B), focus attention on Webster's dramaturgy. A. J. Smith in "The Power of *The White Devil*," pp. 71-91, notes that certain scenes for all their theatricality seem irrelevant to the whole. However, we must "reckon with the force of a calculated randomness": the play is more than the sum of its parts, as proven by its power in the theater. "To think of staging it is to see how much the effects are of a piece, and how far they grow out of a single imaginative perception." In "Webster and the Actor," pp. 23-44, Peter Thomson notes that in two respects Webster makes peculiar demands on the modern actor: he must "die as he has never died before," and he must "demand and . . . relinquish the audience's attention with unrivalled frequency and abruptness." Thomson considers several aspects of the play which would assume particular prominence in the theater. D. C. Gunby's *Webster: "The White Devil"* appeared in 1971.

Most critical attention has been devoted to the Italian tragedies, though remarks on the remainder of the canon are included in Murray, Leech, Scott-Kilvert, Brooke, and Stoll (I,B). T. B. Tomlinson sees *The Devil's Law Case* as an indication of the growing separation of tragic and comic elements in drama (*A Study of Elizabethan and Jacobean Tragedy* [I,B]). The play is considered by D. C. Gunby as serious didactic social comment which ridicules social problems and abuses ("*The Devil's Law Case:* An Interpretation," *MLR* 63 [1968]:545-58); in "*The Devil's Law Case*—an End or a Beginning?", in *John Webster*, ed. Morris (I,B), pp. 115-30, Gunnar Boklund finds the play "firmly connected" with the Italian tragedies "not only in style and workmanship but above all in theme." The characters are trimmed down to life size, and the trivial side of life is Webster's concern, "but this does not make it a trivial play." Inga-Stina Ekeblad, "Webster's Constructional Rhythm," *ELH* 24 (1957): 165-76, examines the claim for Webster's authorship of scenes in *A*

Cure for A Cuckold, finding that certain scenes in the play are built along the same dramatic patterns found in the major tragedies.

B. STATE OF SCHOLARSHIP

The Duchess of Malfi and *The White Devil* continue to provoke interest and controversy. No one denies Webster's power; but critics still disagree over Webster's philosophy and methods and the coherence of his tragic vision. Much of Webster's originality lies in his awareness and dispassionate study of the devious ways of men, and several recent studies have tended to stress this originality instead of describing any unity of tone or moral viewpoint. In 1968 Norman Rabkin noted in his introduction to *Twentieth Century Interpretations of "The Duchess of Malfi"* the kinship between Webster's plays and recent absurdist drama. This parallel with a drama in which "conventional form" does not lead to a "conventional conclusion," he states, may provide readers and viewers with a "concept of the play which makes academic attempts to moralize and tame the play into Christian orthodoxy appear as superfluous as it does earlier tendencies to reject Webster's conventions as unselfconsciously 'barbarous.'" This approach is often reflected in the essays in *John Webster*, ed. Morris (I,B): comparison is made more frequently with the works of Pinter, Beckett, and Ionesco than with any Jacobean dramatist; and Webster increasingly becomes our contemporary rather than Shakespeare's. Yet for many critics still, Webster, particularly in *The Duchess of Malfi*, achieves a sense of meaning and ultimate affirmation which is beyond the grasp of the modernists.

Don D. Moore, in *John Webster and His Critics, 1617-1964* (1966), considers academic and theater criticism in detail over three centuries. The Rabkin collection centers on modern approaches to *The Duchess of Malfi*; G. K. and S. K. Hunter, ed., *John Webster* (1969) offer critical excerpts from past and present.

III. CANON

A. PLAYS IN CHRONOLOGICAL ORDER

This listing follows the order in Alfred Harbage, *Annals of English Drama, 975-1700*, rev. S. Schoenbaum (1964). The acting date is in italics preceding the semicolon; the second date is that of the first edition. The early editions are described in W. W. Greg, *Bibliography of the English Printed Drama to the Restoration*, 4 vols. (1939-59);

E. K. Chambers, *The Elizabethan Stage* (1923), vol. 3, discusses the canon. References are made below to Lucas's edition and to G. E. Bentley, *The Jacobean and Caroline Stage*, vols. 4–5 (1956).

Sir Thomas Wyatt, with Dekker (and others?); history (*1602–7;* 1607)

Parts *1* and *2 Lady Jane* may be incorporated in *Sir Thomas Wyatt*, 1604; see Phillip Shaw, "*Sir Thomas Wyatt* and the Scenario of *Lady Jane*," *MLQ* 13 (1952): 227–38.

Westward Ho, with Dekker; comedy (*1604;* 1607)

Peter B. Murray, "The Collaboration of Dekker and Webster in *Northward Ho* and *Westward Ho*," *PBSA* 56 (1962):482–86, studies the colloquial contractions in the *Ho* plays and concludes that Webster wrote about forty per cent of each play.

Induction to *The Malcontent*, with Marston; tragicomedy (*1600–1604;* 1604)

The third edition of the plays adds the induction and "additions" "written by John Webster." There was earlier debate over the extent to which the additions could be ascribed to Marston; Lucas, following Stoll (1905), credits with certainty only the induction to Webster. M. L. Wine, in his edition of *The Malcontent*, RRDS (1964), notes that if Webster did collaborate on the additions, "it is a thankless task to try to distinguish his fragments from Marston."

Northward Ho, with Dekker; comedy (*1605;* 1607)

Fredson T. Bowers, in *The Dramatic Works of Thomas Dekker*, vol. 2 (1955), asserts that "Webster's share in the writing does not seem to have been extensive." See *Westward Ho*, above.

The White Devil, tragedy (*1609–12;* 1612)

J. R. Brown, in his Revels edition of *The White Devil* (1960; 2nd ed. 1966) limits the date of the first performance to early 1612, possibly February. Among his evidence is the dedication to Dekker's *If It Be Not Good, the Devil Is in It*, published 1612, wherein Dekker, addressing the Queen's Men, wishes good fortune to the "Next New-play" by his "worthy friend." Brown reasonably identifies Webster as the author and notes Webster's reference to the poorly received winter production.

The Duchess of Malfi, tragedy *(1612–14;* 1623)

There may have been a revision 1617–23; see Lucas, vol. 2, p. 405, and Bentley, vol. 5, p. 1252. J. R. Brown in his Revels edition (1964) argues against possible revision, noting that Antonio's lines concerning the French court in I.i do not necessarily refer to Louis XIII's *coup d'etat* in 1617, citing Elyot's *Image of Governance* (1541) as a literary source. He dates first performance as spring or autumn of 1614, or perhaps the winter of 1613–14. All editors note the death of William Ostler, the original Antonio, in Decemוer, 1614; Brown further emphasizes the several borrowings from the *Arcadia,* republished in 1613.

The Devil's Law Case, tragicomedy *(1610–19;* 1623)

J. R. Brown, "The Date of *The Devil's Law Case,*" *N&Q* 5 (1958):100–101, suggests 1616 as the earliest date, based in part on Webster's borrowings from Jonson's *The Devil Is an Ass* (1616), disagreeing with Bentley, vol. 5, p. 1251, who suggests 1610, the time of the action in the play. Lucas, vol. 2, pp. 213–16, notes several allusions to events ca. 1620 and places the first performance at that time.

Anything for a Quiet Life, with Middleton?; comedy (ca. *1620–21;* 1662)

The title page assigns authorship to Middleton. H. D. Sykes in *Sidelights on Elizabethan Drama* (1924; from his *N&Q* articles in 1921) first suggested Webster's co-authorship, which was accepted by Lucas in vol. 4, pp. 66–68. Bentley, vol. 5, p. 860, states that Lucas was "taken in" by Sykes's collection of "Websterean" phrases, and assigns the play in its entirety to Middleton.

Monuments of Honor, civic pageant *(1624;* 1624)

Appius and Virginia, with T. Heywood?; tragedy (ca. *1608–34[?];* 1654)

R. Brooke, *John Webster and the Elizabethan Drama* (1916), first suggested Heywood's authorship with Webster as reviser of two scenes. Lucas, vol. 2, pp. 121–30, effectively proves Webster's greater share and assigns first performance as 1625–27. R. G. Howarth, "Webster's *Appius and Virginia,*" *PQ* 46 (1967):135–37, claims that the unity of the work suggests Webster as sole author. In "John Webster's Burial," *N&Q 1* (1954):114-15, Howarth notes that if Webster did not die until 1638, he could have been indebted to Heywood's later vocabulary.

A Cure for a Cuckold, with W. Rowley (and Heywood?); comedy (*1624-*ca. *1625;* 1661)

Lucas suggests Heywood as reviser (vol. 3, pp. 10-18), following H. D. Gray's case for Heywood in *"A Cure for a Cuckold* by Heywood, Rowley, and Webster," *MLR* 22 (1927):389-97. Inga-Stina Ekeblad looks at dramatic patterns in "Webster's Constructional Rhythm," *ELH* 24 (1957):165-76, and attributes to Webster a major share of composition.

B. UNCERTAIN ASCRIPTIONS AND APOCRYPHA

For detailed discussions, see the Anonymous Plays sections of this series.

The Weakest Goeth to the Wall, pseudo-history (ca. *1599-1600;* 1600)

This play was first assigned to Webster and Dekker by Edward Phillips in *Theatrium Poetrarium* (1675); the ascription was dismissed by Langbaine (1691) and all others. See the essay in the Anonymous Plays section of this volume.

The Thracian Wonder, comedy (*1590-* ca. *1600;* 1661)

Kirkman, publishing the play in 1661 along with *A Cure for a Cuckold*, ascribed authorship to Webster and Rowley, placing their names on the title page. Lucas dismisses the ascription on the basis of style and the high fatuousness of the play. See the essay in the Anonymous Plays sections of this volume.

I Lady Jane, history (*1602;* lost)

With Chettle, Dekker, Heywood, Wentworth Smith. See *Sir Thomas Wyatt*, above.

Caesar's Fall, tragedy (*1602;* lost)

With Dekker, Drayton, Middleton, Munday.

Christmas Comes But Once a Year, comedy (*1602;* lost)

With Chettle, Dekker, Heywood.

Additions to *The Spanish Tragedy* (1601-2)

Lamb, in *Specimens* (1808), first suggested Webster rather than Jonson as the author of the additions; Lucas rejects the ascription on the basis of style and the fact that the additions are better than Webster could have effected at that time.

The Guise, tragedy (?) (*1614-23;* lost)

R. G. Howarth, "Webster's *Guise*," *N&Q* 13 (1966): 294-96, gives evidence that the play was in print as late as 1633, and suggests it was a comedy ca. 1615.

The Late Murder in White Chapel, or Keep the Widow Waking, comedy and tragedy (*1624;* lost)

With Ford, Dekker, W. Rowley.

The Fair Maid of the Inn, comedy (*1626;* 1647)

Lucas accepts the view of H. D. Sykes (*Sidelights on Elizabethan Drama* [1924]) that the writing was shared by Massinger and Webster, with some contribution by Ford; according to Lucas, the play was licensed to take advantage of Fletcher's popularity. Bentley, vol. 3, p. 338, firmly disagrees and admits only that Fletcher may have had collaborators or revisers.

C. CRITIQUE OF THE STANDARD EDITION

F. L. Lucas's *The Complete Works of John Webster* (1927) evoked acclaim such as that of W. W. Greg: "I do not know that what Mr. Lucas has written about Webster could be bettered" (*RES* 4 [1928]:449); and several reviewers immediately labeled it as definitive. Lucas re-edited the Italian tragedies in 1958, and his work continues to stand as "a monument of scholarship" (Scott-Kilvert, *John Webster*). Lucas summarized all that was known and thought about John Webster in an edition that is conservative and highly readable. It is, in fact, aimed at the lay reader, its purpose being, as Lucas wrote, "to get Webster enjoyed." We now, thanks to advances in the study of dramatic manuscripts and critical bibliography, know more about Webster's methods; J. R. Brown's excellent introductions to the Italian tragedies in the Revels editions reflect a more sophisticated critical approach. Nevertheless, Lucas's commentaries remain persuasive.

D. TEXTUAL STUDIES

An important survey is J. R. Brown's "The Printing of John Webster's Plays," in three parts: *SB* 6 (1954): 117–40; 8 (1956): 113–28; and 15 (1962):57–69. Brown shows that *The Duchess of Malfi*, Q1, was set up by two compositors, one setting the first four pages, the other the second four, thus accounting for many early text mislineations. The editions by Brown, Lucas, Brennan, and Mulryne (III,E) also include textual consideration.

E. SINGLE-WORK EDITIONS OF THE PLAYS

J. R. Brown's Revels editions of *The White Devil* (1960; rev. ed. 1966) and *The Duchess of Malfi* (1964) are unusually valuable for cogent introductions, insights into stage action, and careful collation of texts. F. L. Lucas re-edited the two tragedies for separate editions in 1958; useful paperbacks are Elizabeth M. Brennan's New Mermaid editions of *The Duchess of Malfi* (1964) and *The White Devil* (1966). J. R. Mulryne has edited *The White Devil*, RRDS (1969), which includes a good introduction; Travis Bogard's introduction to *The White Devil* (1961) is also useful but his edition contains few notes. Clive Hart edited *The White Devil* for the Fountainwell series (1970). Paperback editions of *The Duchess of Malfi* include those of Louis B. Wright and Virginia LaMar (1959) and Vincent F. Hopper and Gerald Keogh (1960). Frances A. Shirley's edition of *The Devil's Law Case*, RRDS, appeared in 1972, as did D. C. Gunby's one-volume Penguin edition of the Italian tragedies and *The Devil's Law Case*.

IV. SEE ALSO

A. GENERAL

Adams, John Cranford. *The Globe Playhouse: Its Design and Equipment.* 1942.
Adams, Henry Hitch. *English Domestic or, Homiletic Tragedy, 1575–1642.* 1943.
Adams, Martin. "Webster—A Museum Piece?" *Arts Quarterly* 1 (1950):50–52.
Anderson, Marcia Lee. "John Webster's Debt to Guazzo." *SP* 36 (1929): 192–205.
Ansari, K. H. *John Webster: Image Patterns and Canon.* 1969.
Baker, Herschel. *The Wars of Truth.* 1952.

Baldini, Gabriele. *John Webster e il linguaggio della tragedia.* 1953.

Barber, C. L. *The Idea of Honour in the English Drama 1591–1700.* 1957.

Bastiaenen, J. A. *The Moral Tone of Jacobean and Caroline Drama.* 1930.

Bentley, Eric, ed. *The Importance of "Scrutiny."* 1948.

Bentley, G. E. "John Cotgrave's *English Treasury of Wit and Language* and the Elizabethan Drama." *SP* 40 (1943):186–203.

Birrell, F. "John Webster." *Empire Review* 47 (1928):123–29.

Bowden, William R. *The English Dramatic Lyric, 1603–42: A Study in Stuart Dramatic Technique.* 1951.

Bowers, Fredson T. *Elizabethan Revenge Tragedy: 1587–1642.* 1940.

Bradbrook, M. C. *English Dramatic Form: A History of Its Development.* 1965.

Bradford, Gamaliel. *Elizabethan Women.* 1936.

Briggs, K. M. *The Anatomy of Puck: An Examination of Fairy Beliefs among Shakespeare's Contemporaries and Successors.* 1958.

Broadbent, J. B. *Poetic Love.* 1964.

Brown, J. R. "On the Dating of Webster's *The White Devil* and *The Duchess of Malfi.*" *PQ* 31 (1952):353–62.

Buxton, John. *Elizabethan Taste.* 1963.

Cazamian, Louis. *The Development of English Humor.* 1952.

Cecil, David. *Poets and Storytellers.* 1949.

Cook, David. "The Extreme Situation: A Study of Webster's Tragedies." *Komos* 2 (1969):9–15.

Cookman, A. V. "Shakespeare's Contemporaries on the English Stage." *SJ* 94 (1958):29–41.

Craig, Hardin. *English Religious Drama of the Middle Ages.* 1955.

Cunliffe, J. W. *The Influence of Seneca on Elizabethan Tragedy.* 1925.

Davison, Richard A. "John Webster's Moral View Re-examined." *MSpr* 63 (1969):213–23.

Dent, R. W. "John Webster's Debt to William Alexander." *MLN* 65 (1950): 73–82.

Doran, Madeleine. *Endeavors of Art: A Study of Form in Elizabethan Drama.* 1954.

Eaton, Walter P. *The Drama in English.* 1930.

Edwards, W. A. "John Webster." *Scrutiny* 2 (1933):12–23.

Elton, Oliver. *The English Muse.* 1933.

Feldman, A. Bronson. "The Yellow Malady: Short Studies of Five Tragedies of Jealousy." *L&P* 6 (1956):38–52.

Forker, Charles R. "Robert Baron's Use of Webster, Shakespeare, and Other Elizabethans." *Anglia* 83 (1965):176–98.

———. "Two Notes on John Webster and Anthony Munday: Unpublished Entries in the Records of the Merchant Taylors." *ELN* 6 (1968):26–34.

Frost, David L. *The School of Shakespeare.* 1968.

Harbage, Alfred. *Shakespeare and the Rival Traditions.* 1952.

Hart, Clive. "Press Variants in *The Duchess of Malfi* and *The White Devil.*" *N&Q* 16 (1969):292–93.

Hawarth, Peter. *English Hymns and Ballads and Other Studies in Popular Literature.* 1927.

Herndl, George C. *The High Design: English Renaissance Tragedy and the Natural Law.* 1970.

Herrick, Marvin T. *Italian Tragedy in the Renaissance.* 1965.

Holmes, Elizabeth. *Aspects of Elizabethan Imagery.* 1929.

Hook, F. S. "Marlowe, Massinger, and Webster Quartos," *N&Q* 4 (1957):53–57.

Howarth, R. G. "A Note on John Webster." *TLS*, 2 Nov. 1933, p. 751.

———. *Literature of the Theatre: Marlowe to Shirley.* 1953.

———. "John Webster's Burial." *N&Q* 190 (1954):114–15.

———. "John Webster's Classical Nescience." *Sydney University Recorder*, 14 Oct. 1954, pp. 224–26.

———. "Two Notes on Webster." *N&Q* 9 (1962): 334–36.

———. *A Pot of Gillyflowers: Studies and Notes.* 1964.

———. "John Webster, Property Owner?" *N&Q* 12 (1965):236–37.

———. "A Commendatory Sonnet by John Webster." *ESA* 9 (1966):109–16.

———. "The Model Source of John Webster's *A Monumental Column.*" *ESA* 11 (1968):127–34.

Hunter, G. K. "Notes on Webster's Tragedies." *N&Q* 202 (1957):53–55.

Irgat, Mina. "Disease Imagery in the Plays of John Webster." *Litera* (Istanbul University English Department) 2 (1955):1–26.

Jenkins, Harold. "The Tragedy of Revenge in Shakespeare and Webster." *ShS* 14 (1961):45–55.

Jobson, D. "The Webster Family." *N&Q* 150 (1926):394.

Kernan, Alvin. *The Cankered Muse: Satire of the English Renaissance.* 1959.

Knight, G. Wilson. *The Burning Oracle: Studies in the Poetry of Action.* 1939.

———. *The Golden Labyrinth: A Study of the British Drama.* 1962.

Krutch, Joseph Wood. "Corruption's Poet." *Nation*, 4 Sept. 1937, p. 243.

Lagarde, Fernand. "Les emprunts de John Webster." *EA* 16 (1963):243–50.

Lawrence, W. J. *Pre-Restoration Stage Studies.* 1927.

Leech, Clifford. "The Implications of Tragedy." *English* 6 (1947):177–82.

Lucas, F. L. "Some Notes on the Text of Webster." *N&Q* 15 (1926):183–86, 232–52.

———. "An Unexplained Allusion in Webster and Rowley." *TLS*, 15 April 1926, p. 283.

———. "Was John Webster a Member of the Middle Temple?" *TLS*, 28 Oct. 1926, p. 746.

———. "Did Dr. Forman Commit Suicide?" *TLS*, 7 April 1927, p. 250.

Manifold, J. S. *The Music In English Drama: From Shakespeare to Purcell.* 1956.

Moore, Don D. "John Webster in the Modern Theatre." *ETJ* 17 (1965):314–21.

Morgan, F. C. "A Deed of Gift and John Webster." *N&Q* 192 (1947):496.

Oliphant, E. H. C. *The Plays of Beaumont and Fletcher.* 1927.

Padgett, Lawrence E. "An Entry from Guevara in Webster's Commonplace Book?" *N&Q* 4 (1957):145–46.

Parr, Johnstone. *Tamburlaine's Malady and Other Essays on Astrology in Elizabethan Drama.* 1953.

Parrott, Thomas Marc, and Ball, Robert Hamilton. *A Short View of Elizabethan Drama.* 1943.

Prior, Moody E. *The Language of Tragedy.* 1947.

Reed, Robert R., Jr. *Bedlam on the Jacobean Stage.* 1952.

Ribner, Irving. "Webster's Italian Tragedies." *TDR* 5 (1961):106–18 (rpt. in *Jacobean Tragedy* [1962], pp. 97–122).

Ridley, M. R. *Second Thoughts.* 1965.

Salingar, L. G. "Tourneur and the Tragedy of Revenge." In *The Age of Shakespeare* (1955; vol. 2 of *The Pelican Guide to English Literature,* ed. Boris Ford), pp. 355–68.

Schelling, Felix. *Elizabethan Playwrights: A Short History of the English Drama from Mediaeval Times to the Closing of the Theatres in 1642.* 1925.

Schücking, Levin Ludwig. "The Baroque Character of the Elizabethan Tragic Hero." *PBA* 24 (1938):85–111.

Serpieri, Alessandro. *John Webster.* 1966.

Sharpe, Robert B. *Irony in the Drama.* 1959.

Sisson, Charles J. *Lost Plays of Shakespeare's Age.* 1936.

Smet, Robert de [Romain Sanvic]. *Le Théâtre élizabéthain.* 1955.

Smith, James. "The Tragedy of Blood." *Scrutiny* 8 (1939):265–80.

Spencer, Theodore. *Death and Elizabethan Tragedy: A Study of Convention and Opinion in the Elizabethan Drama.* 1936.

Spens, Janet. *Elizabethan Drama.* 1922.

Squire, J. C. "John Webster." *The Observer* (London), 12 Feb. 1928, p. 4.

Squire, Tom. "John Webster." *Theatre Arts* 21 (1937):981–84.

Stoll, Elmer Edgar. *Shakespeare Studies.* 1927.

———. *Shakespeare and Other Masters.* 1940.

Stroup, Thomas B. *Microcosmos: The Shape of the Elizabethan Play.* 1965.

Sypher, Wylie. *Four Stages of Renaissance Style.* 1955.

Thorp, Willard. *The Triumph of Realism in Elizabethan Drama.* 1928.

Wagner, B. M. "New Verses by John Webster." *MLN* 46 (1931):403–5.

Wells, Henry W. *Elizabethan and Jacobean Playwrights.* 1939.

Williams, Phillip. "The Composition of the Pied Bull *Lear.*" *SB* 1 (1948):59–68.

B. INDIVIDUAL PLAYS

The White Devil

Akrigg, G. P. V. "Webster and Raleigh." *N&Q* 193 (1948):427–28.

———. "John Webster's 'Devil in Crystal.' " *N&Q* 1 (1954):52.

Anderson, Marcia L. "Hardy's Debt to John Webster in *The Return of the Native.*" *MLN* 54 (1939):497–501.

Bax, Clifford. *The Life of the White Devil.* 1940.

Brennan, Elizabeth M. " 'An Understanding Auditory': An Audience for John Webster." In *John Webster,* ed. Brian Morris (1970), pp. 3–19.

Brown, J. R. "The Papal Election in John Webster's *The White Devil.*" *N&Q* 4 (1957):490–94.

Cauthen, I. B., Jr. "Another Webster Allusion in *The Wasteland.*" *MLN* 73 (1958):498–99.

Cohen, Hennig. "Melville and Webster's *White Devil.*" *ESQ* 29 (1962):33.

Cross, Gustav. "A Note on *The White Devil.*" *N&Q* 3 (1956):99–100.

———. "Webster and Marston: A Note on *The White Devil.*" *N&Q* 7 (1960):337.

Davison, Richard A. "A Websterian Echo in *The Cenci.*" *AN&Q* 6 (1967):53–54.

Dent, R. W. "John Webster and Nicolas de Montreaux." *PQ* 35 (1956):418–21.

Franklin, H. Bruce. "The Trial Scene of Webster's *The White Devil* Examined in Terms of Elizabethan Rhetoric." *SEL* 1 (1961):35–51.

Freeman, Arthur. "A Note on *The White Devil.*" *N&Q* 7 (1960):421.

———. "*The White Devil*: an Emendation." *N&Q* 10 (1963):101–2.

Hart, Clive. "Wild-Fire, St. Anthony's Fire, and *The White Devil.*" *N&Q* 15 (1968):375–76.

H. H. "*The White Devil.*" *The Observer* (London), 24 March 1935, p. 17.

Lagarde, Fernand. "Les Sources de *The White Devil.*" *EA* 11 (1958):303–9.

———. "*The White Devil*: Esquisse de panorama critique." *EA* 23 (1970):415–24.

Landau, Jack. "Elizabethan Art in a Mickey Spillane Setting." *Theatre Arts* 39 (1955):25, 87.

Lucas, F. L. "Playing the Devil." *New Statesman*, 17 Oct. 1925, pp. 11–13.

Mooschein, Henry. "A Note on *The White Devil.*" *N&Q* 13 (1966):296.

Pratt, S. M. "Webster's *White Devil*, V, iv, 115." *Expl* 29 (1970):10.

Reed, A. W. "Erasmus and John Webster." *TLS*, 14 June 1947, p. 295.

Royde-Smith, N. G. "Drama." *Outlook* 56 (1925):277.

Spencer, Hazelton. "Nahum Tate and *The White Devil.*" *ELH* 1 (1934):235–49.

Sternlicht, Stanford. "Brachiano in *The White Devil.*" *AN&Q* 3 (1965):84.

Stroup, Thomas B. "Flamineo and the 'Comfortable Words.' " *RenP*, 1965, pp. 12–16.

Summers, Montague. "Webster and Cardano." *N&Q* 163 (1932):424.

Wadsworth, Frank W. "Webster's *White Devil*, III, ii, 75–80." *Expl* 11 (1953):28.

The Duchess of Malfi

Akrigg, G. P. V. "A Phrase in Webster." *N&Q* 193 (1948):454.

———. "The Name of God and *The Duchess of Malfi.*" *N&Q* 195 (1950):231–33.

———. "John Webster and *The Book of the Homilies.*" *N&Q* 6 (1959):217–18.

Brown, Ivor. "*The Duchess of Malfi* at the Embassy." *The Observer*, 20 Jan. 1935, p. 13.

Brückl, O. "Sir Phillip Sydney's *Arcadia* as a Source for John Webster's *Duchess of Malfi.*" *ESA* 8 (1965):31–55.

Cross, Gustav. "Ovid Metamorphosed: Marston, Webster, and Nathaniel Lee." *N&Q* 3 (1956):244–45, 508–9.

Davies, Cecil W. "The Structure of *The Duchess of Malfi*: An Approach." *English* 12 (1958):89–93.

Ekeblad, Inga-Stina. "Webster's 'Wanton Boyes.' " *N&Q* 2 (1955):294–95.

Eliot, T. S. "*The Duchess of Malfy.*" *The Listener*, 18 Dec. 1941, pp. 825–26.

Emslie, McDonald. "Motives in *Malfi.*" *Essays in Criticism* 9 (1959):391–405.

Fieler, Frank B. "The Eight Madmen in *The Duchess of Malfi.*" *SEL* 7 (1967): 343–50.

Forker, Charles R. "A Possible Source for the Ceremony of the Cardinal's Arming in *The Duchess of Malfi.*" *Anglia* 87 (1969):398–403.

Frye, Northrop. *The Anatomy of Criticism.* 1957.

Fussell, Edwin. "Poe's 'Raven'; Or, How to Construct a Popular Poem from Almost Nothing at All." *ELN* 2 (1964):36–39.

Gassner, John. "The Theater Arts." *Forum* 106 (1946):510.

Giannetti, Louis. "A Contemporary View of *The Duchess of Malfi.*" *CompD* 3 (1969):297–307.

Gilder, Rosamond. "Each in His Own Way—Broadway in Review." *Theatre Arts* 30 (1946):695–96.

Glen, Enid. "Webster and Lavater." *TLS*, 11 April 1936, p. 316.

Goldie, Grace W. *"The Duchess of Malfi." The Listener*, 2 Feb. 1938, p. 240.

Gross, Seymour. "A Note on Webster's Tragic Attitude." *N&Q* 4 (1957):374-75.

Gunby, D. C. "Further Borrowings by Webster." *N&Q* 13 (1966):296-97.

———. "Webster: Another Borrowing from Jonson's *Sejanus?*" *N&Q* 17 (1970): 214.

Hayakawa, S. I. "A Note on the Mad Scene in *The Duchess of Malfi." PMLA* 42 (1932):907-9.

Hewes, Henry. "Comedy of Inevitability." *Saturday Review*, 6 April 1957, p. 26.

Howarth, R. G. "Webster's Vincentio Lauriola." *N&Q* 2 (1955):99-100.

Joseph, B. L. "Lewis Theobald and Webster." *Comparative Literature Studies* (Cardiff) 18 (1945):29-31.

Kaul, R. K. "What Theobald Did to Webster." *Indian Journal of English Studies* 2 (1961):138-44.

Knight, G. Wilson. *"The Duchess of Malfi." Malahat Review* 4 (1967):88-113.

Krutch, Joseph Wood. "Drama." *The Nation* 168 (1946):510.

Leech, Clifford. "An Addendum to Webster's Duchess." *PQ* 38 (1958): 253-56.

Loftis, John. *"The Duchess of Malfi* on the Spanish and English Stages." *RORD* 12 (1969):25-31.

Lucas, F. L. *"The Duchess of Malfi." New Statesman*, 1 March 1924, pp. 602-3.

———. *"The Duchess of Malfi." TLS*, 13 July 1956, p. 423.

Moore, Don D. *"The Duchess of Malfi* by John Webster and R. H. Horne." *Essays in Honor of E. L. Marilla*, ed. T. A. Kirby and W. J. Olive (1970), pp. 166-73.

Nathan, George Jean. "Cyrano and the Duchess." *American Mercury*, Jan. 1947, pp. 53-56.

Olivero, Frederico. *Studi Britannici.* 1931.

Parr, Johnstone. "The Horoscope in Webster's *The Duchess of Malfi." PMLA* 60 (1945):760-65.

Praz, Mario. *"The Duchess of Malfi." TLS*, 16 June 1954, p. 393.

———. "John Webster and *The Maid's Tragedy." ES* 37 (1956):252-58.

Rexroth, Kenneth. "Classics Revisited." *Saturday Review*, 4 March 1961, p. 21.

Riewald, J. G. "Shakespearean Burlesque in John Webster's *The Duchess of Malfi." ES* 45 (1964):177-89.

Sastri, J. S. "The Latent Motive for Ferdinand's Conduct in *The Duchess of Malfi." Osmania Journal of English Studies* 2 (1962):13-27.

———. "Webster's Masque of Madmen." *Indian Journal of English Studies* 3 (1962):33-43.

———. "Two Machiavellians of Shakespeare and Webster." *Osmania Journal of English Studies* 4 (1964):19-34.

Thayer, C. G. "The Ambiguity of Bosola." *SP* 54 (1957):162-71.

Thomas, Sidney. "Webster and Nashe." *N&Q* 3 (1956):13.

Thornton, R. K. R. "The Cardinal's Rake in *The Duchess of Malfi." N&Q* 16 (1969):295-96.

Todd, F. M. "Webster and Cervantes." *MLR* 51 (1956):321-23.

Ure, Peter. *"The Duchess of Malfi*: Another Debt to Sir William Alexander." *N&Q* 13 (1966):296.

Wadsworth, Frank W. "Webster's *Duchess of Malfi* in the Light of Some Contemporary Ideas on Marriage and Remarriage." *PQ* 35 (1956):394–407.
———. "Some Nineteenth Century Revivals of *The Duchess of Malfi.*" *Theatre Survey* 8 (1967):67–83.
———. "Shorn and Abated: British Performances of *The Duchess of Malfi.*" *Theatre Survey* 10 (1969):89–104.
———. "Webster, Horne, and Mrs. Stowe: American Productions of *The Duchess of Malfi.*" *Theatre Survey* 11 (1970):151–66.
Warren, Roger. "*The Duchess of Malfi* on the Stage." In *John Webster*, ed. Brian Morris (1970), pp. 45–68.
"Webster's Women." *TLS*, 1 Feb. 1947, p. 65.
Whitman, Robert F. "Webster's *Duchess of Malfi.*" *N&Q* 6 (1959):174–75.
Young, Stark. "*The Duchess of Malfi.*" *New Republic*, 28 Oct. 1946, pp. 556–57.

Appius and Virginia

Ekeblad, Inga-Stina. "Storm Imagery in *Appius and Virginia.*" *N&Q* 3 (1956): 5–7.
Gray, H. D. "*Appius and Virginia* by Webster and Heywood." *SP* 24 (1927): 275–89.
Seiden, Melvin. "Two Notes on Webster's *Appius and Virginia.*" *PQ* 35 (1956): 408–17.

The Devil's Law Case

Larkin, Daniel I. "Hooker and Webster." *N&Q* 5 (1958):437.
Reynolds, G. F. *The Staging of Elizabethan Plays.* 1941.

A Cure for a Cuckold

Gray, H. D. "*A Cure for a Cuckold* by Heywood, Rowley, and Webster." *MLR* 22 (1927):389–97.

THOMAS HEYWOOD

Joseph S. M. J. Chang   James P. Hammersmith

The standard edition is by R. H. Shepherd, *The Dramatic Works of Thomas Heywood* (1874).

I. GENERAL

A. BIOGRAPHICAL

The only full-length study of Thomas Heywood since Arthur Melville Clark published his authoritative *Thomas Heywood: Playwright and Miscellanist* (1931) is Michel Grivelet's *Thomas Heywood et le drame domestique élizabéthain* (1959). The scope of Grivelet's book is extensive, including the whole of Elizabethan domestic tragedy. He supplies a new biography which supports Allan Holaday ("Thomas Heywood and the Puritans," *JEGP* 49 [1950]:192–203) in disputing Clark's position that Heywood became a Puritan in his later years; instead, Heywood remained steadfast in his Anglicanism.

In "Thomas Heywood and the Low Countries," *MLN* 66 (1951): 16–19, Holaday adds a few more details to Heywood's biography, noting that the playwright was in the Low Countries from 1613 to 1614.

B. GENERAL STUDIES OF THE PLAYS

Grivelet further contributes a full treatment of Renaissance attitudes toward marriage, as represented in literary and dramatic texts. The concentration on themes and ideas, a major difference from Clark's study, offers a counterbalance to the unfortunate conception of Heywood as a purely expedient dramatist lacking either an artistic conscience or a thematic center. Perhaps Grivelet goes too far, but with Clark's opinion as the standard (". . . of all the dramatists Heywood was the most compliant with the public and yielded with an easy acquiescence and whole-hearted surrender"), overcompensation is understandable. According to Grivelet, Heywood is not merely a pliant dramatist shaped by his age; he is, rather, a dramatist who was chiefly instrumental in rescuing domestic themes from decay. Grivelet also reconsiders domestic drama. While his remarks should be measured against the more conservative positions of Madeleine Doran (*Endeavors of Art: A Study of Form in Elizabethan Drama* [1954]) and Henry Hitch Adams (*English Domestic or, Homiletic Tragedy, 1575–1642* [1943]), Grivelet is stimulating as he questions the desirability of defining the genre in terms of plot, middle-class characters and taste, and homiletic intent. The appendices provide a useful catalogue of the Heywood canon, with information on dates, texts, and sources, as well as a brief analysis of each work.

Though recent studies of Heywood and Elizabethan dramatic form have supplanted Freda L. Townsend's "The Artistry of Thomas Heywood's Double Plots," *PQ* 25 (1946):97–119, this essay still deserves consideration for being among the first to give serious thought to Heywood's use of several plots to affirm a central theme. Peter Ure successfully builds on the Townsend conclusions in arguing that theme and character in Heywood's plays are completely integrated and thereby create a tragic intensity ("Marriage and the Domestic Drama in Heywood and Ford," *ES* 32 [1951]:200–216). Though Heywood fully accepts contemporary doctrines on marriage, his purpose goes beyond homiletic intentions, dramatizing the complex problems of husband and wife. In *A Woman Killed with Kindness*, there is at the play's end a fusion of "the profound appeal of his domestic theme with the new state of the dramatic characters."

George C. Herndl devotes a chapter of *The High Design: English Renaissance Tragedy and the Natural Law* (1970) to "The New Meaning of Tragedy: Heywood and Webster." Herndl's basic contention is that "the traditional natural law" which had governed earlier Elizabethan drama gives way in Heywood to a "code morality," and that "morality abstracted from nature becomes a code the inability of which to accommodate circumstance provides some of the basis of tragedy." Since codes tend to be mechanical, Heywood's plays seem to hinge always upon the same basic themes and situations. In an extensive treatment of *A Woman Killed with Kindness*, Herndl comes to the conclusion that the play "fails as tragedy because it fails to crystallize any vision of intelligible law." Anne's adultery, for example, is an inconsistency of character. In reality, her objections to it are entirely in character, while "the act of adultery is mechanically superimposed on that character." Insofar as the characters of *The English Traveller* "violate the decalogue, not any natural law," Herndl views the play as a "virtual rewriting" of *A Woman Killed*, the situations and themes being nearly identical. Herndl briefly traces similar patterns in *1* and *2 Edward IV* and *The Rape of Lucrece*, emphasizing always that "code ethics," even in Heywood's romance-adventures, supply the situation and conflict.

F. S. Boas, *Thomas Heywood* (1950), provides the student unfamiliar with Heywood's work with a comprehensive and sound introduction. Boas briefly summarizes and comments on the plays, mentioning the pertinent disputes without becoming entangled in them. Whenever possible, Boas allows the author to speak for himself through extensive quotation. The picture of Heywood which emerges is of a versatile and prolific writer. Also useful as an introduction is "Thomas Heywood's Dramatic Art," by Arthur Brown, in *Essays on Shakespeare and Elizabethan Drama in Honor of Hardin Craig*, ed. Richard Hosley (1962), pp. 327-39.

Samuel A. Tannenbaum's *Thomas Heywood: A Concise Bibliography* was published in 1939, reprinted in *Elizabethan Bibliographies*, vol. 3 (1967), and continued by Dennis Donovan, *Elizabethan Bibliographies Supplements II: Thomas Dekker, Thomas Heywood, and Cyril Tourneur* (1967). A selected list appears in Irving Ribner, *Tudor and Stuart Drama*, Goldentree Bibliographies (1966).

II. CRITICISM OF INDIVIDUAL PLAYS AND STATE OF SCHOLARSHIP

A. INDIVIDUAL PLAYS

A Woman Killed with Kindness

David Cook, in "*A Woman Killed with Kindness*: An Unshakespearian Tragedy," *ES* 45 (1964):353-72, offers a markedly new approach to Heywood's masterpiece. Instead of defending the play in terms of dramatic convention or Elizabethan ethics, Cook abandons the historical approach in favor of an essentially impressionistic analysis. Cook is more sympathetic with Anne and Wendoll than is usual; indeed, he places the tragic focus on Anne rather than on Frankford. She is "tragic in meeting an irreconcilable clash of emotions and remaining true to herself, and within her powers, to those she cares for," whereas Frankford retreats into "inflexible morality." The conventional judgment, that Heywood's tragedies are about lesser men, takes on new meaning with Cook: "Frankford's tragedy is, then, the tragedy of an ordinary, limited man, enlightened enough, on the one hand, to be incapable of primitive high action demanding death; but not knowing, on the other hand, the great-hearted emancipation from emotional constraint which would allow him to forgive." Though Cook supports his position by contrasting Heywood's dramatic technique with Shakespeare's, the validity of his position rests ultimately on one's view of the characters. It is entirely fitting, then, that he concludes with a plea for a new production of the play, where his own conception might be realized.

In "Heywood's *A Woman Killed with Kindness,*" *ESA* 4 (1961): 54–57, A. G. Hooper reacts to several comments by T. S. Eliot. Hooper particularly takes issue with the statement that the theme of the subplot involves a man ready to prostitute his sister as payment for a debt of honor. In "A Note on Heywood's *A Woman Killed with Kindness,*" *MLR* 58 (1963):64–65, Lloyd E. Berry elaborates on R. W. Van Fossen's suggestion (in his Revels Plays edition of the play, 1961) that I.ii is structurally related to I.i as a burlesque parallel.

John Canuteson agrees that the plots of *A Woman Killed with Kindness* are thematically linked, for "the subplot functions as a testing ground for the moral principle established in the main plot" ("The Theme of Forgiveness in the Plot and Subplot of *A Woman Killed with Kindness,*" *RenD* 2 [1969]:123–47). In making the plots parallel, Heywood is concerned mainly with working out "moral dilemmas." Canuteson feels that the primary moral matter is "charity rather than chastity," and in this respect the solutions effected in the two plots reflect upon one another. With charity the foremost issue, according to Canuteson, the subplot demonstrates that "punishment for sin can be too severe and that one can carry the notion of honor too far, and the parallels with the main plot confirm our suspicion that Frankford is not a tragic figure but a despicable one."

In "Heywood's Sources for the Main Plot of *A Woman Killed with Kindness,*" in *Studies in the English Renaissance Drama in Memory of Karl Julius Holzknecht,* ed. J. W. Bennett et al. (1959), pp. 188–211, Waldo F. McNeir suggests that the source is Gascoigne's "The Adventures of Master F. J.," from the *Hundreth Sundrie Flowers* (1573), rather than Painter's *Palace of Pleasure.* A study of revenge as treated by Gascoigne, Greene, and Heywood illustrates how much they deviated from the *novella* tradition and the Senecan tradition, both of which lie behind the Elizabethan revenge tragedy.

The English Traveller

Norman Rabkin's "Dramatic Deception in Heywood's *The English Traveller*," *SEL* 1 (1961):1-16 fills the gaps left by Townsend (I,B) concerning the double plots of this play and *The Captives*. While there is only a slender relationship between the plots in *The English Traveller*, they are parallel in dramatic technique, both first violating convention and later affirming it. Thus the comic implications of the May and January relationship between Wincott and his young wife are initially suppressed and then realized when Dalavill's conquest is revealed. The play, at both plot levels, is a serious treatment of the problem of appearance and reality, with all expectations overturned.

The Ages

New evidence to support Frederick G. Fleay's proposal, that the *Ages* are derived from earlier works (*A Biographical Chronicle of the English Drama* [1891]), is presented by Allan Holaday in "Heywood's *Troia Britannica* and the *Ages*," *JEGP* 45 (1946):430-39. *The Golden Age* is simply a dramatization of the *Troia Britannica*, while *The Silver Age* and *The Brazen Age* are modernizations of the old *Hercules* plays of the Admiral's men. With some uncertainty, Holaday associates *The Iron Age* with Henslowe's old Troy play. Holaday's reliance on Henslowe's property and wardrobe list is questioned by Ernest Schanzer, who cites the popularity of plays on Hercules in "Heywood's *Ages* and Shakespeare," *RES* 11 (1960):18-28. Schanzer proposes more proximate sources for Heywood in Shakespeare's *Winter's Tale* and *Pericles*. Though the verbal echoes are not very substantial, Schanzer dates the composition of the first three plays between the end of 1610 and 1611.

Love's Mistress, or The Queen's Masque

In his brief article, "Th' Untun'd Kennel: Note sur Thomas Heywood et le théâtre sous Charles 1er," *EA* 7 (1954):101-6, Michel Grivelet identifies lines from the long religious poem *The Hierarchy of the Blessed Angels* (1635) as being still another of Heywood's responses to attacks by Thomas Carew. The rivalry began with certain dedicatory verses included in the 1630 quarto of Davenant's *The Just Italian*, which Heywood reacted to in *Love's Mistress* (1634).

The Rape of Lucrece

"Thomas Heywood's 'The Gentry to the King's Head' in *The Rape of Lucrece* and John Wilson's Setting" is the subject of a brief article by John P. Cutts in *N&Q* 8 (1961):384–87. The text for the song furnished by Cutts is shorter by ten lines than the version in Holaday's edition (III,E), but it includes two new lines. Cutts publishes the musical setting, composed by Wilson, and he suggests that this may well have been the version used in the performance by Beeston's Boys. Also included is a checklist of Wilson's compositions for lyrics by Beaumont, Fletcher, Shakespeare, Ford, Brome, and Jonson.

B. OVER-ALL STATE OF CRITICISM

Because Heywood was a versatile and prolific writer, the state of criticism remains chaotic. It is perhaps too much to ask for a comprehensive statement of Heywood's achievement, but the various threads (of Heywood the playwright, the pamphleteer, the miscellanist) need pulling together. His acknowledged high-quality works are frequently stressed at the expense of a large body of lesser material which receives mention only in biographical or historical treatments. Such unbalanced critical attention often results in a distorted picture of Heywood's literary accomplishments. Boas's work (I,B), useful in drawing an over-all view, might well serve as a basis for a more thorough study of Heywood's broad literary interests.

III. CANON

A. PLAYS IN CHRONOLOGICAL ORDER

The list follows the chronology of Alfred Harbage, *Annals of English Drama, 975–1700*, rev. Samuel Schoenbaum (1964). The dates in parentheses are those of the first performance (in italics preceding the semicolon) and of the original date of publication. For bibliographical descriptions of the early editions, see W. W. Greg, *A Bibliography of the English Printed Drama to the Restoration*, 4 vols. (1939–59). A discussion of the canon may be found in E. K. Chambers, *The Elizabethan Stage*, 4 vols. (1923).

Joan as Good as My Lady, comedy (*1599;* lost)

War without Blows and Love without Suit (or *Strife*), comedy (?) (*1598–1599;* lost)

The Four Prentices of London with the Conquest of Jerusalem, heroical romance (*1592–*ca. *1600;* 1615)

Albere Galles, with Wentworth Smith; pseudo-history (?) (*1602;* lost [?])

Christmas Comes But Once a Year, with Chettle, Dekker, and Webster; comedy (?) (*1602;* lost)

Cutting Dick, topical play (*1602;* lost)

1 Lady Jane, with others; history (*1602;* lost [?])

Marshal Osric, with Wentworth Smith; tragicomedy (?) (*1602;* lost [?])

The Royal King and the Loyal Subject, with Wentworth Smith (?); tragicomedy (*1602–18;* 1637)

The Blind Eats Many a Fly, comedy (*1602–3;* lost)

1 The London Florentine, with Henry Chettle; comedy (?) (*1602–3;* lost)

A Woman Killed with Kindness, tragedy (*1603;* 1607)

How to Learn of a Woman to Woo, comedy (*1604;* lost [?])

1 If You Know Not Me You Know Nobody, or The Troubles of Queen Elizabeth, history (*1603–5;* 1605)

The Wise Woman of Hogsdon, comedy (ca. *1604;* 1638)

2 If You Know Not Me You Know Nobody, with the Building of the Royal Exchange, and the Famous Victory of Queen Elizabeth, history (*1605;* 1606)

The Rape of Lucrece, tragedy (*1606–8;* 1608)

Fortune by Land and Sea, with William Rowley; comedy (ca. *1607-9;* 1655)

1 The Fair Maid of the West, or A Girl Worth Gold, comedy (*1597-1610;* 1631)

Robert K. Turner, Jr., in his edition for the Regents Renaissance Drama Series (III,C), cautiously dates Part 1 "somewhat earlier than 1604" and Part 2 "some twenty-five or thirty years after Part 1."

The Golden Age, or The Lives of Jupiter and Saturn, classical legend (*1609-11;* 1611)

The Brazen Age, classical legend (*1610-13;* 1613)

The Silver Age, classical legend (*1610-12;* 1613)

1 The Iron Age, classical legend (*1612-13;* 1632)

2 The Iron Age, classical legend (*1612-13;* 1632)

The Captives, or The Lost Recovered, tragicomedy (*1624;* MS)

In his edition of *The Captives* (1921), Alexander Corbin Judson discusses authorship and date. Among internal evidences, he cites metrics, style (including the domestic scenes), and the type of humor as being completely characteristic of Heywood. Judson supports these matters by noting that the play is entered in the "MS. Office-Book" of Sir Henry Herbert under the date 3 September 1624, and metrically it "corresponds more nearly than any other play of Heywood's to *The English Traveller*, which seems to have been first acted during or not long after 1625." Judson's edition was conceived to improve and replace A. H. Bullen's edition in *A Collection of Old English Plays* (1885).

The English Traveller, tragicomedy (*1621-33;* 1633)

Calisto, or The Escapes of Jupiter, classical legend (ca. *1620-41;* MS)

2 The Fair Maid of the West, or A Girl Worth Gold, comedy (ca. *1630-31;* 1631)

London's Jus Honorarium, civic pageant (*1631;* 1631)

Londini Artium et Scientiarum Scaturigo, or London's Fountain of Arts and Sciences, civic pageant (*1632;* 1632)

Londini Emporia, or London's Mercatura, civic pageant (*1633;* 1633)

A Maidenhead Well Lost, comedy (ca. *1625–34;* 1634)

The Late Lancashire Witches, with Richard Brome; topical play (*1634;* 1634)

The Life and Death of Sir Martin Skink, with the Wars of the Low Countries, with Richard Brome; history (ca. *1633–41;* lost)

Love's Mistress, or The Queen's Mask, classical legend (*1634;* 1636)

A Challenge for Beauty, tragicomedy (*1634–36;* 1636)

Londini Sinus Salutis, or London's Harbour of Health and Happiness, civic pageant (*1635;* 1635)

Pleasant Dialogues and Dramas, dialogues (*1635 [Stationers' Register]* unacted [?]; 1637)

Londini Speculum, or London's Mirror, civic pageant (*1637;* 1637)

Porta Pietatis, or The Port or Harbour of Piety, civic pageant (*1638;* 1638)

Londini Status Pacatus, or London's Peaceable Estate, civic pageant (*1639;* 1639)

Love's Masterpiece, comedy (*1640 [Stationers' Register]*; lost)

B. UNCERTAIN ASCRIPTIONS; APOCRYPHA

Considering the difficulties in establishing Heywood's canon, one might well begin with Samuel Schoenbaum's *Internal Evidence and Elizabethan Dramatic Authorship: An Essay in Literary History and Method* (1966). In the course of his examination of attributions of authorship made in the past, Schoenbaum notes that critics advance Heywood as author of plays or passages regarded as stylistically deficient.

The Jew of Malta, revisions of Marlowe; tragedy (ca. *1589–90;* 1633)

Robert Ford Welsh adds his voice to those disputing Fleay's and Clark's suggestion that the 1633 quarto contains revisions by Heywood ("Evidence of Heywood Spellings in *The Jew of Malta,*" *RenP*, 1963, pp. 3–9).

2 Godfrey of Boulogne, heroical romance (?) (*1594;* lost)

A Knack to Know an Honest Man, tragicomedy (*1594;* 1596)

The Book of Sir Thomas More, history (ca. *1593–1601;* MS)

Captain Thomas Stukeley, history (*1596;* 1605)

1 and 2 Edward IV, history (*1592–99;* 1599)

A Warning for Fair Women, tragedy (ca. *1598–99;* 1599)

The Trial of Chivalry, pseudo-history (*1599–1603;* 1605)

The Fair Maid of the Exchange, comedy (1594–*1607;* 1607)

Arthur Brown and Peter H. Davison have edited the play for the Malone Society (1963), but the doubts expressed by Otelia Cromwell (*Thomas Heywood*, 1928), Clark, and Grivelet concerning Heywood's authorship are not resolved.

How a Man May Choose a Good Wife from a Bad, comedy (ca. *1601–2;* 1602)

The Bold Beauchamps, history (?) (ca. *1600–1607;* lost)

The Martyred Soldier, tragedy (*1627;* 1638)

Appius and Virginia, tragedy (ca. *1608–34 [?];* 1654)

A Cure for a Cuckold, comedy (ca. *1624–25;* 1661)

Dick of Devonshire, tragicomedy (*1626;* MS)

The Apprentice's Prize, comedy (?) (ca. *1633–41;* lost)

Since Holaday believes that Heywood remained an Anglican, he disputes Clark's inclusion of the two anonymous pamphlets, *A Revelation of Mr. Brightman's Revelation* (1641) and *Machiavel as He Lately Appeared* (1641), in the Heywood canon (see I,A).

C. CRITIQUE OF THE STANDARD EDITION

R. H. Shepherd's 1874 edition is badly outdated by modern bibliographical standards. While the need for modern editions is gradually being supplied by single-work editions, Shepherd's remains the only collection which is even remotely "complete." Heywood's entire canon must be reviewed and re-edited if there is to be a useful standard edition of his works. Arthur Brown's projected edition (III,D, below) has not materialized.

D. TEXTUAL STUDIES

In "The Early Quartos of Heywood's *A Woman Killed with Kindness,*" *Library* 25 (1970):93–104, Keith M. Sturgess undertakes to establish the relationship of the quarto of 1607 to that of 1617. Sturgess argues that the 1617 text is, as its title page claims, the third edition, while the 1607 text is the first edition, not the second. A missing quarto therefore intervened. After a full bibliographical analysis of the extant texts, Sturgess not only identifies the type-setter of the 1617 text as Compositor B of Shakespeare's First Folio, but also demonstrates strong bibliographical links between Heywood's two quartos. Hence, "it would be easy to assume that Q1607 was B's copy-text, no copy of Q? being available." However, if such was the case, W. S. Kable's "copy-reflecting words" technique ("Compositor B, the Pavier Quartos, and Copy Spellings," *SB* 21 [1968]:131–61) ought to be applicable. But the failure of Kable's method indicates that "B did *not* use Q1607 as copy-text," while the bibliographical links strongly argue "a short line of descent between the quartos." Sturgess draws the logical conclusion, that "Q? intervened but that it was based entirely on Q1607," which renders Q1607 the authoritative text.

By rigorous textual examination, in "The Text of Heywood's *The Fair Maid of the West,*" *Library* 22 (1967):299–325, Robert K.

Turner, Jr., discovers irregularities in the composition of the text which are not explained by the quality of the copy used by the compositor. Between similarities and differences adduced from the two parts of the play, Turner finds the most reasonable explanation to be that the play was set from a transcript prepared by a scribe for examination by officials arranging for the court performances of 1630–31.

E. A. J. Honigmann, in *The Stability of Shakespeare's Text* (1965), claims to have proof that *The Captives* was printed from the author's fair copy, thereby opposing W. W. Greg, who believed the manuscript used was foul papers with annotations by a bookkeeper (*The Shakespeare First Folio* [1955]). More recently, however, Anthony Low, in support of Greg, states that the manuscript reveals "an author in the process of creation," citing as evidence a number of revisions, which, due to their position within the line (not above or below), could not be errors of scribal or authorial transcription ("Thomas Heywood's Authorship of *The Captives,*" *N&Q* 15 [1968]:252).

In "Two Notes on Thomas Heywood," *MLR* 50 (1955):497–98, Arthur Brown presents new evidence that Heywood is the author of *The Captives*, since the unusual spelling of "Ey" for "aye" is found also in the 1632 edition of *The Four Prentices of London*. Furthermore, there are several parallels between *The Captives* and the *Apology for Actors*. To this evidence Low adds a parallel to *A Woman Killed with Kindness*.

In an address promising a new edition of Heywood, Arthur Brown calls attention to the special opportunity allowed by Heywood's orthographic idiosyncrasies for establishing the rest of the canon ("An Edition of the Plays of Thomas Heywood: A Preliminary Survey of Problems," *RenP*, 1954, pp. 71–76). Brown states that notwithstanding Heywood's professed lack of interest in the printing of his plays, there is enough evidence to indicate that certain variants can be attributed to corrections by the author. He supports the claim that the second edition of *Four Prentices of London* (1632) had been "newly revised" by the author, which Clark disputed.

In "Two Compositors in Heywood's *London's Ius Honorarium* (1631)," *SB* 22 (1969):223–26, David M. Bergeron discovers that Nicholas Okes employed two compositors to set this relatively short pamphlet. An examination of running-titles and a check of spelling tests indicate that sheets A and C differ markedly from sheet B. The disparity is further supported by type recurrences which correspond to the distinctive running-titles. Bergeron then notes that sheet B is heavily corrected while obvious errors in sheets A and C pass unnoticed. From this evidence he speculates that the compositor setting B was an apprentice whose work was carefully supervised. Bergeron does not claim to have absolute proof for his case, but he adds that the work of his apprentice contains unique characteristics not found again in Okes's shop.

E. SINGLE-WORK EDITIONS

Since it predates Sturgess's article (III,D), R. W. Van Fossen's careful Revels Plays edition of *A Woman Killed with Kindness* (1961) fails to resolve the vexing problem of the relationship between the 1607 and 1617 quartos. Freely confessing his uncertainty, Van Fossen decides to use the first quarto as copy-text. Thus, his edition is the only other besides Pearson's based on that text. The introduction provides a full review of the characteristics of middle-class tragedy and answers the charges of sentimentality leveled by Eliot and Knights. A German translation of the text is available in *Dramen der Shakespearezeit*, ed. Robert Weimann (1964).

Robert K. Turner, Jr., has newly edited *The Fair Maid of the West, Parts I and II* for the Regents Renaissance Drama Series (1967). The bibliographical analysis of the text is presented in the article mentioned above (III,D). The general introduction contains information about the author and sources, and a survey of the major criticism, while the appendices describe the historical events underlying Heywood's play and give the cast for the court performances, as well as supplying a chronology of Heywood's life.

Allan Holaday's edition of *The Rape of Lucrece* (1950) is the only edition since Verity's in 1903. Regrettably, Holaday has not submitted the extant copies of the several quartos to exhaustive bibliographical analysis. The establishment of the text is critical, especially in view of the metamorphosis of the play between 1608 (Q1) and 1638 (Q5). Holaday, who uses the fifth quarto for his copy-text, repeats his contention that the play was first written in 1594, and that the actor Robert Browne was responsible for the alterations in the second quarto of 1609 (cf. his "Robert Browne and the Dates of Heywood's *Lucrece*," *JEGP* 64 [1945]: 171-80). The early date proposed and the revisions by Browne would explain several curious features of the play. Holaday's date places the play close to Shakespeare's *Rape of Lucrece* and helps explain the stylistic proximity to the *Four Prentices*. Heywood revised the play, the argument goes, in

1606 or 1607, incorporating features from *Macbeth*. Finally, Browne added Valerius's role and certain songs. Though plausible, the hypothesis rests on the uncertain evidence of style and conjecture as to Browne's activities between 1599 and 1607. The best evidence is an allusion to a dramatic production of *Lucrece* found in Drayton.

Arthur Brown and R. E. Alton have produced an edition of *The Captives* for the Malone Society (1953).

F. NONDRAMATIC WORKS

In a chapter on "Thomas Heywood and the Dictionaries" (*Classical Myth and Legend in Renaissance Dictionaries* [1955]), DeWitt T. Starnes and Ernest William Talbert demonstrate Heywood's obvious and extensive reliance on contemporary dictionaries. Parallel passages from Heywood's *Earth and Age, Aegeus, Sardanapal, Salmoneus*, and *Gunaikeion* and from the dictionaries of Thomas Cooper and Charles Stephanus are offered. Heywood is mentioned frequently in Douglas Bush's *Mythology and the Renaissance Tradition in English Poetry* (1932; rev. ed. 1963).

K. M. Briggs, in "Heywood's *Hierarchie of the Blessed Angells*," *Folklore* 80 (1969):89–106, finds "a rich mine of folk tradition" buried in this long narrative poem. Through copious citation of examples and analogues, Briggs establishes Heywood's dependence upon the standard story-patterns of popular folk tales. Briggs comments upon the organizational weakness of the poem, noting that Heywood seemed frequently "to produce his anecdotes rather at random."

IV. SEE ALSO

A. GENERAL

Barber, Charles. *The Idea of Honour in the English Drama, 1591–1700.* 1957.

Bevington, David. *Tudor Drama and Politics: A Critical Approach to Topical Meaning.* 1969.

Boas, Frederick S. *An Introduction to Stuart Drama.* 1946.

Bowden, William R. *The English Dramatic Lyric, 1603–42: A Study in Stuart Dramatic Technique.* 1951.

Bowen, Hoyt E. "Thomas Heywood: Teacher of Tradition." *RenP*, 1956, pp. 12–16.

Bradbrook, M. C. *Shakespeare and Elizabethan Poetry.* 1951.

———. *The Rise of the Common Player: A Study of Actor and Society in Shakespeare's England.* 1962.

Briggs, K. M. *The Anatomy of Puck: An Examination of Fairy Beliefs among Shakespeare's Contemporaries and Successors.* 1959.
———. *Pale Hecate's Team.* 1962.
Brooke, C. F. Tucker. "The Royal Fletcher and the Loyal Heywood." In *Elizabethan Studies and Other Essays in Honor of George F. Reynolds,* Univ. of Colorado Studies, Ser. B. Studies in the Humanities, vol. 2, no. 4 (1945), pp. 192–94.
Burns, F. D. A. "Thomas Heywood and the *Annalia Dubrensia,* 1636." *N&Q* 9 (1962):69–70.
Bush, Douglas. "William Painter and Thomas Heywood." *MLN* 54 (1939): 279–80.
———. *English Literature in the Earlier Seventeenth Century.* 1945; 2nd ed., 1962.
Cazamian, Louis. *The Development of English Humor.* 1952.
Craig, Hardin. *The Enchanted Glass.* 1936.
Greenfield, Thelma N. *The Induction in Elizabethan Drama.* 1969.
Greer, David. "Thomas Heywood's Parody of a Lyric by Campion." *N&Q* 12 (1965):333–34.
Greg, W. W. *Pastoral Poetry and Pastoral Drama.* 1905.
Harbage, Alfred. *Shakespeare and the Rival Traditions.* 1952.
Harrison, G. B. *Elizabethan Plays and Players.* 1940.
Herrick, M. T. *Tragicomedy: Its Origin and Development in Italy, France, and England.* 1955.
Jewkes, Wilfred T. *Act Division in Elizabethan and Jacobean Plays, 1583–1616.* 1958.
Messiaen, Pierre. *Théâtre anglaise, moyen age et XVIe siècle.* 1948.
Morris, Harry. "Some Uses of Angel Iconography in English Literature." *CL* 10 (1958):36–44.
Parrott, Thomas Marc, and Robert Hamilton Ball. *A Short View of Elizabethan Drama.* 1943.
Patrides, C. A. "Thomas Heywood and Literary Piracy." *PQ* 39 (1960):118–22.
Praz, Mario, ed. *Teatro elisabettiano: Kyd, Marlowe, Heywood, Marston, Jonson, Webster, Tourneur, Ford.* 1948.
Prior, Moody E. *The Language of Tragedy.* 1947.
Reed, Robert Rentoul, Jr. *The Occult on the Tudor and Stuart Stage.* 1965.
Ribner, Irving. *The English History Play in the Age of Shakespeare.* 1957; rev. ed., 1965.
———. *Jacobean Tragedy.* 1962.
Sherbo, Arthur. *English Sentimental Drama.* 1957.
Stagg, Louis C. *An Index to the Figurative Language of Thomas Heywood's Tragedies.* 1967.
Stroup, Thomas B. *Microcosmos: The Shape of the Elizabethan Play.* 1965.
Velte, Mowbray. *The Bourgeois Elements in the Dramas of Thomas Heywood.* 1966.
Weimann, Robert. "Die Gegensatze in der Kunst Heywoods, und Fletchers." In *Drama und Wirklichkeit in der Shakespearezeit.* 1958.
———. "Le déclin de la scène 'indivisible' élisabéthaine: Beaumont, Fletcher, et Heywood." In *Dramaturgie et société: Rapports entre l'œuvre théâtrale, son interprétation et son public aux XVIe et XVIIe siècles* (1968), pp. 815–27.

Wells, Henry W. *Elizabethan and Jacobean Playwrights.* 1934.
West, Robert H. *The Invisible World: A Study of Pneumatology in Elizabethan Drama.* 1939.

B. INDIVIDUAL WORKS

A Woman Killed with Kindness

Johnston, George Burke. "The Lute Speech in *A Woman Killed with Kindness.*" *N&Q* 5 (1958):525–26.
McDermott, John J. "Henryson's *Testament of Cresseid* and Heywood's *A Woman Killed with Kindness.*" *Renaissance Quarterly* 20 (1967):16–21.
Smith, Hallet D. "*A Woman Killed with Kindness.*" *PMLA* 53 (1938):138–47.

1 The Fair Maid of the West

Roberts, W. E. "Ballad Themes in *The Fair Maid of the West.*" *Journal of American Folklore* 68 (1955):19–23.

Love's Mistress

Bald, R. C. "Francis Kirkman, Bookseller and Author." *MP* 41 (1943):25–26.
Halstead, W. L. "Dekker's *Cupid and Psyche* and Thomas Heywood." *ELH* 11 (1944):182–91.

The Ages

Ochester, Edwin F. "A Source for Shirley's *The Contention of Ajax and Ulysses.*" *N&Q* 17 (1970):217. [*1 Iron Age*]
Reeves, John D. "Perseus and the Flying Horse in Peele and Heywood," *RES* 6 (1955):397–99. [*Silver Age*]

Troia Britannica

Schanzer, Ernest. "Milton's Fall of Mulciber and *Troia Britannica.*" *N&Q* 4 (1957):379–80.

The Fair Maid of the Exchange

Davison, P. H. "An Obscure Reference to Wool Processing in *The Fair Maid of the Exchange.*" *N&Q* 4 (1957):244–45.
———. "*The Fair Maid of the Exchange.*" *Library* 13 (1958):119–20.

Sir Thomas More

Bald, R. C. "*The Booke of Sir Thomas More* and Its Problems." *ShS* 2 (1949): 44–65.
Nosworthy, J. M. "Hand B in *Sir Thomas More.*" *Library* 11 (1956):47–50.
Partridge, A. C. *Orthography in Shakespeare and Elizabethan Drama.* 1964.

London's Jus Honorarium

Bergeron, David M. "Symbolic Landscape in English Civic Pageantry." *Renaissance Quarterly* 22 (1969):32–37.

The Late Lancashire Witches

Barber, Laird H., Jr. *"The Late Lancashire Witches." N&Q* 9 (1962):29.

C. TEXTUAL STUDIES

Boas, Frederick S. *Christopher Marlowe: A Biographical and Critical Study.* 1940.
Brown, John Russell. "The Rationale of Old-Spelling Editions of the Plays of Shakespeare and His Contemporaries." *SB* 13 (1960):49–67.

ANTHONY MUNDAY

Ann Haaker

There is no standard edition of Munday's complete plays.

I. GENERAL

A. BIOGRAPHICAL

Philipp Aronstein reviews Munday's activities as fitting background
for a skilled craftsman who appealed to popular taste in the English
Renaissance in "Ein dramatischer Kunsthandwerker der englischen
Renaissance," *Archiv* 140 (1926):212-18, which he continues in
Archiv 150 (1926):31-62, and summarizes in "Anthony Munday, der
Typus des dramatischen Kunsthandwerkers," in his book *Das
englische Renaissancedrama* (1929). A simplified sketch of Munday's
life, without footnotes or bibliography, can be found in Eustace
Conway's *Anthony Munday and Other Essays* (1927). Julia Celeste
Turner [Wright's] *Anthony Munday: An Elizabethan Man of Letters*
(1928) remains the most complete biography. Her chronological
account of Munday's varied activities affords an interesting comment
on the Elizabethan milieu as well as on Munday's literary achievements. She supplements the study with "Young Anthony Mundy
Again" in *SP* 56 (1959):150-68, which is based on new evidence
establishing Munday's birth date as 1560 rather than 1553 and on a
fresh study of his patrons and publishers. The essay reviews Munday's
career to 1600—his apprenticeship and associates under the printer
John Allde, his probable education under Claudius Hollyband, and his
experiences in Rome as a government spy. Wright feels that the ruin
of Munday's patron, the Earl of Oxford, and the frequent executions
of Catholics probably panicked him into becoming a recusant-hunter.
She concludes by discussing some of his neglected literary achievements.

Although Wright was the first to suggest, in her 1928 monograph,
that 1560 was a more plausible date of birth, I. A. Shapiro in

"Mundy's Birthdate," *N&Q* 3 (1956):2-3, first detected the error in the transcript of an inscription on a church monument quoted in J. Stow's *A Survey of London* (1633), the chief evidence for the 1553 birth date. Both Leslie Hotson, "Anthony Mundy's Birth-Date," *N&Q* 6 (1959):2-4, and Mark Eccles, "Anthony Munday," in *Studies in the English Renaissance Drama in Memory of Karl Julius Holzknecht*, ed. J. W. Bennett, et al. (1959), pp. 95-105, corroborate the 1560 birthdate with the discovery of a 1560 baptismal registry and Munday's testimony at the Consistory Court of London 22 May 1598. Hotson adds that the Munday signature in the latter document is important because it was made at the same time that Munday flourished as a writer. Mark Eccles further establishes Munday's birth date as 1560 and his death at the age of seventy-three with another 1580/1 city record. He derives other details about the author and his family from city records, records of appearances in law courts, production records of London Lord Mayors' shows, and Munday's will.

Three articles discuss Munday's trip to Rome. Beatrice Hamilton Thompson, in an article based on Munday's earlier birth date, "Anthony Munday's Journey to Rome, 1578-9," *DUJ* 34 (1941): 1-14, accuses Munday of being in the employ of Richard Topcliff in connection with priest-hunting during the period when the name "Jesuit" was synonymous with treasonous plotting to overthrow Queen Elizabeth. She claims Munday distorted facts in his account of his activities at the English Seminary at Rome in 1578, in his evidence against Campion at the trial, and in his *A Brief Discourse of the Taking of Campion and Divers Other Papists* (1581). Anthony Kenny, "Anthony Munday in Rome," *Recusant History* 4 (1962): 158-62, on the other hand, authenticates Munday's account in *The English Romayne Lyfe* (1581) with two 1579 lists of scholars, discovered by Godfrey Anstruther among Cardinal Morone's papers in the Vatican Library. The lists include Munday's name, and a letter by Friar Persons which concerns the difficulty of being admitted to the Seminary and Munday's final audience with Gregory III—all of which corroborate Munday's story. Guiseppi Galigani in *"La English Romayne Lyfe* di A. Mundy," *RLMC* 18 (1965):104-22, based on research into the archives of the English College in Rome, reviews the scholarship written after the discovery of the 1560 birth date and the effects of the later date upon the interpretation of Munday's account.

Four other articles by Celeste Turner Wright give further details of Munday's associates and activities in the publishing world. In

"Anthony Munday, 'Edward' Spenser, and E.K.," *PMLA* 76 (1961): 34–39, internal and external evidence suggest that the "E.K." who prefixed verses to Munday's *The Mirrour of Mutability, or Principal Part of the "Mirror for Magistrates"* (1579) was Edward Knight, a possible editor of the *Shepheardes Calendar*. The article investigates the connections between Spenser and Munday, whose mutual friends included Webbe, Harvey, Lyly, Leicester, and the Earl of Oxford. "Anthony Mundy and the Bodenham Miscellanies," *PQ* 40 (1961): 449–61, traces Munday's connections with the Bodenham series, and describes his relationship with the staff and the roles played by Robert Allot, Francis Meres, Nicholas Ling, James Roberts, and Burby. Wright concludes that Munday edited *Belvedere* (1600), influenced the Bodenham editor, Francis Meres, and remained loyal to the publishing Drapers' Guild. "Mundy and Chettle in Grub Street," *BUSE* 5 (1961):129–39, further illustrates the life of hack writers, printers, and booksellers, and their devious practices; it examines the joint activities of Munday and Chettle in the early 1590s. Wright concludes that, in spite of such tactics as Munday's ascribing his translation of Plato's *Axiochus* to Spenser and his epistle in his translation of *Gerileon of England* to "T.N." (Thomas Nashe), his unauthorized editing of Nashe's *Pierce Penniless*, and the Lazarus Pyott trick, Munday was respected by associates in the publishing world as well as in private life. Her "Lazarus Pyott and Other Inventions of Anthony Mundy," *PQ* 42 (1963):532–41, relates further deception practiced by Munday and his confederates: recently published records of the Stationers' Court revealed that Lazarus Pyott, previously thought Munday's rival translator of *Gerileon* (1592), was in fact Anthony Munday; Munday used the pseudonym Pyott in order to circumvent the copyright code. To add credibility to the hoax, his friend Chettle attacked an imaginary Pyott in print as an upstart competing with Munday's first book. Of that and other practices such as smuggling type to book pirates, Wright concludes: "Elizabethan authors, printers, and publishers were numerous and often hungry; perusing their annals we must learn, like them, to condone minor infringements of the copyright code."

Unpublished entries in the Records of the Merchant Taylors suggest that Munday had been granted honorary freedom in the guild for services that he had rendered or might in the future render, according to Charles R. Forker, "Two Notes on John Webster and Anthony Munday," *ELN* 6 (1968):26–34.

B. GENERAL STUDIES OF THE PLAYS

F. S. Boas in *An Introduction to Tudor Drama* (1933) discusses Munday's hand in *Sir Thomas More* and briefly reviews his other plays. C. F. Tucker Brooke's *The Tudor Drama* (1911) only tolerates Munday's romantic dramas, *The Downfall of Robert, Earl of Huntingdon, afterward called Robin Hood* and its sequel *The Death of Robert, Earl of Huntingdon,* and *John a Kent and John a Cumber,* and considers the rest of his work second-rate. I. A. Shapiro in "Shakespeare and Mundy," *ShS* 14 (1961):25-34, reviews Munday's life and appraises him "one of the most prolific and successful of Elizabethan dramatists"; although most of his plays are lost, there is no reason to believe that we have his best efforts. Shapiro points out that Munday was an experienced writer before he began playwriting; his publications in the 1580s to 1590s included political-theological pamphlets, translations from the French, treatises of moral problems and dilemmas, twelve volumes of translations of *Amandis de Gaule,* poetry, and a euphuistic romance. Considering *Fedele and Fortúnio* as Munday's first attempt as a playwright, Shapiro finds it worthy of remembrance for the character of Captain Crack-stone. More important, however, Shapiro feels, is Munday's probable influence upon Shakespeare; his Turnop and Shrimp, among other considerations in *John a Kent,* may have influenced Shakespeare's *Midsummer Night's Dream.* Meres's description in *Palladis Tamia* (1598) of Munday as "our best plotter" and evidence from Henslowe's *Diary* suggest to Shapiro that Munday supplied scenarios for plays, and that some of Shakespeare's plays may have been reinterpretations of old scenarios rather than versions of original sources; he postulates that Munday's influence is evident in Shakespeare's *King John,* and concludes that a fuller knowledge of Munday's works, especially *Sir Thomas More,* "may have had no little influence on Shakespeare's reading, and rendering, of history." Shapiro also feels that Munday's consistent denunciation of those who granted papal supremacy over Queen Elizabeth and those who conceded the pope's claim to "depose her and absolve her subjects from their vows of allegiance" no doubt extended to his histories written in the same patriotic and antipapal vein; Munday's ascribed contribution to *Sir Thomas More,* on the other hand, reveals More as not only a "credible human being but also a truly great man." Gwynneth Bowen, "Shakespeare and His Contemporaries," *Shakespearean Authorship Society* 7 (1962):2-3, also suggests that a revaluation of the life and work of Munday may have effects on the dating of Shakespeare's plays and on the problem of Shakespearean authorship; the 1560 birth date presents the possibility that Munday's work may have been the model for rather than the imitator of some of Shakespeare's plays.

There are descriptions of some of the emblematic devices used by Munday in his Lord Mayors' Pageants in Glynne Wickham's *Early English Stages, 1300–1660,* vol. 2, pt. 1 (1963). David M. Bergeron, "Anthony Munday: Pageant Poet to the City of London," *HLQ* 30 (1967):345–68, reminds us that no history of the evolution of drama can be complete without acknowledgment of Munday's important contribution, both thematically and technically, to Jacobean civic pageants. Bergeron describes Munday's artful manipulation of history, allegory, and mythology in several of the fifteen Lord Mayors' shows attributed to him during the period 1602–23. His emblematic portrayal of "virtues vital to a government's welfare" correlating with historical fact enabled him to sustain a thematic unity which produced in effect a "miniature, pictorial 'mirror for magistrates' "; his method was undoubtedly borrowed by later dramatists.

C. THE WORKS AT LARGE

There are no full-length studies of Munday's nondramatic works. Celeste Turner Wright, "Young Anthony Mundy Again," (I,A), commends Munday's exquisite "Shepherd Tonie" poems in *England's Helicon* (1600). Both Henry Hitch Adams, *English Domestic or, Homiletic Tragedy, 1575–1642* (1943), and Willard Farnham, *The Medieval Heritage of Elizabethan Tragedy* (1936), briefly discuss Munday's *Mirrour of Mutability* and *A View of Sundry Examples.* Both works see justice and man's sin as the cause of man's punishment, an attitude which, according to Farnham, replaces the more usual concept of Fortune's wheel. More recently, Brian Vickers, "*King Lear* and Renaissance Paradoxes," *MLR* 63 (1968):305–14, suggests further connections between the popular collections of paradoxes and Shakespeare's *King Lear*; the similarity was first observed by Professor W. G. Rice in 1932. Vickers points out that parallels occur between *Lear* and Ortensio Landi's *Paradossi* (1534), which was translated into French with several alterations in 1553 by Charles Estienne; Munday in turn translated the French version as *The Defense of Contraries,* which was published in 1593. The form of this Landi-Estienne-Munday collection remains in great part Ciceronian; a familiarity with that form illuminates whole sections of *King Lear,* especially the "bastardy-blindness themes in his subplots."

Geoffrey Creigh, "*Zelauto* and Italian Comedy: A Study in Sources," *MLQ* 29 (1968):161–67, reaffirms the direct relationship between Munday's *Zelauto* and *The Merchant of Venice* and postulates further that the third part of *Zelauto* "may be a prose adaptation of a contemporary Italian dramatic entertainment" witnessed or read by Munday during his stay in Italy. Similarity in general structure, action, plot, dialogue, motif, and characters suggests "a general indebtedness to sixteenth-century Italian comedy."

In 1942 Samuel A. Tannenbaum published a concise bibliography, *Anthony Mundy, Including the Play of "Sir Thomas More,"* which has been supplemented by *Elizabethan Bibliographies Supplements* 9 (1968), for the years 1941–66, ed. Charles A. Pennel and compiled by Robert C. Johnson.

II. CRITICISM OF INDIVIDUAL PLAYS AND STATE OF SCHOLARSHIP

A. INDIVIDUAL PLAYS

John a Kent and John a Cumber

Corrections in the dialogue and the inserted stage directions, written several lines before they are called for in the text of the manuscript in anticipation of production needs, show us the play developing in Munday's hands according to John William Ashton, "Revision in Munday's *John a Kent and John a Cumber*," *MLN* 48 (1933):531–37. Ashton's "Conventional Material in Munday's *John a Kent and John a Cumber*," *PMLA* 49 (1934):752–61, illustrates how Munday elaborates dramatic conventions, as in his contest of magicians, and constructs a unified play. Robert R. Reed, Jr., "The Probable Origin of Ariel," *SQ* 11 (1960):61–65, compares Shakespeare's Ariel in *The Tempest* with Shrimp, the magician's apprentice in *John a Kent*, and feels strongly that Shakespeare was influenced by Munday.

The Downfall of Robert, Earl of Huntingdon

The Death of Robert, Earl of Huntingdon

James A. S. McPeek, "Macbeth and Mundy Again," *MLN* 46 (1931):391–92, notes Shakespeare's possible indebtedness in *Macbeth* to Munday's use of darkness (night) imagery. Malcolm A. Nelson's

"*Look About You* and the Robin Hood Tradition," *N&Q* 9 (1962): 141-43, says that Munday, in *The Downfall*, was "the first Elizabethan playwright to give Robin Hood an earldom." John C. Meagher, "Hackwriting and the Huntingdon Plays: Elizabethan Theatre," in *Elizabethan Theatre*, SuAS, vol. 9 (1966), pp. 197-219, suggests that a study of construction in the Huntingdon plays exemplifies the basic principles of late Elizabethan compositions and more clearly reveals relevant critical standards.

B. STATE OF SCHOLARSHIP

Although Munday still remains something of an enigma, the discovery of the 1560 birth date was responsible for a revaluation of his life, character, and literary contributions. Before the discovery of the new birth date critics regarded him as a "second rate ambitious man of letters turned adventurer" (B. H. Thompson, I,A); as representative of "commercial authorship at its lowest level" which has "more place in the history of police methods than in that of literature" (C. S. Lewis, *English Literature in the Sixteenth Century* [1954]); as "an obsequious timeserver" and hypocrite (W. Farnham, I,C)—all the result of Munday's dubious activities as recusant-hunter and publisher. These sentiments were reflected in the general assessment of his literary achievements; W. J. Courthope's *A History of English Poetry*, vol. 4 (1903), for example, refers to Munday as "a typical representative of the literary 'hack' of the Elizabethan age." Scholarly opinion after the discovery of the 1560 birth date shows greater tolerance for the younger Munday; e.g., Celeste Turner Wright, though admitting that many of the details of Munday's career are unattractive, considers him "talented and versatile" ("Young Anthony Munday Again," I,A). She emphasizes that *Fedele* (which she considers Munday's) "is no mere translation, but the skillful adapting of an Italian comedy—a lively English play." I. A. Shapiro, in "The Significance of a Date," *ShS* 8 (1955):100-105, suggests that we need to "revise our estimate . . . of Munday's activity as dramatist"; Munday may possibly be considered the pioneer of the English history play. Allardyce Nicoll notes (in his preface to *ShS* 8 [1955]: v) that Shapiro's article in that issue is "far-reaching— possibly for an understanding of Shakespeare's career and certainly for our knowledge of early dramatic history." F. D. Hoeniger records Richard Hosley's suggestion in "Informal Minutes of Conference 26" in *RenD*, Suppl. 7 (1964):3-4 that the adaptation of *Fedele and Fortunio* (which Hosley ascribes to Munday) from the second edition of Luigi Pasqualigo's *Il fedele* offers a valuable instance of reconstructing "the process by which a book that influenced the drama entered England from Italy." In the same issue John Leon Lievsay, "Some Research Opportunities in Anglo-Italian Renaissance Drama," pp. 10–12, recommends that more attention should be given to the Italian element in the works of Munday and Chapman. As noted above (I,C), Bergeron stresses Munday's important contribution to Jacobean civic pageantry which in turn influenced drama. In spite of suggested revaluations and the revival of interest, however, there has been little Munday scholarship of any notable length.

III. CANON

A. PLAYS IN CHRONOLOGICAL ORDER

This list follows Alfred Harbage's *Annals of English Drama, 975–1700*, rev. S. Schoenbaum (1964), which is also the source for the type of play, the acting date (in italics preceding semicolon), and the original date of publication. For a further description of printing of early editions, see W. W. Greg, *A Bibliography of the English Printed Drama to the Restoration*, 4 vols. (1939–59); for a discussion of the canon and lost plays, see E. K. Chambers, *The Elizabethan Stage*, 4 vols. (1923); and see G. E. Bentley, *The Jacobean and Caroline Stage*, vol. 4 (1956), for later city pageants.

John a Kent and John a Cumber, pseudo-history (ca. *1587–90;* MS)

In J. W. Ashton's "The Date of *John a Kent and John a Cumber*," *PQ* 8 (1929):225–32, a comparison with *Knack to Know a Knave* and supporting external evidence dates the play the latter half of 1594, for the newly reorganized Lord Strange's Company. By close examination of the ways in which Munday formed his sixes and zeros, I. A. Shapiro's "The Significance of a Date" (II,B), dates the manuscript of *John a Kent* "Decembris 1590"; the 1590 date, replacing the previously accepted 1596 date, explains the "Mar-Martin, John a Cant, his hobbie-horse" allusion in the last of the Marprelate tracts, *The Protestation*, issued about mid-September 1589, as a "typical and skillful double pun" referring to the Archbishop's employment of Munday as his pursuivant and pamphleteer. The new date also upsets assumptions about other plays of the period, dating *More* not later than 1591 and reopening the date for Marlowe's *Dr. Faustus*. It also reverses the assumption that Munday was influenced by Shakespeare; Shakespeare may have taken hints from Munday.

The Downfall of Robert, Earl of Huntingdon, with Chettle; history (*1598;* 1601)

The Death of Robert, Earl of Huntingdon, with Chettle; history (*1598;* 1601)

1 Sir John Oldcastle, with Drayton, Hathway, Wilson; history (*1599;* 1600)

See the Drayton essay in this volume.

The Triumphs of Reunited Britannia, civic pageant (*1605;* 1605)

Campbell, or the Ironmongers' Fair Field, civic pageant (*1609;* 1609)

London's Love to Prince Henry, royal entertainment (*1610;* 1610)

Chryso-Thriambos, civic pageant (*1611;* 1611)

Himatia-Poleos: The Triumphs of Old Drapery, or The Rich Clothing of England, civic pageant (*1614;* 1614)

Metropolis Coronata: The Triumphs of Ancient Drapery, or Rich Clothing of England, civic pageant (*1615;* 1615)

Chrysanaleia: The Golden Fishing, or Honour of Fishmongers, civic pageant (*1616;* 1616)

Siderothriambos, or Steel and Iron Triumphing, civic pageant (*1618;* 1618)

B. UNCERTAIN ASCRIPTIONS; APOCRYPHA

The Rare Triumphs of Love and Fortune, mythological moral (*1582;* 1589)

See the discussion in *The Predecessors of Shakespeare*, pp. 161–64.

Fedele and Fortunio, comedy (*1579–84;* 1585)

Three articles by Richard Hosley advance Munday's authorship of

Fedele and Fortunio over that of Gosson or Chapman. In "Anthony Munday, John Heardson, and the Authorship of *Fedele and Fortunio,*" *MLR* 55 (1960):564–65, he brings forward the following evidence: the initials A. M. are signed in the dedicatory epistle of a special presentation copy (the Collier-Huntington copy); the "Shepherd Tonie" lyric, reprinted in *England's Helicon* (1600) occurs in the play; and it is likely that Munday was associated with the dedicatee, John Heardson, through his brother Thomas, one-time warden of the Drapers's Company. In "The Date of *Fedele and Fortunio,*" *MLR* 57 (1962):385–86, he argues that the text (Hacket's quarto, 1585) is derived from the second edition of Luigi Pasqualigo's *Il fedele* (1579) rather than from the first edition (1576); it follows that *Fedele and Fortunio* was written in 1579 or later, nullifying Chambers's suggestion, in *The Elizabethan Stage*, vol. 4 (1923), that Stephen Gosson may have been the author. Hosley reviews previous scholarship on authorship in "The Authorship of *Fedele and Fortunio,*" *HLQ* 30 (1967):315–30, and presents further evidence supporting Munday's authorship.

A Knack to Know an Honest Man, tragicomedy (*1594;* 1596)

See the discussion in the Anonymous Plays section of this volume.

The Book of Sir Thomas More, history (ca. *1593*–ca. *1601;* MS)

J. M. Nosworthy, "Shakespeare and Sir Thomas More," *RES* 6 (1955):12–15, postulates bibliographical and stylistic evidence that Munday, Chettle, and Dekker wrote *Sir Thomas More* ca. 1600 and that Shakespeare wrote his section of the additions about 1601–2. MacD. P. Jackson, "Anthony Munday and *Sir Thomas More,*" *N&Q* 10 (1963):96, affirms I. A. Shapiro's belief expressed in "Shakespeare and Munday" (II,B) that the original draft of *Sir Thomas More* was conceived and written wholly by Anthony Munday. He takes issue with W. Greg's argument, in his introduction to his Malone Society Reprint (1911), which denies Munday's responsibility for *More* mainly on the basis of the error "fashis" in line 1847. Also supporting Munday's authorship of the first draft of *More* is Karl P. Wentersdorf's "The Date of the Additions in the *Booke of Sir Thomas More,*" *SJ* (1965):305–25, and Scott McMillin's "*The Book of Sir Thomas More*: A Theatrical Review," *MP* 68 (1970):10–24. McMillin's fresh analysis of the arrangement of the scenes with the insertions from the producer's point of view reveals "that the manuscript is a coherent theatrical document, arranged for the personnel of a specific

acting company, and prepared for the copying of actors' parts."
Revisions show intentional visual contrasts, repetitions, and
similarities which stress the *de casibus* theme of the play. More
delivers his final speeches just before his martyrdom on a raised
platform and alludes to the successive locations or sets which represented the various stages of his career. The representative actions for
these locations perhaps took place in a curtained area just below the
platform, which staging visually recalled More's progression toward
sainthood. McMillin concludes that "the visual organization of the
drama and the summoning of locations in the final speeches are
evidence of playwrights more sharply aware of their craft than
perhaps we have been willing to recognize."

The Case Is Altered, comedy, (*1597-98;* 1609)

   Frank L. Huntley in "Ben Jonson and Anthony Munday, or *The
Case Is Altered* Altered Again," *PQ* 41 (1962):205-14, reviews the
canonicity of *The Case Is Altered*, and with external and internal
evidence concludes that "Jonson took an old play written by his
enemies in the poetmachia, and refurbished it to strike back at them,
particularly at Anthony Munday; and that Munday, therefore, had
the greatest hand in the composition of the original play."

Chance Medley, comedy (*1598;* lost)

Mother Redcap, comedy? (*1598;* lost)

Valentine and Orson, romance (*1598;* lost)

The Funeral of Richard Cœur de Lion, history (*1598;* lost)

1 Fair Constance of Rome, classical history? (*1600;* lost)

2 Sir John Oldcastle, history (*1600;* lost)

Owen Tudor, history (*1600;* lost)

The Rising of Cardinal Wolsey, history (*1601;* lost)

Caesar's Fall, tragedy (*1602;* lost)

Jephthah, biblical history (*1602;* lost)

The Set at Tennis, unknown (*1602;* lost)

The Widow's Charm, comedy (*1602;* lost)

Pericles Prince of Tyre, tragicomedy (*1606-8;* 1609)

Janet Spens, *Elizabethan Drama* (1922), devotes a section to Munday in her discussion of the Shakespeare Apocrypha because of the light Munday appears to throw on early Elizabethan drama; she suggests that Shakespeare may possibly have been engaged in some sort of collaboration with Munday during that unknown period in Shakespeare's career, 1584-93.

The Sun in Aries, civic pageant (*1621;* 1621)

D. TEXTUAL STUDIES

Muriel St. Clare Byrne, "Anthony Munday's Spelling as a Literary Clue," *Library* 4 (1924):9-23, reveals how a paleographical study of three autograph manuscripts of Munday's offers "excellent opportunity for studying the relation of the printed text to the author's copy in Elizabethan times." Gerald R. Hayes, "Anthony Munday's Romances of Chivalry," *Library* 6 (1925):57-81, offers a chronology of the romances and the facts of dating and printing pertaining to each. Bibliographical evidence in his "Anthony Munday's Romances: A Postscript," *Library* 7 (1926):31-38, pertains to the recovery of the copy of *The Second Booke of Primaleon of Greece* (1596) and a record of *Palmerin of England*, Part 1 (1609).

Muriel St. Clare Byrne, "Bibliographical Clues in Collaborate Plays," *Library* 13 (1932):21-48, suggests that clues provided by text alterations, versification, stage directions, handwriting, spelling, and typography should be used as checks against stylistic arguments. Bernard Freyd refutes the arguments in F. M. Padelford's Johns Hopkins variorum facsimile edition of *The Axiochus of Plato* (1934) that the translation is a genuine work of Edmund Spenser in "Spenser or Anthony Munday?—A Note on *Axiochus*," *PMLA* (1935): 903-8, and claims Munday was not only the translator, but also the author of "A Sweet Speech or Oration" annexed to the translation. In the same issue (pp. 908-13), Padelford reviews Freyd's note and defends his basic arguments, reinforcing his orginal position by a comparison of style and spelling in some of the artificial analogues in Spenser's *Amoretti* with photostats of expository treatises of Munday, and by a review of manifestations of Stoic philosophy in some of Spenser's mentors. Marshall W. S. Swan uses historical and bibliographical evidence to support his case, in "The Sweet Speech and Spenser's (?) *Axiochus,*" *ELH* 11 (1944):161-81, for Munday's authorship of *Axiochus,*" and the attached final "Sheet D" containing the text of the speech of the Earl of Oxford's page, both of which were usually attributed to Spenser.

S. Schoenbaum's *Internal Evidence and Elizabethan Dramatic Authorship* (1966) regards Munday's consistent preference in autograph manuscripts for doubled medial "o" (*doone, loove, woorthy*) as a literary clue to the authorship of *Love and Fortune, Fedele and Fortunio,* and *The Death of Robert, Earl of Huntingdon.* A. C. Partridge, *Orthography in Shakespeare and Elizabethan Drama* (1964) considers Munday's orthography in the manuscripts of *Sir Thomas More* and *John a Kent.*

E. SINGLE-WORK EDITIONS OF THE PLAYS

The Malone Society reprint of *John a Kent and John a Cumber* (1923) prepared by Muriel St. Clare Byrne is derived from a holograph manuscript described in the introduction, which also includes a discussion of Munday's handwriting. Text revisions, background, and date are discussed in "A Critical Edition of Anthony Munday's *John a Kent and John a Cumber,*" ed. John William Ashton in *The University of Chicago Abstracts of Theses,* Humanistic Series 7 (1928-29): 511-15. J. H. P. Pafford's facsimile edition of *Chrysothriambos, The Triumphs of Gold* (1962), contains a reproduction of the 1611 title page and a bibliography. John C. Meagher prepared two editions for the Malone Society: his *The Downfall of Robert, Earl of Huntingdon* (1965) is based on a collation of the ten known copies of the 1601 quarto, and as reviewed in *YWES* 45 (1965):182 is "scrupulously prepared for the academic reader"; his *The Death of Robert, Earl of Huntingdon* (1967) is based on a collation of six copies of the 1601 quarto. Introductions to both *Downfall* and *Death* include discussions of textual problems and lists of variant readings and of irregular and doubtful readings. Xerographs of the Harvard copy served as the base for both editions.

F. EDITIONS OF NONDRAMATIC WORKS

The Paine of Pleasure (1938), privately printed, is a photostat facsimile of the copy in the Pepysian Library, Cambridge, of the edition edited and printed for Henri Car in 1580. *The English Romayne Lyfe* (1583), ed. G. B. Harrison (1925), has a brief introduction summarizing Munday's activities as recusant hunter, and four woodcuts depicting the martyrdom of Richard Atkins at Rome. Jack Stillinger discusses structure, source, influence, style, and characterization in the introduction to his edition of *Zelauto, The Fountaine of Fame* (1963); he used the single extant Bodleian copy of *Zelauto* as copy-text. Appendices include emendations, explanatory notes, and a modernized index of proverbs, sententiae, comparisons, and allusions.

IV. SEE ALSO

A. GENERAL

Brown, Arthur. "The Play within a Play: An Elizabethan Dramatic Device." *E&S* 13 (1960):36–48.

Churchill, R. C. *Shakespeare and His Betters.* 1958.

Dodds, M. Hope. "Anthony Munday." *N&Q* 146 (1924):331.

Geraldine, Sister M. "Erasmus and the Tradition of Paradox." *SP* 61 (1964): 41–63.

Koskenniemi, Inna. *Studies in the Vocabulary of English Drama, 1550–1600, Excluding Shakespeare and Ben Jonson.* 1962.

Krzyzanowski, J. "Some Conjectural Remarks on Elizabethan Dramatists." *N&Q* 193 (1948):233–34.

Lloyd, Bertram. "Anthony Munday, Dramatist." *N&Q* 152 (1927):98.

Mehl, Dieter. "Forms and Functions of the Play within a Play." *RenD* 8 (1965):41–61.

Miller, Henry Knight. "The Paradoxical Encomium with Special Reference to Its Vogue in England, 1600–1800." *MP* 53 (1956):145–78.

Muir, Kenneth. "Elizabethan Remainders." *Library* 13 (1958):56–57.

Mundy, P. E. "Anthony Munday and His Connections." *N&Q* 147 (1924):261.

Nicoll, Allardyce. *British Drama: An Historical Survey from the Beginnings to the Present Time.* 1925; 5th ed. 1962.

Phialas, Peter G. "Middleton and Munday." *TLS*, 23 Nov. 1956, p. 697; see also letter by Jean Robertson, *TLS*, 7 Dec. 1956, p. 731.

Smart, George K. "English Non-Dramatic Blank Verse in the Sixteenth Century." *Anglia* 61 (1937):387.

Sykes, H. Dugdale. "The Dramatic Works of Henry Chettle." *N&Q* 144 (1923): 263–65, 283–86, 303–6, 324–27, 345–47, 365–66, 386–89 (continuous from 7 April to 19 May 1923).

Wilson, Dover. "The New Way With Shakespeare's Texts, III." *ShS* 9 (1956): 69–80.

Worthington, F. L. "Tudor Plays on the Way to Production." *Ashland Studies for Shakespeare*, ed. Margery Bailey. 1957. [Not seen.]

B. INDIVIDUAL PLAYS

Sir Thomas More

Bald, R. C. "*The Booke of Sir Thomas More* and Its Problems." *ShS* 2 (1949):44-65.

Crundell, H. W. "Anthony Munday and *King Leir.*" *N&Q* 166 (1934):310-11.

———. "Arden of Feversham. *Arden* and *Richard III.*" *N&Q* 166 (1934):456-58.

Jenkins, Harold. "Readings in the Manuscript of *Sir Thomas More.*" *MLR* 43 (1948):512-14.

———. *A Supplement to Sir Walter Greg's Edition of "Sir Thomas More."* Malone Society, 1961.

MICHAEL DRAYTON

Richard F. Hardin

Drayton is something of an anomaly in this volume. Although he is known to have written (mostly in collaboration) twenty or more plays, only one of these survives. It was thought proper to include him, however, because of his importance in the Elizabethan literary scene and because of his inclusion in Chambers's *Elizabethan Stage*. The standard edition is *The Works of Michael Drayton*, ed. J. William Hebel, with introductions, notes, and variant readings by Kathleen Tillotson and Bernard H. Newdigate, 5 vols. (1931–41). A corrected edition, with revised bibliography by Bent Juel-Jensen, appeared in 1961.

I. GENERAL

A. BIOGRAPHICAL

Most of the facts known about Drayton's life come from his own writings, though there is a handful of contemporary references to him. These have all been drawn into a carefully documented account by B. H. Newdigate, *Michael Drayton and His Circle* (1941), which reproduces virtually all of the poet's autobiographical statements, including his sporadic correspondence with Drummond. Much is provided (perhaps too much) on Drayton's "circle," especially his patrons and Anne Goodere, for whom Drayton supposedly had a life-long infatuation (which Newdigate earlier explored in "Michael Drayton and His *Idea*," *Dublin Review* 200 [1937]:79-92). Since Newdigate a few items have come to light. In "Drayton at Poles-worth," *N&Q* 194 (1949):496, I. A. Shapiro presents evidence that Drayton may have known Donne through Henry Goodere. Dick Taylor, in "Drayton and the Countess of Bedford," *SP* 49 (1952): 214-28, shows that Drayton's publishers were responsible for keeping the dedications to Lucy Countess of Bedford in his books even after his break with her; Lucy is the "Selena" of the 1606 eighth eclogue. More recently Christopher Whitfield gives an account of the Rainsford home near Stratford, where Drayton frequently stayed, in "Clifford Chambers: The Muses' Quiet Port," *N&Q* 12 (1965): 362–75.

B. GENERAL STUDIES OF THE PLAYS

The only extant play in which Drayton had a hand is *The First Part of Sir John Oldcastle*, written with Munday, Richard Hathway, and Robert Wilson in 1599. Kathleen Tillotson has included the play in the *Works*, with a full introduction and notes, even though, as she says, it is impossible to ascertain Drayton's part in the work.

C. THE WORKS AT LARGE

After the appreciative studies by Oliver Elton (*Michael Drayton* [1905]) and H. H. Child (in the *Cambridge History of English Literature*, vol. 4[1909]), Drayton went into an eclipse. F. L. Lucas in *Authors Dead and Living* (1926) placed him between fifteenth-century sluggishness and Cavalier gallantry. Mario Praz was even less appreciative in "Drayton," *ES* 28 (1947):97–107, complaining of the woodenness of the poet's historical characters. A possible renewal of interest is seen in the appearance of several recent books. Paul Gerhard Buchloh's *Michael Drayton, Barde und Historiker, Politiker und Prophet* (1964), relates Drayton to the political and social issues of his age, concentrating mostly on *Poly-Olbion*. Buchloh sees the view of history in this poem as deliberately varied in order to show the differing attitudes toward English history then in vogue; Part Two of the poem ushers in a decline of patriotic spirit motivated by Drayton's hostility to the Court in later years. Joseph A. Berthelot's volume in the Twayne series, *Michael Drayton* (1967), takes us through the poems by genre, and concludes with an examination of Drayton's poetics and his reputation. While an enthusiastic introduction to the poet, the book is somewhat marred by errors of fact (Drayton's *Harmony* was not confiscated, there is no book by Wiatt on the *Epistles*, the maps in *Poly-Olbion* are not from Saxton's *Atlas*).

John Buxton's chapter in *A Tradition of Poetry* (1967) expands his earlier introduction to the Muses' Library edition of Drayton. Buxton sees Drayton as temperamentally aloof, with "no wish to play an active part in the affairs of his own time"; in *Nimphidia* he found a "congenial method of laughing at his contemporaries." A longer study appears in Joan Grundy's *The Spenserian Poets* (1969), which devotes two chapters to the heroic poems and *Poly-Olbion*. Drayton figures largely elsewhere in this book, especially in the chapter on pastorals. Grundy explores the relation between love and the heroic in the *Epistles;* in *Poly-Olbion* she finds a sympathy with nature that contrasts with the anthropocentric spirit of his predecessors' pastorals. Richard F. Hardin, *Michael Drayton and the Passing of Elizabethan England* (1973), sees Drayton as essentially a patriotic poet in an age when the values of the nation were in flux. All of the poetry is discussed, but the focus is on the historical poems and satires: these served to exhort and admonish the people in the pattern of greatness.

Today Drayton is perhaps best known for his sonnets, his persistent revisions of which have attracted much attention. Rosemond Tuve, in *Elizabethan and Metaphysical Imagery* (1947), thinks the revisions were intended to clarify the meaning and logical structure of the poems; the chief influence was Donne and his circle. Metaphysical influence is also argued in Jörg Schönert, "Draytons Sonett-Revisionen: Zum Problem des Übergangsdichters," *Anglia* 85 (1967): 161–83. In contrast, F. Y. St. Clair, "Drayton's First Revision of His Sonnets," *SP* 36 (1939):40–59, argues that the chief influence is Drayton's dramatic writing, a point earlier made in Janet G. Scott's *Les sonnets élisabéthains* (1929), probably still the most stimulating introduction to the sonnets. Scott also considers the influence of De Pontoux (none) and Sidney (very much). A novel interpretation that "*Idea* is essentially a comic sonnet sequence, its subject the unsuccessful attempt to avoid conventionality," has been proposed by Walter R. Davis, " 'Fantastickly I Sing': Drayton's *Idea* of 1619," *SP* 66 (1969):204–16.

The historical poetry receives an informed sympathy from Homer Nearing, Jr., in *English Historical Poetry, 1599–1641* (1945), where Drayton is "*the* historical poet of the English Renaissance." Anthony LaBranche, "Drayton's *Barons Warres* and the Rhetoric of Historical Poetry," *JEGP* 62 (1963):82–95, finds the rhetoric of the poem to be modeled on Books I and VIII of Lucan. Elsewhere (again writing on *The Barons Warres*) LaBranche shows how Drayton manipulates his readers' responses ("Poetry, History, and Oratory: The Renaissance Historical Poem," *SEL* 9 [1969]:1–19). *Englands Heroicall Epistles* are seen as a unified series of poems with a patriotic purpose in Richard F. Hardin, "Convention and Design in Drayton's *Heroicall*

Epistles," *PMLA* 83 (1968): 35-41. The same work is approached from a stylistic point of view in N. Christoph de Nagy's monograph, *Michael Drayton's "England's Heroical Epistles"*: *A Study in Themes and Compositional Devices* (1968), which seeks to contribute to "the elucidation of the phenomenology of Elizabethan poetry." The chief means used to this end is the comparison of Drayton's rhetoric with that of Ovid in the *Heroides*. Drayton's place in the whole European course of the heroic epistle may be seen in Heinrich Dörrie, *Der heroische Brief* (1968).

The pastorals have not attracted as much attention as they deserve, but there are signs of a change in the wind if T. G. Rosenmeyer's *The Green Cabinet: Theocritus and the European Pastoral Lyric* (1969) is any indication. Here Drayton receives a wholly fresh look as a pastoralist, though the insights on his poems are usually found in the author's general discussions of Renaissance pastoral. Michael Bristol, "Structural Patterns in Two Elizabethan Pastorals," *SEL* 10 (1970): 33-48, claims that *The Shepheards Garland* follows a systematic organization similar to that in Virgil's eclogues; Drayton's poems are set in a triadic pattern around a central motif of praise. Geoffrey Hiller, "Drayton's *Muses Elizium*: A New Way over Parnassus," *RES* 21 (1970):1-13, establishes the possibility that *The Muses Elizium* was originally written as a masque-like entertainment for the Dorset family; the nymphalls are influenced by Robert White's "Cupid's Banishment."

Drayton's odes were acknowledged to have a seminal place in the development of the genre in Robert Shafer's *The English Ode to 1660* (1918), and this view is sustained in Carol Maddison, *Apollo and the Nine: A History of the Ode* (1960), where Drayton is "the first proper ode writer in English," even though his attempt to define the genre is unsuccessful and some of the odes should not be so called. A "competitive vitality" is found in the odes by Anthony LaBranche, in "The 'Twofold Vitality' of Drayton's Odes," *CL* 15 (1963):116-29, as native and classical sources confront each other; the odes are compared with those of Horace and Ronsard. Finally, in terms evocative of F. L. Lucas (with whom this section began), D. S. J. Parsons, "The Odes of Drayton and Jonson," *QQ* 75 (1968): 675-84, explains how Drayton "moved from a humanist-medieval to a Cavalier form of expression," though like Jonson he eventually found the ode not suited to his temperament.

Several studies of Drayton from a special point of view bear mentioning, among them two articles by Thomas P. Harrison stressing the poet's inclinations as a naturalist: "Drayton's Herbals," *Texas Studies in English* 22 (1943):15-25 (influence of Henry Lyte, John Gerard, and Rembert Dodoens), and "Drayton's Birds," *Texas Studies in English* 29 (1950):102-17, later developed as a chapter in *They Tell of Birds: Chaucer, Spenser, Milton, Drayton* (1956). Mythological lore in Drayton's *Endimion and Phoebe* and other poems is treated in Douglas Bush's *Mythology and the Renaissance Tradition in English Poetry* (1932; rev. ed. 1963) where Drayton is seen as departing from the erotic vein of his contemporaries. A. Lytton Sells has a chapter on Drayton in *The Italian Influence on English Poetry* (1955); particularly interesting is his comparison of Tasso's *Aminta* with *The Muses Elizium*. In *Elizabethan Poetry in the Eighteenth Century* (1947) Earl Wasserman argues that Drayton was widely read by the Augustans, adding to the findings of Russell Noyes's monograph, *Michael Drayton's Literary Vogue Since 1631* (1935). The *Concise Bibliography* by Samuel Tannenbaum was published in 1941 and reprinted in *Elizabethan Bibliographies*, vol. 2 (1967). A continuation by George R. Guffey appears in *Elizabethan Bibliographies Supplements VII* (1967).

II. CRITICISM OF INDIVIDUAL PLAYS AND STATE OF SCHOLARSHIP

A. INDIVIDUAL PLAYS

Sir John Oldcastle

Sir John Oldcastle has drawn little scholarly attention in its own right; the interest has centered on Oldcastle's relation to Falstaff and on the Reformation backgrounds of the story. For those not inclined to read Wilhelm Baeske, *Oldcastle-Falstaff in der englischen Literatur bis zu Shakespeare* (1905), there is Leslie Mahin Oliver, "Sir John Oldcastle: Legend or Literature?" *Library* 1 (1946):179-83, or Rudolph Fiehler, "How Oldcastle Became Falstaff," *MLQ* 16 (1955): 16-28. Oliver denies the existence of a villainous Oldcastle supposed by some in popular legend. Fiehler omits a few minor sources found in Baeske, but does clarify Oldcastle's significance to English Reformers. This subject as it relates specifically to Drayton's play is explored in Mary Grace Muse Adkins, "Sixteenth-Century Religious and Political Implications in *Sir John Oldcastle*," *Studies in English* (Univ. of Texas) 22 (1942):86-109. Today we may find her version

of Elizabethan religion and politics a little too simple, but the article
does provide helpful comments on the play and its milieu. Readers
should know that it might have been William Lord Cobham, not his
son Henry, who took offense at Shakespeare's Oldcastle: see John
Dover Wilson, "The Origins and Development of Shakespeare's *Henry
IV,*" *Library* 26 (1945):2-16. A minor character in the play has been
found to originate in Fabyan's chronicles by R. E. Bennett, "The
Parson of Wrotham in *Sir John Oldcastle,*" *MLN* 45 (1930): 142-44.
The only discussion of the play in recent years occurs in Irving
Ribner's *The English History Play in the Age of Shakespeare* (1957;
rev. ed. 1965), where it is acknowledged as a successful instance of
biographical drama. Ribner agrees with Adkins that the play was
written to affirm the Puritans' loyalty to Queen Elizabeth.

B. STATE OF SCHOLARSHIP

Drayton has been more attractive to literary historians than critics,
perhaps because his poems lack a density of texture. This may
explain why Douglas Peterson's *English Lyric from Wyatt to Donne*
(1967) gives an entire chapter to Fulke Greville's *Caelica* as against
two pages for Drayton's poetry. Much can be said about Drayton as
an artist, however: his habits of revision (beyond the sonnets), the
effect of dramatic writing on his style, the qualities of his diction and
prosody. He is also an especially rich and largely untapped mine for
the social historian: his resentment of the Court, his anatomy of
Jacobean society in the satires, his nostalgia and antiquarian inclinations, his affiliations with the rural gentry, all would seem to invite
the attention of historians (including literary historians) grappling
with the problematic character of England in the decades from
Elizabeth to the Civil War. Nevertheless, as indicated in the sections
above, there has been a modest flurry of interest in his poetry from
several points of view in the past decade.

III. CANON

A. PLAYS IN CHRONOLOGICAL ORDER

The information on dating, type of play, and lost plays is from
Alfred Harbage, *Annals of English Drama, 975-1700*, rev. Samuel
Schoenbaum (1964). The dates in parentheses are first performance
(italics) and first publication. Dates following the lost plays are entry

dates in the *Annals*. E. K. Chambers discusses canon and dates in *The Elizabethan Stage*, vol. 3 (1923). W. W. Greg describes early editions in *A Bibliography of the English Printed Drama to the Restoration*, 4 vols. (1939-59).

1 Sir John Oldcastle, history (*1599;* 1600)

See above, I,B.

The following lost plays have been ascribed, in whole or in part, to Drayton. Not all were completed.

The Famous Wars of Henry I and the Prince of Wales, 1598; *1 Black Bateman of the North*, 1598; *1* and *2 Earl Godwin and His Three Sons*, 1598; *Pierce of Exton*, 1598; *The Funeral of Richard Cœur de Lion*, 1598; *Chance Medley*, 1598; *1, 2,* and *3 The Civil Wars of France*, 1598; *Connan Prince of Cornwall*, 1598; *1* and *2 Worse (A)feared Than Hurt (Hannibal and Hermes)*, 1598; *The Madman's Morris*, 1598; *Pierce of Winchester*, 1598; *Mother Redcap*, 1598; *William Longbeard*, 1599; *1 Fair Constance of Rome*, 1600; *2 Sir John Oldcastle*, 1600; *Owen Tudor*, 1600; *The Rising of Cardinal Wolsey*, 1601; *Caesar's Fall*, 1602.

B. UNCERTAIN ASCRIPTIONS; APOCRYPHA

H. W. Crundell was the last to see Drayton's hand in *Edward III*, in "Drayton and *Edward III*," *N&Q* 176 (1939):258-60. His argument is weakened, however, by Kathleen Tillotson's reply in pages 318-19 of the same volume.

Drayton's authorship of *The Merry Devil of Edmonton* has not been seriously advanced by any editor since Dodsley, and is dismissed by William A. Abrams in his edition of that play (1942). Thus Karl J. Holzknecht's mention of Drayton as possible author is misleading (*Outlines of Tudor and Stuart Plays* [1947]). See the discussion in the section on anonymous plays in this volume.

The London Prodigal, comedy (*1603-5;* 1605)

Harbage's *Annals* lists Drayton as one candidate for the authorship of this play, apparently owing to an extremely tenuous argument by Fleay. This theory has been convincingly rejected by Baldwin Maxwell, "Conjectures on *The London Prodigal*," in *Studies in Honor of T. W. Baldwin*, ed. D. C. Allen (1958), pp. 171-84.

C. CRITIQUE OF THE STANDARD EDITION

J. William Hebel's *The Works of Michael Drayton* (1931–41) is a thorough, accurate edition, not likely to be superseded. Hebel died before finishing the work, and the fifth volume, containing notes and introductions to the works, was prepared by Kathleen Tillotson and B. H. Newdigate, with bibliography by Geoffrey Tillotson. A corrected edition was issued in 1961, with a far more extensive bibliography by Bent Juel-Jensen.

Hebel's text is readable and well edited, and the variant readings appear to be the results of nearly exhaustive collations. *Ideas Mirrour* and *Idea* are printed separately, as are the early and late versions of the pastorals and legends. Introduction and notes to *Poly-Olbion* are by Newdigate, while those to other works are by K. Tillotson. The edition includes separate indexes to the notes and to *Poly-Olbion*, a glossary compiled with the assistance of C. T. Onions, a finding-list of Drayton's sonnets, and an extensive chronology of the author. Selden's "illustrations" to *Poly-Olbion* are given but not annotated. Juel-Jensen's "Bibliography of the Early Editions of the Writings of Michael Drayton," in the 1961 corrected edition, must be studied by anyone wishing to do serious work on the poems. Each edition of the works, including important editions of the eighteenth century, receives a careful bibliographical description with comments on the publishing history and provenance of Drayton's books.

A less expensive edition based on Hebel's text is *Poems of Michael Drayton*, edited by John Buxton (1953). Annotation in these two compact volumes is necessarily sparse, but there is new material on *The Owle*.

D. TEXTUAL STUDIES

In recent years the study of Drayton's text has been almost wholly in the domain of Bent Juel-Jensen (though see also Taylor, I, A, and Cohen, IV, below). His " '*Polyolbion*', '*Poemes Lyrick and Pastorall*', '*Poemes*' 1619, '*The Owle*', and a Few Other Books by Michael Drayton," *Library* 8 (1953):145–62, casts new light on the printing history of Drayton's later works, and discusses the genesis of Hole's engraving of Prince Henry, though he later modifies his findings in "Fine and Large-Paper Copies of *S. T. C.* Books, and Particularly of Drayton's *Poems* (1619) and *The Battaile of Agincourt* (1627)," *Library* 19 (1964):226–30. Juel-Jensen gives an account of his experience collecting Drayton, with interesting facts on the provenance of some books, in "A Drayton Collection," *Book Collector* 4 (1955):133–43. In "An Oxford Variant of Drayton's *Polyolbion*," *Library* 16 (1961):53–54, he reports finding a hitherto unknown issue of the long poem, printed as *The Faerie Land.* The autograph MS of Drayton's letter to Drummond of 22 November 1620 has been discovered and published by him in *Library* 21 (1966):328–30.

IV. SEE ALSO

Ackerman, Catherine A. "Drayton's Revision of *The Shepheards Garland." CLAJ* 3 (1959):106–13.

Allen, Don Cameron. *The Legend of Noah: Renaissance Rationalism in Art, Science, and Letters.* 1949.

Ball, Lewis F. "The Background of the Minor English Renaissance Epics." *ELH* 1 (1934):63–89.

Benjamin, E. B. "Fame, Poetry, and the Order of History in the Literature of the English Renaissance." *SRen* 6 (1959):64–84.

Bradbrook, Muriel C. *Shakespeare and Elizabethan Poetry.* 1951.

Briggs, K. M. *The Anatomy of Puck: An Examination of Fairy Beliefs among Shakespeare's Contemporaries and Successors.* 1959.

Bullitt, John M. "The Use of Rhyme Link in the Sonnets of Sidney, Drayton, and Spenser." *JEGP* 49 (1950):14–32.

Buxton, John. *Elizabethan Taste.* 1963.

———. *Sir Philip Sidney and the English Renaissance.* 1964.

Cawley, Robert R. "Drayton and the Voyagers." *PMLA* 38 (1923): 530–56.

———. "Drayton's Use of Welsh History." *SP* 22 (1925):234–55.

Cohen, Hennig. "Michael Drayton's *Poly-Olbion." RenP*, 1956, pp. 110–11.

Crundell, H. W. "*Love's Labour's Lost:* A New Shakespeare Allusion." *N&Q* 183 (1942):44–45.

Davenport, A. "The Seed of a Shakespeare Sonnet?" *N&Q* 182 (1942):242–44.

Donow, Herbert S. *A Concordance to the Sonnet Sequences of Daniel, Drayton, Shakespeare, Sidney, and Spenser.* 1969.

Drayton, Michael. *Poems. 1619.* 1969. [Facsimile Reprint.]

———. *The First Part of Sir John Oldcastle.* Ed. with Intro. by John Robertson Macarthur. 1907.

Duclos, P.-C. "Michael Drayton." *RLV* 20 (1954):276–84.

Eagle, R. L. "Anthony Cooke." *N&Q* 191 (1946):170. (See also reply by J. B. Whitmore, pp. 239–40.)

Evans, Maurice. *English Poetry in the Sixteenth Century.* 1955.

Fowler, Alastair. *Triumphal Forms: Structural Patterns in Elizabethan Poetry.* 1970.

Friedman, Stanley. "*Antony and Cleopatra* and Drayton's *Mortimeriados." SQ* 20 (1969):481–84.

Friedrich, Gerhard. "The Genesis of Michael Drayton's Ode 'To the Virginian Voyage.'" *MLN* 72 (1957):401–6.

Grundy, Joan. "Brave Translunary Things." *MLR* 59 (1964):501-10.
Hardin, Richard F. "The Composition of *Poly-Olbion* and *The Muses Elizium.*" *Anglia* 86 (1968):160-62.
Heffner, Ray L., Jr. "Drayton's 'Lady I. S.'" *N&Q* 5 (1958):376-81.
Heltzel, Virgil B. *Fair Rosamond: A Study of the Development of a Literary Theme.* 1947.
Ing, Catherine. *Elizabethan Lyrics.* 1951.
Jenkins, Raymond. "The Sources of Drayton's *Battaile of Agincourt.*" *PMLA* 41 (1926):280-93.
Juel-Jensen, Bent. "Drayton and His Patron." *TLS*, 7 Dec. 1956, p. 731.
———. "Three Lost Drayton Items." *Book Collector* 9 (1960):78-79.
Le Comte, Edward S. *Endymion in England: The Literary History of a Greek Myth.* 1944.
Lever, J. W. *The Elizabethan Love Sonnet.* 1956.
Macdonald, Charlotte. "Drayton's 'Tidy' and Chaucer's 'Tidif.'" *RES* 21 (1945):127-33.
McManaway, James G. "A New Shakespeare Document." *SQ* 2 (1951):119-22. [On *Oldcastle.*]
Maxwell, Baldwin. *Studies in the Shakespeare Apocrypha.* 1956.
Meyerstein, E. H. W. "A Drayton Echo in Tennyson." *TLS*, 2 June 1950, p. 341.
Miles, Josephine. *Renaissance, Eighteenth Century, and Modern Language in English Poetry: A Tabular View.* 1960.
Miller, Edwin H. *The Professional Writer in Elizabethan England.* 1959.
Miner, Paul. "William Blake: Two Notes on Sources." *BNYPL* 62 (1958):203-7.
Moore, William H. "Sources of Drayton's Conception of *Poly-Olbion.*" *SP* 65 (1968):783-803.
Morris, Helen. *Elizabethan Literature.* 1958.
Newdigate, B. H. "Cotswold Sheep in *Poly-Olbion.*" *N&Q* 181 (1941):142.
Nicolson, Marjorie Hope. *Mountain Gloom and Mountain Glory: The Development of the Aesthetics of the Infinite.* 1959.
Richmond, Hugh H. *The School of Love: The Evolution of the Stuart Love Lyric.* 1964.
Riggs, E. S. "A Little Learning." *AN&Q* 3 (1965):135.
Schaar, Claes. *Elizabethan Sonnet Themes and the Dating of Shakespeare's "Sonnets."* 1962.
Scoular, Kitty W. *Natural Magic: Studies in the Presentation of Nature in English Poetry from Spenser to Marvell.* 1965.
Smith, Hallett. *Elizabethan Poetry.* 1952.
Strong, Roy C. "The Popular Celebration of the Accession Day of Queen Elizabeth." *JWCI* 21 (1958):86-103.
———. *Tudor and Jacobean Portraits.* 2 vols. 1969.
Thomas, Sir William Beach. "What Drayton Admired." *Hertfordshire*, 1950, pp. 236-44.
Tillotson, Geoffrey. "Contemporary Praise of *Polyolbion.*" *RES* 16 (1940):181-83.
Tillotson, Kathleen. "The Language of Drayton's *Shepheards Garland.*" *RES* 13 (1937):272-81.
———. "Drayton and Richard II: 1597-1600." *RES* 15 (1939):172-79.

———. "Michael Drayton as a 'Historian' in the 'Legend of Cromwell.' " *MLR* 34 (1939):186–200.

Tillyard, E. M. W. *Some Mythical Elements in English Literature.* 1961.

West, Michael. "Drayton's 'To the Virginian Voyage': From Heroic Pastoral to Mock-Heroic." *RenQ* 24 (1971):501–6.

White, Helen C. *Tudor Books of Saints and Martyrs.* 1963.

Wilson, Frank Percy. *Elizabethan and Jacobean.* 1945.

Winters, Yvor. *Forms of Discovery.* 1967.

Zocca, Louis. *Elizabethan Narrative Poetry.* 1950.

ANONYMOUS PLAYS

Anne Lancashire   Jill Levenson

Books and articles consulted date from the publication of E. K. Chambers, The Elizabethan Stage, *4 vols. (1923), to the end of 1967; works published 1920–23 and not cited in Chambers are included, as are some post-1967 works. For additional information, see: G. E. Bentley,* The Jacobean and Caroline Stage, *7 vols. (1941–68); W. W. Greg,* A Bibliography of the English Printed Drama to the Restoration, *4 vols. (1939-59); Alfred Harbage,* Annals of English Drama, *975–1700, rev. Samuel Schoenbaum (1964), and the* Supplement *by Schoenbaum (1966). A list of works dealing generally with a large number of anonymous plays will appear in the next volume of this series,* The New Intellectuals. *The dates following play titles indicate the preferred date of first performance (in italics) and the date of the first edition from the* Annals *and the* Supplement; *type classifications are from the* Annals. *Full bibliographical citation is given only for the first reference to a work in each essay; short titles are used for subsequent references. In longer essays, a shortened title of the section in which the work is first cited ("Edition," "Text," etc.) is usually given in parentheses following the short title.*

A Knack to Know an Honest Man, tragicomedy (*1594;* 1596)

Editions

The play is available in microprint in Henry W. Wells, ed., *Three Centuries of Drama* (Readex Microprint Corp., 1955–56).

Text

The 1596 text is generally agreed to be a bad quarto. Evelyn May Albright, *Dramatic Publication in England, 1580–1640* (1927), declares that the play was published [presumably legitimately] "in what may well be a stage version"; but other scholars comment on the corrupt state of the text. Robert Boies Sharpe, *The Real War of the Theaters* (1935), calls it "confused and probably surreptitious" (cf. E. K. Chambers, *Elizabethan Stage* [1923], vol. 4). Leo Kirschbaum, "A Census of Bad Quartos," *RES* 14 (1938):20–43, lists it as a bad quarto; see also his *Shakespeare and the Stationers* (1955) and "An Hypothesis concerning the Origin of the Bad Quartos," *PMLA* 60 (1945): 697–715, the latter work maintaining that all bad quartos are products of memorial reconstruction. Wilfred T. Jewkes, *Act Division in Elizabethan and Jacobean Plays, 1583–1616* (1958), believes the printer's copy to have been a playhouse version, either a reconstructed shortened acting text or a report of an actual performance. Dora Jean Ashe includes *Knack to Know an Honest Man* in her article, "The Non-Shakespearean Bad Quartos as Provincial Acting Versions," *RenP*, 1954, pp. 57–62; she believes these quartos to have been memorially reconstructed for provincial performance by poor and drifting acting companies. General characteristics of the texts, she points out, are economy of casting and staging requirements, brevity, often over-prominent comedy, and plague-period date. See also her 1953 Univ. of Virginia Ph.D. dissertation, "A Survey of Non-Shakespearean Bad Quartos" (*DA* 14 [1954]: 1070–71), in which she suggests that the reporters of the *Knack to Know an Honest Man* text were the actors of the parts of the Duke of Venice and Lelio, and gives additional information.

The Play

The only extended treatment of *Knack to Know an Honest Man* is found in Arthur Sherbo's *English Sentimental Drama* (1957) and is wholly in terms of why the play is not a sentimental work: *Knack to Know an Honest Man* contains, Sherbo asserts, numerous sentimental situations and speeches, but is episodic and naive, with an emphasis on action and an "almost impersonal" quality as in folk literature. In *Tudor Drama and Politics* (1968), David Bevington states that the play, which was "written [in late 1594] seemingly in response to the anti-Puritan *A Knack to Know a Knave*, appeals to ideas of conscience above law and of retreat from the norms of decadent society"; its heroes place virtue above loyalty to the state, and justify their conduct according to Christian divine law. Sharpe, *Real War*, comments that *Knack to Know an Honest Man* "is romantic and tragi-comic in type," with resemblances to *Measure for Measure* and

Antonio and Mellida; it was probably written in emulation of *Knack to Know a Knave* and seems to have influenced *The Merchant of Venice* and to have been perhaps influenced by early Shakespearean work. Possibly, Sharpe suggests, it was performed by the Admiral's Men at court on 6 Jan. 1594/95. Sharpe also comments that the author might be Heywood or, more probably, Munday (the play having a strong Italian flavor); indeed *Knack to Know an Honest Man* "may even contain work by Wilson, Chettle, and Chapman." In a discussion of Elizabethan plays which are primarily social satires, Louis B. Wright, "Social Aspects of Some Belated Moralities," *Anglia* 54 (1930):107–48, declares that *Knack to Know an Honest Man* makes no effort at really serious treatment of social conditions and is an attempt to capitalize on the popularity of *Knack to Know a Knave*.

Other Studies

Friendship material in the play is dealt with by Laurens J. Mills in *One Soul in Bodies Twain* (1937) and in a footnote in T. W. Baldwin's *Shakspere's Five-Act Structure* (1947). Mills suggests that the play was hastily written, to compete with *Knack to Know a Knave*. Ola Elizabeth Winslow, *Low Comedy as a Structural Element in English Drama from the Beginnings to 1642* (1926), points out that the comic character Franco, revealing his master's complicity in Lelio's escape, is a determining plot agent, but that his determining part appears to be accidental. Dieter Mehl, *The Elizabethan Dumb Show* (1965; German ed. 1964), calls the "pompious shew" a kind of exemplum illustrating for Sempronio his statement, *Vanitas vanitatum*.

See Also

Adams, Joseph Quincy. "Hill's List of Early Plays in Manuscript." *Library* 20 (1939–40):71–99.
Cellini, Benvenuto, ed. *Drammi pre-Shakespeariani*. Collana di Letterature Moderne, no. 4 (1958).
Jorgensen, Paul A. *Redeeming Shakespeare's Words*. 1962.
McNeir, Waldo F. "Trial by Combat in Elizabethan Literature." *NS* 65 (1966): 101–12.

A. L.

The Tragedy of Alphonsus Emperor of Germany, tragedy *(1594;*
1654)

Editions

The play is available in microprint in Henry W. Wells, ed., *Three
Centuries of Drama* (Readex Microprint Corp., 1955–56).

Date

Most scholars since 1923 have assigned to the play a date in the
1590s. H. Dugdale Sykes, *Sidelights on Elizabethan Drama* (1924)
[the chapter on *Alphonsus* is reprinted from *N&Q*, 1916], states that
the style of *Alphonsus* is that of the pre-Shakespearean drama of
Marlowe, Greene, and Peele, and that the play is a Machiavellian
revenge drama influenced by the works of Kyd and Marlowe and
written ca. 1590; in "Peele's Borrowings from Du Bartas," *N&Q* 147
(1924): 368–69, he calls it the latest of Peele's extant plays, ca.
1594. J. M. Robertson, *The Shakespeare Canon*, pt. 1 (1922),
declares *Alphonsus* to be an old play and places it after 1590; in *An
Introduction to the Study of the Shakespeare Canon* (1924) he
speculates that it may predate—and have inspired—Greene's *Alphonsus
King of Aragon* and therefore be dated originally "as far back as
1589." The 1654 edition is "late and revised." Finally, in *Marlowe:
A Conspectus* (1931), he dates the work 1590 and posits a later
"drastic reconstruction" during which the German matter was
inserted. Mario Praz, "Machiavelli and the Elizabethans," *PBA* 14
(1928):49–97 (Annual Italian Lecture), dates *Alphonsus* not long
after Marlowe's works, though stating that it was only performed in
1636 [see below for scholarship on this performance date]; Robert
Boies Sharpe, *The Real War of the Theaters* (1935), places the play
in the 1590s, perhaps 1595. In the most extended treatment of date,
"The Date and Composition of *Alphonsus, Emperor of Germany*,"
Harvard Studies and Notes in Philology and Literature 15 (1933):
165–89, Fredson Thayer Bowers states that the archaic stylistic
devices, anti-Spanish bias, portrait of Edward, contempt of foreigners,
and meter all seem to belong to the years immediately after the
Spanish Armada of 1588. The play, he believes, also contains
resemblances to several late sixteenth-century plays and shows no
evidence of revision and no influence of Fletcher. Bowers places it
after *Titus Andronicus* (1593–94) and probably after *King John*
(?1596–97), and before *The Malcontent* (1604) and *Antonio and*

Mellida and *Antonio's Revenge* (1599): thus 1594–99, with the probability being for 1597–99. Taylor Starck, in a companion article to Bowers's, "The German Dialogue in *Alphonsus, Emperor of Germany*, and the Question of Authorship," *Harvard Studies and Notes in Philology and Literature* 15 (1933):147–64, cites Bowers, and, finding *Alphonsus* to have been written probably by an English actor who had traveled in Germany (see below, "Authorship—Others"), also favors a date of composition at the end of the sixteenth century, and no later revision. He states that the Dutch-German of *Alphonsus* is closer to that found in late sixteenth-century plays than to that found in Stuart drama, that few new English actors traveled to Germany after the start of the Thirty Years War, and that members of the original touring companies "were nearly all dead by the close of the first quarter of the seventeenth century." See also Allardyce Nicoll, *The British Drama* (1962), and Harold M. Dowling (below, "Authorship—Chapman").

The traditional critical identification of *Alphonsus* with the *Alfonso* performed in 1636 at the Blackfriars theater in honor of the Elector Palatine is plausibly rejected by Starck, "German Dialogue." (See also Bowers, "Date and Composition.") Starck points out that the play's political subject matter would not have been suitable for such a performance, and, moreover, that in 1636 *Alphonsus* was neither a recent play nor a famous revival. In 1924 Sykes (see above and below) takes for granted the *Alphonsus-Alfonso* identification, as do many other scholars: e.g., Praz, "Machiavelli and the Elizabethans," and Irwin Smith, *Shakespeare's Blackfriars Playhouse* (1964). Cf. G. E. Bentley, *Jacobean and Caroline Stage*, vol. 6 (1968).

Connections between *Alphonsus* and other plays (and nondramatic works) of its period are mentioned by several scholars, although not always in relation to the play's date. See: J. M. Robertson, *An Introduction* [*Titus Andronicus, Alphonsus King of Aragon*]; Mario Praz, "Machiavelli and the Elizabethans" [*Alphonsus* influenced by *Richard III, Jew of Malta, Spanish Tragedy*]; Fredson Thayer Bowers, "*Alphonsus, Emperor of Germany*, and the *Ur-Hamlet*," *MLN* 48 (1933): 101–8, and "Date and Composition" [*2 Tamburlaine, Soliman and Perseda, Spanish Tragedy, Jew of Malta*, Nashe's *Unfortunate Traveler*, a *Hamlet* play, *Antonio's Revenge, Titus Andronicus, The Malcontent, King John*]; M. C. Bradbrook, *Themes and Conventions of Elizabethan Tragedy* (1935) [Chettle's *Hoffman* and his lost *Orphan's Tragedy*]; Sharpe, *Real War* [*Blind Beggar of*

Alexandria, Doctor Faustus, Jew of Malta, Tamburlaine, Massacre at Paris, Spanish Tragedy, Hamlet, Nashe's *Unfortunate Traveler, Lust's Dominion*]; Fredson Thayer Bowers, *Elizabethan Revenge Tragedy, 1587–1642* (1940) [*Ur-Hamlet, Titus Andronicus,* Marlowe's work, other revenge dramas]; William Wells, *"Alphonsus, Emperor of Germany," N&Q* 179 (1940):218–23, 236–40 [*Titus Andronicus, 3 Henry VI, Richard II, Arden of Feversham, Julius Caesar,* Greene's *Orlando Furioso*].

Authorship

Chapman

The 1654 title-page attribution to Chapman has been generally rejected. See: Felix E. Schelling, *Foreign Influences in Elizabethan Plays* (1923); H. Dugdale Sykes, *Sidelights;* J. M. Robertson, *An Introduction* [summarizing previous scholarship on the Chapman attribution]; Franck L. Schoell, *Études sur l'humanisme continental en Angleterre* (1926); Mario Praz, "Machiavelli and the Elizabethans"; Bowers, "Date and Composition"; Havelock Ellis, *Chapman* (1934); Bradbrook, *Themes and Conventions;* Paul V. Kreider, *Elizabethan Comic Character Conventions* (1935); Wells, *"Alphonsus, Emperor of Germany";* Jean Jacquot, *George Chapman (1559–1634)* (1951); S. Schoenbaum, *Internal Evidence and Elizabethan Dramatic Authorship* (1966). Sharpe (*Real War*), however, accepts Chapman as a possible (though not the sole) author, and links the authorship of *Alphonsus* with that of *Lust's Dominion.* Georg Frohberg, "Das Fortleben des elisabethanischen Dramas im Zeitalter der Restauration," *SJ* 69 (1933): 61–86, assumes that the play is by Chapman; and Harold M. Dowling, "Peele and Some Doubtful Plays," *N&Q* 164 (1933): 366–70, suggests that *Alphonsus* "is an old Peele play [ca. 1590] revised by Chapman for a special occasion [royal performance] before 1634" with the assistance of a German collaborator. The German scenes "form an integral part of the play and are necessary to the action," and show an "intimate knowledge of German customs and modes of expression." The German dialogue in *Alphonsus* is also referred to by Schelling, *Foreign Influences.* For a lengthy treatment of the subject, see below, "Others."

Peele

Kirkman's seventeenth-century attribution of *Alphonsus* to Peele has been supported by a number of scholars. J. M. Robertson, *Shake-*

speare Canon, pt. 1, believes that Peele had a hand in the play; and H. Dugdale Sykes gives the entire play to Peele. In *Sidelights,* mentioning Robertson, Sykes cites, as proof, seventeenth- and eighteenth-century attributions, and parallels between *Alphonsus* and Peele's known work and *The Troublesome Reign of King John, Jack Straw* (both of which he believes to be Peele's), *Locrine,* and *Selimus* (in both of which he finds Peele's hand); in "Peele's Borrowings," he finds support for the Peele attribution in his discovery (mentioned in a footnote in *Sidelights* and not in the original 1916 article) that the opening soliloquy of *Alphonsus* is based on Du Bartas's "Les Artifices," which Peele uses extensively in his *David and Bethsabe.* (Cf. Robertson, *Shakespeare Canon,* pt. 1, pt. 2 [1923], *An Introduction,* and *Marlowe.*) Probably "in the existing text Peele's work has undergone some alteration by a later hand" ("Peele's Borrowings"). In *Sidelights* Sykes solves the problem of the German dialogue (the problem being that Peele nowhere else in his work shows an acquaintance with German language and customs) by suggesting that someone knowing German either assisted Peele in the original composition or revised the play for the revival performance in 1636. (Against Sykes's attribution methods, see M. St. C. Byrne, "Bibliographical Clues in Collaborate Plays," *Library* 13 [1932-33]: 21-48.)

E. H. C. Oliphant, in "How Not to Play the Game of Parallels," *JEGP* 28 (1929):1-15, accepts Sykes's case for Peele as excellent, though in general attacking Sykes's methods of attribution, and in *The Plays of Beaumont and Fletcher* (1927) assumes Peele's authorship of the anonymous play. See also Harold M. Dowling (above, "Chapman").

There have also been, however, some dissenting voices: see, for example, Bowers, "Date and Composition," who says that he is "unimpressed" by Robertson's theory. Arthur M. Sampley, " 'Verbal Tests' for Peele's Plays," *SP* 30 (1933):473-96, attacks the methods used by Sykes and Robertson in their attributions, and in "Plot Structure in Peele's Plays as a Test of Authorship," *PMLA* 51 (1936):689-701, finds that all Peele's known plays are badly constructed, and that *Alphonsus,* which is well constructed, cannot therefore by by Peele. Wells, "The Authorship of *King Leir,*" *N&Q* 177 (1939):434-38, and *"Alphonsus, Emperor of Germany,"* rejects the Peele attribution, though the latter article accepts the possibility of a later revision by Peele of an original by someone else.

Others

Wells (see above, two articles) argues for Kyd as author. In *"Alphonsus, Emperor of Germany"* he states implausibly that the play has typically Kydian construction, characterization, versification, and diction, and argues against Sykes's views especially. Kyd, he believes, may have plagiarized from Peele's work, or perhaps Peele later revised Kyd's original. In both articles Wells claims common Kydian authorship for *King Leir, The Troublesome Reign of King John*, and *Alphonsus*.

In *Shakespeare Canon*, pt. 1, Robertson gives the opening scene of *Alphonsus* to Marlowe (after 1590), and a hand in the work to Peele; in *An Introduction* he suggests collaborate authorship by Kyd (as plot-constructor), Peele, Greene, and Marlowe (to whom again he gives the opening scene); in *Marlowe* he states that the play, adapted from the Italian, was controlled by Kyd, with Marlowe writing the opening and with Peele participating in the work, with later "drastic reconstruction" during which the German matter was inserted.

Mario Praz, "Machiavelli and the Elizabethans," declares that the play was possibly written by a John Poole, to whom it is ascribed in the Stationers' Register entry of 1653. Cf. E. K. Chambers, *Elizabethan Stage* (1923), vol. 4, and G. E. Bentley, *Jacobean and Caroline Stage*, (1956) vol. 5. (Praz's *Il dramma Elisabettiano: Webster-Ford* [1940] and *The Flaming Heart* [1958] contain material on *Alphonsus* identical to that in his *PBA* lecture.)

The problem of authorship in relation to the German dialogue in *Alphonsus* is dealt with at length by Bowers, "Date and Composition," and Starck, "German Dialogue." Bowers points out that the entire theory of a German reviser or collaborator at work on *Alphonsus* developed because of the 1654 title-page attribution of the play to Chapman; when this attribution is rejected, the theory becomes unnecessary. The play, he states, is of the late sixteenth century; it contains no evidence of revision; the German parts are integral to the whole; and the style is uniform throughout. *Alphonsus* is, he maintains, a work of single authorship, unrevised, and the author is not Chapman. Starck, in his companion article, cites Bowers, and argues that the mixture of High and Low German dialect forms in the peasant scenes of *Alphonsus*, and the phonetic imitations of German mispronunciations of English words, could not have been written by a German. (He is especially concerned with disposing of the theory that George Rudolf Weckherlin was involved in the play's composition.) Moreover, he states, these would not have been unusual on the Elizabethan stage, though the play is indeed unique in its author's knowledge of Germany and in his extended use of High German. His conclusion is that the author must have known Germany at first hand, and was probably an English actor who had traveled and acted there. (Bowers, "Date and Composition," concurs.)

Harold Dowling, "Peele and Some Doubtful Plays," briefly summarizes attribution work to ca. 1933; Leonard R. N. Ashley, *Authorship and Evidence* (1968), provides a more up-to-date summary and sensibly concludes that on the evidence now available the play must be left as anonymous.

See also Heinz Reinhold, "Die metrische Verzahnung als Kriterium für Fragen der Chronologie und Authentizität...," *Archiv* 182 (1943):7-24.

The Play

Bowers, *Elizabethan Revenge Tragedy*, points out that the play is not the Kydian type of revenge tragedy, since the protagonists are a villain king and a villainous revenger of blood, and revenge is made subsidiary to the interest in villainous intrigue. The drama, he states, owes little to Seneca except in language and flavor. Allardyce Nicoll, *British Drama*, calls Alphonsus a monster of vice and the play a display of horror-incidents; "theatricality runs riot." In the plot, "Marlowe and Kyd ... meet." Sharpe, *Real War*, declares *Alphonsus* to be a tragedy in the Senecan vein, imitating Kyd and Marlowe, in which the Senecan horrors clash with the pastoral elements; Robertson, *An Introduction*, suggests Italian ancestry for the "intricacies of plot" and horrors, and in *Marlowe* believes the play to be an adaptation from the Italian.

René Wellek, "Bohemia in Early English Literature," *Slavonic and East European Review* 21 (1943):114-46, calls the drama "obviously crude anti-Spanish propaganda," and comments on the author's use of Bohemian history.

Other Studies

Mario Praz, "Machiavelli and the Elizabethans," states that Lorenzo is a caricature of Machiavelli and that Alphonsus is modeled on Cesare Borgia. The banquet at which Alphonsus tries to poison his enemies is also similar, Praz believes, to the famous historical banquet of Pope Alexander VI. Bowers, "Date and Composition," states that part of the play is derived from the German *Golden Bull* (probably in the original rather than in the English translation of 1619). Robertson, *Shakespeare Canon*, pt. 1, declares that the play contains an allusion to Cassius which suggests the existence of a now-lost sequel to the action we see in Shakespeare's *Julius Caesar*; perhaps there was another *Julius Caesar* prior to Shakespeare's. Edward M. Wilson includes *Alphonsus* in his "Family Honour in the Plays of Shakespeare's Predecessors and Contemporaries," *E&S* 6 (1953):19–40. For staging points, see Irwin Smith, *Shakespeare's Blackfriars Playhouse*, and Albert B. Weiner, "Elizabethan Interior and Aloft Scenes: A Speculative Essay," *Theatre Survey* 2 (1961):15–34. See also Bradbrook, *Themes and Conventions*.

See Also

Barber, C. L. *The Idea of Honour in the English Drama, 1591–1700.* 1957.

Foxon, D. F. *Thomas J. Wise and the Pre-Restoration Drama.* Supplement to the Bibliographical Society's Transactions, no. 19. 1959.

Linton, Marion. "The Bute Collection of English Plays." *TLS*, 21 Dec. 1956, p. 772.

Loane, George G. "More Notes on Chapman's Plays." *MLR* 38 (1943):340–47.

Maxwell, J. C. "Peele and Shakespeare: A Stylometric Test." *JEGP* 49 (1950): 557–61.

The article by B. A. P. van Dam, "R. Greene's *Alphonsus*," *ES* 13 (1931): 129–42, cited by G. E. Bentley, *Jacobean and Caroline Stage*, vol. 5 (1956), under *Alphonsus Emperor of Germany*, deals with Greene's *Alphonsus King of Aragon*.

A. L.

Edmond Ironside, or War Hath Made All Friends, history (*1595;* MS)

Editions

Since 1923, *Edmond Ironside* has been edited by Eleanore Boswell in the Malone Society series (1928, for 1927) and by Ephraim Bryson Everitt in a 1955 Ph.D. dissertation for the University of Pennsylvania, "*Edmund Ironside*: A Modern Edition with a Descriptive Analysis" (*DA* 15 [1955]:1853). Everitt also has included the play in his and R. L. Armstrong's *Six Early Plays Related to the Shakespeare Canon*, Anglistica, vol. 14 (1965).

Boswell describes the manuscript, which she finds to be scribal copy, and identifies the hand as being "of a very formal and distinctly legal type," dating "any time within a generation or so before or after 1600." The scribe's work has been gone over by a stage reviser, "whose work shows that the play was prepared for acting and was in all probability acted." There are also, she states, one or more other hands in the manuscript, making alterations and deletions; the written-in actors' names show that the play was performed in the fourth decade of the seventeenth century; and, as suggested by F. S. Boas, perhaps the manuscript was a prompt copy for provincial performance (although the play was not necessarily, as Boas believes, performed by a regular London company). Boswell gives a brief history of the collection of plays (MS. Egerton 1994) in which *Ironside* is found, and declares that the play is to be dated much earlier than the "about 1647" assigned to it by Halliwell-Phillipps. It has "many characteristics of the semi-Senecan school which flourished in the early nineties," together with other indications of an early date, including lack of dramatic structure and a close depen- dence on the source, Holinshed. The unknown author, she believes, lacks dramatic skill, shows some familiarity with the classics, and is addicted to proverbs; and perhaps the play is to be identified with the lost *Knewtus* (performed 3 Nov. 1597 by the Admiral's Men), or perhaps *Knewtus* was a second part of *Ironside*. Certainly *Iron- side* is "the most important extant dramatization of Anglo-Saxon history."

Everitt's dissertation deals with the manuscript (a prompt copy, Everitt states, written in a Legal Secretary hand and containing actors' names from the 1630s), internal evidence for a date of ca. 1590, and sources (chiefly Holinshed, Everitt believes, with Grafton for one long speech, and the influence of the *Homilies*). "The dramatization of eleventh-century military history is interspersed with fictitious scenes, some humorous," and the pattern is episodic. In a history play of this early date, "the use of dumb-show solely for condensation of action and the apparently independent development of a Machiavellian villain impute some originality to the undeter- mined author. The closest dramatic affinity of the play seems to be with *The Troublesome Raigne of King John*, printed in 1591." In his printed edition, Everitt also includes a brief discussion of the manu- script, dates the play 1590 or earlier (for various reasons, including the "archaic" diction, dumb shows, and chorus), and assigns it to Shakespeare, taking the manuscript as being in his autograph. Histori- cal background from the *Anglo-Saxon Chronicle* is also given. The theme of the troubles of a land with two strong kings is sym- metrically opposed, Everitt states, to the theme of *Woodstock*.

Text and Date

Frederick S. Boas, *Shakespeare and the Universities* (1923), states that there is insufficient evidence for determining whether the manuscript, a playhouse prompt copy, is in the author's autograph. He dates the play ca. 1590, on the evidence of style, but points out that the actors' names in the manuscript come from the fourth decade of the seventeenth century and that all the other plays collected in Egerton 1994 belong to the Stuart period. Cuts have been made in the manuscript text, some perhaps because of the censor, but most "for theatrical reasons only." M. Hope Dodds, *"Edmond Ironside* and *The Love-sick King,"* MLR 19 (1924):158–68, finds a probable date of ca. 1590 suggested by the play's style, construction, and apparent connection with Anthony Brewer's *The Lovesick King.* E. K. Chambers, *William Shakespeare* (1930), vol. 1, states that the manuscript may belong, as the play more clearly does, to the sixteenth century, and that its main hand is probably that of a professional scribe. Corrections and additions of different dates and in different hands point, he states, to seventeenth-century revivals. W. W. Greg, *Dramatic Documents from the Elizabethan Playhouses* (1931), "Commentary" [vol. 1], describes the manuscript in detail, finding it to be a playhouse copy written by a scribe who may have been a scrivener, with additions in one or more other hands, and no evidence of censorship. The play, he declares, was apparently revived in the 1620s. Alfred Hart, *Stolne and Surreptitious Copies* (1942), discusses the abridgement of the manuscript text by the actors.

In *The Young Shakespeare: Studies in Documentary Evidence*, Anglistica, vol. 2 (1954), E. B. Everitt argues for the manuscript as being in Shakespeare's (the author's) hand, and links *Ironside* with plays such as *The Troublesome Reign of King John, King Leir, Edward III,* and *The Second Maiden's Tragedy.* He believes that *Ironside* was written for Alleyn in the role of Edmond. Everitt's Shakespeare arguments are successfully attacked by Robert Adger Law in "Guessing About the Youthful Shakespeare," *Studies in English* (Univ. of Texas) 34 (1955): 43–50, and are also totally rejected by Irving Ribner, *The English History Play in the Age of Shakespeare* (1957; rev. ed. 1965). Everitt also calls *Ironside* a Queen's Men play written just before the summer of the Spanish Armada, perhaps in rivalry with *Tamburlaine.*

Robert Boies Sharpe, *The Real War of the Theaters* (1935), believing *Ironside* to contain "various reminders of historical and literary matters of about 1598," dates the play accordingly. Ribner, *English History Play*, accepts a date of ca. 1590, and David Bevington, *Tudor Drama and Politics* (1968), one of ca 1590–1600.

General Studies

The play has received a fair amount of critical attention. F. S. Boas, *Shakespeare and the Universities*, devotes an entire chapter to it; he discusses its historical subject matter, and calls it a chronicle-history "with the naïveté and the inconsecutiveness of the type," but admires the portrait of Edricus (a Machiavellian intriguer) and the choice and disposition of incidents. There is, he believes, a serious attempt to portray Edricus, Ironside, and Canute. He also states that the audiences for the seventeenth-century production must have been old-fashioned—perhaps mainly in the provinces—to have enjoyed such a play at that date, that the unknown author was well educated, and that the author's source was Holinshed, freely used. M. Hope Dodds, "*Edmond Ironside*," in suggesting that Anthony Brewer's *The Lovesick King* may borrow from *Ironside*, comments on the literary qualities of *Ironside* (its blank verse, lack of structural unity, and longwindedness) and the close following of Holinshed's *Chronicles* by the anonymous author. *Ironside* "seems to be a first part, and concludes with ominous mutterings of the disasters that are to come." Irving Ribner, *English History Play*, sees the play as a serious attempt to portray three actual historic figures (Edmond Ironside, Canute, and Edricus Duke of Mercia); the source is Holinshed, closely followed, with Edricus perhaps modeled on Shakespeare's Richard III. The play, Ribner suggests, may be an attempt to warn against the havoc wrought by internal treachery, but the work is confused and uncertain. He believes that *Ironside* was written originally for the Admiral's Men and probably had a sequel—perhaps *Knewtus* (as suggested by Boswell in her Malone Society edition), which is perhaps the Admiral's Men *Hardicanute* of 1598; and he states that the play was performed, probably in provincial touring, in the seventeenth century.

In *Shakespeare and the Allegory of Evil* (1958), Bernard Spivack includes *Ironside* in his discussion of the attempt in Elizabethan drama to fuse homiletic and naturalistic elements in the human villain who had evolved from the old Vice figure of the moralities. Edricus, in the leading role, belongs partly to Holinshed, partly to homiletic allegory, and so is not a consistent human character but one "dramatized in two contradictory dimensions, of which one is the pragmatic morality of the historic person, the other the naked homiletic exposition of the moral personification"; the Vice element dominates. Stitch, Spivack believes, is a tool villain, in which character type survives the farce element of the old Vice figure, and is left alive at the play's end only because *Ironside* is the first half of a two-part play; the second part, now lost, probably continued through the death of Edmond. *Ironside* as a whole, Spivack states, contains many of the stock techniques and motifs of the Elizabethan chronicle play.

David Bevington, *Tudor Drama*, and Robert Boies Sharpe, *Real War*, both find specific Elizabethan political applications in the play. Bevington suggests that the drama is connected with Essex, and believes that it offended the censor because of its "theme of Catholic betrayal at court permitting successful invasion of England . . . and its glorification of the military leader who is a friend of the poor and the common soldier." Sharpe had suggested thirty-three years earlier that the play might contain a parallel between Edricus and Essex, and some references to contemporary matters of ca. 1598. The subtitle (*War Hath Made All Friends*), he had pointed out, might refer to the surface reconciliation at the beginning of 1598 of conflicting court factions for and against Essex. The lost *Knewtus*, Sharpe believes, may underlie *Ironside*.

Other Studies

Clifford Leech, "The Two-Part Play. Marlowe and the Early Shakespeare," *SJ* 94 (1958): 90–106, briefly suggests that *Ironside* may be the first part of an uncompleted two-part drama conceived under the influence of *1* and *2 Tamburlaine*. MacD. P. Jackson, "Shakespeare and *Edmund Ironside*," *N&Q* 10 (1963): 331–32, dealing with authorship, cites Everitt's *The Young Shakespeare*, points out that an image cluster mentioned by Kenneth Muir in *Shakespeare as Collaborator* (1960) as peculiarly Shakespearean is also to be found in *Ironside*, and shows other image-linkages between *Ironside* and early Shakespearean works, but in the end casts general doubt on the use of image clusters as evidence for authorship.

See Also

Black, Matthew. "Enter Citizens." In *Studies in the English Renaissance Drama in Memory of Karl Julius Holzknecht*, ed. Josephine W. Bennett, Oscar Cargill, and Vernon Hall, Jr. (1959), pp. 16–27.
Braun, Margareta. *Symbolismus und Illusionismus im englischen Drama vor 1620.* 1962.

Cellini, Benvenuto, ed. *Drammi pre-Shakespeariani*. Collana di Letterature Moderne, no. 4 (1958).

McNeir, Waldo F. "Trial by Combat in Elizabethan Literature." *NS* 65 (1966): 101–12.

Reynolds, George Fullmer. *The Staging of Elizabethan Plays at the Red Bull Theater, 1605–1625*. 1940.

> The play is not included in E. K. Chambers's *Elizabethan Stage*.

A. L.

Captain Thomas Stukeley, history (*1596;* 1605)

Editions

Since Richard Simpson edited *Captain Thomas Stukeley* in his *School of Shakspere* (1878), vol. 1, there has been only one modern edition of the play: the 1968 Harvard University dissertation of Judith Charlotte Levinson. She is now preparing a reprint edition for the Malone Society.

In the introduction to her dissertation edition, Levinson first treats the question of sources, showing that *Stukeley* incorporates a wide variety of material and explaining why the origins of some of the play's details may never be known. Her section on date, after it reviews and challenges previous theories of composition, offers a new theory. When considering authorship, Levinson examines earlier scholarship, particularly the influential article by Joseph Quincy Adams, Jr. (below, "Attribution"); concludes that attributions to date rest on unsubstantial evidence; admits that she has no candidate to suggest; and attempts to construct a portrait of the anonymous dramatist from internal evidence offered by the play. She also discusses the genre of *Stukeley* and its themes, structure, and literary style. Her introduction ends with a thorough study of the text.

The 1605 text of *Stukeley* is available in microprint in Henry W. Wells, ed., *Three Centuries of Drama* (Readex Corp., 1955–56).

Attribution

Joseph Quincy Adams, Jr., in *"Captaine Thomas Stukeley," JEGP* 15 (1916):107–29, claims the Stukeley scenes in the play for Thomas Heywood, an ascription which has found favor among later scholars. In *The Plays of Beaumont and Fletcher: An Attempt to Determine Their Respective Shares and the Shares of Others* (1927), E. H. C. Oliphant finds Heywood's hand in the Stukeley portion of the play and elsewhere in it; in addition, he proposes that five other dramatists, including Marlowe, contributed to it. (See also Oliphant's "The Plays of Beaumont and Fletcher: Some Additional Notes," *PQ* 9 [1930]:7-22.) Otelia Cromwell, *Thomas Heywood: A Study in the Elizabethan Drama of Everyday Life* (1928), attempting to corroborate Adams's ascription, argues for Heywood's authorship on the basis of *Stukeley*'s loose plot, idealization of English virtues, patriotism, focus on the middle class, humor, and simple literary style. Michel Grivelet, *Thomas Heywood et le drame domestique élizabéthain* (1957), agrees with Adams's conclusions about Heywood, as does M. T. Jones-Davies, *Un peintre de la vie londonienne: Thomas Dekker* (1958), vol. 2. (Jones-Davies takes issue with Fleay's attribution of the play to Dekker.) David Bevington, *Tudor Drama and Politics* (1968), thinks that Heywood may have contributed. Levinson finds no sign of Heywood's work in *Stukeley*, nor does Arthur Melville Clark, *Thomas Heywood: Playwright and Miscellanist* (1931).

Both Harold M. Dowling, "Peele and Some Doubtful Plays," *N&Q* 164 (1933): 366-70, and Thorleif Larsen, "The Historical and Legendary Background of Peele's *Battle of Alcazar*," *PTRSC* 33 (1939), sec. ii: 185-97, disagree with earlier scholars who think that Peele was connected with *Stukeley*. Two other critics, like Levinson, believe that the identity of the author of *Stukeley* is unknowable: G. C. Duggan, *The Stage Irishman: A History of the Irish Play and Stage Characters from the Earliest Times* (1937), and Leonard R. N. Ashley, *Authorship and Evidence* (1968).

Date and Sources

There is general agreement that *Stukeley* was written several years before its entry in the Stationers' Register in 1600. William J. Lawrence, *Pre-Restoration Stage Studies* (1927), finds a correspondence with Marlowe's *2 Tamburlaine the Great* (1588) in the anonymous play which suggests to him a date earlier than 1596 (the date usually assigned). Oliphant, *The Plays of Beaumont and Fletcher*, concurs with earlier scholarship which fixes the *terminus ad quem* at 1598; Duggan considers *Stukeley* as an early Elizabethan play written close to the time when Stukeley and Shane O'Neill were figures of public significance; and Larsen says simply that *Stukeley* probably dates much before 1600 (all in "Attribution"). In *The English History Play in the Age of Shakespeare* (1957; rev. ed. 1965),

Irving Ribner assumes that the play was on the stage in 1596 and describes the contemporary meaning it had at that time. John Yoklavich, ed., *The Battle of Alcazar*, in *The Dramatic Works of George Peele*, in the Yale *Life and Works of George Peele*, gen. ed. Charles T. Prouty, (1961) vol. 2, provides evidence to show that *Stukeley* must be dated before 1600; David Beers Quinn, *The Elizabethans and the Irish*, Folger Monographs on Tudor and Stuart Civilization (1966), maintains that the date of the play is 1596 or earlier. Bevington ("Attribution") says that *Stukeley* "is an updating (ca. 1599) of earlier dramatic accounts of the title figure."

The views about sources which Levinson puts forth in her edition are restated in her article "The Sources of *Captain Thomas Stukeley*," *ELN* 9 (1971):85–90. Both Larsen ("Attribution") and Yoklavich (above) think that *Stukeley* may be based in part on ephemeral literature: ballads, chapbooks, tracts. Yoklavich also believes that oral tradition influenced the anonymous playwright. In *"Captain Thomas Stukeley,"* *N&Q* 10 (1963):96–98, he claims that the principal sources are still unknown and offers evidence to suggest that a few details in one plot derive from a tract entitled *The Explanation. Of the True and Lawfull Right and Tytle, of the Moste Excellent Prince, Anthonie . . .* [1585].

Theories of Composition

As Levinson, Larsen, and Yoklavich point out and corroborate in their studies, most scholars now concur on two important issues in their theories about the play's composition: an original version, called "stewtley," was recorded by Henslowe in 1596; and that version was crudely revised as *Stukeley*. Clark, Jones-Davies (both in "Attribution"), and Ribner ("Date") seem confident of that theory; Oliphant, *The Plays* ("Attribution"), bases an elaborate and unconvincing theory of composition on it. Levinson proposes that the revision might have been done for printing rather than for stage revival. In his 1923 work for the Malone Society, *Two Elizabethan Stage Abridgements: "The Battle of Alcazar" & "Orlando Furioso":An Essay in Critical Bibliography*, W. W. Greg said that there was probably some connection between the two plays. Grivelet ("Attribution") thinks that the two dramas are probably identical. Some writers apparently prefer not to link the two plays: see, for example, Cromwell and Larsen (both in "Attribution"); and Robert Boies Sharpe, *The Real War of the Theaters: Shakespeare's Fellows in*

Rivalry with the Admiral's Men, 1594-1603 (1935). Useful reviews of scholarship about theories of composition appear in the two works of Yoklavich's cited above ("Date"), and in Levinson's dissertation edition.

Greg suggests on the basis of a passage in *Satiromastix* (1601) that Dekker may have borrowed material from Peele's *Battle of Alcazar* (1589) for both "stewtley" and *Stukeley*, whereas Sharpe maintains that a fragment of the Peele play is used in *Stukeley*. In the opinion of Ashley (1968; "Attribution"), it is useful to look at the two plays together; though Yoklavich in his 1961 edition ("Date") had implied that such a comparison would be fruitless, since it cannot be proved that either playwright borrowed from the other. (See also Yoklavich's article, in "Date.") Ernest A. Gerrard, *Elizabethan Drama and Dramatists, 1583-1603* (1928), believes that an early Peele or Marlowe play probably lay behind both *Stukeley* and *The Battle of Alcazar*; and Greg proposes that *Stukeley* may contain whatever survives of *Muly Molloco* (1599).

Literary Connections and Miscellaneous

R. P. Cowl, *Sources of the Text of "Henry the Fourth"* (1929), finds an echo of *2 Henry IV* in *Stukeley*; Sharpe ("Theories of Composition") and Ribner ("Date") point out imitations of Marlowe's *Tamburlaine* in the anonymous play.

The genre of *Stukeley*, biographical history, receives attention from Cromwell ("Attribution"); Willard Farnham, *The Medieval Heritage of Elizabethan Tragedy* (1936); Ribner ("Date"); and Yoklavich (edition and article, in "Date").

The background and/or characterization of the play's protagonist are considered by Cromwell and Larsen (both in "Attribution"); Sharpe ("Theories of Composition"); G. Geoffrey Langsam, *Martial Books and Tudor Verse* (1951); and Robert Kimbrough, *Shakespeare's "Troilus and Cressida" and Its Setting* (1964).

Several writers discuss the use of Irish characters, language, or topography: Duggan ("Attribution"); Florence R. Scott, "Teg—The Stage Irishman," *MLR* 42 (1947):314-20; J. O. Bartley, *Teague, Shenkin, and Sawney* (1954; see also his article "The Development of a Stock Character," *MLR* 37[1942]:438-47); and Quinn ("Date").

Concerned with textual matters, Duggan ("Attribution") comments on Simpson's edition of *Stukeley*, and Wilfred T. Jewkes, *Act Division in Elizabethan and Jacobean Plays, 1583-1616* (1958), find evidence that the text is playhouse copy if not the official prompt-book or a transcript from it. The function of the dumb show in the play receives consideration from both B. R. Pearn, "Dumb-Show in Elizabethan Drama," *RES* 11 (1935):385–405, and Dieter Mehl, *The Elizabethan Dumb Show* (1966; German ed. 1964). Samuel C. Chew, *The Crescent and the Rose* (1937), remarks that the last two acts of *Stukeley* are incoherent.

See Also

Baldwin, T. W. *On the Literary Genetics of Shakspere's Plays, 1592-1594.* 1959.

Cawley, Robert Ralston. *Unpathed Waters: Studies in the Influence of the Voyagers on Elizabethan Literature.* 1940.

Doran, Madeleine. *Endeavors of Art: A Study of Form in Elizabethan Drama.* 1954.

Harbage, Alfred. *Shakespeare and the Rival Traditions.* 1952.

Harrison, G. B. *Elizabethan Plays and Players.* 1940.

Hinton, Edward M. *Ireland Through Tudor Eyes.* 1935.

Horne, David H. *The Life and Minor Works of George Peele.* In the Yale *Life and Works of George Peele*, gen. ed. Charles T. Prouty, vol. 1 (1952).

Izon, John. *Sir Thomas Stucley, c. 1525-1578: Traitor Extraordinary.* The Rogues Gallery, no. 4 (1956).

Jones, Eldred D. *Othello's Countrymen: The African in English Renaissance Drama.* 1965.

Larsen, Thorleif. "The Growth of the Peele Canon." *Library* 11 (1930):300–311.

Lebel, Roland. *Le Maroc chez les auteurs anglais du XVIe au XIXe siècle.* 1939.

Linton, Marion. "The Bute Collection of English Plays." *TLS*, 21 Dec. 1956, p. 772.

———. "National Library of Scotland and Edinburgh University Library Copies of Plays in Greg's *Bibliography of the English Printed Drama.*" *SB* 15 (1962): 91–104.

Nicoll, Allardyce. " 'Tragical-Comical-Historical-Pastoral': Elizabethan Dramatic Nomenclature." *BJRL* 43 (1960):70–87.

Reynolds, George Fullmer. *The Staging of Elizabethan Plays at the Red Bull Theater, 1605-1625.* 1940.

Roberts, Donald R. " 'Miching Mallico.' " *TLS*, 18 April 1936, p. 336.

Sherbo, Arthur. *English Sentimental Drama.* 1957.

Tillyard, E. M. W. *Shakespeare's History Plays.* 1944.

Velte, F. Mowbray. *The Bourgeois Elements in the Dramas of Thomas Heywood.* 1924.

Wright, Louis B. "Elizabethan Sea Drama and Its Staging." *Anglia* 51 (1927): 104–18.

———. *Middle-Class Culture in Elizabethan England.* 1935.

J. L.

A Larum for London, or The Siege of Antwerp, history (*1599;* 1602)

Editions

A Larum for London is available in microprint in Henry W. Wells, ed., *Three Centuries of Drama* (Readex Microprint Corp., 1955–56).

Authorship

Recent authorship candidates include Kyd, Lodge, Marlowe, Barnaby Rich, and Robert Wilson. No one attribution has been generally accepted.

Marlowe

Marlowe authorship is briefly rejected by Tucker Brooke, "The Marlowe Canon," *PMLA* 37 (1922):367–417, and by John Bakeless, *The Tragicall History of Christopher Marlowe* (1942), vol. 2, but is favored by J. M. Robertson and Marion Bodwell Smith. Robertson, in *An Introduction to the Study of the Shakespeare Canon* (1924), suggests that the play was written before 1594 by Marlowe and Lodge as collaborators, or that Marlowe began the play and Lodge later finished it; and Marston may have had a hand in it. In *Marlowe: A Conspectus* (1931) he states that the drama was begun by Marlowe ca. 1590 and was completed and perhaps revised by Lodge, and rejects the Marston possibility. Smith, *Marlowe's Imagery and the Marlowe Canon* (1940), finds that "the proportion of images to lines in this play [*A Larum for London*] accords well with the norm for Marlowe's works, while its imagery pattern resembles closely that of *The Massacre at Paris*," and so believes Marlowe to be the play's chief author.

Wilson

S. R. Golding, "Robert Wilson and *Sir Thomas More*," *N&Q* 154 (1928): 237–39, declares *A Larum for London* to be perhaps "a recast by Wilson of an earlier play, probably one of which he was the author"; other "Wilson" plays in which he finds parallels with *A Larum* include *Fair Em, Sir John Oldcastle, Knack to Know a Knave,* and *Look About You.* ·E. H. C. Oliphant, "How Not to Play the Game of Parallels," *JEGP* 28 (1929):1–15, successfully attacks Golding's attribution methods.

Lodge, Rich, Kyd

Robert Boies Sharpe, *The Real War of the Theaters* (1935), briefly suggests that the play was perhaps written by Lodge as early as 1590-94 and revived at the Spanish scares of 1597 and 1599. See also Robertson (above). Fernando Ferrara summarizes and evaluates some previous authorship attributions and argues at length for the authorship of Barnaby Rich, in "Barnabe Riche, difensore del soldato inglese e autore di *A Larum for London*," *EM* 8 (1957):21-54. Ferrara finds similarities between *A Larum* and Rich's known works, including some in departures of *A Larum* from its source (Gascoigne's *The Spoyle of Antwerpe*), and views Stump as "una oggettivazione drammatica dello stesso autore." The play, he believes, was written under the influence of *A Looking Glass for London and England*, and probably influenced *The Massacre at Paris*. Finally, A. Bronson Feldman, "The Rape of Antwerp in a Tudor Play," *N&Q* 5 (1958): 246-48, in passing gives the play to Kyd; *A Larum* "is pungently thick with reminders of his [Kyd's] *Jeronimo*."

General Studies

Scholars generally agree that *A Larum* is above all a politically didactic work about the vulnerability to attack and destruction of a city (specifically, London) indifferent to military preparations and defense. See: Evelyn May Albright, *Dramatic Publication in England, 1580-1640* (1927); Fernando Ferrara, "Barnabe Riche"; A. Bronson Feldman, "Rape of Antwerp"; Bernard Beckerman, *Shakespeare at the Globe, 1599-1609* (1962); David Bevington, *Tudor Drama and Politics* (1968); Mary Crapo Hyde, *Playwriting for Elizabethans, 1600-1605* (1949). These scholars also have, however, other points to make about the play. Albright states that the drama probably was acted some years before its Stationers' Register entry of 1600 and was printed [in 1602] because of current alarm over the possible betrayal of England to Spain. Ferrara views the play as a human and social document rather than as a work of literary importance, and dates it 1587-88, believing it to show the influence of *Tamourlaine* but to predate the Spanish Armada of 1588. Feldman maintains that Stump, who "exemplifies the ideal of the Christian warrior upheld by his countryman Erasmus," is vitally portrayed, although the rest of the drama "is mere dumbshow and noise." Some version of the play, he believes, may have been current on the London stage shortly after the event of Nov. 1576 which the drama portrays; and the author's source for the twelfth scene may have been a lost tragedy named

Timoclea at the Siege of Thebes (performed at court in Feb. 1574 and doubtless inspired by Plutarch) or perhaps Plutarch directly. Beckerman calls *A Larum* a play of a single theme—that the English will be destroyed by external enemies and internal treachery unless they forego personal profit and turn to the defense of the state—but with "a multiple reflection of its theme in a number of independent scenes, each having equal emphasis." The structure, he says, is split: the story moves one way, then shifts direction after the first half of the drama. Beckerman also comments on staging.

David Bevington sees the play in specific political terms, as an example of extremist support of the Earl of Essex, and as anti-Catholic propaganda, "based on raw pamphlet and ballad accounts of a continental atrocity against Protestants." Mary Crapo Hyde finds the play to resemble documentary reporting, and declares that it is not a pure history play.

A Larum is seen by S. M. Pratt, "Antwerp and the Elizabethan Mind," *MLQ* 24 (1963):53–60, as belonging to the "genre of alarm," which developed from the religious tradition of denouncing sin. He states that the play is one of a number of Elizabethan works about Antwerp which view that city's fall as a moral example for mankind, and that the source is Gascoigne's *The Spoyle of Antwerpe* (1576).

Other Studies

Links between *A Larum* and Shakespeare's works are posited by R. P. Cowl, "Echoes of *Henry the Fourth* in Elizabethan Drama," *TLS*, 22 Oct. 1925, p. 697, and George C. Taylor, "Hermione's Statue Again," *ShAB* 13 (1938):82–86. Cowl finds echoes of *1* and *2 Henry IV* in *A Larum*, though he admits the possibility that Shakespeare's work may echo the anonymous play, which he dates 1594–1600. Taylor believes that the mock-death of Alva in *A Larum* (or the statue device in *The Trial of Chivalry*) may have suggested to Shakespeare the statue device in *The Winter's Tale*; for a different view, see Ferrara, "Barnabe Riche."

Leo Kirschbaum, *Shakespeare and the Stationers* (1955), declares the 1600 Stationers' Register entry to have been a blocking entry (see also Albright, *Dramatic Publication*), and the 1602 quarto to have been perhaps unauthorized. The printer's copy, he states, seems to have been authorial, not playhouse, copy. Wilfred T. Jewkes, on the other hand, in *Act Division in Elizabethan and Jacobean Plays, 1583–1616* (1958), believes the play to have been printed from "bad" copy, probably memorially reconstructed for performance. William J. Lawrence, *Pre-Restoration Stage Studies* (1927), points out a necessary emendation of "horse" to "hearse."

See Also

Black, Matthew. "Enter Citizens." In *Studies in the English Renaissance Drama in Memory of Karl Julius Holzknecht,* ed. Josephine W. Bennett, Oscar Cargill, and Vernon Hall, Jr. (1959), pp. 16–27.
Jorgensen, Paul A. "Shakespeare's Use of War and Peace." *HLQ* 16 (1952–53): 319–52.
Langsam, G. Geoffrey. *Martial Books and Tudor Verse.* 1951.
Paul, Emil. "Über *A Larum for London or The Siege of Antwerpe.*" Erlangen dissertation, 1921: printed two-page summary [not seen].
Wasson, John Marvin. "The Elizabethan History Play: A Study of its Types and Dramatic Techniques." Ph.D. dissertation, Stanford Univ.: *DA* 20 (1959): 1358–59.

A. L.

Look About You, comedy (*1599;* 1600)

Editions

Look About You has been edited by Anne Charlotte Begor in a 1965 Ph.D. dissertation for Harvard University, "*Look About You*: A Critical Edition" (*DA* 32 [1971|:907A). The modern-spelling text is accompanied by an introduction, textual notes, critical commentary on the text, and eight appendices; the introduction deals with genre, sources, Shakespeare connections, date and title, authorship, literary analysis, text, and previous modern editions. The play, Begor asserts, is not only a multiple-disguise comedy but also a genuine history play, and its sources are basically chronicle history, Robin Hood tradition, the legend of Fair Rosamond, and stories of the Bastard Faulconbridge. She declares that it is linked definitely to *1 Henry IV* and possibly to *Comedy of Errors* and *King John,* and was probably written between late 1598 and early 1599; and there is no evidence that it was ever known by a title different from its present one. The author she believes to be probably Henry Chettle or Anthony Munday, or a special combination of the two (Munday as plot-designer, Chettle as dialogue-writer); and in structure, characterization, and style the play is superior to most other minor Elizabethan dramas. The text was partially proofread and corrected while being printed, and appears to have been set up from authorial foul papers or fair copy, presumably legally obtained. "Headline analysis reveals that the first four gatherings of the play were printed with one skeleton but the last seven gatherings with two."

Look About You is also available in microprint in Henry W. Wells, ed., *Three Centuries of Drama* (Readex Microprint Corp., 1955-56).

Authorship

S. R. Golding, in "Robert Wilson and *Sir Thomas More,*" *N&Q* 154 (1928):237-39, takes *Look About You* to be Wilson's; the attribution is summarily dismissed by E. H. C. Oliphant in "How Not to Play the Game of Parallels," *JEGP* 28 (1929):1-15, and is not even considered by other scholars, who variously suggest as the *Look About You* author Henry Chettle, Anthony Munday, Antony Wadeson, and others. Chettle has been put forward as sole author (though perhaps in collaboration with Munday) by H. Dugdale Sykes, "The Dramatic Work of Henry Chettle," *N&Q* 144 (1923): 263-65, 283-86, 303-6, 324-27 (especially), 345-47, 365-66, 386-89, who bases his attribution on entirely untenable parallels; his case is accepted, however, by Fred L. Jones, "*Look About You* and *The Disguises,*" *PMLA* 44 (1929):835-41, who calls *Look About You* one of Chettle's earliest plays and identifies it with the supposedly-lost *The Disguises* of 1595. Harold Jenkins, Chettle's only book-length biographer (*The Life and Work of Henry Chettle* [1934]), attacks Sykes's attribution methods—as does M. St. C. Byrne, "Bibliographical Clues in Collaborate Plays," *Library* 13 (1932-33): 21-48—and points out that the similarities between *Look About You* and Chettle's known work are typical of much of the drama of the period. Participation by Chettle in the composition of *Look About You* is not impossible, "but the same might be said of almost any other anonymous play dated between 1593 and 1606." Malcolm A. Nelson, "*Look About You* and the Robin Hood Tradition," *N&Q* 9 (1962):141-43, also remains unconvinced by Sykes's Chettle parallels.

William J. Lawrence, *Pre-Restoration Stage Studies* (1927), rejects Fleay's attribution of *Look About You* to Anthony Wadeson and, following Sykes, suggests collaborate Munday-Chettle authorship (the play, he states, is probably by two authors); but Jenkins, *Henry Chettle*, considers Wadeson to be a possibility, at least as part-author, and Wilfred T. Jewkes, *Act Division in Elizabethan and Jacobean Plays, 1583-1616* (1958), assumes *Look About You* likely to be Wadeson's. M. T. Jones-Davies, *Un peintre de la vie londonienne, Thomas Dekker* (1958), 2 vols., declines, in spite of similarities between *Look About You* and Dekker's work, to challenge Greg's Wadeson attribution. See also Sharpe, below.

Previous authorship work is summarized by Jenkins, *Henry Chettle*.

Title and Date

Look About You, because of its indefinite title and lack of Stationers' Register entry, has often been identified, though without plausible evidence, with various recorded and supposedly lost plays of the 1590s. Jones, *"Look About You,"* believes it to be *The Disguises* of 1595 because of its relationship to *The Downfall of Robert Earl of Huntingdon, The Death of Robert Earl of Huntingdon, The Blind Beggar of Alexandria,* and *John a Kent and John a Cumber*; Robert Boies Sharpe, *The Real War of the Theaters* (1935), also makes this identification, giving the authorship to Munday, and argues that the 1595 play was then rewritten in 1599 as Dekker's *Bear a Brain*. A *Bear a Brain* identification is suggested as a possibility by Jenkins, *Henry Chettle*, and is rejected by Lawrence, *Pre-Restoration Stage Studies*, who also denies a *The Disguises* identification and proposes that *Look About You* is possibly Chettle's "lost" *'Tis No Deceit to Deceive the Deceiver*.

Karl J. Holzknecht, "Theatrical Billposting in the Age of Elizabeth," *PQ* 2 (1923):267–81, calls the play-name *Look About You* simply a catch title to attract attention, an instance of "good showmanship."

Jenkins, *Henry Chettle*, and Nelson, *"Look About You,"* both reject Jones's 1595 date; Jenkins places the play probably not before 1598, and Nelson dates it in late 1598 or early 1599, both scholars finding the drama to postdate *The Downfall* and *The Death* in its use of Robin Hood tradition, and Nelson pointing out that *Look About You* echoes *1 Henry IV*, especially in Prince John's resemblance to Shakespeare's Hotspur. William E. Simeone, "Renaissance Robin Hood Plays," in *Folklore in Action: Essays for Discussion in Honor of MacEdward Leach*, ed. Horace P. Beck (1962), pp. 184–99, declares that the play was probably acted in 1599, after *The Downfall* and *The Death*; and Anne B[egor] Lancashire, *"Look About You* as a History Play," *SEL* 9 (1969): 321–34, points out a probable specific political parallel in the work which agrees with a date of late 1598 to early 1599.

The Play

Look About You has attracted critical attention as a Robin Hood drama, a multiple-disguise comedy, and a history play. Lawrence, *Pre-Restoration Stage Studies,* discusses *Look About You* as "the best complex-disguise play of its period," and calls it not a comedy but "a chronicle history humorously told." Skink, according to Lawrence, is the mainspring of the action. Sharpe, *Real War,* agrees that *Look About You* is "the cleverest and jolliest" of the multiple-disguise plays, and discusses it in this context, but also remarks that the "closing lines, read in the light of the play's marked anti-abdication propaganda, seem designed to foster those bitter suspicions of Essex which the party hostile to him were diffusing from 1597 until his downfall." The dual comical-historical nature of the play is also mentioned by M. C. Bradbrook, *Shakespeare and Elizabethan Poetry* (1951), who finds in *Look About You* "the tone and atmosphere of revelry, horseplay, good fellowship, and patriotic fervour." The play is in the English comic tradition of "Merry England, where the king revelled and reigned as king of good fellows." E. M. W. Tillyard, *Shakespeare's History Plays* (1944), and Irving Ribner, *The English History Play in the Age of Shakespeare* (1957; rev. ed. 1965), believe the play to be almost entirely unhistorical, Ribner calling it a "historical romance" focused on Robin Hood legend and disguise comedy; but Anne B. Lancashire, "*Look About You,*" points out definitely historical subject matter and purpose in the work. The anonymous author draws extensively on chronicle history (especially on Holinshed's *Chronicles*), and uses the play for purposes of "political didacticism, and the stimulation of patriotism, in relation to contemporary political problems," referring specifically to the monarchical aspirations of the Earl of Essex ca. 1598–99.

Simeone, "Renaissance Robin Hood Plays," deals with *Look About You* as one of a group of Robin Hood plays, and finds it to be unique in using only the historical (and not the pastoral) tradition of Robin Hood; he denies Ribner's claim that the play's focus is on Robin Hood tradition, and discusses Robin as "one of several equally important characters" in the work. For other treatments of Robin Hood material in *Look About You,* see Jones, "*Look About You,*" Jenkins, *Henry Chettle,* and Nelson, "*Look About You,*" though Jones views the drama above all as a multiple-disguise play.

Other Studies

Ruth Wallerstein, *King John in Fact and Fiction* (1921), mentions *Look About You* as a play in which John appears as a villainous character (Richard, she says, is the hero of the work), and calls the drama "incoherent, mingling true dignity in some scenes with the greatest coarseness and impossible farce in others"; somewhat the same criticism is made by Ola Elizabeth Winslow, *Low Comedy as a Structural Element in English Drama from the Beginnings to 1642* (1926), who states that the play sins against decorum in its use of low comedy.

Staging points are made by Lawrence, *Pre-Restoration Stage Studies*, and by Louis B. Wright, "Stage Duelling in the Elizabethan Theatre," *MLR* 22 (1927):265–75. Lawrence also finds Jaques's "All the world's a stage" speech in *As You Like It* to have been inspired by the seven parts played by one actor in *Look About You*.

Sharpe, *Real War*, finds an influence of *Look About You* on *Fair Maid of the Exchange*, and a link between *Look About You* and *King John*. Elmer Edgar Stoll, *Shakespeare Studies* (1927), points out an echo in *Look About You* of *1 Henry IV*.

Jewkes, *Act Division*, declares that the 1600 quarto appears to have been printed from an author's manuscript and contains little evidence of playhouse preparation.

See Also

Albright, Evelyn May. *Dramatic Publication in England, 1580–1640.* 1927.
Bowden, William R. *The English Dramatic Lyric, 1603–42.* 1951.
Heltzel, Virgil B. *Fair Rosamond: A Study of the Development of a Literary Theme.* 1927.
Mehl, Dieter. *The Elizabethan Dumb Show.* 1965; German ed. 1964.
Reese, Gertrude Catherine. "The Question of the Succession in Elizabethan Drama." *Studies in English* (Univ. of Texas) 22 (1942):59–85.

A. L.

The Thracian Wonder, comedy (*1599;* 1661)

Authorship

The 1661 quarto title-page attribution to Webster and William Rowley has been generally rejected. See: Marvin T. Herrick, *Tragicomedy* (1955)– "there is no good reason for attributing it to Webster"; S. Schoenbaum, *Internal Evidence and Elizabethan Dramatic Authorship* (1966); F. L. Lucas, ed., *The Complete Works of John Webster* (1927), vol. 4, who summarizes attribution scholar-ship to 1910, and says that Webster may possibly have done a quick revision of the play, but no more. The old Heywood attribution is cited but called "very problematical" by Mowbray Velte, *The Bourgeois Elements in the Dramas of Thomas Heywood* (1922), and is entirely rejected by Arthur Melville Clark, *Thomas Heywood: Playwright and Miscellanist* (1931). Clark states that the play is "like an inexperienced playwright's imitation of a fashion that had gone out before Heywood's arrival."

The play is not treated as Webster's in the compendious *John Webster* (1968) of Fernand Lagarde.

Other Studies

Herrick, *Tragicomedy*, calls the play an interesting example of a "tragical-comical-historical-pastoral play" comparable to *Pericles* and *The Winter's Tale*; Clark, *Thomas Heywood*, speaks of *"The Thracian Wonder*'s vulgar, stupid amalgam of courts and sheep-cotes, kings and shepherds," and calls the style at best undramatic. In *Tudor Drama and Politics* (1968) David Bevington states that the play shows the courtly vogue for genteel escapism, with its debt to Spenser and Lyly, love debates, courtiers in rustic disguise, and pagan gods. The pastoral here, he suggests, is elitist, artificial and detached. J. H. P. Pafford in his Arden edition (1963) of *The Winter's Tale* mentions the similarity (pointed out in older scholarship) between the plots of *The Winter's Tale* and *The Thracian Wonder*, and the anonymous play's resemblance (previously noted by Hatcher, *MLN*, 1908) to Greene's *Orlando Furioso*.

The play is used by Richard Hosley, "Was there a Music-room in Shakespeare's Globe?" *ShS* 13 (1960):113–23, as evidence for the Elizabethan music room being equipped with curtains, located above the stage, and sometimes used for dramatic action.

See Also

Bowers, Fredson. "The First Series of Plays Published by Francis Kirkman in 1661." *Library* 2 (1947–48):289–91.

Gibson, Strickland. "A Bibliography of Francis Kirkman." *Oxford Bibliographical Society Publications* 1 (1947):47–148.

Mehl, Dieter. *The Elizabethan Dumb Show.* 1965; German ed. 1964.

Pearn, B. R. "Dumb-Show in Elizabethan Drama." *RES* 11 (1935):385–405.

A. L.

A Warning for Fair Women, tragedy (*1599;* 1599)

Editions

A Warning for Fair Women has been edited by Dorothy Cohen in a
1957 Radcliffe College Ph.D. dissertation (not in *DA* and nowhere
described), and by Charles Dale Cannon, "*A Warning for Fair Women:
A Critical Edition*," as a Ph.D. dissertation for the University of
Missouri (*DA* 25 [1964]:1889–90). Cannon examines the text,
source, authorship, staging, and date, gives an account of past criticism, and evaluates the play as a literary work. The printer's copy, he
finds, was probably authorial fair copy, with the possible exception
of signature H, where the printer appears to have been working from
prompt copy; the primary source is Arthur Golding's *A Brief Discourse* (1573; rpt. 1577); evidence is insufficient to establish the
play's author, but sufficient to show that the drama cannot be
attributed to either Kyd or Heywood. Internal evidence suggests to
him public performance, possibly but not certainly at the Globe. The
play, he states, is to be dated between the mid 1580s and 1599, and
is one of the best extant domestic tragedies, surpassed only by *Arden
of Feversham* and *A Woman Killed with Kindness*.

 A Warning for Fair Women is also available in microprint in Henry
W. Wells, ed., *Three Centuries ˙of Drama* (Readex Microprint Corp.,
1955–56).

Authorship

 Drayton, Thomas Heywood, Kyd, and Lodge have all been authorship candidates, but no firm case has been made for any one dramatist. Wilfred T. Jewkes, *Act Division in Elizabethan and Jacobean
Plays, 1583–1616* (1958), believes the Heywood attribution to be the
strongest; but Heywood has been queried or rejected as author by
other scholars since 1922. Mowbray Velte, *The Bourgeois Elements in
the Dramas of Thomas Heywood* (1922), cannot accept Heywood as
author without further proof; Otelia Cromwell, *Thomas Heywood: A
Study in the Elizabethan Drama of Everyday Life* (1928), finds
similarities between *A Warning for Fair Women* and Heywood's
known works, in atmosphere, some stylistic details, ethics, and
simplicity, but differences in structure and sentiment, style, and
thought, and points out that Heywood's plays usually contain comic
relief but *A Warning for Fair Women* does not. Moreover, she asserts,
A Warning for Fair Women has artistic merit beyond Heywood's

capabilities, though Heywood might possibly have written an original rough draft, based on a plot by someone else, which was then revised by another dramatist into the play we know. Arthur Melville Clark, *Thomas Heywood: Playwright and Miscellanist* (1931), summarizes previous attributions and states that the characters, structure, style, and vocabulary are all unlike Heywood; and the attribution is also rejected by Michel Grivelet in his *Thomas Heywood et le drame domestique élizabéthain* (1957).

J. M. Robertson moves, in three books, from a hesitant to a definite acceptance of Kyd's authorship (suggested earlier by Sykes). *The Shakespeare Canon*, pt. 1 (1922), cautiously states that *A Warning for Fair Women* might well be a late work of Kyd's, and that Drayton's hand in the piece is barely possible; *An Introduction to the Study of the Shakespeare Canon* (1924) suggests Kyd, and possibly Marston in the Induction, but leaves the matter open, and definitely rejects Lodge; *Literary Detection* (1931) argues for Kyd, but with Lodge or another as possibly associated with Kyd in the Induction or even in the play. See also *The Shakespeare Canon*, pt. 4, div. 1 (1930). Robert Boies Sharpe, *The Real War of the Theaters* (1935), puts forward Lodge as a possible author; H. W. Crundell, "Drayton and *Edward III*," *N&Q* 176 (1939):258–60, points out that *A Warning for Fair Women* (a "Holinshed play") contains verse in Drayton's manner.

Literary Connections and Date

See: J. M. Robertson, *Shakespeare Canon*, pt. 1 [*Richard III, Macbeth, Julius Caesar, Arden of Feversham*], *An Introduction* [*Macbeth, Julius Caesar, Arden*], *Literary Detection* [*Macbeth, Arden, Soliman and Perseda*]; Sharpe, *Real War* [*Arden, Spanish Tragedy, Hamlet, Edward II, Doctor Faustus, Locrine, Battle of Alcazar, Sir John Oldcastle, Henry V, Macbeth, Julius Caesar*, Marston's *Antonio* plays]; Grivelet, *Thomas Heywood* [*Arden*]. Robertson, *Literary Detection*, dates the play ca. 1595. See also Sharpe, *Real War*.

Henry Hitch Adams, *English Domestic or, Homiletic Tragedy, 1575 to 1642* (1943), calls the opening of *A Warning for Fair Women* "an evident imitation" of the beginning of Robert Yarington's *Two Lamentable Tragedies* (ca. 1594). Sources of the play, he states, are *A Brief Discourse* and Stow's *Chronicle*.

Clark, *Thomas Heywood*, dates the play several years before 1599; Crundell, "Drayton and *Edward III*," places it in 1598–99.

The Play

Criticism of *A Warning for Fair Women* as a dramatic work invariably focuses on the genre of domestic tragedy: as, for example, in Grivelet's *Thomas Heywood*. Sharpe, *Real War*, suggests that the play began an important revival of domestic tragedies ca. 1598, the genre having lapsed since ca. 1592. Adams, *English Domestic or, Homiletic Tragedy*, above all uses the play as an example of the moral instructiveness of domestic tragedy. *A Warning for Fair Women*, he declares, insists on Christian morality and shows how sin is punished by Divine Providence. It contains allegorical characters, thus preserving a morality-play framework, and shows the growth of vice infecting the soul. Browne's repentance at the end echoes the prodigal son plays. The author tries to depict everyday life realistically, but his emphasis on theological exhortation brings the action to a standstill; the "combination of psychological and theological approach failed to occur to the writer." The same accusation—of moralistic overemphasis which "seriously clogs the action" (Doran) is made by Madeleine Doran, *Endeavors of Art: A Study of Form in Elizabethan Drama* (1954), who calls the play a dramatized sermon and sees it as combining Senecan tragedy and the native English moral play, and by Frederick S. Boas, *An Introduction to Tudor Drama* (1933). Dieter Mehl, *The Elizabethan Dumb Show* (1965; German ed. 1964), deals above all with how in *A Warning for Fair Women* scenes of realistic tragedy alternate with morally instructive allegorical dumb shows, creating two levels in the play, in two different styles. The style of the popular histories and interludes blends, he declares, with the tradition of classical drama, and the allegoric figures of the frame establish contact between the audience and the characters of the play. According to Mehl, the dramatist is above all concerned with staging exciting events, not with deeper motives and inner conflicts behind the action; even developments within characters are presented as visible actions. The aim is to please a wide public and to offer moral instruction. Mehl deals at length with the individual dumb shows, and declares that an original element of the play is that an event "decisive for the advance of the plot [Anne's change in attitude towards Browne] is only represented in the form of an allegorical mime." He views the play as part of a general pattern of development in English drama.

Willard Farnham, *The Medieval Heritage of Elizabethan Tragedy* (1936), and Dieter Mehl, "Forms and Functions of the Play within a

Play," *RenD* 8 (1965):41–61, both focus on the Induction (which is commented on and quoted by many scholars because of its "definitions" of dramatic genres). Farnham views it as showing the popularity of "the Kydian drama of intrigue" and as suggesting the kinship of domestic tragedy with the Kydian form. Kyd's type of drama, he states, probably stimulated interest in the dramatization of famous, everyday murders. He believes that the play itself, like *Arden of Feversham*, has a realistic effectiveness, and is simpler in structure than *The Spanish Tragedy*. Mehl believes that the Induction characterizes the play distinctly as a play and brings out the moral message of the action. A. P. Rossiter, *English Drama from Early Times to the Elizabethans* (1950), comments on the mixture of realism and moral abstraction, and sees the play as exemplifying the "moral" trend in the staging of "history," since the murder it dramatizes is not recent but from the past. David Bevington, *Tudor Drama and Politics* (1968), briefly calls the play a homiletic tragedy emphasizing God as an avenger who works not only through providential miracle and individual conscience but also through human legal institutions.

In *The British Drama* (1962), Allardyce Nicoll states that some scenes are almost melodramatically absurd, but that some are realistic, showing that the author was seeking a "documentary" effect and was to some extent skilled in recording common speech and characters. G. B. Harrison, *Elizabethan Plays and Players* (1940), finds the play, as a domestic tragedy, to be a good mixture of tragedy, horror, pathos, and edification. The verse, he states, is never excellent but is seldom utter doggerel. Grivelet, *Thomas Heywood*, believes that sensationalism dominates; Robertson, *Literary Detection*, calls the verse generally plodding and prosaic. Otelia Cromwell, *Thomas Heywood*, briefly discusses the play, pointing out that it gives a sympathetic portrayal of middle-class ideals and that Anne Sanders becomes real as a tragic heroine only in the closing scenes, and compares it to *Arden*.

Other Studies

J. Wilson McCutchan, "Justice and Equity in the English Morality Play," *JHI* 19 (1958): 405–10, traces the evolution of the concept and treatment of Justice, as a personified abstraction, in English morality plays of the fifteenth and sixteenth centuries. Justice begins, he states, as a predominantly theological concept, related only to

God's judgment, but becomes secularized and changes from a feminine to a masculine personification. In *A Warning for Fair Women*, he points out, Justice is masculine and is a civil rather than a theological force.

The trial scene is examined by Joseph H. Marshbaum, "*A Cruell Murder Donne in Kent* and Its Literary Manifestations," *SP* 46 (1949):131–40, who finds its style and diction to be "strikingly suggestive of the court records of the period." Perhaps the author took the indictment in the play from the coroner's inquisition-post-mortem for Kent; certainly "the writer . . . was not unfamiliar with courtroom procedure." Marshbaum compares the various extant accounts, including *A Warning for Fair Women*, of the murder of George Sanders.

Ola Elizabeth Winslow, *Low Comedy as a Structural Element in English Drama from the Beginnings to 1642* (1926), points out that the dreams of the servants echo the portents of the main story; Hardin Craig, "Morality Plays and Elizabethan Drama," *SQ* 1 (1950): 64–72, finds the play to be "moralistic in technique"; Sharpe, *Real War*, assigns the play to the Chamberlain's Men. Staging points are made by Allardyce Nicoll, " 'Passing Over the Stage,' " *ShS* 12 (1959):47–55, and Bernard Beckerman, *Shakespeare at the Globe, 1599–1609* (1962); and F. S. Boas, *An Introduction*, comments on the execution and declares that the play follows the details of the source pamphlet "with pedantic closeness."

Both Leo Kirschbaum, *Shakespeare and the Stationers* (1955), and Wilfred T. Jewkes, *Act Division*, examine the 1599 text. Kirschbaum believes that the printer's copy did not originate in the playhouse; Jewkes suggests that the copy was authorial manuscript, possibly prepared for performance. One word in the text, "looks," is emended to "locks" by Arthur O. Lewis, Jr., "*A Warning for Faire Women* (Line 143)," *N&Q* 1 (1954):18–19, who suggests that "looks" may even be not a printer's error but a variant spelling of "locks."

See Also

Anderson, Donald K., Jr. "The Banquet of Love in English Drama (1595–1642)." *JEGP* 63 (1964):422–32.
Blayney, Glenn H. "Field's Parody of a Murder Play." *N&Q* 2 (1955):19–20.
Cairncross, A. S. *The Problem of "Hamlet": A Solution.* 1936.
Pearn, B. R. "Dumb-Show in Elizabethan Drama." *RES* 11 (1935):385–405.

A. L.

Charlemagne, or The Distracted Emperor, tragedy (*1600;* MS)

Editions

The two modern editions of *Charlemagne* have been done by Franck L. Schoell (1920), and by John Henry Walter for the Malone Society (1938, for 1937). These editions contain the only overall studies of the play.

In his introduction, Schoell describes briefly the manuscript, the play's genre (he calls it a chronicle history), and its probable date of composition, ca. 1598–99. The bulk of the introduction and most of the notes, however, deal with the question of authorship. Schoell attempts to prove that Chapman wrote *Charlemagne* by citing numerous parallels between the anonymous play and Chapman's known work, resemblances in content, the development of plot, characterization, and prosody. An appendix discusses sources: for one part of the plot, Charlemagne's love for the body of the dead Theodora, the dramatist used a letter written by Petrarch in 1333 (see *Epistolae familiares* [1601]); some details may have come from Étienne Pasquier's *Recherches de la France* (1596) or Sebastiano Erizzo's *Le sei giornate* (1567). When Schoell describes the choice and use of sources, he again points out signs of Chapman's workmanship.

Walter's introduction provides a detailed account of the manuscript, which is apparently a fair copy made by the author. With convincing external evidence, Walter suggests that the play was written early in the reign of James I, and he reviews the sources. In commenting on attribution, he explains why Schoell's argument for Chapman is weak. Impressed by the crudity of *Charlemagne*, Walter thinks that "the play seems most likely to be the work of an amateur—influenced, possibly, by the work of Chapman."

Attribution, Date, and Sources

Schoell's argument for attributing *Charlemagne* to Chapman evidently persuaded at least three scholars to accept the ascription: Felix E. Schelling, *Foreign Influences in Elizabethan Plays* (1923); Havelock Ellis, *Chapman* (1934); and Jean Jacquot, *George Chapman (1559–1634): Sa vie, sa poésie, son théâtre, sa pensée* (1951). However, neither Millar MacLure, *George Chapman: A Critical Study* (1966), nor S. Schoenbaum, *Internal Evidence and Elizabethan Dramatic Authorship* (1966), feels that Schoell has proved his case.

Allardyce Nicoll, ed., *The Works of Cyril Tourneur* (1930), dismisses Bullen's suggestion that Tourneur may have contributed, and M. T. Jones-Davies, *Un peintre de la vie londonienne: Thomas Dekker* (1958), vol. 2, disagrees with Fleay's ascription of the play to Dekker.

Schelling thinks that the date of *Charlemagne* may be a little earlier than 1598-99, the period suggested by Schoell. On the other hand, Ellis proposes a date ca. 1600. Jacquot, whose discussion of date seems to derive from that of Walter, tentatively posits a date later than 1589 and implies that he means the beginning of the seventeenth century. MacLure remarks that the play probably dates ca. 1604.

Summarized by Schoell and Walter, early scholarship on the sources of *Charlemagne* has received no substantial additions or qualifications.

Literary Connections and Miscellaneous

Arthur Acheson, *Shakespeare, Chapman, and "Sir Thomas More"* (1931), explains what he takes to be an allusion in the anonymous drama *Soliman and Perseda* (1590) to *Charlemagne*. In *Playwriting for Elizabethans, 1600-1605* (1949), Mary Crapo Hyde links it with other plays which romanticize historical events.

Similarities in the manuscripts of *Charlemagne* and the anonymous play *Thomas of Woodstock* (1592) are noted by both Frederick S. Boas, *Shakespeare and the Universities* (1923), and Wilhelmina P. Frijlinck in her edition of *Woodstock* for the Malone Society (1929; checked by W.W. Greg). Frijlinck finds the appearance of the same hand, that of a stage manager, in both manuscripts, and uses this information to help determine the stage history of *Woodstock*.

The manuscript receives attention also from W. W. Greg in *Dramatic Documents from the Elizabethan Playhouses* (1931), vol. 2, where he gives a detailed description of it. Greg mentions the manuscript again in *The Editorial Problem in Shakespeare* (1942), saying that it appears to be in the hand of its author. Disagreeing with this view, Ludwig Borinski, "Vers und Text in den Dramenmanuskripten der Shakespearezeit," *Anglia* 75 (1957):391-410, considers the manuscript to be a copyist's.

Some bits of stage business in *Charlemagne* are discussed briefly by M. C. Bradbrook, *Themes and Conventions of Elizabethan Tragedy* (1935; cf. Alfred Harbage, "Elizabethan Acting," *PMLA* 54 [1939]: 685-708); Robert H. Bowers, "Gesticulation in Elizabethan Acting,"

SFQ 12 (1948):267–77; and Marvin Rosenberg, "Elizabethan Actors: Men or Marionettes?" *PMLA* 69 (1954):915–27.

See Also

Craig, Hardin. "Textual Degeneration of Elizabethan and Stuart Plays: An Examination of Plays in Manuscript." *RIP* 46 (1960):71–84.

Harbage, Alfred. "Elizabethan and Seventeenth-Century Play Manuscripts." *PMLA* 50 (1935):687–99.

Hart, Alfred. "Acting Versions of Elizabethan Plays." *RES* 10 (1934):1–28.

Horne, David H. *The Life and Minor Works of George Peele.* In the Yale *Life and Works of George Peele,* gen. ed. Charles T. Prouty, vol. 1 (1952).

Jewkes, Wilfred T. *Act Division in Elizabethan and Jacobean Plays, 1583–1616.* 1958.

Lawrence, William J. *Pre-Restoration Stage Studies.* 1927.

Schoell, Franck L. *Études sur l'humanisme continental en Angleterre à la fin de la Renaissance.* Bibliothèque de la *Revue de Littérature Comparée,* vol. 29 (1926).

Sharpe, Robert Boies. *The Real War of the Theaters: Shakespeare's Fellows in Rivalry with the Admiral's Men, 1594–1603.* 1935.

Smidt, Kristian. *Iniurious Imposters and "Richard III."* NSE, vol. 12 (1964).

Sykes, H. Dugdale. *Sidelights on Elizabethan Drama.* 1924.

J. L.

Lust's Dominion, or The Lascivious Queen, tragedy (*1600*; 1657)

Editions

Lust's Dominion has been edited twice since the publication of E. K. Chambers's *The Elizabethan Stage* (1923): by J. Le Gay Brereton for Materials for the Study of the Old English Drama, gen. ed. Henry De Vocht, vol. 5 (1931); and by Fredson Bowers in his edition of *The Dramatic Works of Thomas Dekker,* vol. 4 (1961).

After a brief description of four copies of the play, Brereton's introduction focuses on the question of attribution. It thoroughly reviews earlier ascription scholarship and considers five of the playwrights put forward as candidates for authorship: Marlowe, Chettle, Dekker, Haughton, and Day. Brereton favors the theory that the play is collaborate, one contributor being Dekker; and he thinks that it may have been composed before 1599 and revised later. In his discussion of sources, he points out that the origins of the plot have not yet been discovered; he speculates that Dekker, influenced by Marlowe's *Jew of Malta* (1589) and Shakespeare's *Titus Andronicus* (1594), may have invented the plot. Brereton concisely describes characterization in the play, then devotes his attention to two adaptations of it: Aphra Behn's *Abdelazer, or The Moor's Revenge* (1676), and Edward Young's *The Revenge* (1721).

Bowers assumes that *Lust's Dominion* is either completely or partly Dekker's work. His introduction, which concentrates on textual matters, offers a complete textual description of the duodecimo *Lust's Dominion* published in 1657 by Francis Kirkman and a list of editions of the play between 1814 and 1961.

The 1657 edition of *Lust's Dominion* is available in microprint in Henry W. Wells, ed., *Three Centuries of Drama* (Readex Corp., 1955–56).

Attribution

H. Dugdale Sykes, "*The Spanish Moor's Tragedy* or *Lust's Dominion*," *N&Q* 1 (1916):81–84 (rpt. with slight changes in Sykes's *Sidelights on Elizabethan Drama* [1924]), accepts J. P. Collier's suggestion that *Lust's Dominion* is identical with *The Spanish Moor's Tragedy* (1600), for which Henslowe's *Diary* records a payment to Dekker, Haughton, and Day. Comparing *Lust's Dominion* with Dekker's known work, Sykes finds the dramatist's hand throughout the anonymous play. He speculates about the shares of Haughton and Day.

Collier's identification and the ascription which follows from it have received support, tentative or wholehearted, throughout the twentieth century: see, for example, C. F. Tucker Brooke, "The Marlowe Canon," *PMLA* 37 (1922):367–417; H. Dugdale Sykes, "The Dramatic Work of Henry Chettle," *N&Q* 12 (1923):386–89; W. W. Greg, ed., *English Literary Autographs, 1550–1650*, pt. 1 (1925); William J. Lawrence, *The Physical Conditions of the Elizabethan Public Playhouse* (1927); Robert Boies Sharpe, *The Real War of the Theaters: Shakespeare's Fellows in Rivalry with the Admiral's Men, 1594–1603* (1935); Samuel C. Chew, *The Crescent and the Rose* (1937); K. Gustav Cross, "The Authorship of *Lust's Dominion*," *SP* 55 (1958):39–61; Eldred D. Jones, *Othello's Countrymen: The African in English Renaissance Drama* (1965); and Ernest L. Rhodes, " 'Me Thinks This Stage Shews Like a Tennis Court,' " *RenP*, 1968, pp. 21–28.

Those scholars have various reasons for their agreement with Collier and various arguments for and against other ascriptions. Brooke thinks that metrical evidence corroborates Collier's identification; he also finds in *Lust's Dominion* signs of Marlowe's influence but not his authorship and evidence perhaps of Kyd's workmanship. (Agreeing with Brooke, H. W. Herrington, "Christopher Marlowe—Rationalist," in *Essays in Memory of Barrett Wendell* [1926], pp. 119–52, feels that the tone of the anonymous tragedy shows Kyd's influence; he discovers stylistic features which argue against Marlowe's authorship.) Chew accepts Collier's ascription because he sees in the play substantial evidence of Dekker's work and occasional signs of Day's. Cross elaborates on Collier's theory and the studies of Sykes and Brereton; having agreed that Dekker, Haughton, and Day contributed to *Lust's Dominion*, he tries to prove that Marston collaborated as well. His case rests on parallels in content, theme, and language between the anonymous play and Marston's known efforts, and on some questionable external evidence.

A few scholars in addition to Brooke, Herrington, and Brereton consider attributions of the play to Marlowe. Felix E. Schelling, *Elizabethan Playwrights* (1925), says that Marlowe's authorship is difficult to conceive. In *Marlowe's Imagery and the Marlowe Canon* (1940), Marion Bodwell Smith examines the imagery in *Lust's Dominion* in relation to Marlowe's use of imagery and concludes that this stylistic evidence tends to refute the ascription. John Bakeless, *The Tragicall History of Christopher Marlowe* (1942), vol. 2, who provides a helpful review of attribution scholarship, looks carefully at internal and external evidence for Marlowe's authorship, decides the evidence is inconclusive, and suggests, like Brooke, that Marlowe influenced but did not write *Lust's Dominion*. (See also Bakeless's brief remarks on authorship in his *Christopher Marlowe: The Man in His Time* [1937].)

Three other opinions about attribution remain to be cited. M. T. Jones-Davies, *Un peintre de la vie londonienne: Thomas Dekker* (1958), vol. 2, accepts with mild reservations Brereton's assignment of part of the play to Dekker. In *Elizabethan Drama and Dramatists, 1583–1603* (1928), Ernest A. Gerrard disagrees with Collier's identification and assigns the play to Tourneur. S. R. Golding, "The Authorship of *Lust's Dominion*," *N&Q* 155 (1928):399–402, takes issue with all previous attribution scholarship, especially Sykes's. Discovering flaws in both the internal and external evidence put forward for various authorship candidates, he concludes that only two statements about ascription are justified: the play was composed originally by a dramatist imitating Marlowe, and it was later revised.

Date and Sources

Most critics agree that *Lust's Dominion* was either written or revised ca. 1600: see, for example, Brereton's edition; Sharpe, Smith, Bakeless, and Rhodes (all in "Attribution"); Gustav Cross, "The Vocabulary of *Lust's Dominion*," *NM* 59 (1958):41–48; and Fernand Lagarde, *John Webster*, vol. 1 (1968). Brooke ("Attribution") speculates that the play may have been created in 1591, when Marlowe and Kyd were sharing a chamber, and Willard Farnham, *The Medieval Heritage of Elizabethan Tragedy* (1936), says that it may have been composed before 1600.

Bakeless ("Attribution") believes that the source is, as Collier indicated, a pamphlet published in 1589: *True and Brief Declaration of the Sickness and Last Words of Philip the Second, King of Spain.* In "More's *Historie of Kyng Rycharde the Thirde* and *Lust's Dominion*," *N&Q* 4 (1957):198-99, Gustav Cross cites the pamphlet as a source and adds that Sir Thomas More's *Life of Richard III* (1513-14) may have influenced the composition of the second and third acts. Like Brereton, Jones-Davies ("Attribution"; vol. 1) thinks that the source is unknown.

Literary Connections and Genre

R. P. Cowl, *Sources of the Text of "Henry the Fourth"* (1929), finds a borrowing in Shakespeare's *1 Henry IV* from *Lust's Dominion*, whereas Fred L. Jones, "Echoes of Shakspere in Later Elizabethan Drama," *PMLA* 45 (1930):791-803, discovers what he believes are allusions to Shakespearean plays in *Lust's Dominion*.

As noted above, critics have recognized the influence of Marlowe and Shakespeare on the play, which imitates *The Jew of Malta* and *Titus Andronicus* in particular. For comments about this influence, see, for example: Brooke, Golding, Chew, Smith, Jones, and Rhodes (all in "Attribution"); Fredson T. Bowers, *Elizabethan Revenge Tragedy, 1587-1642* (1940—Kydian reminiscences are also noted); M. C. Bradbrook, *Shakespeare and Elizabethan Poetry* (1951); Cross's 1958 *SP* article ("Attribution") and his 1958 *NM* article ("Date"—Cross notes parallels with Chettle's *Hoffman, or a Revenge for a Father* [1602] in both articles); Jones-Davies (vols. 1 and 2—"Attribution"); Bernard Spivack, *Shakespeare and the Allegory of Evil* (1958—Spivack notes parallels also with Chettle's *Hoffman*); Richard Levin, "The Eager Queen and the Melancholy Moor," *AN&Q* 4 (1965):35-36; Lagarde ("Date"—Lagarde sees connections with Webster's *The Devil's Law Case* [1617]).

Both Cross, 1958 *SP* article, and Jones-Davies (both in "Attribution") mention the adaptations of *Lust's Dominion* done by Aphra Behn and Edward Young, and discussed by Brereton in his edition. In "The Relationship of *Lust's Dominion* and John Mason's *The Turke*," *ELH* 20 (1953):194–99, Frank W. Wadsworth argues that John Mason's *The Turk (Mulleasses the Turk)* (1607) was either influenced by or based on *Lust's Dominion*; he builds his case upon internal evidence from both plays. Levin (above) says that *The Turk* is indebted to the anonymous play.

The genre of *Lust's Dominion*, a tragedy whose theme is ambition, receives attention from Bowers, *Elizabethan Revenge Tragedy*, and Bradbrook (both above); Mary Crapo Hyde, *Playwriting for Elizabethans, 1600–1605* (1949); Cross, 1958 *SP* article ("Attribution") and 1958 *NM* article ("Date"); Jones ("Attribution"); and Lagarde ("Date").

Miscellaneous

Cross's 1958 *SP* article ("Attribution") theorizes briefly about the copy behind Kirkman's 1657 edition, which Bowers discusses thoroughly in his edition, and Wilfred T. Jewkes, *Act Division in Elizabethan and Jacobean Plays, 1583–1616* (1958), finds it difficult to determine the kind of copy from which the printer worked. Fredson Bowers, *Bibliography and Textual Criticism* (1964), looks at an anomaly in the 1657 text and then examines the running-titles to see what they reveal about the printing of the tragedy.

Lawrence ("Attribution") remarks some stage directions, and Rhodes ("Attribution") attempts to describe the stage on which *Lust's Dominion* was performed. Eldred D. Jones, "The Physical Representation of African Characters on the English Stage during the Sixteenth and Seventeenth Centuries," *Theatre Notebook* 17 (1962): 17–21, and *Othello's Countrymen* ("Attribution"), briefly discusses the use of make-up in the play.

Several writers focus on the character of Eleazar. Lawrence Babb, *The Elizabethan Malady: A Study of Melancholia in English Literature from 1580 to 1642* (1951), sees the Moor as a sometimes melancholy villain (see also Babb's "Sorrow and Love on the Elizabethan Stage," *ShAB* 18 [1943]: 137–42, and Eldred D. Jones, "Aaron and Melancholy in *Titus Andronicus*," *SQ* 14 [1963]: 178–79). Spivack ("Literary Connections") views Eleazar as a villain with features of the medieval vice-figure. Levin ("Literary

Connections") concentrates on the kind of sexuality the Moor represents (see also Lawrence Babb, "The Physiological Conception of Love in the Elizabethan and Early Stuart Drama," *PMLA* 56 [1941]: 1020-35). Other topics which receive notice include: the conduct and conclusion of the action (M. C. Bradbrook, *Themes and Conventions of Elizabethan Tragedy* [1935]); characterization, and the function of a ruse and the fairies (Hyde, in "Literary Connections"); vocabulary (Cross's 1958 *NM* article, in "Date"); and Machiavellism, with special emphasis on Eleazar and the Queen (Lagarde, in "Date").

See Also

Bald, R. C. "Francis Kirkman, Bookseller and Author." *MP* 41 (1943):17-32.

Bowden, William R. *The English Dramatic Lyric, 1603-42: A Study in Stuart Dramatic Technique.* 1951.

Bowers, Fredson. "Kyd's Pedringano: Sources and Parallels." *Harvard Studies and Notes in Philology and Literature* 13 (1931):241-49.

Brooke, C. F. Tucker. "The Reputation of Christopher Marlowe." *Transactions of the Connecticut Academy of Arts and Sciences* 25 (1922):347-408.

Bullen, A. H., ed. *The Works of John Day.* Rpt. from the collected edition of 1881 with a new Introduction by Robin Jeffs. 1963.

Eckhardt, Eduard. *Das englische Drama der Spätrenaissance: Shakespeares Nachfolger.* 1929.

Frohberg, Georg. "Das Fortleben des elisabethanischen Dramas im Zeitalter der Restauration." *SJ* 69 (1933):61-86.

Hewett-Thayer, Harvey W. "Tieck and the Elizabethan Drama: His Marginalia." *JEGP* 34 (1935):377-407.

Hunter, G. K. "Elizabethans and Foreigners." *ShS* 17 (1964):37-52.

Jaggard, William. "Marlowe: Stage History." *N&Q* 178 (1940):233.

Linton, Marion. "National Library of Scotland and Edinburgh University Library Copies of Plays in Greg's *Bibliography of the English Printed Drama.*" *SB* 15 (1962):91-104.

Praz, Mario. *The Flaming Heart.* 1958.

Reed, Robert Rentoul, Jr. *The Occult on the Tudor and Stuart Stage.* 1965.

Reynolds, George Fullmer. *The Staging of Elizabethan Plays at the Red Bull Theater, 1605-1625.* 1940.

Schoenbaum, S. *Internal Evidence and Elizabethan Dramatic Authorship.* 1966.

Sibly, John. "The Duty of Revenge in Tudor and Stuart Drama." *REL* 8 (1967):46-54.

Sorelius, Gunnar. *"The Giant Race Before the Flood": Pre-Restoration Drama on the Stage and in the Criticism of the Restoration.* Acta Universitatis Upsaliensis. Studia Anglistica Upsaliensia, no. 4 (1966).

Stroup, Thomas B. *Microcosmos: The Shape of the Elizabethan Play.* 1965.

Thompson, Alan Reynolds. "Melodrama and Tragedy." *PMLA* 43 (1928):810-35.

J. L.

Thomas Lord Cromwell, history (*1600;* 1602)

Editions

The play will appear in G. R. Proudfoot's forthcoming edition of the *Shakespeare Apocrypha,* and is also available in microprint in Henry W. Wells, ed., *Three Centuries of Drama* (Readex Microprint Corp., 1955–56).

Origin and Date

Three scholars have developed separate theories of the origin and date of the play. Arthur Acheson, *Shakespeare, Chapman and "Sir Thomas More"* (1931), believes that *Cromwell* was written 1582–83 and belonged before 1589 to the old Oxford's company, then passed in 1591 to Pembroke's Men, then in 1594 to the Chamberlain's Men, was revised by Dekker, and finally went to Henslowe and Alleyn, whose authors Chettle, Drayton, Munday, and Smith used it in writing *Cardinal Wolsey;* it was at last sent to the press in 1602. This elaborate line of development is queried by Baldwin Maxwell, *Studies in the Shakespeare Apocrypha* (1956), and no other scholar has ventured to create so complex a progress for the play. Robert Boies Sharpe, *The Real War of the Theaters* (1935), states that *Cromwell* was probably produced by the Chamberlain's Men in 1601, but that the text we have, which seems old-fashioned in style for 1601 performance, may be that of an older play which was revised for an early seventeenth-century revival, the revised version not being extant. Maxwell, *Shakespeare Apocrypha,* examines the text and finds it to fall into two parts, a skillfully written I–III.ii and an episodic, shapeless second half, and suggests that our text is a telescoping into one play of a two-part original. Other possibilities are: (1) that the play is a collaborate work by two authors of unequal ability; (2) that the play was begun by one dramatist and finished by another. The text we have—original or revision—should be dated, Maxwell believes, ca. 1599–1600, because Cromwell was Earl of Essex, and the play shows signs of censorship involving Cromwell's honors; for a few years after 1599 a favorable stage portrait of an Earl of Essex would have been difficult to present. Moreover, Maxwell points out, the play has possible debts to *Henry V* and *Julius Caesar,* and is related to the lost Admiral's Men *Wolsey* (1601–2) and to *Sir Thomas More* (late 1590s).

R. P. Cowl, *The Authorship of "Pericles." The Date of "The Life and Death of the Lord Cromwell"* (no date), finds two "echoes" of *2 Henry IV* in *Cromwell*, and a parallel father-son situation which is not in Foxe's *Acts and Monuments* (on which *Cromwell* is based), and so places the anonymous drama after *2 Henry IV*. David Bevington, *Tudor Drama and Politics* (1968), gives a date of ca. 1597–1602.

Authorship

Thomas Lord Cromwell has been attributed in the past to a variety of Elizabethan dramatists, including Drayton, Heywood, and Shakespeare. The Shakespeare attribution has by now been almost entirely dismissed: see, for example, E. K. Chambers, *William Shakespeare* (1930), vol. 1, Acheson, *Shakespeare, Chapman*, Clara Longworth de Chambrun, *Shakespeare: A Portrait Restored* (1957), and Irving Ribner, *The English History Play in the Age of Shakespeare* (1957; rev. ed. 1965), two of whom reject the attribution in one sentence. A. W. Titherley, in *Shakespeare's Identity* (1952), however, persists in holding to the view that *Cromwell* is an early play by "Shakespeare" (i.e., the sixth Earl of Derby, William Stanley) which was discarded by the author as unworthy of revision. The Heywood and Drayton attributions have also been generally rejected. Arthur Melville Clark, *Thomas Heywood: Playwright and Miscellanist* (1931), finds *Cromwell* too bad to be Heywood's, and Ribner, *English History Play*, states that although the play's bourgeois sentiments make it somewhat resemble the work of Heywood, there is no real evidence of his authorship. William R. Bowden, however, in *The English Dramatic Lyric, 1603–42* (1951), lists the work as Heywood's, in commenting on a song in the play. Fleay's Drayton attribution is dismissed by Bernard H. Newdigate, *Michael Drayton and His Circle* (1941), as "irresponsible," and is summarily rejected by Ribner, *English History Play*; and J. M. Robertson, *The Shakespeare Canon*, pt. 1 (1922), in a footnote declares *Cromwell* to diverge at some points from the *Legend of Cromwell* and to be too poor a work to be Drayton's. Baldwin Maxwell, *Shakespeare Apocrypha*, argues against Fleay on political grounds: the first Earl of Bedford, great-grandfather of Drayton's patron, the third earl, is favorably portrayed in *Cromwell*, but Drayton had broken with the Bedfords before the date Fleay gives to the play's composition. Also, Maxwell states, Drayton's *Legend of Great Cromwell* does not present Cromwell as the paragon of virtues we find him to be in the play.

Other authorship candidates rejected (in one sentence) by Ribner, *English History Play*, are Chettle, Dekker, Munday, William Sly, and Wentworth Smith. Two scholars make positive attribution arguments. Acheson, *Shakespeare, Chapman*, gives the play to Chapman and Munday, in collaboration, in 1582–83, and posits a 1594 revision by Dekker. Maxwell, *Shakespeare Apocrypha*, also suggests Munday, who shared in the work on both *Sir Thomas More* and *Wolsey*, had had some personal experiences similar to Cromwell's (see also Acheson, *Shakespeare, Chapman*), was a militant Protestant, and had apparently read Foxe's life of Cromwell, on which the play is based. Perhaps, Maxwell comments, collaborators also worked with Munday on the drama—some of the same dramatists who had written *More* or *Wolsey* with him; and Wentworth Smith may have shared in the work, and perhaps revised or condensed the play ca. 1599–1600.

Literary Connections

Four scholars view the play in the light of other plays of its time dealing with the same historical period. Acheson, *Shakespeare, Chapman*, compares *Cromwell* with *Sir Thomas More*, and believes that parts of *Cromwell* were used by the authors of the lost *Wolsey*, and, via *Wolsey*, passed on into *Henry VIII*, which is a rewriting of *Wolsey* by "Burbage's writers" after Shakespeare's retirement. Sharpe, *Real War*, suggests that *Thomas Lord Cromwell* and *Henry VIII* are plays produced by the Chamberlain's Men as rival pieces to one or more Admiral's Men plays on Wolsey, the two companies "competing to show their parties' ancestors in the most favorable light, the Admiral's men by blackening Wolsey and exalting Norfolk [uncle of the Lord Admiral], the Chamberlain's by showing the Howards' enemies [i.e., Cromwell] in a more agreeable way." There seems, Sharpe suggests, to be a parallel between Cromwell and the 1590s Earl of Essex. Baldwin Maxwell, *Shakespeare Apocrypha*, citing Acheson, also finds a relationship between the Admiral's Men *Wolsey* and the Chamberlain's Men *Cromwell*, believing *Wolsey* to predate *Cromwell*, and uses this to date and to find an author for the latter play. Finally, Irving Ribner, *English History Play*, suggests that *Cromwell* may be involved in the Admiral's-Chamberlain's rivalry, perhaps as a counter-blow (1600) to *Sir John Oldcastle*, and mentions Sharpe's theory of *Cromwell*'s connection with the lost Admiral's Men plays on Wolsey. Like Sharpe, he treats the play in terms of the political affiliations of its company and the dramatic portraits it

contains of historical political characters related to contemporary
personages. Cromwell had been Earl of Essex; and the Chamberlain's
Men in the 1590s were friendly towards the faction of the contemporary Essex. David Bevington, *Tudor Drama and Politics* (1968),
also views the drama as possibly a Chamberlain's Men response to the
Admiral's Men *Sir John Oldcastle.*

Links between *Cromwell* and other literary works of its time,
besides those already cited in other connections, are made by Ola
Elizabeth Winslow, *Low Comedy as a Structural Element in English
Drama from the Beginnings to 1642* (1926), Sharpe, *Real War,*
Kathleen Tillotson, "Michael Drayton as a 'Historian' in the *Legend
of Cromwell," MLR* 34 (1939):186–200, and E. H. C. Oliphant, *The
Plays of Beaumont and Fletcher* (1927). Winslow notes parallel
episodes in *Cromwell* and *Sir John Oldcastle*; Sharpe suggests a
reference in *Cromwell* to Shakespeare's *Troilus and Cressida*, and
connects *Cromwell* in locale with *Two Maids of More-Clacke* and
Westward Ho; Tillotson states that the play influenced Drayton's
poem on Cromwell; and Oliphant speculates that the 1613 edition of
Cromwell was published because of the successful production then of
Henry VIII.

The Play

There have been a number of general critical assessments of the
play. Maxwell, *Shakespeare Apocrypha*, calls it "a loosely-constructed
. . . mixture of historical fact, fiction, hearsay, and propaganda," with
little or no characterization, some good comedy, and "a glorification
of homely virtues." The first half, he states, shows technical skill in
plotting and action. Mary Crapo Hyde, *Playwriting for Elizabethans,
1600–1605* (1949), views the drama as a "tragic history" which "in
execution is closer to comedy"; she believes the characterization of
Cromwell to be gently satiric. E. M. W. Tillyard, *Shakespeare's
History Plays* (1944), finds *Cromwell* to have only a touch of
thought about history, in the Chorus's statement of the *de casibus*
theme; Willard Farnham, *The Medieval Heritage of Elizabethan
Tragedy* (1936), regards the play as a primitive tragedy, with a
structure close to that of *de casibus* tragedy but not the spiritual
force of *de casibus* drama, and very little characterization. "*Cromwell*
is perhaps a perfect example of the biographical play," maintains
Irving Ribner, *English History Play*; the work is episodic in structure,
with a *de casibus* theme and medieval world view. Its political

purpose, Ribner states, is a defense of Cromwell and thus, by impli-
cation, a defense of the contemporary Earl of Essex and an attack on
the Howards; and it is strongly Protestant.

David Bevington, *Tudor Drama*, views the play above all as
religious propaganda (see also Acheson, *Shakespeare, Chapman*),
though admitting the possibility of its Essex connections and purpose. *Cromwell*, he states, glorifies the cause of religious reform, and
with no warnings against Puritan excess. Its biased interpretation of
Cromwell "was accessible in Foxe's *Acts and Monuments*," and
Cromwell's grandson was a defender of Puritanism in the English
parliament, 1571-89. Acheson, *Shakespeare, Chapman*, Maxwell,
Shakespeare Apocrypha, and Ribner, *English History Play*, all also
find Foxe to be the source.

Other Studies

Bernard Beckerman, *Shakespeare at the Globe, 1599–1609* (1962),
deals with the structure of the play, which he finds to be split: the
play moves one way, then shifts direction in the second half. The
pattern, he maintains, is episodic, unity being achieved through the
central figure of Cromwell, and the delayed reprieve for Cromwell is
a structural substitute for a judge-figure. Beckerman also comments
on staging.

Louis B. Wright, *Middle-Class Culture in Elizabethan England*
(1935), points out that the anonymous author (as noted previously
by Felix E. Schelling, *The English Chronicle Play* [1902]) extolls
Cromwell's citizen virtues: thrift and capacity in trade, temperance,
piety, and staunch Protestantism. See also Tillotson, "Michael
Drayton."

The text is examined by Leo Kirschbaum, *Shakespeare and the
Stationers* (1955), and Wilfred T. Jewkes, *Act Division in Elizabethan
and Jacobean Plays, 1583–1616* (1958). Kirschbaum declares that the
"copyright history of the play is muddled," and that the work
probably did not belong to the Chamberlain's Men. The printer's
copy, he states, seems to have been authorial manuscript, or a
transcript from it, rather than a playhouse book. Jewkes (who also
comments on the choruses) calls the text "rather confused and
truncated," and finds evidence in it of a reworking of the primary
text by a hand other than the original author's. He believes that the
copy text was probably author's manuscript worked over but not
prepared for playhouse use.

See Also

Albright, Evelyn May. *Dramatic Publication in England, 1580–1640.* 1927.
Hart, Alfred. *Stolne and Surreptitious Copies.* 1942.
Knights, L. C. *Drama and Society in the Age of Jonson.* 1937.
Moore, John Robert. "The Songs of the Public Theaters in the Time of Shakespeare." *JEGP* 28 (1929):166–202.
Rausch, Heinrich. *Der "Chorus" im englischen Drama bis 1642.* 1922.

A. L.

The Weakest Goeth to the Wall, pseudo-history (*1600;* 1600)

Editions

Two editions of *The Weakest Goeth to the Wall (WGW)* have appeared since the publication of E. K. Chambers's *The Elizabethan Stage* (1923): E. B. Everitt's edition in *Six Early Plays Related to the Shakespeare Canon*, ed. E. B. Everitt and R. L. Armstrong, Anglistica, vol. 14 (1965); and Jill Levenson's 1967 Harvard University dissertation.

In the introduction to his edition, Everitt briefly discusses earlier editions and attribution scholarship. Using external evidence, he decides that 1586–87 is a reasonable date for *WGW*. He compares the play with its source, Barnaby Riche's "Sappho Duke of Mantona," the first of eight novellas in *Riche His Farewell to Militarie Profession* (1581), and concludes by describing themes and techniques used in *WGW* which, in his opinion, suggest Shakespeare's authorship of the anonymous play. (J. C. Maxwell's review of the edition in *N&Q* 13 [1966]:152–55, and that of Franklin B. Williams, Jr., in *SQ* 17 [1966]:430, provide helpful appraisals of Everitt's work.)

Levenson's introduction begins by examining earlier attribution scholarship which ascribes *WGW* to at least four different playwrights: Webster, Chettle, Munday, and Dekker. She concludes that there is evidence for attributing the comic scenes and parts of the serious portions to Dekker, but none for assigning the body of the play to any particular dramatist. She then discusses the relation of the play to its source, Riche's novella, and its genre. She employs both internal and external evidence to establish a date between 1595 and 1600, probably ca. 1597 or 1598. Her introduction ends with a critical evaluation of *WGW* and a thorough analysis of its text.

The 1600 text of *WGW* is available in microprint in Henry W. Wells, ed., *Three Centuries of Drama* (Readex Corp., 1955–56).

Attribution

The question of authorship remains unresolved. The only thorough and convincing study of ascription has been made by Mary Leland Hunt, *Thomas Dekker: A Study* (1911), who believes that Dekker wrote the humorous portions. In a footnote to her study of Dekker, Hunt assigns the major portion of *WGW* to Chettle; that attribution rests on unsubstantial evidence.

Only one scholar agrees totally with Hunt's ascription of *WGW* to both Dekker and Chettle: M. T. Jones-Davies, *Un peintre de la vie londonienne: Thomas Dekker* (1958), vol. 2. Two critics in addition to Levenson accept the Dekker attribution but not the Chettle: H. Dugdale Sykes, *Sidelights on Elizabethan Drama* (1924); and Julia Celeste Turner [Wright], *Anthony Mundy: An Elizabethan Man of Letters* (1928). Gerald J. Eberle, "Dekker's Part in *The Familie of Love*," in *Joseph Quincy Adams Memorial Studies*, ed. James G. McManaway et al. (1948), pp. 723-38, thinks that Dekker probably contributed to *WGW*.

Arthur Acheson, *Shakespeare, Chapman, and "Sir Thomas More"* (1931), believes that Munday wrote *WGW* very early in his career. (Turner had found no evidence for Munday's authorship of the play.)

Several scholars feel that there is insufficient evidence for making any attribution: F. L. Lucas, ed., *The Complete Works of John Webster* (1927), vol. 4; Harold Jenkins, *The Life and Work of Henry Chettle* (1934); Thomas M. Cranfill, "Barnaby Rich's 'Sappho' and *The Weakest Goeth to the Wall*," *Studies in English* (Univ. of Texas) 25 (1945-46):142-71; and Marvin T. Herrick, *Tragicomedy* (1955).

Date and Source

There has been little discussion of date outside of that in the two editions. E. K. Chambers, *William Shakespeare* (1930), vol. 1, sees no reason to date *WGW* much earlier than its 1600 publication date. Acheson ("Attribution") uses unconvincing external evidence to date the play ca. 1580-81.

D. T. Starnes, "Barnabe Riche's 'Sappho Duke of Mantona': A Study in Elizabethan Story-Making," *SP* 30 (1933):455-72, corroborates earlier scholarship which suggested that Riche's "Sappho" was the source of *WGW*. He traces the sources of the novella, showing that the story has a composite character; points out how closely the play follows the tale; and thus establishes that the dramatist and Riche could not possibly have used a common source. Cranfill

("Attribution") attempts to supplement Starnes's evidence and support his conclusions; having reviewed earlier source scholarship, he adds at least sixteen more sources for Riche's "Sappho" to Starnes's eight to show that the anonymous dramatist undoubtedly borrowed from Riche and that the two writers did not use a common source. He examines closely the relationship between *WGW* and Riche's "Sappho" to prove decisively that the play depends upon the story. (In conjunction with Cranfill's discussion of sources in his 1945–46 *Studies in English* article, see his remarks on the subject in Thomas M. Cranfill and Dorothy Hart Bruce, *Barnaby Rich: A Short Biography* [1953], and in his edition of *Rich's Farewell to Military Profession* [1959].) (Both modern editors accept the theory that Riche's "Sappho" is the source.)

Literary Connections and Miscellaneous

A number of scholars find in a phrase in Shakespeare's *All's Well That Ends Well*, II.iii, a reference to *WGW*: see, for example, Chambers ("Date"); Karl Wentersdorf, "Shakespearean Chronology and the Metrical Tests," in *Shakespeare-Studien: Festschrift für Heinrich Mutschmann*, ed. Walther Fischer and Karl Wentersdorf (1951), pp. 161–93; Geoffrey Bullough, *Narrative and Dramatic Sources of Shakespeare*, vol. 2 (1958); and Robert Kimbrough, *Shakespeare's "Troilus and Cressida" and Its Setting* (1964). G. K. Hunter, ed., *All's Well That Ends Well* (1959; third Arden), thinks that there is no substantial argument for connecting the line with *WGW*.

The genre of *WGW*, a mixture of romance, comedy, and pseudo-history, receives attention in Levenson's edition and from Mary Crapo Hyde, *Playwriting for Elizabethans, 1600–1605* (1949); Herrick ("Attribution"); and Robert Grams Hunter, *Shakespeare and the Comedy of Forgiveness* (1965). Two scholars focus on the roles of the comic characters in the action: Olive Mary Busby, *Studies in the Development of the Fool in the Elizabethan Drama* (1923); and Ola Elizabeth Winslow, *Low Comedy as a Structural Element in English Drama from the Beginnings to 1642* (1926).

William J. Lawrence, *Pre-Restoration Stage Studies* (1927), explains why *WGW* appears to have been an inn-yard play and discusses the dumb show which opens it. Other critics who consider the function of the dumb show in *WGW* are B. R. Pearn, "Dumb-Show in Elizabethan Drama," *RES* 11 (1935):385–405; Hyde (above); and Dieter Mehl, *The Elizabethan Dumb Show* (1966; German ed. 1964).

A few scholars briefly treat the songs in *WGW*: John Robert Moore, "The Songs of the Public Theaters in the Time of Shakespeare," *JEGP* 28 (1929):166–202; William R. Bowden, *The English Dramatic Lyric, 1603–42: A Study in Stuart Dramatic Technique* (1951); and Vincent Duckles, "The Music for the Lyrics in Early Seventeenth-Century English Drama: A Bibliography of the Primary Sources," in *Music in English Renaissance Drama*, ed. John H. Long (1968), pp. 117–60.

Hyde (above) discusses the treatment of several characters and scenes in *WGW*, and Kimbrough (above) refers briefly to the play's attitudes towards love, lust, and honor.

In "Conjectural Remarks on Elizabethan Dramatists (Pt. III)," *N&Q* 195 (1950):400–402, Juliusz Krzyzanowski corrects two readings in W. W. Greg's edition of *WGW* for the Malone Society (1912). Wilfred T. Jewkes, *Act Division in Elizabethan and Jacobean Plays, 1583–1616* (1958), thinks that the copy for the play was probably an author's manuscript which had been made ready for performance on the public stage.

See Also

Abrams, William Amos, ed. *"The Merry Devil of Edmonton": 1608.* 1942.

Bevington, David. *Tudor Drama and Politics.* 1968.

Brewster, Paul G. "Games and Sports in Sixteenth- and Seventeenth-Century English Literature." *WF* 6 (1947):143–56.

Dawson, Giles E. "An Early List of Elizabethan Plays." *Library* 15 (1935):445–56.

Draper, John W. "Falstaff, 'A Fool and Jester.'" *MLQ* 7 (1946):453–62 (appears as "Falstaff, a 'Knave-Fool,'" in *Stratford to Dogberry* [1961], pp. 189–99).

Empson, William. *Some Versions of Pastoral.* 1935.

Greg, W. W., ed. *English Literary Autographs, 1550–1650.* Pt. 1. 1925.

Huizinga, J. "Engelschen en Nederlanders in Shakespeare's Tijd." *De Gids*, 1 May 1924, pp. 219–35.

Jorgensen, Paul A. "Barnaby Rich: Soldierly Suitor and Honest Critic of Women." *SQ* 7 (1956):183–88.

Linton, Marion. "National Library of Scotland and Edinburgh University Library Copies of Plays in Greg's *Bibliography of the English Printed Drama.*" *SB* 15 (1962):91–104.

Schelling, Felix E. *Foreign Influences in Elizabethan Plays.* 1923.

Schoenbaum, S. *Internal Evidence and Elizabethan Dramatic Authorship.* 1966.

Sharpe, Robert Boies. *The Real War of the Theaters: Shakespeare's Fellows in Rivalry with the Admiral's Men, 1594–1603.* 1935.

Ward, B. M. *The Seventeenth Earl of Oxford, 1550–1604. From Contemporary Documents.* 1928.

J. L.

The Trial of Chivalry, pseudo-history (*1601;* 1605)

Introduction and Attribution

No one has edited *The Trial of Chivalry* recently, and scholarship on the play is meager.

The question of attribution remains unsettled. Frederic L. Jones, "*The Trial of Chivalry*, A Chettle Play," *PMLA* 41 (1926):304–24, assumes that two dramatists collaborated on *Trial.* He attempts to prove that Chettle produced most of the play by citing figures of speech, ideas, a classical allusion, character types, and structural features in the anonymous drama which have parallels in Chettle's acknowledged work. After briefly summarizing earlier scholarship which suggested that the collaborator might have been Munday, Day, or Heywood, he concludes that "Heywood seems . . . to be the likeliest guess." Harold Jenkins, *The Life and Work of Henry Chettle* (1934), discovers in Jones's argument no convincing evidence for ascribing *Trial* to Chettle. Arthur Melville Clark, *Thomas Heywood: Playwright and Miscellanist* (1931), who provides a short review of attribution scholarship, does not find Heywood's hand in either the serious or the comic portions of the play. He proposes that an inexperienced playwright like William Stanley, Earl of Derby, may have written the old-fashioned romantic plot, whereas Dekker or the author of *The Merry Devil of Edmonton* (1602) created the character Dick Bowyer. In *The Real War of the Theaters: Shakespeare's Fellows in Rivalry with the Admiral's Men, 1594–1603* (1935), Robert Boies Sharpe remarks that Heywood apparently made the additions of "Cutting Dick" for Worcester's Men in 1602. For unspecified reasons, Ernest A. Gerrard, *Elizabethan Drama and Dramatists, 1583–1603* (1928), assigns *Trial* to Dekker with Drayton.

Date and Sources

Of the scholars cited above, only Jones and Clark mention the date of *Trial.* Jones believes that the play was written much earlier than 1602 (the date Bullen assigned it), and Clark suggests it may have been composed more than ten years before its publication.

In "Another Source for *The Trial of Chivalry*," *PMLA* 47 (1932): 668–70, Frederic L. Jones agrees with C. R. Baskervill, "Sidney's *Arcadia* and *The Tryall of Chevalry*," *MP* 10 (1912):197–201, that the *Arcadia* served as the principal source for the main plot of *Trial.* He adds that the "enveloping action" comes from Robert Greene's

Carde of Fancie (1587). Jones thinks that *Trial* may be the sequel to an earlier play which depended on the *Carde of Fancie* for its main plot.

Literary Connections and Miscellaneous

R. P. Cowl points out echoes in *Trial* of Shakespeare's *Henry IV* plays in *W. Shakespeare: "King Henry the Fourth" and Other Plays: An Experiment with "Echoes"* (1927) and *Sources of the Text of "Henry the Fourth"* (1929). Several scholars have briefly compared the scene in *Trial* where the statue of Ferdinand comes alive with *The Winter's Tale*, V.iii: H. Carrington Lancaster, "Hermione's Statue," *SP* 29 (1932):233-38; George C. Taylor, "Hermione's Statue Again," *ShAB* 13 (1938):82-86; Kenneth Muir, *Shakespeare's Sources*, vol. 1, *Comedies and Tragedies* (1957; rpt. with new appendices, 1961); John Lawlor, "*Pandosto* and the Nature of Dramatic Romance," *PQ* 41 (1962):96-113; M. C. Bradbrook, *English Dramatic Form: A History of Its Development* (1965); and Robert Grams Hunter, *Shakespeare and the Comedy of Forgiveness* (1965). W. W. Greg, *Dramatic Documents from the Elizabethan Playhouses* (1931), vol. 2, notices some thought-provoking resemblances between *Trial* and the plot of *2 Fortune's Tennis* (1602).

Clark ("Introduction") speculates about why *Trial* had two different titles—*The Trial of Chivalry* and *This Gallant Cavaliero Dick Bowyer*—when it appeared in 1605. Wilfred T. Jewkes, *Act Division in Elizabethan and Jacobean Plays, 1583-1616* (1958), thinks that copy for the play derived from an authorial manuscript or a nontheatrical transcript. Bernard Spivack, *Shakespeare and the Allegory of Evil* (1958), analyzes Roderick, Duke of Orléans, in *Trial*, a character influenced by the medieval vice-figure. Laurens Joseph Mills, *One Soul in Bodies Twain* (1937), discusses the use of friendship conventions in the play, and Samuel Schoenbaum, "The 'Deformed Mistress' Theme and Chapman's *Gentleman Usher*," *N&Q* 7 (1960):22-24, remarks the occurrence of the "deformed mistress" theme in it. In *Shakespeare's "Troilus and Cressida" and Its Setting* (1964), Robert Kimbrough describes attitudes expressed in *Trial* towards love, war, and honor. David Bevington, *Tudor Drama and Politics* (1968), also comments on the play's attitude towards war.

See Also

Greg, W. W., ed. *English Literary Autographs, 1550-1650.* Pt. 1. 1925.

Hyde, Mary Crapo. *Playwriting for Elizabethans, 1600-1605.* 1949.

Schelling, Felix E. *Foreign Influences in Elizabethan Plays.* 1923.
Schoenbaum, S. *Internal Evidence and Elizabethan Dramatic Authorship.* 1966.
Sykes, H. Dugdale. *Sidelights on Elizabethan Drama.* 1924.
Velte, F. Mowbray. *The Bourgeois Elements in the Dramas of Thomas Heywood.* 1924.
Wright, Louis B. "Stage Duelling in the Elizabethan Theatre." *MLR* 22 (1927): 265–75.

J. L.

The Fair Maid of the Exchange, comedy (*1602;* 1607)

Editions

The two modern editions of *The Fair Maid of the Exchange (FME)* are Karl E. Snyder's 1949 Northwestern University dissertation (*Doctoral Dissertations* 16 [1948–49]:150), and Peter H. Davison and Arthur Brown's edition for the Malone Society (1963, for 1962).

In the introduction to the Malone Society edition, Davison and Brown list and briefly describe seventeenth-century editions of the comedy. After a concise review of attribution scholarship, they conclude that *FME* should remain anonymous until more convincing evidence about its authorship appears. They fix the *terminus a quo* at 1593/94 and the *terminus ad quem* at 1601/2, but a lack of substantial evidence makes it impossible to establish a more precise date. Finally, the editors describe the 1607 edition and try to determine the nature of the copy behind it.

The 1607 quarto is available in microprint in Henry W. Wells, ed., *Three Centuries of Drama* (Readex Corp., 1955–56).

Attribution, Date, and Sources

The question of attribution has received little attention and remains unresolved. Felix E. Schelling, *Elizabethan Playwrights* (1925), finds in the humor and pathos of *FME* signs of Dekker's early work and hints of Heywood's authorship. In *Thomas Heywood: A Study in the Elizabethan Drama of Everyday Life* (1928), Otelia Cromwell focuses on the authorship issue. After examining previous attribution scholarship, she considers the suggestion that Heywood produced *FME*; discussing the absence of the distinctive features which characterize Heywood's known work, she decides that if he contributed at all, he merely outlined the plots, some situations, and the characters. Arthur Melville Clark changed his views about attribution between 1922 and 1931: in "Thomas Heywood as a Critic,"

MLN 37 (1922):217–23, he assumed that Heywood was the author, but in *Thomas Heywood: Playwright and Miscellanist* (1931), he sees little evidence of Heywood's hand and remarks that if the dramatist had a share in the comedy at all, his contribution was small. (In conjunction with Clark's comments about *FME* in his book about Heywood, see his article "A Bibliography of Thomas Heywood," *Oxford Bibliographical Society: Proceedings & Papers* 1 [1922–26]: 97–153.) Joseph Quincy Adams in his edition of *Oenone and Paris* (1594) by "T.H." for the Folger Shakespeare Library (1943) is convinced by internal evidence that Heywood had a "main finger" in the composition of *FME*. Alden Brooks, *Will Shakspere and the Dyer's Hand* (1943), suggests no particular candidate for authorship but thinks that whoever the anonymous playwright was, he knew much about the relationship between Nashe and Shakespeare, and tried through *FME* to publicize his knowledge.

There is not much discussion of the date outside of the Davison-Brown edition. W. W. Greg, ed., *English Literary Autographs, 1550–1650*, pt. 1 (1925), places the comedy ca. 1602. Cromwell, remarking that it was written before 1607, believes that it must have been composed during Heywood's most productive years (a fact which makes the dramatist's sole authorship of *FME* seem unlikely to her). Clark is uncertain about the date of composition; although internal evidence suggests that the play dates from the end of the stage quarrel, the passages he cites as evidence may have been later additions to the text, which he thinks underwent a great deal of revision. Robert Boies Sharpe, *The Real War of the Theaters: Shakespeare's Fellows in Rivalry with the Admiral's Men, 1594–1603* (1935), reasons that the comedy's imitations of Shakespeare and Jonson fix its date ca. 1602. He also provides evidence to propose that *FME* may have been performed at court by Worcester's company on 3 January 1602.

None of the recent scholarship on *FME* deals with sources.

Literary Connections and Genre

Several scholars have noticed phrases borrowed from Shakespeare's *Venus and Adonis* in *FME*: see, for example, Alfred Bruce Black and Robert Metcalf Smith, *Shakespeare Allusions and Parallels*, Lehigh Univ. Publication, vol. 5, no. 3; The Institute of Research, Circular no. 51; Studies in the Humanities, no. 8 (1931); Brooks ("Attribution"–he notices citations from *Much Ado about Nothing* as well); and Clara Longworth, Comptesse de Chamᴏrun, *Shakespeare: A Portrait Restored* (1957; French ed. 1947). Adamᴣ ("Attribution") finds parallels with *Venus and Adonis*, some Shakespearean plays, and *Oenone and Paris* by "T.H." Both Clark in his 1922 *MLN* article and Sharpe (both in "Attribution") think that *FME* may be burlesquing such contemporary dramatists as Chapman, Jonson, and Marston. In *Shakespeare's "Troilus and Cressida" and Its Setting* (1964), Robert Kimbrough briefly compares Mall Berry in *FME* with Cressida in Shakespeare's *Troilus and Cressida*. Richard H. Perkinson, "Topographical Comedy in the Seventeenth Century," *ELH* 3 (1936): 270–90, suggests that *FME* had some influence on the writing of Jonson's *Bartholomew Fair* (1614), and he also points out resemblances between the anonymous comedy and Lording Barry's *Ram Ally, or Merry Tricks* (1608).

Both Agnes Mure Mackenzie, *The Playgoer's Handbook to the English Renaissance Drama* (1927), and Sharpe ("Attribution") comment on the genre of *FME*, a combination of romantic adventure and English domestic drama. Sharpe, in addition, groups *FME* with other contemporary plays in which disguises play an important role. Clark, *Thomas Heywood* ("Attribution"), calls *FME* "a comedy of manners, midway between the style of Dekker and that of Middleton."

Miscellaneous

A few critics consider the staging of *FME*. In *The Staging of Elizabethan Plays at the Red Bull Theater, 1605–1625* (1940), George Fullmer Reynolds finds evidence in the play's text that it has a shop-setting. Richard Hosley, "The Gallery Over the Stage in the Public Playhouse of Shakespeare's Time," *SQ* 8 (1957):15–31, groups *FME* with twenty-one other contemporary plays produced at the Red Bull between 1605 and 1625, dramas which did not require a gallery as an acting area. Allardyce Nicoll, " 'Passing Over the Stage,' " *ShS* 12 (1959):47–55, discusses the way characters enter the stage at the beginning of the third act. William J. Lawrence, *Pre-Restoration Stage Studies* (1927), shows why the table of character distribution for *FME* is "inoperative."

In *"The Fair Maid of the Exchange," Library* 13 (1958):119–20, P. H. Davison provides evidence that V. Sims was the printer of the first edition (1607) and describes the proofreader's marks in a copy of the third edition (1637), corrections generally designed to restore the 1637 compositor's setting to his copy, the 1625 edition. Wilfred T. Jewkes, *Act Division in Elizabethan and Jacobean Plays, 1583–1616* (1958), concludes that "the copy for this play seems to have done duty in the playhouse . . . . "

The songs in *FME* receive attention from Edward Bliss Reed, ed., *Songs from the British Drama* (1925); John Robert Moore, "The Songs of the Public Theaters in the Time of Shakespeare," *JEGP* 28 (1929):166–202; and William R. Bowden, *The English Dramatic Lyric, 1603–42: A Study in Stuart Dramatic Technique* (1951).

Louis B. Wright, "Vaudeville Dancing and Acrobatics in Elizabethan Plays," *Englische Studien* 63 (1928):59–76, describes the use of trick dancing in *FME*. To Sharpe ("Attribution"), the names of the London characters seem real rather than descriptive. In *Playwriting for Elizabethans, 1600–1605* (1949), Mary Crapo Hyde briefly discusses the trick conclusion of the play and the functions of three characters in the plot. P. Davison, "An Obscure Reference to Wool Processing in *The Fair Maid of the Exchange*," *N&Q* 4 (1957): 244–45, traces the allusion to "tentering" on fol. D1^V of the 1607 edition and then interprets the passage in which the allusion appears.

See Also

Bastiaenen, Johannes Adam. *The Moral Tone of Jacobean and Caroline Drama.* 1930.

Bevington, David. *From "Mankind" to Marlowe: Growth of Structure in the Popular Drama of Tudor England.* 1962.

Boas, Frederick S. *An Introduction to Stuart Drama.* 1946.

Bradbrook, M. C. *The Growth and Structure of Elizabethan Comedy.* 1955.

Craig, Hardin. *The Literature of the English Renaissance, 1485–1660.* In *A History of English Literature*, vol. 2, ed. Hardin Craig (1950).

Dawson, Giles E. "An Early List of Elizabethan Plays." *Library* 15 (1935): 445–56.

Greg, W. W. "Authorship Attributions in the Early Play-Lists, 1656–1671." *Edinburgh Bibliographical Society Transactions* 2 (1938–45):303–29.

Ives, E. W. "Tom Skelton—a Seventeenth-Century Jester." *ShS* 13 (1960): 90–105.

Jente, Richard. "The Proverbs of Shakespeare with Early and Contemporary Parallels." *Washington Univ. Studies,* Humanistic Ser. 13 (1926):391–444.

Linton, Marion. "National Library of Scotland and Edinburgh University Library Copies of Plays in Greg's *Bibliography of the English Printed Drama.*" *SB* 15 (1962):91–104.

Schoenbaum, S. *Internal Evidence and Elizabethan Dramatic Authorship.* 1966.

Sykes, H. Dugdale. *Sidelights on Elizabethan Drama.* 1924.

Velte, F. Mowbray. *The Bourgeois Elements in the Dramas of Thomas Heywood.* 1924.

Wright, Celeste Turner. "The Usurer's Sin in Elizabethan Literature." *SP* 35 (1938):178–94.
Wright, Louis B. "The Male-Friendship Cult in Thomas Heywood's Plays." *MLN* 42 (1927):510–14.

J. L.

How a Man May Choose a Good Wife from a Bad, comedy (*1602;* 1602)

Introduction, Attribution, Date, Sources

How a Man May Choose a Good Wife from a Bad (HMMC) was notably popular during the seventeenth century, as several scholars have pointed out: see, for example, Willard Thorp, *The Triumph of Realism in Elizabethan Drama, 1558–1612* (1928); Arthur Melville Clark, *Thomas Heywood: Playwright and Miscellanist* (1931); George Fullmer Reynolds, *The Staging of Elizabethan Plays at the Red Bull Theater, 1605–1625* (1940), and "*Mucedorus,* Most Popular Elizabethan Play?" in *Studies in the English Renaissance Drama in Memory of Karl Julius Holzknecht,* ed. J. W. Bennett et al. (1959), pp. 248–68.

Modern critics, however, have paid little attention to this anonymous play. There is no recent edition, for instance (although the 1608 text is available in microprint in Henry W. Wells, ed., *Three Centuries of Drama* [Readex Corp., 1955–56]), and comprehensive studies of the comedy are rare. Overall studies do appear in two books about Thomas Heywood: Otelia Cromwell, *Thomas Heywood: A Study in the Elizabethan Drama of Everyday Life* (1928); and Michel Grivelet, *Thomas Heywood et le drame domestique élizabéthain* (1957).

Cromwell briefly discusses earlier scholarship concerning date and the location of performances, then focuses upon the play's genre (domestic drama combining the themes of faithful wife and prodigal husband), setting, structure, and style. She explains that the sources have already been established: a story originally appearing in Cinthio's *Hecatommithi,* III.5, and probably used in the Elizabethan version made by Barnaby Riche in *Riche His Farewell to Militarie Profession* (1581). (Other scholars who accept Cinthio and/or Riche as the anonymous playwright's sources are Thorp and Grivelet [both above]; Thomas P. Harrison, Jr., "The Literary Background of Renaissance Poisons," *Studies in English* [Univ. of Texas] 27 [1948]:35–67; Thomas M. Cranfill and Dorothy Hart Bruce, *Barnaby*

Rich: A Short Biography [1953].) Cromwell concludes by reviewing attribution scholarship, comparing *HMMC* with Heywood's acknowledged work, and deciding that a convincing case for Heywood's authorship requires more external evidence than presently exists.

Grivelet, convinced by both internal and external evidence that Thomas Heywood wrote *HMMC*, concentrates on the way the playwright used Riche's version of the story by Cinthio. According to Grivelet, the changes Heywood made in the tale increase its dramatic interest and show the dramatist's skill in constructing plays. He believes also that with *HMMC*, Heywood invented the genre of domestic romance, and he suggests that the anonymous play may have influenced dramas by Marston and Shakespeare (cf. Grivelet's remarks on this subject in the introduction to his edition of *Measure for Measure* [1957; Aubier, Collection Bilingue]). Finally, Grivelet proposes a date of 1601 or early 1602; suggests that the play was performed by Worcester's Men while they occupied the Boar's Head; relates that six successive quartos followed the first edition of 1602; and explains that though Heywood's main source was Riche's story, the dramatist also drew on the popular domestic literature of the Elizabethan period.

Outside of the scholarship cited above, reference to attribution, date, and sources is sparse. W. W. Greg, ed., *English Literary Autographs, 1550–1650*, pt. 1 (1925), speculates that if Heywood wrote *HMMC*, then the playwright must have been writing for Worcester's company before their appearance in Henslowe's *Diary*. Like Grivelet, Clark believes that the comedy was written while Worcester's Men were still at the Boar's Head; he adds that it was slightly revised before its printing in 1602. In *Italian Popular Comedy* (1934) vol. 2, K. M. Lea considers the influence of the *commedia dell'arte* on *HMMC*.

Literary Connections and Genre

Thorp suggests that *HMMC* may have influenced the anonymous author of *The Fair Maid of Bristow* (1604), and Clark notes revealing parallels between *HMMC* and both Marlowe's *Jew of Malta* (1589) and the anonymous *Yorkshire Tragedy* (1606). R. P. Cowl, *Some "Echoes" in Elizabethan Drama of Shakespeare's "King Henry the Fourth," Parts I and II, Considered in Relation to the Text of Those Plays* (1926), finds an allusion to *1 Henry IV* in *HMMC*; Donald Joseph McGinn, *Shakespeare's Influence on the Drama of his Age, Studied in "Hamlet"* (1938), points out an allusion to *Hamlet*.

A number of critics in addition to Cromwell and Grivelet consider the genre of *HMMC*, focusing upon the manner in which the play employs prodigal son and patient Griselda motifs, or combines tragedy and comedy: see, for example, John B. Moore, *The Comic and the Realistic in English Drama* (1925); Thorp; Clark; Mary Crapo Hyde, *Playwriting for Elizabethans, 1600–1605* (1949); M. C. Bradbrook, *The Growth and Structure of Elizabethan Comedy* (1955); and Marvin T. Herrick, *Tragicomedy* (1955). Whereas Frederick T. Wood, "The Beginnings and Significance of Sentimental Comedy," *Anglia* 55 (1931): 368–92, sees resemblances between *HMMC* and the Augustan comedy of sentiment, Arthur Sherbo, *English Sentimental Drama* (1957), stresses that the overall effect of the play is not sentimental because comedy persistently undermines sentiment. Harold S. Wilson, "Dramatic Emphasis in *All's Well That Ends Well*," *HLQ* 13 (1950):217–40, groups *HMMC* with other contemporary plays about wronged wives and compares them all with *All's Well That Ends Well* to illustrate Shakespeare's superior handling of the theme. In *Shakespeare's "Troilus and Cressida" and Its Setting* (1964), Robert Kimbrough notes the moral implications of the domestic plot in *HMMC*.

Miscellaneous

William J. Lawrence, *Pre-Restoration Stage Studies* (1927), provides internal and external evidence to show that *HMMC* was an inn-yard play. Reynolds, *The Staging of Elizabethan Plays* ("Introduction"), who discusses some of the comedy's stage directions, thinks that it was probably performed sometime during the period of its continued popularity at the Red Bull. In "The Gallery Over the Stage in the Public Playhouse of Shakespeare's Time," *SQ* 8 (1957): 15–31, Richard Hosley groups *HMMC* with twenty-one other contemporary plays produced at the Red Bull between 1605 and 1625, dramas which did not require a gallery as an acting area.

Olive Mary Busby, *Studies in the Development of the Fool in the Elizabethan Drama* (1923), briefly discusses the function of Pipkin in *HMMC*, and Harrison ("Introduction") considers the way the device of a sleeping potion is used.

Wilfred T. Jewkes, *Act Division in Elizabethan and Jacobean Plays, 1583–1616* (1958), says that "the text is good, and probably not far removed from the author's original."

See Also

Boas, Frederick S. *Christopher Marlowe: A Biographical and Critical Study.* 1940.

———. *An Introduction to Stuart Drama.* 1946.

Brodwin, Leonora Leet. "The Domestic Tragedy of Frank Thorney in *The Witch of Edmonton.*" *SEL* 7 (1967):311–28.

Clark, Arthur Melville. "A Bibliography of Thomas Heywood." *Oxford Bibliographical Society: Proceedings & Papers* 1 (1922–26):97–153.

Dawson, Giles E. "An Early List of Elizabethan Plays." *Library* 15 (1935): 445–56.

Holaday, Allan. "Thomas Heywood and the Puritans." *JEGP* 49 (1950):192–203.

Linton, Marion. "National Library of Scotland and Edinburgh University Library Copies of Plays in Greg's *Bibliography of the English Printed Drama. SB* 15 (1962):91–104.

Myers, Aaron Michael. *Representation and Misrepresentation of the Puritan in Elizabethan Drama.* 1931.

Niemeyer, P. *Das bürgerliche Drama in England im Zeitalter Shakespeares.* 1930.

Schaefer, Elisabeth. "Zur Datierung von Shakespeare's *All's Well That Ends Well.*" *SJ* 59/60 (1923–24):86–108.

Sharpe, Robert Boies. *The Real War of the Theaters: Shakespeare's Fellows in Rivalry with the Admiral's Men, 1594–1603.* 1935.

Sykes, H. Dugdale. *Sidelights on Elizabethan Drama.* 1924.

Ure, Peter. "Marriage and the Domestic Drama in Heywood and Ford." *ES* 32 (1951):200–216.

Velte, F. Mowbray. *The Bourgeois Elements in the Dramas of Thomas Heywood.* 1924.

J. L.

The Merry Devil of Edmonton, comedy (*1602;* 1608)

Editions

The Merry Devil of Edmonton has been edited by E. H. C. Oliphant in *Shakespeare and His Fellow Dramatists* (1929), vol. 1, and in *Elizabethan Dramatists Other than Shakespeare* (1931); by A. K. McIlwraith in *Five Elizabethan Comedies* (1934); and by William Amos Abrams as *"The Merry Devil of Edmonton": 1608* (1942). The introductions to the texts in the anthologies are brief. Oliphant describes the extant text; states that the source of the main plot is a chapter in the prose pamphlet *The Famous Historie of Fryer Bacon* (first extant edition 1627) and that an analogue for the underplot is the prose tract *The Life and Death of the Merry Devil of Edmonton* . . . (Stationers' Register entry 1608) by Anthony Brewer; thinks that the play may date 1592 or earlier; notes indications that *Merry Devil* has been altered; and says that the anonymous comedy, attributed to Drayton, seems to have been written by a single dramatist. McIlwraith devotes his attention to the roles of comedy, magic, and realism in the play.

Abrams's lengthy and thorough introduction begins by giving the early bibliographical and stage history. In discussing sources and analogues, he agrees with the conclusions of John Manly, an earlier editor of the play, which were adopted by Oliphant. He speaks about the possible influence of *Wily Beguiled* (1602); about a jest which is the basis of IV.ii; and about the legends surrounding places and families in *Merry Devil*, which he considers to be a topographical comedy (cf. Robert Boies Sharpe, *The Real War of the Theaters: Shakespeare's Fellows in Rivalry with the Admiral's Men, 1594–1603* [1935], whose research on the legends is cited by Abrams). After reviewing scholarship about the date, Abrams gathers internal and external evidence to conjecture that the play may have been performed just before the closing of the theaters in 1603. He then analyzes the 1608 text, speculates about the nature of the copy behind it, and examines editions to date. His introduction ends with a study of the attribution problem. Rejecting earlier ascriptions of the play to Shakespeare, Anthony Brewer, Drayton, and Heywood, Abrams builds a case for Dekker's authorship primarily on internal evidence such as style, characters, and plot. In two appendices, he reprints Brewer's pamphlet on the Merry Devil and the jest which inspired IV.ii (see above).

Useful reviews of Abrams's edition include those of G. I. Duthie in *MLR* 39 (1944):193–95; Robert Adger Law in *JEGP* 42 (1943): 589–94; and J. B. Leishman in *RES* 20 (1944):316–17. W. W. Greg's judicious and detailed assessment of Abrams's work in *Library* 25 (1944/45):122–39, establishes why the edition is competent but not definitive. Greg takes issue with some of Abrams's conclusions about both the manuscript which underlay the 1608 edition (see also Wilfred T. Jewkes, *Act Division in Elizabethan and Jacobean Plays, 1583–1616* [1958]) and the relation between Brewer's chapbook and the play. He criticizes portions of the editorial work on the text and adds to the bibliographical notes provided for the title page.

The 1608 edition is available in microprint in Henry W. Wells, ed., *Three Centuries of Drama* (Readex Corp., 1955–56). Karl J. Holzknecht summarizes the plot in *Outlines of Tudor and Stuart Plays, 1497–1642* (1947), and Arthur Brown, comp., gives three excerpts from the play in *"A Whole Theatre of Others": An Anthology of Elizabethan and Jacobean Dramatists Other Than Shakespeare* (1960).

Attribution

Outside of Abrams's study, scholarship on attribution does little to solve the question of authorship. Harvey W. Hewett-Thayer, "Tieck and the Elizabethan Drama: His Marginalia," *JEGP* 34 (1935): 377–407, points out that Tieck, after denying Shakespeare's authorship of *Merry Devil*, later ascribed the comedy to Shakespeare and Middleton. E. K. Chambers, *William Shakespeare* (1930), vol. 1, thinks that the Shakespeare assignment deserves no support, and Richard Proudfoot, "Shakespeare and the New Dramatists of the King's Men, 1606–1613," in *Later Shakespeare*, SuAS, vol. 8 (1966), pp. 234–61, suggests that the Shakespeare ascription may have resulted from the knowledge that *Merry Devil* was part of the repertory of the King's Men between 1606 and 1613.

Fleay's attribution to Drayton has met with strong reservations or rejection: see, for example, J. M. Robertson, *The Shakespeare Canon*, pt. 1 (1922); Bernard H. Newdigate, *Michael Drayton and His Circle* (1941); and Holzknecht ("Editions"). Arthur Melville Clark, *Thomas Heywood: Playwright and Miscellanist* (1931), disagrees with earlier scholars who assigned *Merry Devil* to Heywood.

Like Abrams, Gerald J. Eberle, "Dekker's Part in *The Familie of Love*," in *Joseph Quincy Adams Memorial Studies*, ed. James G. McManaway et al. (1948), pp. 723–38, finds Dekker's hand in *Merry Devil*. M. T. Jones-Davies, *Un peintre de la vie londonienne: Thomas Dekker* (1958), vol. 2, accepts and summarizes Abrams's arguments for Dekker.

On the subject of attribution, see also Elizabeth Dorothy Worman, *The Authorship of "The Merry Devil of Edmonton"* (1925; in the Folger; not seen).

Date and Sources

Modern scholars tend to fix a date for *Merry Devil* early in the seventeenth century, between 1600 and 1604: see, for instance, Abrams; William J. Lawrence, *The Physical Conditions of the Elizabethan Public Playhouse* (1927); Sharpe ("Editions"); John Bakeless, *The Tragicall History of Christopher Marlowe* (1942), vol. 1; Jones-Davies ("Attribution"); and Katharine M. Briggs, *Pale Hecate's Team* (1962). However, Hardin Craig, *The Literature of the English Renaissance, 1485–1660*, in *A History of English Literature*, vol. 2, ed. Hardin Craig (1950), believes that the play may belong to the end of the sixteenth century. In *Pre-Restoration Stage Studies* (1927),

William J. Lawrence maintains that providing a date is a matter of speculation.

Sources have received little consideration recently. Sharpe ("Editions") believes that part of *Merry Devil* derives from Brewer's pamphlet and traces the origins of some family and place names in the play. Holzknecht ("Editions"), like Oliphant and Abrams, sees the pamphlet as an analogue, and he proposes that the love story may be the dramatist's invention.

Literary Connections and Genre

Imitations in *Merry Devil* of Shakespearean plays have been noticed by: Felix E. Schelling, *Elizabethan Playwrights* (1925); R. P. Cowl, *Some "Echoes" in Elizabethan Drama of Shakespeare's "King Henry the Fourth," Parts I and II, Considered in Relation to the Text of Those Plays* (1926), and *W. Shakespeare: "King Henry the Fourth" and Other Plays: An Experiment with "Echoes"* (1927); Donald Joseph McGinn, *Shakespeare's Influence on the Drama of His Age, Studied in "Hamlet"* (1938); *Catalogue of the Pierpont Morgan Library Exhibition on English Drama from the Mid-Sixteenth to the Later Eighteenth Century* (1946); Holzknecht ("Editions"); Robert H. Bowers, "Gesticulation in Elizabethan Acting," *SFQ* 12 (1948):267–77; and Proudfoot ("Attribution").

Scholars who remark the influence of Marlowe's *Doctor Faustus* (1592) on *Merry Devil* include: C. F. Tucker Brooke, "The Reputation of Christopher Marlowe," *Transactions of the Connecticut Academy of Arts and Sciences* 25 (1922):347–408; M. C. Bradbrook, *Themes and Conventions of Elizabethan Tragedy* (1935); Bakeless and Briggs ("Date"); and Joseph Horrell, "Peter Fabell and Dr. Faustus," *N&Q* 183 (1942):35–36. Both C. F. Tucker Brooke, in *A Literary History of England*, ed. Albert C. Baugh (1948), and M. C. Bradbrook, *The Growth and Structure of Elizabethan Comedy* (1955), view *Merry Devil* as a descendant of the plays of Greene.

Few critics treat genre. Sharpe ("Editions") uses the play to illustrate a genre he calls "Family Drama." The *Catalogue of the Pierpont Morgan Library* (above), and Madeleine Doran, *Endeavors of Art: A Study of Form in Elizabethan Drama* (1954), both consider *Merry Devil* a romantic comedy.

Text and Staging

H. Dugdale Sykes, "Notes on the Text of *The Merry Devil of Edmonton*," *N&Q* 153 (1927):187, briefly discusses two corrupt passages in the text, and J. Krzyzanowski, "Some Conjectural Remarks on Elizabethan Dramatists," *N&Q* 192 (1947):276–77, provides a reading for a line in the Induction. Lawrence, *Pre-Restoration Stage Studies* ("Date"), says that the text is corrupt. In *Shakespeare and the Stationers* (1955), Leo Kirschbaum suggests that *Merry Devil* was first printed from a corrupt private transcript and without the permission of the King's Men. Giles E. Dawson, "Copyright of Plays in the Early Seventeenth Century," *English Institute Essays* 6 (1947):169–92, reconstructs the early copyright history. (For textual matters, consult also "Editions.")

Lawrence, *Physical Conditions of the Elizabethan Public Playhouse* ("Date"), is concerned with the set for V.ii in *Merry Devil*. He discusses the staging of the Induction and the use of a chiming device in "Bells on the Elizabethan Stage," *Fortnightly Review* 116 (1924): 59–70; *Pre-Restoration Stage Studies* ("Date"); and *Those Nut-Cracking Elizabethans* (1935). Bowers ("Literary Connections") uses the play to illustrate a point about Elizabethan acting styles and staging. J. W. Saunders briefly considers the staging and sets of IV.ii and V.i in "Vaulting the Rails," *ShS* 7 (1954):69–81, and "Staging at the Globe, 1599–1613," *SQ* 11 (1960):401–25. In "The Discovery-Space in Shakespeare's Globe," *ShS* 12 (1959):35–46, Richard Hosley points out that *Merry Devil* requires a discovery-space. Bernard Beckerman, *Shakespeare at the Globe, 1599–1609* (1962), gives thought to the properties needed and to a matter of staging.

Miscellaneous

John William Ashton, "Conventional Material in Munday's *John a Kent and John a Cumber*," *PMLA* 49 (1934):752–61, compares the magic contests in *John a Kent and John a Cumber* (1589) and *Merry Devil*. In " 'I Serve the Good Duke of Norfolk,' " *MLQ* 10 (1949): 364–66, Rudolph Fiehler attempts to explain fifteen repetitions of a line in *Merry Devil*. Mary Crapo Hyde, *Playwriting for Elizabethans, 1600–1605* (1949), briefly refers to characterization and a ruse in the anonymous comedy; John V. Curry, *Deception in Elizabethan Comedy* (1955), mentions the play's use of disguise. William R. Bowden, *The English Dramatic Lyric, 1603–42: A Study in Stuart Dramatic Technique* (1951), notes a possibility for song; Katharine M. Briggs, *The Anatomy of Puck* (1959), and *Pale Hecate's Team* ("Date"), describes the sympathetic treatment of magic in the comedy.

See Also

Adams, Joseph Quincy. "Hill's List of Early Plays in Manuscript." *Library* 20 (1939):71–99.

Albright, Evelyn May. *Dramatic Publication in England, 1580–1640.* 1927.

Bartlett, Henrietta C. *Mr. William Shakespeare.* 1922.

Bentley, G. E. *The Jacobean and Caroline Stage.* Vol. 1. 1941.

———. *Shakespeare and His Theatre.* 1964.

Bradley, Jesse Franklin, and Joseph Quincy Adams. *The Jonson Allusion-Book.* 1922.

Brooke, C. F. Tucker. "Elizabethan 'Nocturnal' and 'Infernal' Plays." *MLN* 35 (1920):120–21.

Brooks, Alden. *Will Shakspere and the Dyer's Hand.* 1943.

Carrère, Félix, ed. *"Arden de Faversham": Étude critique et traduction.* 1950.

Crofts, Alfred. "The Canon of Thomas Heywood's Dramatic Writing." *Doctoral Dissertations* 3 (1935–36):86.

Cromwell, Otelia. *Thomas Heywood: A Study in the Elizabethan Drama of Everyday Life.* 1928.

Dawson, Giles E. "An Early List of Elizabethan Plays." *Library* 15 (1935): 445–56.

Forsythe, Robert S. "Comic Effects in Elizabethan Drama." *Quarterly Journal of the Univ. of North Dakota* 17 (1927):266–92.

Frohberg, Georg. "Das Fortleben des elisabethanischen Dramas im Zeitalter der Restauration." *SJ* 69 (1933):61–86.

Gerrard, Ernest A. *Elizabethan Drama and Dramatists, 1583–1603.* 1928.

Greg, W. W. "Authorship Attributions in the Early Play-Lists, 1656–1671." *Edinburgh Bibliographical Society Transactions* 2 (1938–45):303–29.

Jente, Richard. "The Proverbs of Shakespeare with Early and Contemporary Parallels." *Washington Univ. Studies,* Humanistic Ser. 13 (1926):391–444.

Judges, A. V. *The Elizabethan Underworld.* 2nd ed. 1965.

Kimbrough, Robert. *Shakespeare's "Troilus and Cressida" and Its Setting.* 1964.

Kreider, Paul V. *Elizabethan Comic Character Conventions as Revealed in the Comedies of George Chapman.* 1935.

Lawrence, William J. "A Plummet for Bottom's Dream." *Fortnightly Review* 111 (1922):833–44.

———. *Speeding up Shakespeare.* 1937.

Linton, Marion. "National Library of Scotland and Edinburgh University Library Copies of Plays in Greg's *Bibliography of the English Printed Drama.*" *SB* 15 (1962):91–104.

Lüdeke, H. *Ludwig Tieck und die Brüder Schlegel, Briefe mit Einleitung und Anmerkungen.* 1930.

Myers, Aaron Michael. *Representation and Misrepresentation of the Puritan in Elizabethan Drama.* 1931.

Nicoll, Allardyce. *A History of Restoration Drama, 1660–1700.* 2nd ed. 1928.

Niemeyer, P. *Das bürgerliche Drama in England im Zeitalter Shakespeares.* 1930.

Oliphant, E. H. C. *The Plays of Beaumont and Fletcher: An Attempt to Determine Their Respective Shares and the Shares of Others.* 1927.

———. "The Shakespeare Canon." *QR* 259 (1932):32–48.

Parks, Edd Winfield. "Simms's Edition of the Shakespeare Apocrypha." In *Studies in Shakespeare*, ed. Arthur D. Matthews and Clark M. Emery (1953), pp. 30-39.

Schoenbaum, S. *Internal Evidence and Elizabethan Dramatic Authorship.* 1966.

Sorelius, Gunnar. *"The Giant Race Before the Flood": Pre-Restoration Drama on the Stage and in the Criticism of the Restoration.* Aeta Universitatis Upsaliensis. Studia Anglistica Upsaliensia, no. 4 (1966).

Steele, Mary Susan. *Plays and Masques at Court during the Reigns of Elizabeth, James, and Charles.* 1926.

Tiddy, R. J. E. *The Mummers' Play.* 1923.

Wright, Louis B. "Animal Actors on the English Stage Before 1642." *PMLA* 42 (1927):656-69.

———. *Middle-Class Culture in Elizabethan England.* 1935.

Zocca, Louis R. *Elizabethan Narrative Poetry.* 1950.

J. L.

The Fair Maid of Bristow, comedy (*1604;* 1605)

Editions

The play is available in microprint in Henry W. Wells, ed., *Three Centuries of Drama* (Readex Microprint Corp., 1955-56).

Text

Wilfred T. Jewkes, Leo Kirschbaum, and Dora Jean Ashe concur in finding the 1605 edition of *Fair Maid of Bristow* to be a bad quarto. In *"The Faire Maid of Bristow* (1605), Another Bad Quarto," *MLN* 60 (1945):302-8, Kirschbaum provides evidence: the play's brevity, broken-down blank verse, and other characteristics of memorial reconstruction. "The emphasis in the original must have been on Vallenger as the rake who reforms and on Anabell, his long-suffering wife." The character of Florence, he states, is powerfully drawn. In *Shakespeare and the Stationers* (1955) he queries whether the performance information given in the Stationers' Register entry of the play and on the title page of the 1605 quarto can be trusted. See also his "An Hypothesis concerning the Origin of the Bad Quartos," *PMLA* 60 (1945):697-715. Ashe includes *Fair Maid of Bristow* in her study, "The Non-Shakespearean Bad Quartos as Provincial Acting Versions," *RenP*, 1954, pp. 57-62, as one of a number of texts memorially reconstructed for drifting acting companies performing in the provinces, and therefore being characterized by brevity, economical casting and staging requirements, often over-prominent comedy, and plague-period date. In the abstract of her 1954 Ph.D.

dissertation for the University of Virginia, "A Survey of Non-Shakespearean Bad Quartos," *DA* 14 (1954):1070-71, she further suggests that *Fair Maid of Bristow* may have been a group reconstruction. Jewkes, *Act Division in Elizabethan and Jacobean Plays, 1583-1616* (1958), believes the printer's copy to have been a text memorially reconstructed for performance, and gives examples of the corrupt state of the text.

The Play

The play is sometimes discussed as one of a group of Elizabethan domestic dramas on the theme of the abused wife or the prodigal husband. See Elisabeth Schäfer, "Shakespeare und das Domestic-Drama," *Germanisch-Romanische Monatsschrift* 13 (1925):202-18, 286-95, and "Zur Datierung von Shakespeare's *All's Well That Ends Well,*" *SJ* 59/60 (1924):86-108, Willard Thorp, *The Triumph of Realism in Elizabethan Drama, 1558-1612* (1928), Marvin T. Herrick, *Tragicomedy* (1955), and Robert Y. Turner, "Dramatic Conventions in *All's Well That Ends Well,*" *PMLA* 75 (1960):497-502. Thorp points out similarities especially between *Fair Maid of Bristow* and *How a Man May Choose a Good Wife from a Bad*, and suggests that the former may even have been inspired by the latter play. The plot, he states, is apparently the invention of the author, and the *mise en scène*, except for the character of Richard I, is contemporary. Robert Boies Sharpe, *The Real War of the Theaters* (1935), finds the play to belong to a dramatic type which he calls "family drama": plays in which characters represent (and are named for) real country families "of solid rather than lofty Elizabethan importance, and of secondary importance in earlier history," and which consist basically of domestic scenes, somewhat romantic and somewhat realistic, in a slight historical frame, with detailed local references and a low-comedy underplot. *Fair Maid of Bristow*, he admits, untypically has little or no local color. Sharpe speculates that *Fair Maid of Bristow* "may have been written for a Bristol visit [by the King's Men] during the plague interim" 1603-4, identifies characters with their real contemporary counterparts, and finds similarities in character types (noted in older scholarship) and in names and places, "which hint at their interchangeability," between *Fair Maid of Bristow* and *The London Prodigal, How a Man May Choose a Good Wife from a Bad*, and *The Miseries of Enforced Marriage*. The close resemblance between *Fair Maid of Bristow* and *How a Man May Choose* "may perhaps be due to disputed ownership of an underlying older play." Sharpe also links *Fair Maid of Bristow* with the earlier Admiral's Men multiple-disguise comedies such as *Look About You*.

Other Studies

Other criticism of the play consists almost entirely of miscellaneous comments in general surveys of Elizabethan drama; the lengthiest of such treatments is by Bernard Beckerman in *Shakespeare at the Globe, 1599–1609* (1962). Beckerman discusses above all the structure of the drama: its contrived finale, and its "mirror" structural pattern of two stories balanced, contrasted, and interwoven with one another. The structure, he maintains, is good, though the play lacks strong characterization, "richness of poetic texture," and a fresh approach to the prodigal son theme. His book also includes remarks on Anabell as the typical "faithful wife," and on staging details and disguise.

Marvin T. Herrick, *Tragicomedy*, calls *Fair Maid of Bristow* a tragicomedy comparable to the mature tragicomedies of Fletcher, Massinger, and Shirley; Michel Grivelet, *Thomas Heywood et le drame domestique élizabéthain* (1957), briefly discusses the play and declares it to be from *How a Man May Choose* and Marston's *Dutch Courtesan*; Irving Ribner, *The English History Play in the Age of Shakespeare* (1957; rev. ed. 1965), calls *Fair Maid of Bristow* a historical romance, into which the English king is introduced only as a *deus ex machina*. Richard Proudfoot, "Shakespeare and the New Dramatists of the King's Men, 1606–1613," in *Later Shakespeare*, SuAS, vol. 8 (1966), pp. 235–61, finds the play to be influenced by *Measure for Measure*. Ola Elizabeth Winslow, *Low Comedy as a Structural Element in English Drama from the Beginnings to 1642* (1926), states that the love element of Frog and Douse bridges a time gap; and identification of the play with the *Bristow Tragedy* by John Day recorded in Henslowe's *Diary* is rejected by Henry Hitch Adams, *English Domestic or, Homiletic Tragedy, 1575 to 1642* (1943).

A description of the play is given in *New Theatre Magazine* 5, pt. 2 (1964):24, in connection with the production of *Fair Maid of Bristow* in the Bristol Shakespeare Festival, 1964, by the Department of Drama at the University of Bristol and under the direction of Marion Jones. It is stated that Shakespeare probably acted in the 1603/4 performance of the play before James I, and that the author, who was not Shakespeare, was an excellent craftsman but not a great poet, with "a sure insight into popular taste." "The play is ... a melodrama, and one of the best extant examples of sheer 'box-office' entertainment from this period."

                                                                    A. L.

1 Jeronimo, with the Wars of Portugal, pseudo-history (*1604;* 1605)

Editions

1 Jeronimo has recently appeared as the first of the two plays in Andrew S. Cairncross's edition (1967; RRDS) of Kyd's *The First Part of Hieronimo* and *The Spanish Tragedy*. Cairncross takes the extant *Jeronimo* text to be a memorial version of a longer original first part (*The Spanish Comedy*) of *The Spanish Tragedy*, by Kyd, and supports his stand by reference to apparent corruptions in the text and to stylistic features and other elements, such as the intricate nature of the plot, common to *1 Jeronimo* and *The Spanish Tragedy*. Discrepancies between the two plays, he maintains, may be accounted for as due to the faulty memory of the reporter of *1 Jeronimo*, and in fact would have been less likely to have occurred if *Jeronimo* had been written by a hack writer following *The Spanish Tragedy*. *1 Jeronimo* is a play about the opposition of honor and policy; and "the emphasis falls on incident, structure, and suspense more than on character." The work's foundations are "melodramatic and Senecan," and the probable date of composition is between 1585 and 1587.

Origin and Date

The problem of the origin of *1 Jeronimo* is complex, but scholars examining the text, between 1923 and 1967, generally adopt one of two basic theories about the play: (1) that it is an imitation or burlesque of *The Spanish Tragedy*, written after it (a) at some unspecified date or (b) not before 1600; (2) that it is an old play (a) of unspecified origin or (b) which was written as a fore-piece to *The Spanish Tragedy*. Theory 2 has been less favored than 1 for many years, but is now coming back into critical repute.

Theory 1 has been held, with variations, by: Felix E. Schelling, *Foreign Influences in Elizabethan Plays* (1923) [a]; W. W. Greg, ed., *The Spanish Tragedy with Additions* (1925; Malone Society) [b]; Fredson Thayer Bowers, "Kyd's Pedringano: Sources and Parallels," *Harvard Studies and Notes in Philology and Literature* 13 (1931):

241-49 [b]; Frederick S. Boas, *An Introduction to Tudor Drama* (1933) [b]; Robert Boies Sharpe, *The Real War of the Theaters* (1935) [b]; Mary Crapo Hyde, *Playwriting for Elizabethans, 1600-1605* (1949) [b]; Félix Carrère, *Le théâtre de Thomas Kyd* (1951) [b]; Benvenuto Cellini, ed., *Drammi pre-Shakespeariani*, Collana di Letterature Moderne, no. 4 (1958) [a]; Bernard Spivack, *Shakespeare and the Allegory of Evil* (1958) [b]; Philip Edwards, ed., Kyd's *The Spanish Tragedy* (1959; Revels ed.) [a]. Only some of these scholars elaborate upon, develop, or argue for their point of view. Greg, believing that *1 Jeronimo* "manifestly parodies" *Spanish Tragedy* and "is inconsistent with *The Spanish Tragedy* both in character and incident," points out apparent references in the text to the year of Jubilee in Rome (1600) and to a boy playing the part of Jeronimo, and so places the drama after 1600. He moves, however, towards theory 2 in suggesting that *1 Jeronimo* may be "possibly based in some distant manner on earlier work." Boas dates the play, a "burlesque piece," ca. 1605; Bowers gives a date of 1600-1605. Sharpe believes it to be a Chamberlain's Men play, written and acted in 1602 as a burlesque on the old-fashioned *Spanish Tragedy* at that time being revived by the Admiral's Men, and then stolen by the Revels Children, who acted in it with the additional burlesque touch of giving the role of Jeronimo to one of the smallest among them. Hyde calls *1 Jeronimo* an "adaptation" and intentional burlesque of *Spanish Tragedy*; Cellini finds the play to be a parody and to be inconsistent with *Spanish Tragedy*, and consequently rejects Kyd as a possible author. Carrère emphasizes the mediocrity of *1 Jeronimo* and finds references to the Jubilee of 1600 and to the Chapel Children's 1604 performance of *The Spanish Tragedy*, together with inconsistencies between *Spanish Tragedy* and *1 Jeronimo*; he concludes that the work is by an unknown dramatist profiting from the 1602 revival of *Spanish Tragedy*. Spivack cites and accepts the views of Boas in his 1901 edition of Kyd's *Works*, dating the play ca. 1603. Edwards states that *1 Jeronimo* is "almost certainly intended as a burlesque," and was stolen from the King's Men and adapted by the Children of the Queen's Revels.

Theory 2 has not had as many adherents as 1 between 1923 and 1967. In 1931 Arthur Acheson, *Shakespeare, Chapman and "Sir Thomas More,"* developing an elaborate theory, calls *1 Jeronimo* a revision by Marston, for the Chapel Children, of a much-revised original by Kyd. Kyd's original play, Acheson believes, was revised by Marlowe (1587-89), then altered (1589-92) "by Peele and his assistants," who divided it into two works, *The Spanish Comedy* and *The Spanish Tragedy*, which were played by Lord Strange's Men in 1592; after 1594 and before 1599–1600 *The Spanish Comedy* was stolen from the Chamberlain's Men by Jonson and Marston, and was revised by Marston into *1 Jeronimo*. A. S. Cairncross, *The Problem of "Hamlet": A Solution* (1936), comments that "*Ieronimo*, like *The Spanish Tragedy* with which it is associated, is generally dated about 1585–6," though "it continued to be acted even after 1600." William Wells, "*Alphonsus, Emperor of Germany*," *N&Q* 179 (1940): 236–40, finds the extant *Jeronimo* to be a revised version of an original by Kyd, and John Bakeless, *The Tragicall History of Christopher Marlowe* (1942), vol. 1, believes that the play was "probably first produced in 1588 and certainly acted in 1591," and is probably Kyd's. In *Shakespeare and the Rival Traditions* (1952), Alfred Harbage states that the play "could only have been written as a fore-piece to *The Spanish Tragedy*" and apparently assumes Kyd's authorship. Finally, in 1967 Arthur Freeman, *Thomas Kyd: Facts and Problems*, suggests that *1 Jeronimo* is the original "*Spanish Comedy*" [of 1592], "borrowed and burlesqued, or perhaps reconstructed," by the Children of the Chapel, "perhaps in conjunction with their theft" of *The Spanish Tragedy* (the *Malcontent* Induction referring, he believes, to that play). The plot of *1 Jeronimo* is therefore probably close, he states, to that of the early fore-piece. Freeman finds in *1 Jeronimo* literary echoes of *Julius Caesar* and *Hamlet*, and a semi-parodic imitation of *The Gentleman Usher*, which place the extant text much later than 1592, and points out that this makes Kyd's authorship impossible, as does the style, which is not his. He does not accept, however, the existence of a reference in the text to the Jubilee of 1600, though he does note both the allusions to Jeronimo's smallness and a probable play on the name of a Chapel actor, William Ostler. He specifically rejects Edwards's view of the play as an adaptation of a Chamberlain's Men original.

For the most recent critical opinion, see Cairncross's edition.

Authorship

A few scholars comment on the authorship of the play without involving themselves directly in the problem of origin and date. A. Bronson Feldman, "The Rape of Antwerp in a Tudor Play," *N&Q* 5 (1958):246–48, apparently assumes *1 Jeronimo* to be Kyd's, and links it with *A Larum for London*. Dieter Mehl, however, in *The Elizabethan Dumb Show* (1965; German ed. 1964), comments that the play "is almost certainly not by Kyd"; and Ernest A. Gerrard, *Elizabethan Drama and Dramatists, 1583-1603* (1928), in a brief paragraph maintains that the "workmanship" of the drama is not like Kyd's but resembles that of Greene.

T. W. Baldwin, "On the Chronology of Thomas Kyd's Plays," *MLN* 40 (1925):343-49, calls Boas correct in rejecting *1 Jeronimo* as a first part by Kyd of *The Spanish Tragedy*.

See also J. C. Maxwell, "Peele and Shakespeare: A Stylometric Test," *JEGP* 49 (1950):557-61.

Other Studies

Spivack, *Allegory of Evil*, gives a critique of the play separated from the issues of origin, authorship, and date, in his book discussing the attempts in Elizabethan drama to fuse old homiletic and new naturalistic elements in the figure of the human villain which developed from the morality Vice. In *1 Jeronimo*, he states, Lorenzo is not a believable human villain because he is too much in the Vice tradition; and "the dramatic pattern established by the Vice is prominent not in action but in the homiletic method on its verbal level."

Schelling, *Foreign Influences*, states that the play purports to be derived from Spanish annals but that no real source has yet been found; Bakeless, *Tragicall History*, believes the work to imitate Marlowe. In *Die Geisterszene in der Tragödie vor Shakespeare*, Palaestra, vol. 225 (1958), Gisela Dahinten compares the play with *The Spanish Tragedy;* Hyde, *Playwriting*, remarks that "the old [*Spanish Tragedy*] plot has been subjected to the strong influence of low comedy" and that Jeronimo himself begins as a dignitary but ends as a clown, without heroic stature. The play itself, however, she declares, has stirring dramatic action. Hyde also comments on the opening dumb show. Wells, "*Alphonsus, Emperor of Germany*," finds links between *1 Jeronimo* and *Julius Caesar*, and Mehl, *Elizabethan Dumb Show*, comments on the ceremony of Jeronimo's installation as marshal and states that the play is like a popular history drama.

The text is mentioned by both Leo Kirschbaum, *Shakespeare and the Stationers* (1955), and Wilfred T. Jewkes, *Act Division in Elizabethan and Jacobean Plays, 1583-1616* (1958). Kirschbaum points out that the copy for Pavier's 1605 quarto came not from the King's Men but in some way from the Queen's Revels. He notes the Epilogue's reference to Jeronimo's short stature and believes *1 Jeronimo* to be the play referred to in the *Malcontent* Induction.

Jewkes calls the extant text apparently "a much adapted and reconstructed version, which was probably used as the basis of a promptbook." It has, he believes, been much cut, and perhaps is the basis of the version stolen from the King's Men by the boys and mentioned in the *Malcontent* Induction. Cairncross, *Problem of "Hamlet,"* in 1936 suggested that *Jeronimo* is one of a number of piracies from the same hand, the group including the *Romeo and Juliet, Henry V,* and *Merry Wives of Windsor* bad quartos, and *The Massacre at Paris.*

See Also

Baldwin, T. W. *The Organization and Personnel of the Shakespearean Company.* 1927.
Pearn, B. R. "Dumb-Show in Elizabethan Drama." *RES* 11 (1935):385–405.
Sisson, Charles J., ed. *Thomas Lodge and Other Elizabethans.* 1933.
Spencer, Hazelton. "The Elizabethan 'To Board.' " *MLN* 44 (1929):531–32.
Wright, Louis B. "Stage Duelling in the Elizabethan Theatre." *MLR* 22 (1927): 265–75.

A. L.

The London Prodigal, comedy *(1604;* 1605)

Editions

Since 1920 *The London Prodigal* has appeared in foreign-language editions only. A German translation of the play is included by Albert Ritter in *Der unbekannte Shakespeare* (1923); Diego Angeli translates the drama into Italian in his *Opere attribuite a Shakespeare* (1934), vol. 2; and there is a French adaptation by Henri Ghéon, *Le prodigue de Londres* (1947), which is based on the German version by Ernst Kamnitzer, *William Shakespeare: Der Londoner verlorene Sohn* [1931]. All editions contain a brief introduction (an afterword in Kamnitzer's edition).

The London Prodigal will appear in G. R. Proudfoot's forthcoming edition of the *Shakespeare Apocrypha,* and is also available in microprint in Henry W. Wells, ed., *Three Centuries of Drama* (Readex Microprint Corp., 1955–56).

Authorship

The attribution of *The London Prodigal* to Shakespeare is now generally rejected. (But see the foreign-language editions listed above.) E. K. Chambers, *William Shakespeare* (1930), vol. 1, dismisses Shakespeare's candidacy in one sentence; Baldwin Maxwell, "Conjectures on *The London Prodigal*," in *Studies in Honor of T. W. Baldwin*, ed. Don Cameron Allen (1958), pp. 171-84, finds the play to be entirely unlike Shakespeare's work; see also Maxwell's *Studies in the Shakespeare Apocrypha* (1956) and Leo Kirschbaum's *Shakespeare and the Stationers* (1955). Clara Longworth de Chambrun, however, in *Shakespeare: A Portrait Restored* (1957), implausibly gives Shakespeare a hand in the work, finding him to have corrected or rewritten parts of another's original.

Bernard H. Newdigate, *Michael Drayton and His Circle* (1941), dismisses Fleay's claim for Drayton's hand in the play as "irresponsible"; and Drayton is also rejected by Maxwell, "Conjectures," who turns down Marston as well, but will consider Dekker if the play can be dated ca. 1601. M. T. Jones-Davies, *Un peintre de la vie londonienne, Thomas Dekker* (1958), 2 vols., finds many Dekkerian elements in the work, in theme, situations, characters, vocabulary, and comic effects, and accepts Dekker as a possible sole or collaborate author. In *Thomas Heywood et le drame domestique élizabéthain* (1957), Michel Grivelet finds Heywood's influence in the play, but leaves the work as anonymous (and briefly discusses it).

Glenn H. Blayney, "Enforcement of Marriage in English Drama (1600-1650)," *PQ* 38 (1959):459-72, refers in a footnote to a 1925 Cornell University dissertation by G. S. Greene, "George Wilkins," which attributes *London Prodigal* to that dramatist. Maxwell, "Conjectures," summarizes attribution work to 1900. See also Charles Barber, "A Rare Use of the Word *Honour* as a Criterion of Middleton's Authorship," *ES* 38 (1957):161-68.

Date

Maxwell, "Conjectures," gives previous scholarship on date, and himself places the play between 1591 or 1595 (the date of *Romeo and Juliet*, which he believes to be echoed or parodied in *London Prodigal*) and 1605 (the date of *London Prodigal* publication), and tries to narrow the time spread by reference to the physical characteristics of the *London Prodigal* characters compared to the characteristics of the specific King's Men actors who presumably played the roles. Daffidill he believes to have been originally a more comic character than in the extant text, the part having been cut because of the 1603 or 1604 death of Thomas Pope. He concludes that *London Prodigal* was written before James became king, and was revised after the death of Pope, when the theaters reopened in 1604.

The Play

The London Prodigal is often discussed as one of a number of "abused wife" or "prodigal son" plays of the sixteenth and seventeenth centuries. See: Grivelet, *Thomas Heywood*; Robert Y. Turner, "Dramatic Conventions in *All's Well That Ends Well*," *PMLA* 75 (1960):497–502; Elisabeth Schäfer, "Shakespeare und das Domestic-Drama," *Germanisch-Romanische Monatsschrift* 13 (1925):202–18, 286–95, who views it as one of a number of domestic plays including *King Lear, Fair Maid of Bristow*, and *Measure for Measure*, and "Zur Datierung von Shakespeare's *All's Well That Ends Well*," *SJ* 59/60 (1924):86–108; Willard Thorp, *The Triumph of Realism in Elizabethan Drama, 1558–1612* (1928), who calls *London Prodigal* "one of the first naturalistic dramas in English"; Arthur Sherbo, *English Sentimental Drama* (1957), who quotes Thorp's views on the play though he does not wholly agree with them; Bernard Beckerman, *Shakespeare at the Globe, 1599–1609* (1962). Thorp, Sherbo, and Frederick T. Wood, the last in his "The Beginnings and Significance of Sentimental Comedy," *Anglia* 55 (1931):368–92, are concerned with the play above all in relation to eighteenth-century sentimental drama; and both Wood and Thorp believe that *London Prodigal* approaches the eighteenth-century type of sentimental play but differs from it in that the young prodigal in the Elizabethan work is not fundamentally good. Wood points out that the hero's reformation is accomplished only by a character change; Thorp calls this conversion "a kind of baptism" through "the regenerative power" of the virtue of the prodigal's wife. Sherbo classifies the play, not as a sentimental drama, but as a domestic comedy with a large element of the serious.

John Doebler, "Beaumont's *The Knight of the Burning Pestle* and the Prodigal Son Plays," *SEL* 5 (1965):333–44, discusses *London Prodigal* as one of a group of dramas, part of the prodigal son tradition, "which deal with the proper use of money"; he also notes that it is a middle-class play and an Italianate comedy of intrigue. Glenn H. Blayney, "Enforcement of Marriage," suggests that the play was intended to comment adversely on parentally enforced marriage and that it does not succeed on these terms. See also his "Wardship in English Drama (1600–1650)," *SP* 53 (1956):470–84.

Robert Boies Sharpe, *The Real War of the Theaters* (1935), views *London Prodigal* as a type of what he calls "family drama": plays in which the "leading roles are given to real families, some of them openly named, of solid rather than lofty Elizabethan importance, and of secondary importance in earlier history." These plays, he asserts, also have somewhat romantic domestic scenes, in a very slight framework of history, with detailed local references and a low-comedy underplot. According to Sharpe, in *London Prodigal* the characters have descriptive names but are unmasked as real people by a local allusion, and Sir Launcelot Spurcock is in reality one Sir Richard Bulkeley; and in *London Prodigal, Fair Maid of Bristow, How a Man May Choose a Good Wife from a Bad,* and *Miseries of Enforced Marriage,* character types (as noted in older scholarship), names and places are similar from one play to another.

Clara Longworth de Chambrun, *Shakespeare,* calls *London Prodigal* a comedy of manners in Jonson's style.

Other Studies

Beckerman, *Shakespeare at the Globe,* comments on the play's split structure and staging; other scholarly criticism is extremely miscellaneous. Kenneth Muir, *Shakespeare's Sources,* vol. 1 (1957), suggests Shakespeare's use of *London Prodigal* for Edgar's dialect in IV.vi of *King Lear;* Leslie Hotson, *Shakespeare's Sonnets Dated and Other Essays* (1949), explains the play's use of the expression, "Dun is the mouse"; Chambrun, *Shakespeare,* calls the play "hastily composed," perhaps to fill in the gap left in the King's Men repertory by the censorship of *Gowry;* Thomas Whitfield Baldwin, *The Organization and Personnel of the Shakespearean Company* (1927), rejects (in a footnote) Fleay's suggestion that Robert Armin played the part of Flowerdale, as does Maxwell, "Conjectures." A twentieth-century French production by Henri Ghéon is mentioned by Paul Blanchart, "Le théâtre contemporain et les élisabéthains," *EA* 13 (1960): 145–58.

Leo Kirschbaum, *Shakespeare and the Stationers,* asks how, if the quarto title-page attribution to Shakespeare is rejected, as it generally is, one can trust the title-page assignment of the play to the King's Men? Cf. Maxwell, "Conjectures," who is not so ready to reject the King's Men connection, though in his *Shakespeare Apocrypha* he notes that both the printer and the publisher of the 1605 quarto text were unscrupulous. Finally, Wilfred T. Jewkes, *Act Division in Elizabethan and Jacobean Plays, 1583–1616* (1958), states that the play was apparently printed from authorial manuscript or a transcript from it; there are no signs in the text of playhouse preparation.

See Also

Curry, John V. *Deception in Elizabethan Comedy.* 1955.

Cutts, John P. *La musique de scène de la troupe de Shakespeare.* 1959.

Hastings, William T. "*Exit* George Wilkins?" *ShAB* 11 (1936):67–83.

Herrick, Marvin T. *Tragicomedy.* 1955.

Hoskins, Frank L. "Misalliance: A Significant Theme in Tudor and Stuart Drama." *RenP*, 1956, pp. 72–81.

Kamnitzer, E. "*Der verlorene Sohn.* Warum darf und muss man den Namen Shakespeares über den Londoner verlorenen Sohn setzen?" *Germania*, Das neue Ufer, 34 (1929) [not seen].

Partridge, Edward B. *The Broken Compass.* 1958.

Proudfoot, Richard. "Shakespeare and the New Dramatists of the King's Men, 1606–1613." In *Later Shakespeare*, SuAS, vol. 8 (1966), pp. 235–61.

A. L.

The Wit of a Woman, comedy (*1604;* 1604)

Editions

The play is available in microprint in Henry W. Wells, ed., *Three Centuries of Drama* (Readex Microprint Corp., 1955–56).

Studies

The only modern critical work focused on *Wit of a Woman* is June J. Morgan's "Toward a Textual Study of *The Wit of a Woman,*" *ESRS* 15 (1966):8–17. Morgan discusses the order in which the five extant copies of the 1604 quarto came from the press, comments on the "mangled condition of the text," and attempts to reconstruct the plot. Internal stylistic evidence, especially of Italian influence, suggests to her a date in the early 1590s or in 1598; and the character name "Goffo" in the text might possibly be the name of the actor Robert Goffe (Goughe). Morgan deals briefly with the Italian characteristics of the play—character types, situation, comedy, plot, motifs, settings, technique, and form—but admits that no major Italian source is known. The play could, she declares, be a direct translation from the Italian, which is likely, or be indirectly connected with Italian drama or a *novella*; it differs, however, in one plot element from other Italianate and English comedy. Malone's attribution of the play to Chettle is rejected; possible candidates put forward are Chapman and Munday; perhaps *Wit of a Woman* is the play recorded in Henslowe's *Diary* as Chapman's "the [y]lle of A Womon" (15 June 1595), or Munday's "Comodey for the corte"

(Aug. 1598). Morgan argues at some length that internal and external evidence, plus textual study, points to Munday as the probable author.

Other critical comments on the play are brief. K. M. Lea, *Italian Popular Comedy* (1934), vol. 2, points out similarities between *Wit of a Woman* and Italian popular comic drama. "There is no need to ransack Italian fiction for the source of this comedy which gives us the clearest instance of the influence of the Commedia dell'arte. Properly speaking it has no story, but is constructed from the simple materials of the theme of a double love-interest and a couple of disguise manoeuvres." Robert Boies Sharpe, *The Real War of the Theaters* (1935), calls the play "rather amateurish and bourgeois" and assigns it possibly to the Chamberlain's Men, possibly to Worcester's. Wilfred T. Jewkes, *Act Division in Elizabethan and Jacobean Plays, 1583-1616* (1958), comments that the text is "one of the most confused of the period," and that it is "almost impossible to say what the [printer's] copy for this play must have been." He finds *Wit of a Woman* to be unidentifiable as belonging to the public or to the private theater, "except on the flimsy ground of a similarity of tone with other children's plays," and notes that other children's plays extant are not very corrupt texts.

Ola Elizabeth Winslow, *Low Comedy as a Structural Element in English Drama from the Beginnings to 1642* (1926), sees in the play an example of the tendency she finds in English drama after 1600 unjustifiably to interrupt or to delay the main action for the sake of comic matter.

See Also

Bowden, William R. *The English Dramatic Lyric, 1603-42.* 1951.

A. L.

Nobody and Somebody, with the True Chronicle History of Elydure, pseudo-history (*1605;* [ca. 1606])

Editions

The only twentieth-century edition of *Nobody and Somebody (N&S)* is David L. Hay's 1970 Bowling Green State University dissertation (*DA* 31 [1971]:6551A). In his introduction, Hay discusses attribution, date, text, and the play's peculiar stress on the disorder of the world.

The 1606 text is available in microprint in Henry W. Wells, ed., *Three Centuries of Drama* (Readex Corp., 1955–56).

Attribution, Date, and Sources

The question of attribution has received very little consideration and remains unsettled. Earlier scholarship had suggested that the extant *N&S* was the revision of an older play done by Heywood and Wentworth Smith for Henslowe. Arthur Melville Clark, *Thomas Heywood: Playwright and Miscellanist* (1931), who has no candidate for authorship, is not completely convinced that Heywood and Wentworth Smith ever revised the play. (In conjunction with Clark's comments about *N&S* in his book about Heywood, see his article "A Bibliography of Thomas Heywood," *Oxford Bibliographical Society: Proceedings & Papers* 1 [1922–26]:97–153.) Michel Grivelet, *Thomas Heywood et le drame domestique élizabéthain* (1957), accepting the suggestion of earlier scholars, says that if one identifies the title "albere galles" in Henslowe's *Diary* with the character Archigallo in *N&S*, then one must conclude that Heywood and Smith together revised the pseudo-history in September 1602.

Scholars have not yet established a date for the play. Clark, *Thomas Heywood*, thinks that the extant *N&S* is a revision of a play written in the early 1590s, when dramas about mythical kings of Britain were popular. The older piece may have been revised more than once: in 1602 for Henslowe and again after the accession of King James (Clark cites allusions in the play to events early in James's reign to support his claim for a second revision). In *Ralegh and Marlowe: A Study in Elizabethan Fustian* (1941), Eleanor Grace Clark remarks a possible reference to Essex in *N&S* which would fix the play's date during the Elizabethan period. Gertrude Catherine Reese, "The Question of the Succession in Elizabethan Drama," *Studies in English* (Univ. of Texas) 22 (1942):59–85, says that *N&S* was written after 1587. Grivelet thinks that it dates ca. 1590 and that the 1606 edition shows signs of revisions after James's accession. Like Clark, *Thomas Heywood*, and Grivelet, Irving Ribner, *The English History Play in the Age of Shakespeare* (1957; rev. ed. 1965), believes that the extant text dates from the beginning of James's reign; he suggests that the play was written originally ca. 1592.

Clark, *Thomas Heywood*, Grivelet, and Ribner agree that the primary source of *N&S* was Geoffrey of Monmouth's account of King Elidure's reign.

Literary Connections and Genre

Olive Mary Busby, *Studies in the Development of the Fool in the Elizabethan Drama* (1923), notices a possible connection between a scene in *N&S* and one in Shakespeare's *As You Like It*. Geoffrey Bullough, *Narrative and Dramatic Sources of Shakespeare*, vol. 5 (1964), agreeing with at least two editors of *Antony and Cleopatra* (see M. R. Ridley's revised version of R. H. Case's edition of *Antony and Cleopatra* [1954; ninth Arden]), finds some verbal resemblances between Shakespeare's play and *N&S* which lead him to conclude that Shakespeare probably wrote his tragedy in 1606. Paul E. Bennett, "A Critical Edition of *A Knack to Know a Knave*," (*DA* 13 [1953]:226–27), states that the anonymous play *A Knack to Know a Knave* (1592) and *N&S* are closely related because of their literary affinities with both the morality play and pseudo-historical romance. Both Gerta Calmann, "The Picture of Nobody: An Iconographical Study," *JWCI* 23 (1960):60–104, and Samuel C. Chew, *The Pilgrimage of Life* (1962), think that the reference in *The Tempest*, III.ii, to "the picture of Nobody" may be an allusion to the woodcut on the title page of *N&S*. (Most modern editors of *The Tempest* remark this possibility in their notes to III.ii.125: see, for example, Sir Arthur Quiller-Couch and John Dover Wilson's edition [1921; Cambridge], or Frank Kermode's edition [1954; sixth Arden].)

The genre of *N&S*, which combines morality-play features, romance, satire, and comedy, receives brief mention from Clark, *Thomas Heywood*, and Grivelet (both in "Attribution"); E. P. Vandiver, Jr., "The Elizabethan Dramatic Parasite," *SP* 32 (1935): 411–27; Bennett (above); and Alan C. Dessen, "The 'Estates' Morality Play," *SP* 62 (1965):121–36.

Political Implications

Reese ("Attribution") believes that *N&S* takes a stand on the issue of succession: hereditary right is the legitimate means of determining the succession as long as it is supported by good government. In *Shakespeare's History Plays* (1944), E. M. W. Tillyard maintains that Somebody in *N&S* represents disregard for order and degree. According to Grivelet ("Attribution"), the play offers a political and social critique which emphasizes the social responsibility of every man. Ribner ("Attribution") finds the political purpose of *N&S* perfectly lucid. He feels that in its sharp attacks on the abuses of law, wealth, power, and tyranny, the pseudo-history issues two warnings: one against the civil chaos which tyranny inevitably brings; the other against the miseries a state incurs through an irresponsible king. Ribner suggests also that the play may contain some allusions to Elizabeth and her court. Dessen ("Literary Connections") explains how *N&S* attacks social and political evils on two levels by means of its two plots; although the play indulges itself in comedy at times, social issues are still its main concern.

Calmann ("Literary Connections") provides a description of the Nobody and Somebody types which helps to clarify the play's political implications. She concentrates on the way these figures were represented pictorially and lists several books where reproductions of Nobody can be found.

Miscellaneous

Clark, *Thomas Heywood* ("Attribution"), briefly explains that *N&S* was acted on the Continent in the early 1590s and translated into German as *Niemand und Jemand* (printed 1620); Calmann ("Literary Connections"), discusses in some detail the play's success on the Continent, and its many translations and revisions between the early seventeenth century and the late nineteenth. In her edition of Massinger's *Great Duke of Florence* (1933), Johanne M. Stochholm concisely describes two seventeenth-century German adaptations of *N&S*.

Richard Hosley, "The Gallery Over the Stage in the Public Playhouse of Shakespeare's Time," *SQ* 8 (1957):15–31, groups *N&S* with twenty-one other contemporary plays produced at the Red Bull between 1605 and 1625, dramas which did not require a gallery as an acting area. Wilfred T. Jewkes, *Act Division in Elizabethan and Jacobean Plays, 1583–1616* (1958), thinks that the copy for the play probably came from the playhouse. Kenneth Muir, "An Unfinished Prompt-Book," *SQ* 9 (1958): 420–22, describes a copy of the first quarto of *N&S* in the Folger Shakespeare Library and speculates about who its original owner might have been.

Louis B. Wright, "Stage Duelling in the Elizabethan Theatre," *MLR* 22 (1927):265–75, gives a brief account of the wrestling match in the play, and William J. Lawrence, *Speeding up Shakespeare* (1937), proposes that Tarlton may have played the part of the clown.

See Also

"Antiquarian Notes: Elizabethan Plays in Germany." *TLS*, 26 April 1941, p. 208.

Baesecke, Anna. *Das Schauspiel der englischen Komödianten in Deutschland: Seine dramatische Form und seine Entwicklung.* Studien zur englischen Philologie, vol. 87 (1935).

Boas, Frederick S. *Thomas Heywood.* 1950.

Brewster, Paul G. "Games and Sports in Sixteenth- and Seventeenth-Century English Literature." *WF* 6 (1947):143–56.

Brockbank, J. P. "The Frame of Disorder—*Henry VI.*" In *Early Shakespeare,* SuAS, vol. 3 (1961), pp. 72–99.

Dawson, Giles E. "An Early List of Elizabethan Plays." *Library* 15 (1935): 445–56.

Fredén, Gustaf. *Friedrich Menius und das Repertoire der englischen Komödianten in Deutschland.* 1939.

———. " 'Those That Play Your Clowns . . . .' " *MSpr* 58 (1964):317–31.

Kramer, Frederic J. "*Nobody and Somebody:* A Study of the English and Two German Versions." *Ohio State Univ. Abstracts of Doctors' Dissertations* 20 (1935–36):61–70; and *Doctoral Dissertations* 3 (1935–36):91.

Lawrence, William J. *Pre-Restoration Stage Studies.* 1927.

Nicoll, Allardyce. " 'Tragical-Comical-Historical-Pastoral': Elizabethan Dramatic Nomenclature." *BJRL* 43 (1960):70–87.

Reynolds, George Fullmer. *The Staging of Elizabethan Plays at the Red Bull Theater, 1605–1625.* 1940.

Riewald, J. G. "New Light on the English Actors in the Netherlands, c. 1590–c. 1660." *ES* 41 (1960):65–92.

Sykes, H. Dugdale. *Sidelights on Elizabethan Drama.* 1924.

Velte, F. Mowbray. *The Bourgeois Elements in the Dramas of Thomas Heywood.* 1924.

Wright, Celeste Turner. "Some Conventions Regarding the Usurer in Elizabethan Literature." *SP* 31 (1934):176–97.

J. L.

A Yorkshire Tragedy, tragedy (*1606;* 1608)

Editions

Several editions of *A Yorkshire Tragedy (All's One, or One of the Four Plays in One) (YT)* appear in anthologies: H. F. Rubinstein, ed., *Great English Plays* (1928); E. H. C. Oliphant, ed., *Shakespeare and His Fellow Dramatists* (1929), vol. 2; Oliphant's *Elizabethan Dramatists Other Than Shakespeare* (1931); *A Book of Short Plays: XV–XX Centuries* (1940); J. V. Cunningham, ed., *The Renaissance in England* (1966); and Keith Sturgess, ed., *Three Elizabethan Domestic Tragedies* (1969). The play has also been edited by Barry Joseph Gaines as a 1971 University of Wisconsin dissertation (*DA* 32 [1971]:3248A–3249A), and by Diego Angeli in *Opere attribuite a Shakespeare* (1934), vol. 1 (in Italian translation).

Most of the anthology editions have brief introductions. Rubinstein, focusing on attribution, speculates that a minor dramatist of the period is probably responsible for *YT*. Oliphant finds reason to reject ascriptions to Shakespeare, Middleton, and Wilkins; in addition, he considers the questions of date, source, and the relation between *YT* and Wilkins's *The Miseries of Enforced Marriage* (1606). The general introduction to Cunningham's edition mentions how the play reflects class distinctions in Renaissance England. Concise but comprehensive, Sturgess's discussion covers genre, sources, themes, dramatic conventions, the connection between *YT* and Wilkins's *Miseries*, attribution, staging, and text. (In an appendix, Sturgess reprints part of the pamphlet *Two Unnatural Murders* [1605], which is the play's source.) The introduction to Gaines's dissertation edition deals with authorship, sources, date, and text, and provides a critical evaluation of *YT*.

The 1608 edition is available in microprint in Henry W. Wells, ed., *Three Centuries of Drama* (Readex Corp., 1955-56). Allardyce Nicoll, ed., *Readings from British Drama* (1928), prints an excerpt from the tragedy, and Karl J. Holzknecht, *Outlines of Tudor and Stuart Plays, 1497-1642* (1947), summarizes the plot.

General

A key to the issues which most concern students of *YT* is provided by Baldwin Maxwell's comprehensive analysis of the play in *Studies in the Shakespeare Apocrypha* (1956). Maxwell discusses the relation between the play and its pamphlet source; the addition of the puzzling first scene, which seems unconnected to the rest of the tragedy; and the inaccurate accounts of Walter Calverley's history before the murder of his sons. He takes issue with earlier critics who assume that the relationship between *YT* and *Miseries of Enforced Marriage* is extremely close, and with Fleay and Sykes's theory that the anonymous play is part of *Four Plays in One* (see H. Dugdale Sykes, "The Authorship of *A Yorkshire Tragedy*," *JEGP* 16 [1917]: 437-53, rpt. in *Sidelights on Shakespeare* [1919], pp. 77-98). Considering the question of date, Maxwell presents evidence which suggests the later part of 1605 for *YT* and the beginning of 1606 for *Miseries*. In the section on attribution, he reviews ascriptions to Shakespeare, Heywood, and Wilkins, and concludes: "A convincing identification of the author or authors of *A Yorkshire Tragedy*, if it is ever to be accomplished, must await our clearer knowledge of what were the peculiar characteristics of the various Jacobean dramatists."

Useful reviews of Maxwell's book are those of G. K. Hunter in *MLR* 52 (1957):587-88, and M. A. Shaaber in *MLN* 72 (1957):290-92. Less detailed than Maxwell's study, A. C. Cawley's *English Domestic Drama: "A Yorkshire Tragedy"* (1966), a pamphlet, also treats the play comprehensively. Cawley describes at length the relationship between the play and its source; mentions that the connection between *YT* and *Miseries* is "obscure"; and puzzles over the dissociation of the first scene from the other nine. In his discussion of attribution, he considers Shakespeare's claim to the anonymous play. Finally, Cawley makes critical observations about genre, the theme of demonic possession, and the way the Calverley murders have excited the popular imagination up to the present day.

Attribution

Most modern scholarship on *YT* rejects the Shakespeare ascription: see, for example, E. K. Chambers, *William Shakespeare* (1930), vol. 1; C. F. Tucker Brooke, in *A Literary History of England*, ed. Albert C. Baugh (1948); Leo Kirschbaum, *Shakespeare and the Stationers* (1955). Richard Proudfoot, "Shakespeare and the New Dramatists of the King's Men, 1606-1613," in *Later Shakespeare*, SuAS, vol. 8 (1966), pp. 234-61, suggests that the ascription may have resulted because *YT* was performed by the King's Men. In *Shakespeare: A Portrait Restored* (1957; French ed. 1947), Clara Longworth, Comtesse de Chambrun, is willing to concede that Shakespeare may have taken a small part in composing or staging the play, perhaps collaborating with Wilkins.

Heywood's claim has been argued most extensively by Arthur Melville Clark, *Thomas Heywood: Playwright and Miscellanist* (1931). After commenting on earlier attribution scholarship, Clark builds his case for Heywood by comparing *YT* with the dramatist's known work (which, in his opinion, apparently includes the anonymous play *How a Man May Choose a Good Wife from a Bad* [1602]). His internal evidence includes plot development, characterization, literary style, and use of sources. (In conjunction with Clark's discussion of authorship in his book about Heywood, see his article "A Bibliography of Thomas Heywood," *Oxford Bibliographical Society: Proceedings & Papers* 1 [1922-26]:97-153.) T. S. Eliot, "Thomas Heywood," in *Elizabethan Essays* (1934), pp. 101-16, thinks that Clark's ascription is a "valuable" one, and W. Bridges-Adams, *The Irresistible Theatre*, vol. 1 (1957), considers the Heywood attribution a better speculation than the Shakespeare assignment. However,

Frederick S. Boas, *Thomas Heywood* (1950), remains unconvinced by Clark's argument, and Michel Grivelet, *Thomas Heywood et le drame domestique élizabéthain* (1957), suggests that Heywood contributed but reaches no decision about authorship.

The remaining attribution scholarship does little to solve the problem of authorship. E. H. C. Oliphant, *The Plays of Beaumont and Fletcher: An Attempt to Determine Their Respective Shares and the Shares of Others* (1927), who sees no evidence of Shakespeare's or Beaumont's work in *YT*, hints that Middleton may have contributed (cf. Oliphant's later opinion about attribution in his editions of the tragedy ["Editions"]). Rubinstein's edition ("Editions") proposes that a minor dramatist might have produced the play. In *"Exit George Wilkins?"* *ShAB* 11 (1936):67–83, William T. Hastings points out weaknesses in Sykes's argument (see "General") that Wilkins wrote the play. After considering both the Shakespeare and Wilkins ascriptions, Marc Friedlaender, "Some Problems of *A Yorkshire Tragedy,"* *SP* 35 (1938):238–53, reasons that conclusive proof for Wilkins's authorship is lacking and the first scene may be Shakespeare's. Sturgess ("Editions"), after reviewing attribution scholarship, concludes: "It is probably more sensible, and it is certainly easier, to see *A Yorkshire Tragedy* as a product of its circumstances rather than to try to identify a particular author for it." Gaines ("Editions") thinks that the author is elusive.

Date and Sources

Outside of the editions and comprehensive studies of *YT*, there has been very little discussion of date. In general, scholars date the play no earlier than 1606, though Maxwell ("General") and Gaines ("Editions") place it in the latter half of 1605. Typically, William J. Lawrence, *Pre-Restoration Stage Studies* (1927), thinks that the tragedy could not have been produced more than two years at most before its publication.

The source and analogues—the Calverley story treated by Stow, a ballad, two pamphlets, and another play—receive attention from: Clark, *Thomas Heywood*, Hastings, and Friedlaender (all in "Attribution"); Henry Hitch Adams, *English Domestic or, Homiletic Tragedy, 1575-1642* (1943); Holzknecht ("Editions"); and Glenn H. Blayney in two articles, "Wardship in English Dram. (1600–1650)," *SP* 53 (1956):470–84, and "Wilkins's Revisions in *The Miseries of Inforst Mariage,"* *JEGP* 56 (1957):23–41, and in his edition of *The Miseries of Enforced Marriage* for the Malone Society (1964, for 1963).

Yorkshire Tragedy and *Miseries of Enforced Marriage*

Three scholars focus their attention on the relationship between *YT* and *Miseries*.

Clark, *Thomas Heywood* ("Attribution"), following the suggestion of P. A. Daniel, argues that the two plays together constituted *The Four Plays in One* mentioned in the head-title of *YT*. After providing evidence to support this view, Clark attempts to determine the four parts of *The Four Plays in One*. (Kenneth Muir in the introduction to his edition of George Wilkins's *The Painfull Adventures of Pericles, Prince of Tyre,* Liverpool Reprints, no. 8 [1953], finds Clark's theories plausible.)

Friedlaender ("Attribution") disagrees with earlier scholars who conjecture that *YT* and *Miseries* were one play. He argues, however, that the anonymous tragedy may have been the last part of a play whose first part was drastically revised to become *Miseries*. According to Friedlaender, censorship of the original play, which was done to avoid offending the Calverley and Cobham families, accounts for the cutting of the original drama, the revisions which produced *Miseries*, and the addition of the first scene to *YT*.

Glenn H. Blayney speaks about the relation between the two plays in his edition of *Miseries* ("Date") and several articles: "Massinger's Reference to the Calverley Story," *N&Q* 1 (1954):17–18; "Variants in Q1 of *A Yorkshire Tragedy,*" *Library* 11 (1956):262–67; his 1956 *SP* article and his 1957 *JEGP* article (both in "Date"). In his most detailed discussion of the matter, the 1957 *JEGP* article, he disagrees with critics who hypothesize a structural link between the two plays. Blayney feels that textual and bibliographical evidence suggests that *YT* and *Miseries* are separate plays and that Wilkins's drama originally had a different ending from its present one which had no direct connection with the anonymous play. Supporting his view that the earlier ending of *Miseries* was tragic, Blayney cites and explains an allusion in Massinger's *The Guardian* (1633) to the Calverley story (an argument he treated at greater length in his 1954 *N&Q* article [above]). Finally, in this article, Blayney rejects Friedlaender's censorship theory in favor of the theory that Wilkins revised his ending for *Miseries* not from *YT* but from his own earlier draft of a conclusion unlike the anonymous tragedy. Blayney's 1956 *Library* article (above) also undermines the view that the two plays are structurally linked. Here the critic suggests that careful textual study of *YT* may help to show that the textual histories of the anonymous play and *Miseries* are presently not compatible. (In conjunction with this article, see Blayney's "Variants in the First Quarto of *The Miseries of Inforst Mariage,*" *Library* 9 [1954]:176-84.) In his edition of Wilkins's play ("Date"), Blayney reviews earlier scholarship on the relation between the two dramas, and in his 1956 *SP* article ("Date") he contrasts the treatment of wardship and enforced marriage in them.

A few scholars deal briefly with the connection between *YT* and *Miseries.* M. C. Bradbrook, *Themes and Conventions of Elizabethan Tragedy* (1935), comments that the anonymous play seems to be an alternative fifth act for Wilkins's drama; in her view, *YT* probably belonged to a series of plays based on a single theme. Adams ("Date") remarks the similar origins of both plays; pointing out that scene one of *YT* alludes to events in *Miseries*, he conjectures that either the audience is expected to have the required background information or the information was given by one of the earlier plays of *The Four Plays in One.* Holzknecht ("Editions") compares the two plays and, like Adams, mentions that *Miseries* clarifies the confusing first scene of *YT.*

Genre

The genre of *YT*, generally held to be domestic tragedy, receives attention from: Alan Reynolds Thompson, "Melodrama and Tragedy," *PMLA* 43 (1928):810-35; Willard Thorp, *The Triumph of Realism in Elizabethan Drama, 1558-1612* (1928); Felix Sper, "The Germ of the Domestic Drama," *Poet Lore* 40 (1929):544-51; Clark ("Attribution"); Adams ("Date"); *Catalogue of the Pierpont Morgan Library Exhibition on English Drama from the Mid-Sixteenth to the Later Eighteenth Century* (1946); Madeleine Doran, *Endeavors of Art: A Study of Form in Elizabethan Drama* (1954); Arthur Sherbo, *English Sentimental Drama* (1957); José Axelrad and Michèle Willems, *Shakespeare et le théâtre élizabéthain* (1964); Sturgess ("Editions").

Adams provides the most extensive treatment of genre, interpreting *YT* according to his carefully worked-out definition of domestic tragedy. Also helpful, Sherbo's study compares the anonymous seventeenth-century tragedy with three eighteenth-century plays derived from it to show how domestic tragedy differs from sentimental drama (cf. John Homer Caskey, *The Life and Works of Edward Moore* [1927], who also examines later dramatic versions of YT).

Staging, Text, and Miscellaneous

In "The Discovery-Space in Shakespeare's Globe," *ShS* 12 (1959): 35–46, Richard Hosley concludes that *YT* does not seem to require a discovery-space. J. W. Saunders, "Staging at the Globe, 1599–1613," *SQ* 11 (1960):401–25, comments on the staging of the fifth scene, and Bernard Beckerman, *Shakespeare at the Globe, 1599–1609* (1962), discusses briefly the staging of three scenes, a puzzling stage direction, and the properties needed for the play.

J. Krzyzanowski, "Some Conjectural Remarks on Elizabethan Dramatists," *N&Q* 192 (1947):276–77, offers a reading for a line in the second scene. Glenn H. Blayney contributes three articles relating to textual matters. In "An Error in Microfilms," *Library* 8 (1953): 126–27, he describes irregularities in a microfilm of the Kemble-Devonshire copy of *YT*, 1608, in the Huntington Library, and warns readers to beware of inaccuracies in reproductions of printed books on microfilm. His 1956 *Library* article (cited in "*Yorkshire Tragedy* and *Miseries of Enforced Marriage*" above) describes what is revealed by his textual collation of the six copies of Q1 and suggests that investigation of the text's origin and transmission is needed. He discusses the use of dramatic pointing in "Dramatic Pointing in the *Yorkshire Tragedy*," *N&Q* 4 (1957):191–92. Kirschbaum ("Attribution") includes *YT* in his survey of the "so-called '1619 quartos' " printed by William Jaggard. Wilfred T. Jewkes, *Act Division in Elizabethan and Jacobean Plays, 1583–1616* (1958), maintains that the text of this play is the manuscript of either the author or a reviser.

Lawrence Babb, *The Elizabethan Malady: A Study of Melancholia in English Literature from 1580 to 1642* (1951), succinctly diagnoses the Husband's melancholy. In "Family Honour in the Plays of Shakespeare's Predecessors and Contemporaries," *E&S* 6 (1953):19–40, Edward M. Wilson describes how the theme of marital dishonor is treated. Robert Rentoul Reed, Jr., *The Occult on the Tudor and Stuart Stage* (1965), speaks about the concept of devil-possession (cf. Cawley ["General"] and Adams ["Date"]).

See Also

Barker, Richard Hindry. *Thomas Middleton.* 1958.

Bartlett, Henrietta C. *Mr. William Shakespeare.* 1922.

Blayney, Glenn H. "G. Wilkins and the Identity of W. Calverley's Guardian." *N&Q* 198 (1953):329–30. (See the reply of Baldwin Maxwell in the same volume of *N&Q*, p. 450.)

Boas, Frederick S. *Shakespeare and the Universities*. 1923.

———. *An Introduction to Stuart Drama*. 1946.

Carrère, Félix, ed. *"Arden de Faversham": Étude critique et traduction*. 1950.

Chapman, Raymond. *"Arden of Faversham:* Its Interest Today." *English* 11 (1956):15–17.

Craig, Hardin. *The Literature of the English Renaissance, 1485–1660*. In *A History of English Literature*, vol. 2, ed. Hardin Craig (1950).

Cunningham, J. V. *Woe or Wonder: The Emotional Effect of Shakespearean Tragedy*. 1951.

Cutts, John P., ed. *La musique de scène de la troupe de Shakespeare, the King's Men, sous le règne de Jacques Ier*. 1959.

Dawson, Giles E. "An Early List of Elizabethan Plays." *Library* 15 (1935): 445–56.

———. "Robert Walker's Editions of Shakespeare." In *Studies in the English Renaissance Drama in Memory of Karl Julius Holzknecht*, ed. J. W. Bennett et al. (1959), pp. 58–81.

Evans, Ifor. *A Short History of English Drama*. 1948; rev. ed. 1965.

Gerrard, Ernest A. *Elizabethan Drama and Dramatists, 1583–1603*. 1928.

Gibson, H. N. *The Shakespeare Claimants*. 1962.

Gillet, Louis. *"Arden de Feversham."* In *Le théâtre élizabéthain* (special issue of *CS* 10 [1933]:154–61, rpt. with additions 1940, pp. 197–207, and in a translation by Max Bluestone in *Shakespeare's Contemporaries*, ed. Max Bluestone and Norman Rabkin [1961], pp. 149–56).

Harbage, Alfred. *Shakespeare and the Rival Traditions*. 1952.

Hoffman, Calvin. *The Murder of the Man Who Was "Shakespeare."* 1955.

Kendall, Lyle H., Jr. "Shakespeare Collections, Quartos, Source and Allusion Books in the W. L. Lewis Collection." In *Shakespeare 1964*, ed. Jim W. Corder (1965), pp. 113–77.

Lawrence, William J. "Horses on the Elizabethan Stage." *TLS*, 5 June 1919, p. 312.

———. *Those Nut-Cracking Elizabethans*. 1935.

Linton, Marion. "National Library of Scotland and Edinburgh University Library Copies of Plays in Greg's *Bibliography of the English Printed Drama*." *SB* 15 (1962):91–104.

Mackenzie, Agnes Mure. *The Playgoer's Handbook to the English Renaissance Drama*. 1927.

Muir, Kenneth. *Shakespeare as Collaborator*. 1960.

Myers, Aaron Michael. *Representation and Misrepresentation of the Puritan in Elizabethan Drama*. 1931.

Newdigate, Bernard H. *Michael Drayton and His Circle*. 1941.

Nicoll, Allardyce. *British Drama*. 1925; 5th ed., 1962.

Niemeyer, P. *Das bürgerliche Drama in England im Zeitalter Shakespeares*. 1930.

Oliphant, E. H. C. "The Shakespeare Canon." *QR* 259 (1932):32–48.

Parks, Edd Winfield. "Simms's Edition of the Shakespeare Apocrypha." In *Studies in Shakespeare*, ed. Arthur D. Matthews and Clark M. Emery (1953), pp. 30–39.

Pellegrini, Giuliano. "Note sulla *Yorkshire Tragedy*." *Convivium*, 1950, pp. 206–15 (also in Pellegrini's *Barocco Inglese* [1953], pp. 223–35).

Praz, Mario. *The Flaming Heart.* 1958.

Ritter, A. *Der unbekannte Shakespeare.* 1923.

Schoenbaum, S. *Internal Evidence and Elizabethan Dramatic Authorship.* 1966.

Sisson, Charles J. *Le goût public et le théâtre élisabéthain jusqu'à la mort de Shakespeare.* 1922.

Una Tragedia nella Contea di York (1952; listed by Gordon Ross Smith in *A Classified Shakespeare Bibliography: 1936–1958* [1963]:C326; not seen).

Wolff, Max J. "Zu *Arden von Feversham.*" *NS* 35 (1927):424–27.

Wood, Frederick T. "The Beginnings and Significance of Sentimental Comedy." *Anglia* 55 (1931):368–92.

J. L.

The Second Maiden's Tragedy, tragedy (*1611;* MS)

Editions

The Second Maiden's Tragedy (SMT) has recently been edited by Harold L. Stenger, Jr., in a University of Pennsylvania Ph.D. dissertation, "*The Second Maiden's Tragedy*: A Modernized Edition with an Introduction" (*DA* 14 [1954]:1423). The four-part introduction deals with manuscript, sources, authorship, and the play as tragic drama. In the first part, Stenger describes and analyzes the text; in the second, he presents analogues to the main plot from the legendary history of Ines de Castro and Don Pedro of Portugal and from the Herod-Mariamne and the Charlemagne-Fastrada legends, and examines in detail the subplot's debt to Cervantes's story of "The Curious Impertinent." In the third and fourth parts, reviewing previous authorship attributions, he assigns the drama to Middleton, and, relating the play to "the Jacobean theatrical environment," sees it as "a new kind of sensational drama, the tragedy of lust."

The play is at present being edited for the Revels series by Anne Lancashire.

Manuscript

The manuscript, a prompt copy dated 1611 and containing literary, playhouse, and censorship revisions by at least three hands other than that of its scribe, has been of special interest to scholars. W. W. Greg, *Dramatic Documents from the Elizabethan Playhouses* (1931), includes in "Reproductions and Transcripts" [vol. 2] a reproduction and transcription of folios 46a, 47a, and 48a, and in "Commentary" [vol. 1] discusses both prompt books in general and the *SMT* manuscript in particular. The book is a transcript by a professional scribe, Greg states; and the two actors' names which are inserted by a playhouse reviser identify the acting company as the King's Men. William J. Lawrence, *Pre-Restoration Stage Studies* (1927), discusses the manuscript as prompt book. Wilfred T. Jewkes, *Act Division in Elizabethan and Jacobean Plays, 1583–1616* (1958), wrongly states that the act headings appear in the author's hand, and comments on the act divisions. The manuscript is incorrectly cited by B. A. P. van Dam, "Shakespeare Problems Nearing Solution. *Henry VI* and *Richard III*," *ES* 12 (1930):81–97, as illustrating that in the Jacobean playhouse the author's fair copy of a play was used in production, no transcript being necessary, not even when a play was shortened. Thomas Whitfield Baldwin, *The Organization and Personnel of the Shakespearean Company* (1927), comments on textual details and uses the manuscript in establishing the typical character parts of the two actors named in it, Richard Robinson and Robert Goffe.

Evelyn May Albright and Eleanor Grace Clark both focus on the censorship of the manuscript. Albright, *Dramatic Publication in England, 1580–1640* (1927), gives examples of how the censor removed from the text references to royal and upper-class vices and two satiric hits at women, together with "impropriety" of language; Clark, *Ralegh and Marlowe: A Study in Elizabethan Fustian* (1941), comments too on the censorship of apparent criticism of James I, and remarks that the censor paid no attention to a possible parallel between the Lady and Arabella Stuart. (The part of Clark's book including *SMT* material was previously published, as *Elizabethan Fustian*, in 1937.)

W. W. Greg's Malone Society series edition of 1909 is the cause of an exchange in *PQ* between Greg and Samuel A. Tannenbaum. In "Textual Errors in the Malone Society's *The Second Maydens Tragedy*," *PQ* 9 (1930):304–6, Tannenbaum lists numerous corrections of Greg's reprinted text, many involving the capitalization or non-capitalization of initial "M" and the difference between inverted semicolons and question marks. Greg replies in "Textual Errors in the Malone Society's *The Second Maiden's Tragedy*," *PQ* 10 (1931):80–82, accepting only twenty-one of Tannenbaum's corrections, and pointing out that word-division, distinction between majuscule and minuscule forms, and distinction between question marks and inverted semicolons are matters on which it is impossible to get agreement, admitting that he himself should not have tried in the edition to distinguish between a query mark and an inverted semicolon. He also notes seven misreadings by Tannenbaum, and concludes by pointing to four errors in Tannenbaum's own list.

Authorship

Much of the critical work done recently on *SMT* has been concerned with the problem of authorship. The manuscript itself contains three ascriptions, in differing, later hands: one to Shakespeare, one to Goffe, one to Chapman; and attributions have also been made to Massinger, Middleton, and Tourneur. Greg, *Dramatic Documents*, calls all three manuscript attributions "worthless"; and all three are also dismissed by Richard H. Barker, "The Authorship of the *Second Maiden's Tragedy* and *The Revenger's Tragedy*," Sh*AB* 20 (1945): 51–62 and 121–33.

Shakespeare

Shakespeare's candidacy has not been seriously considered, although E. B. Everitt, *The Young Shakespeare: Studies in Documentary Evidence*, Anglistica, vol. 2 (1954), believes the manuscript to be in Shakespeare's autograph. Everitt's arguments are convincingly attacked by Robert Adger Law, "Guessing About the Youthful Shakespeare," *Studies in English* (Univ. of Texas) 34 (1955):43–50.

Goffe

Goffe (Gough?) has not recently been put forward as a candidate.

Chapman

Two biographers of Chapman have explicitly rejected, in footnotes, *SMT* as Chapman's: Havelock Ellis, *Chapman* (1934), who says that no author can be assigned to the play with certainty, and Jean Jacquot, *George Chapman (1559–1634)* (1951). A recent article, however, by Leonora Leet Brodwin, "Authorship of *The Second Maiden's Tragedy*: A Reconsideration of the Manuscript Attribution to Chapman," *SP* 63 (1966):51–77, argues at length for Chapman's authorship, though dismissing the Shakespeare and Goffe ascriptions as not meriting serious consideration. Brodwin relies on evidence of philosophical and other similarities between *SMT* and Chapman's known work, especially his *Revenge of Bussy D'Ambois* and *Caesar and Pompey*. "*The Second Maiden's Tragedy* . . . represents romantic situations taken from Chapman's earlier plays and treated in the intellectual, Stoic mood which dominated Chapman's non-romantic tragedies, c. 1611"; it may be "Chapman's finest late tragedy." Possibly there was a revision by a "second, wholly subordinate hand," which is unlikely to have been Massinger's or Tourneur's and could have been Marston's, Ford's, or (though not probably) Middleton's. There are, she states, no authorial corrections in the manuscript.

Massinger

Massinger has also been generally rejected; see A. H. Cruickshank, *Philip Massinger* (1920), Maurice Chelli, *Etude sur la collaboration de Massinger avec Fletcher et son groupe* (1926); W. W. Greg, *Dramatic Documents* [the Massinger attribution has been made "on no very substantial grounds"], Richard H. Barker, "Authorship," and Brodwin, "Authorship." Massinger's authorship has been assumed, however, by Edwin B. Knowles, Jr., *Four Articles on "Don Quixote" in England* (1941).

Tourneur

Cruickshank, *Philip Massinger*, finds a good deal in the play to be in Tourneur's manner, but others have dismissed Tourneur's candidacy. The editor of *The Works of Cyril Tourneur* (1929), Allardyce Nicoll, does not absolutely reject Tourneur as a possible author, but suspects that imitation may account for the similarities between *SMT* and Tourneur's known work, and declines to include the play in the *Works*. Greg, *Dramatic Documents*, declares that the Tourneur attribution has been made "on no very substantial grounds." Tourneur's most recent biographer, Peter B. Murray, *A Study of Cyril Tourneur* (1964), points out in a footnote that Tourneur is a candidate for *SMT* authorship almost entirely because of similarities between *SMT* and *The Revenger's Tragedy*, and that if one discounts *The Revenger's Tragedy* and looks at *SMT* only in relation to Tourneur's and to Middleton's undisputed works, one sees resemblances only to Middleton. Samuel Schoenbaum, *Middleton's Tragedies* (1955), reviews the evidence and rejects the Tourneur attribution.

See also Barker, "Authorship," and Brodwin, "Authorship."

Middleton

Middleton is by far the favored candidate, his strongest supporters being Samuel Schoenbaum (before 1966) and Richard Hindry Barker. In his *ShAB* article, Barker finds similarities between *SMT* and known

Middleton plays, and accounts for the resemblances between *SMT* and *The Revenger's Tragedy* by giving the latter play to Middleton as well. In his *Thomas Middleton* of 1958, he declares, "If any anonymous Jacobean play can be ascribed to an author with almost absolute certainty on internal evidence alone, then this one can." The manuscript hand described by Greg [in the 1909 Malone Society ed.] as that of the "literary Corrector, almost certainly the author," does not seem, Barker admits, to be Middleton's, but the play is certainly his. Schoenbaum, *Middleton's Tragedies*, also denies that Greg's "literary corrector" is the author, and, summing up previous attribution scholarship, and citing many similarities between *SMT* and Middleton's work, declares, as did Barker in "Authorship," that there are only three possible conclusions: (1) that the *SMT* author imitated Middleton (but there are a number of parallels between *SMT* and post-1611 Middleton plays); (2) that Middleton imitated the style of *SMT* (which is unlikely); (3) that Middleton wrote *SMT*. He discusses the play above all as a part of Middleton's dramatic development: his growing interest in the psychology of characters, his use of irony, his verse style. In 1966, however, in *Internal Evidence and Elizabethan Dramatic Authorship*, Schoenbaum is no longer so sure of Middleton's claim, and states that in 1955 he did not attach sufficient weight to the changes made by the literary corrector, which imply knowledge of the author's preference or intention and are not in Middleton's hand.

E. H. C. Oliphant, "The Authorship of *The Revenger's Tragedy*," *SP* 23 (1926):157–68, gives both *Revenger's Tragedy* and *SMT* to Middleton, citing similarities between the two plays and Middleton's known work. In *The Plays of Beaumont and Fletcher* (1927) he reiterates the *SMT* attribution, and in his two anthologies, *Shakespeare and His Fellow Dramatists* (1929), vol. 2, and *Elizabethan Dramatists Other Than Shakespeare* (1931), he declares the play to be "plainly his [Middleton's] on the internal evidence." Two scholars, in general studies, point out that their work supports Middleton as *SMT* author: Charles Barber, "A Rare Use of the Word *Honour* as a Criterion of Middleton's Authorship," *ES* 38 (1957): 161–68, and Ants Oras, *Pause Patterns in Elizabethan and Jacobean Drama: An Experiment in Prosody* (1960). See also Murray, *Cyril Tourneur*, and Everitt, *The Young Shakespeare*; Everitt states that *SMT* is by Middleton and "afford[s] an insight" into the authorship of *Timon of Athens, Two Noble Kinsmen*, and *Henry VIII*, and also "resurrects the question of *Cardenio*."

Brodwin, "Authorship," argues against the Middleton attribution, especially as it is presented by Schoenbaum (in 1955).

The Play

Older criticism finds the play to be flawed, especially in a lack of connection between the main plot and the subplot, but recently more appreciative analyses of the drama have appeared.

In *Elizabethan Revenge Tragedy, 1587–1642* (1940), Fredson Thayer Bowers, considering the place of *SMT* in the development of revenge tragedy, finds the subplot to be "entirely unconnected" with the main plot, and to have been introduced into the play only for the purpose of achieving "sufficient complication of plot." The main plot, he states, has similarities to Kydian tragedy, and "the author borrows, with no functional purpose in mind, from Shakespeare's *Hamlet, The Jew of Malta, Antonio's Revenge, The Malcontent,* but especially from *The Revenger's Tragedy* and *The Atheist's Tragedy.* Yet all these externals of blood and thunder tragedy are used simply as atmosphere for a sentimental romance." There is a "lack of turmoil in the whole idyllic atmosphere of the play," and the revenge motive is softened. The subplot "is no more than a comic *novella* story equipped with a tragic ending." A lack of real connection between the two plots is also condemned by Schoenbaum, *Middleton's Tragedies,* who, however, is more appreciative of the play's subplot, which, he states, shows men and women who fall from reason because of "the lures of pleasure and the pressures of physical attraction" and are eventually destroyed. The tragedy, he maintains, lies in the (ironic) self-destruction of the characters, who are remarkable studies in abnormal psychology. Unnecessary sensationalism at times, however, mars the action, and the main plot is "lurid and fantastic," "unconvincing . . . [and] uninteresting," largely as a result of the influence of Fletcherian melodrama. To Schoenbaum, the play lacks true dramatic force in the main plot or in the close of the subplot, and is important only because of its place in the development of Middleton as a dramatist.

Richard Hindry Barker, *Thomas Middleton,* concurs in calling the play "generally second rate," though he finds the style to be accomplished. Like Schoenbaum, he believes the subplot to be the worthwhile part of the play; its characters are human and interesting, with inner lives, and suffer mentally as well as physically. The final scene of this plot is, however, mere "gratuitous slaughter," and the main plot is simply melodrama. Middleton was combining "domestic drama with the older sort of court intrigue, obviously with imperfect success."

In 1935, however, M. C. Bradbrook, *Themes and Conventions of Elizabethan Tragedy*, enigmatically declares the subplot of *SMT* to be implicitly related to the main plot; and two recent articles deal with the play as an integrated whole. Richard Levin, "The Double Plot of *The Second Maiden's Tragedy*," *SEL* 3 (1963):219-31, cites previous scholarship on the two plots as unconnected and proceeds, in much detail, to show them to be highly integrated. The main plot deals with the "triumphant martyrdom" of a secular saint, which calls forth our admiration and wonder, and which has miraculous consequences: the cleansing of the corrupt court and the restoration of the rightful king. The subplot begins at a similar point in its heroine's career, but shows her failure of the test of her virtue, and her consequent debasement and punishment. The two actions thus begin at the same point but develop in opposite directions, and "reinforce each other ... through our emotional response to the play." The main action is simple, with nonrealistic characters, while the subplot is complex, and "realistic" in its characterization. Brodwin, "Authorship," finds the theme of the play to be the conflict between spiritual goodness and worldly greatness, with freedom of the heavenly mind celebrated, and perfectly achieved only in death. The main plot, she suggests, presents this conflict between characters—the Lady (spiritual goodness) opposed to the Tyrant (worldly greatness)—and the subplot presents it within characters, in "the mind divided against itself." There are similarities and deliberate contrasts in detail between characters, situations, emotions, and actions in the two plots. Brodwin also remarks that in the two plots we see "both the chaste and original adulterous traditions of courtly love represented," love flourishing in difficulty and celebrating death as the highest voucher of its fidelity. The characters have "remarkable depth," and the play is profound and moving, pervasively intellectual, finely crafted.

Literary Connections

For links between *SMT* and other plays of its period, not already cited in other connections, see: Cruickshank, *Philip Massinger* [*Duke of Milan* parallel]; M. C. Bradbrook, *Elizabethan Stage Conditions* (1932) [a staging point related to *Romeo and Juliet*]; Laurens J.

Mills, *One Soul in Bodies Twain* (1937) [Greene's pamphlet *Philomela* (1592)]; Bowers, *Elizabethan Revenge Tragedy* [references to many plays, and the lustful Tyrant as "a Fletcherian development"]; Jacquot, *George Chapman* [*Charlemagne, 2 Tamburlaine, Duke of Milan*]; Samuel Schoenbaum, *Middleton's Tragedies* [*Changeling* and *Revenger's Tragedy* parallels]; Mario Praz, "John Webster and *The Maid's Tragedy*," *ES* 37 (1956):252-58 [*Duchess of Malfi* influenced by *SMT, SMT* influenced by *The Winter's Tale*]; T. A. Dunn, *Philip Massinger* (1957) [*Duke of Milan* adaptation of *SMT*, V.ii]; Samuel Schoenbaum, *"The Widow's Tears* and the Other Chapman," *HLQ* 23 (1959-60):321-38 [a similar character in *Widow's Tears* and *SMT*].

For an extended discussion of the subplot source, Cervantes's "The Curious Impertinent," and the author's use of it, see Schoenbaum, *Middleton's Tragedies*. See also Knowles, *Four Articles*.

Other Studies

Mills, *One Soul*, deals with friendship material in the subplot; Robert Hunter West, *The Invisible World: A Study of Pneumatology in Elizabethan Drama* (1936), is intrigued by the Lady's ghost, which has a providential function, but also "a pagan taint" in its concern over the fate of its body.

Staging points are made by William J. Lawrence, *The Physical Conditions of the Elizabethan Public Playhouse* (1927), and *Pre-Restoration Stage Studies*, M. C. Bradbrook, *Elizabethan Stage Conditions*, J. W. Saunders, "Staging at the Globe, 1599-1613," *SQ* 11 (1960):401-26, and Irwin Smith, *Shakespeare's Blackfriars Playhouse* (1964). John P. Cutts, *La musique de scène de la troupe de Shakespeare* (1959), and Henry L. Snuggs, *Shakespeare and Five Acts* (1960), comment on musical details. See also Praz, "John Webster."

See Also

Boas, Frederick S. *Shakespeare and the Universities.* 1923.
Bowden, William R. *The English Dramatic Lyric, 1603-42.* 1951.
Hunter, G. K. "The Marking of *Sententiae* in Elizabethan Printed Plays, Poems, and Romances." *Library* 6 (1951):171-88.
Korninger, Siegfried. "Die Geisterszene im elisabethanischen Drama." *SJH* 102 (1966):124-45.
Moore, John Robert. "The Songs of the Public Theaters in the Time of Shakespeare." *JEGP* 28 (1929):166-202.

A. L.

The Valiant Welshman, or The True Chronicle History of the Life and Valiant Deeds of Caradoc the Great, history (*1612;* 1615)

Introduction, Attribution, and Source

The Valiant Welshman (VW) has received little attention from modern scholars. There have been no editions of the play since the beginning of this century (although the 1615 edition is available in microprint in Henry W. Wells, ed., *Three Centuries of Drama* [Readex Corp., 1955–56]), and criticism consists primarily of short notices.

The authorship of *VW* is still unknown. One scholar clearly favors Robert Armin as a candidate: Robert Herring, "The Whale Has a Wide Mouth," *Life and Letters To-Day* 36 (1943):44–65. Another thinks that Armin may have been responsible for the play: M. C. Bradbrook, *Shakespeare the Craftsman* (1969). Two consider the Armin ascription doubtful: W. J. Hughes, *Wales and the Welsh in English Literature from Shakespeare to Scott* (1924), and J. O. Bartley, *Teague, Shenkin, and Sawney* (1954). Two find no reason for the attribution: Irving Ribner, *The English History Play in the Age of Shakespeare* (1957; rev. ed. 1965), and Charles S. Felver, *Robert Armin, Shakespeare's Fool: A Biographical Essay*, Kent State Univ. Bulletin, vol. 49, no. 1; Research Series, 5 (1961). In "The Authorship of *The Valiant Welshman*," *N&Q* 197 (1952):425–27 (article prepared for publication by Sylvia Lloyd), Bertram Lloyd finds the Armin ascription untenable and argues that Robert Anton wrote *VW* by a comparison of the anonymous play with Anton's known work. Two critics take issue with nineteenth-century scholars who assigned *VW* to Chettle and Drayton: H. Dugdale Sykes, "The Dramatic Work of Henry Chettle," *N&Q* 12 (1923):386–89; and Harold Jenkins, *The Life and Work of Henry Chettle* (1934).

There has been no recent discussion of date. Ribner, who treats the question of sources, says that the anonymous playwright seems to have used Holinshed without consideration for historical accuracy.

Literary Connections and Miscellaneous

Donald Joseph McGinn, *Shakespeare's Influence on the Drama of His Age, Studied in "Hamlet"* (1938), finds several allusions to *Hamlet* in *VW*. Ribner discovers little in the anonymous play which is not borrowed from earlier dramas; comparing *VW* with Fletcher's *Bonduca* (1613), he sees no connection between the two plays except the appearance of Caradoc in each; he agrees with earlier scholarship which suggested that Shakespeare's *Antony and Cleopatra* influenced *VW*. Like Ribner, Bradbrook notices the eclectic nature of *VW* and points out allusions to plays by Shakespeare and Jonson. William J. Lawrence, "Welsh Song in Elizabethan Drama," *TLS*, 7 Dec. 1922, p. 810, believes that *VW* may have influenced Jonson's use of music in *The Irish Mask* (1613), and Scott Elledge, "Milton, Sappho (?), and Demetrius," *MLN* 58 (1943):551-53, cites a line in Milton's *Comus* which he thinks was taken literally from the anonymous play.

A few writers consider the use of Welsh characters and language in *VW*; see, for instance, Joseph de Perott, "Welsh Bits in the Tudor and Stuart Drama," *MLN* 36 (1921):352-54; Hughes; J. O. Bartley, "The Development of a Stock Character," *MLR* 38 (1943):279-88, and *Teague, Shenkin, and Sawney*. Dieter Mehl describes the play's induction in both *The Elizabethan Dumb Show* (1966; German ed. 1964), and "Forms and Functions of the Play within a Play," *RenD* 8 (1965):41-61. Herring remarks the use of rant in the play. The music is mentioned by Lawrence (above); John Robert Moore, "The Songs of the Public Theaters in the Time of Shakespeare," *JEGP* 28 (1929):166-202; and William R. Bowden, *The English Dramatic Lyric, 1603-42: A Study in Stuart Dramatic Technique* (1951). Wilfred T. Jewkes, *Act Division in Elizabethan and Jacobean Plays, 1583-1616* (1958), reasons that the copy for *VW* probably originated as "an author's manuscript . . . prepared with a tentative performance in mind . . . ."

See Also

Dawson, Giles E. "An Early List of Elizabethan Plays." *Library* 15 (1935): 445-56.

Hunter, G. K. "The Marking of *Sententiae* in Elizabethan Printed Plays, Poems, and Romances." *Library* 6 (1951):171-88.

Kendall, Lyle H., Jr. "Shakespeare Collections, Quartos, Source and Allusion Books in the W. L. Lewis Collection." In *Shakespeare 1964*, ed. Jim W. Corder (1965), pp. 113-77.

Lawrence, William J. *Pre-Restoration Stage Studies.* 1927.

Linton, Marion. "The Bute Collection of English Plays." *TLS*, 21 Dec. 1956, p. 772.

———. "National Library of Scotland and Edinburgh University Library Copies of Plays in Greg's *Bibliography of the English Printed Drama.*" *SB* 15 (1962): 91-104.

Millett, Fred Benjamin. *The Date and Literary Relations of "Woodstock."* 1934.

Smith, Roland M. "King Lear and the Merlin Tradition." *MLQ* 7 (1946):153-74.

J. L.

The Faithful Friends, tragicomedy (*1614;* MS)

Introduction

The Faithful Friends has been neglected by modern scholars. There is no recent edition of the play, and only one critic attempts a general study of it: Dieter Mehl, "Beaumont und Fletchers *The Faithful Friends,*" *Anglia* 80 (1962):417–24. Mehl discusses the authorship, genre, and date of the play, which he regards as "eine Tragikomödie des zuerst von Beaumont und Fletcher entwickelten und später immer wieder neu abgewandelten Typs." He suggests that *Faithful Friends* belongs to the period between 1609 and 1626. (See also Mehl's brief comments on the authorship of *Faithful Friends* in his book *The Elizabethan Dumb Show* [1966; German ed. 1964].)

Attribution, Date, and Sources

E. H. C. Oliphant, *The Plays of Beaumont and Fletcher: An Attempt to Determine Their Respective Shares and the Shares of Others* (1927), initially feels hesitant about his attribution. He speculates that Beaumont and Fletcher wrote *Faithful Friends* originally, and that Field and Massinger revised it subsequently. In an appendix on the play, however, Oliphant explains that after further consideration of the manuscript he is far more confident about the Massinger ascription. (In conjunction with Oliphant's analysis of authorship in his book, see his article "The Plays of Beaumont and Fletcher: Some Additional Notes," *PQ* 9 [1930]:7–22, where he mentions that Roberta Florence Brinkley, *Nathan Field, the Actor-Playwright* [1928], finds no sign of Field's work in *Faithful Friends*.) In *"The Booke of Sir Thomas Moore" (A Bibliotic Study)* (1927), Samuel A. Tannenbaum assigns a scene in the fourth act of *Faithful Friends* to Massinger. Neither W. W. Greg in his review of Tannenbaum's book, in *Library* 9 (1928):202–11, nor E. K. Chambers, *William Shakespeare* (1930), vol. 1, think that there is any reason to attribute the inserted scene to Massinger. Laurens Joseph Mills, *One Soul in Bodies Twain* (1937), is not convinced that Beaumont or Fletcher wrote *Faithful Friends*, and H. Dugdale Sykes, *Sidelights on Elizabethan Drama* (1924), finds unsubstantial the evidence put forth by scholars who assign the play to Field, Daborne, Beaumont, Fletcher, or Massinger.

Oliphant, *The Plays of Beaumont and Fletcher*, proposes that Field revised *Faithful Friends* no later than 1610–11, and that Massinger's version was probably done ca. 1613–14. Chambers reasons that the play most likely dates no earlier than 1621. There has been no recent discussion of sources.

Text

C. J. Sisson, "Bibliographical Aspects of Some Stuart Dramatic Manuscripts," *RES* 1 (1925):421–30, mentions several kinds of textual anomalies in *Faithful Friends*. In *The Plays of Beaumont and Fletcher*, Oliphant discusses the handwritings which appear on the manuscript in the light of information he received from Samuel A. Tannenbaum. Chambers offers a brief description of the manuscript. R. C. Bald considers the transmission of *Faithful Friends*, IV.v, in both his edition of Middleton's *A Game at Chesse* (1929; Cambridge ed.), and " 'Assembled' Texts," *Library* 12 (1931):243–48. In *Dramatic Documents from the Elizabethan Playhouses* (1931), vol. 2, W. W. Greg distinguishes among the three hands which contributed to the manuscript and conjectures about its connection with the playhouse; he comments on certain additions to the manuscript in *The Editorial Problem in Shakespeare* (1942). Baldwin Maxwell, *Studies in Beaumont, Fletcher, and Massinger* (1939), discusses the "confused" list of dramatis personae which precedes the manuscript. Ludwig Borinski, "Vers und Text in den Dramenmanuskripten der Shakespearezeit," *Anglia* 75 (1957):391–410, remarks some textual corruptions and additions in the manuscript.

Literary Connections and Miscellaneous

Alfred Bruce Black and Robert Metcalf Smith, *Shakespeare Allusions and Parallels*, Lehigh Univ. Publication, vol. 5, no. 3; The Institute of Research, Circular no. 51; Studies in the Humanities, no. 8 (1931), notice two allusions to Shakespearean plays in *Faithful Friends*.

William J. Lawrence remarks a piece of stage business (in *The Physical Conditions of the Elizabethan Public Playhouses* [1927]) and a stage direction (in *Pre-Restoration Stage Studies* [1927]). Mills explains the use of friendship conventions in *Faithful Friends*. The dumb show receives attention from B. R. Pearn, "Dumb-Show in Elizabethan Drama," *RES* 11 (1935):385–405, and Mehl, *Elizabethan Dumb Show*.

See Also

Abend, Murray. "Shakespeare's Influences in Beaumont and Fletcher." *N&Q* 197 (1952):272–74.

Bowden, William R. *The English Dramatic Lyric, 1603–42: A Study in Stuart Dramatic Technique.* 1951.

Chelli, Maurice. *Le drame de Massinger.* 1923.

Craig, Hardin. "Textual Degeneration of Elizabethan and Stuart Plays: An Examination of Plays in Manuscript." *RIP* 46 (1960):71–84.

Cutts, John P., ed. *La musique de scène de la troupe de Shakespeare, the King's Men, sous le règne de Jacques Ier.* 1959.

Harbage, Alfred. "Elizabethan and Seventeenth-Century Play Manuscripts." *PMLA* 50 (1935):687–99.

Hart, Alfred. "Acting Versions of Elizabethan Plays." *RES* 10 (1934):1–28.

Leech, Clifford. *John Ford and the Drama of His Time.* 1957.

Spivack, Bernard. *Shakespeare and the Allegory of Evil.* 1958.

J. L.

OTHER DRAMATISTS

Terence P. Logan   Denzell S. Smith

The figures included here were active in the public theaters at the same time as the major playwrights treated in this volume; they are included because their plays have been the subject of some recent scholarship. Articles and books dealing exclusively or primarily with their nondramatic works are not included. For additional information see: G. E. Bentley, The Jacobean and Caroline Stage, *7 vols. (1941–68), E. K. Chambers,* The Elizabethan Stage, *4 vols. (1923), W. W. Greg,* A Bibliography of the English Printed Drama to the Restoration, *4 vols. (1939–59), Alfred Harbage,* Annals of English Drama, 975–1700, *rev. Samuel Schoenbaum (1964), and the Supplements by Schoenbaum (1966, 1970). The essays on anonymous plays and on appropriate major authors in this volume and in* The Predecessors of Shakespeare, *ed. Terence P. Logan and Denzell S. Smith (1973), include more extensive treatments of the plays of uncertain authorship and the collaborative plays that are dealt with here. Playwrights are discussed in alphabetical order. Entries are listed in chronological order for each playwright and include items listed in the source bibliographies from the publication of* The Elizabethan Stage *(1923) to the end of 1971; the title of each work is followed by a brief summary of its contents.*

BARNABE BARNES

Bayley, A. R. "Barnabe Barnes." *N&Q* 146 (1924):268. The parish register of St. Michael le Belfrey enters Barnes's name under "Christeninges for 1570"; the *DNB* birth-date of 1569 is incorrect.

Eccles, Mark. "Barnabe Barnes." In *Thomas Lodge and Other Elizabethans*, ed. Charles J. Sisson (1933), pp. 165–241. Court records and allusions to Barnes by Campion, Marston, and Nashe are used to reconstruct Barnes's life. Barnes left Oxford without a degree and probably served abroad under Essex; on his return to London he sought Southampton's favor and stayed on the outer fringes of the Essex circle. He was arrested in 1598 and tried before the Star Chamber for the attempted poisoning of John Browne, Recorder of Berwick. Barnes escaped from prison and the charges were dropped after a period of discreet self-exile.

Fellheimer, Jeanette. "Barnabe Barnes' Use of Geoffrey Fenton's *Historie of Guicciardin.*" *MLN* 57 (1942):358–59. Fenton's 1579 translation of Guicciardini is the source of the historical elements in *The Devil's Charter*; an additional parallel passage is offered to support McKerrow's identification of Barnes's source in his 1904 edition of the play.

HENRY CHETTLE

Sykes, H. Dugdale. "The Dramatic Works of Henry Chettle." *N&Q* 144 (1923):263–65, 283–86, 303–6, 324–27, 345–47, 365–66, 386–89. Word frequency patterns establish Chettle's authorship of specific portions of: *1 The Blind Beggar of Bednal Green; The Death of Robert, Earl of Huntingdon; The Downfall of Robert, Earl of Huntingdon; Look about You;* and *Patient Grissil.* Chettle's share in these plays is larger than was previously assumed. His canon includes about fifty plays.

———. *Sidelights on Elizabethan Drama.* 1924. Some of the attributions made in the above *N&Q* articles are restated in summary form.

Jones, Fred L. "*The Trial of Chivalry*, A Chettle Play." *PMLA* 41 (1926):304–24. Plot and stylistic parallels reveal that Chettle was the principal author of the play. Thomas Heywood probably collaborated with Chettle but Heywood's contribution was distinctly minor.

———. "*Look about You* and *The Disguises.*" *PMLA* 44 (1929): 835–41. Chettle is the sole author of *Look about You*, "the most elaborate disguise play in Elizabethan drama." This is probably the same as the "lost" play called *The Disguises. Look about You* was influenced by Munday's *John a Kent and John a Cumber* and by Chapman's *Blind Beggar of Alexandria* and should be dated prior to 1598.

———. "Another Source for *The Trial of Chivalry.*" *PMLA* 47 (1932):668–70. Chettle's main source was the *Arcadia.* Greene's *Carde of Fancie* supplies some of the action and may have furnished the main plot of an earlier Chettle play.

Byrne, Muriel St. Clare. "Bibliographical Clues in Collaborate Plays." *Library* 13 (1932–33):21–48. Sykes and others who make attributions of anonymous plays on the basis of verbal and stylistic parallels are wrong. Munday and Chettle's *The Death of Robert, Earl of Huntingdon* and *The Downfall of Robert, Earl of Huntingdon* are plays which especially illustrate the inadequacies of Sykes's methods.

Jenkins, Harold. *The Life and Works of Henry Chettle.* 1934. Chettle was one of "the humbler and more ordinary wielders of the pen"; the ordinary nature of his life and works makes him an ideal benchmark against which we can measure his outstanding contemporaries. Jenkins includes the known biographical facts, balanced criticism of works positively ascribed to Chettle, a comprehensive account of the evidence for and against uncertain ascriptions, and a list of early editions.

Tillotson, Kathleen. "Drayton and Chettle." *TLS*, 14 Aug. 1937, p. 592. Fenton's "King James His Welcome to London" includes Drayton and Chettle in a list of poets invited to celebrate the arrival of the new monarch.

———. "Drayton and Chettle." *TLS*, 28 Aug. 1937, p. 628. Corrects an error in the note above.

Hard, Frederick. "John Fenton." *TLS*, 25 Dec. 1937, p. 980. Fenton's "King James His Welcome to London" alludes favorably to Chettle, especially to his "England's Mourning Garment."

Halstead, W. L. "Collaborations on the *Patient Grissil.*" *PQ* 18 (1939):381–94. Chettle was the first to be paid by Henslowe; Dekker and Haughton were paid later and may have been merely revising a play originally entirely by Chettle. The contribution of each author is tentatively identified.

Jenkins, Harold. "Chettle and Dekker." *TLS*, 25 Oct. 1941, p. 531. Chettle, not Dekker, is the author of specified songs in their plays.

Herring, Robert. "The Whale Has a Wide Mouth." *Life and Letters Today*, Jan. 1943. *YWES* 24 (1943): "Herring makes a plea for fuller appreciation of so-called Elizabethan plays written after 1615," including *The Tragedy of Hoffman*. [Not seen.]

Halstead, W. L. "Dekker's *Cupid and Psyche* and Thomas Heywood." *ELH* 11 (1944):182–91. Chettle and Day were especially busy at the time the play was written; Dekker may have written most of it unaided. Heywood borrows from *Cupid* in *Love's Mistress*; the borrowing may be due to Heywood's having acted in *Cupid and Psyche*.

Peery, William. "Notes on Bang's Edition of *The Blind Beggar of Bednal Green.*" *RES* 27 (1946):152–55. Bang's edition, in Materialien zur Kunde des älteren englischen Dramas, vol. 1 (1902), contains errors caused by his reliance on a single copy of the quarto text. Corrections are provided.

Hoppe, Harry A. *The Bad Quarto of "Romeo and Juliet": A Bibliographical and Textual Study*. 1948. Chettle may have been the "reporter-versifier" behind John Danter's 1597 pirated edition.

Schlochauer, Ernst J. "A Note on Variants in the Dedication of Chettle's *Tragedy of Hoffman.*" *PBSA* 42 (1948):307–12. A collation of ten copies of the 1631 quarto shows four versions of the dedication to Richard Kilvert.

Bald, R. C. "*The Booke of Sir Thomas More* and Its Problems." *ShS* 2 (1949):44–65. Analysis of the several handwritings establishes that Chettle, Dekker, Munday, and Shakespeare were involved in writing the play. Shakespeare's role may have been that of final reviser.

Feldman, Abraham. "Shakespeare and the Scholars." *N&Q* 194 (1949):556. Chettle's *Kind Harts Dreame* does not include an apology to Shakespeare for Chettle's failure to excise slighting remarks in *Groatsworth of Wit*.

Parsons, Howard. "Shakespeare and the Scholars." *N&Q* 195 (1950):283–84. Feldman is incorrect; *Kind Harts Dreame* does include an apology to Shakespeare.

Maxwell, J. C. "Shakespeare and the Scholars." *N&Q* 195 (1950):349. Feldman is correct; Parsons is wrong.

Parsons, Howard. "Shakespeare and the Scholars." *N&Q* 195 (1950):569–70. An allusion to a crow in Sonnet 70 proves that Shakespeare took offense at Greene's remarks in *Groatsworth of Wit*.

Thomas, Sidney. "Henry Chettle and the First Quarto of *Romeo and Juliet.*" *RES* 1 (1950):8–16. Chettle was Danter's editor for the 1597 edition. There are parallels in style, spelling, imagery, and stage directions with Chettle's known work and he is probably the author of the disputed passages in the pirated text.

Jenkins, Harold. "The 1631 Quarto of *The Tragedy of Hoffman.*" *Library* 6 (1951):88–91. Hugh Perry's dedication to the Chettle play exists in five states and was plagiarized. More than one compositor was involved and the large number of errors necessitated frequent stop-press corrections.

–––, ed. *The Tragedy of Hoffman.* 1951. This Malone Society edition includes a discussion of the printing of the first edition, speculation on possible revision, and a list of variants.

Nosworthy, J. M. *"The Case Is Altered."* *JEGP* 51 (1952):61–70. Jonson wrote the play in collaboration with Henry Porter. Chettle's contribution was small; he may have helped with the plotting. This play may be the same as the "lost" *Hot Anger Soon Cold*.

–––. "Shakespeare and *Sir Thomas More.*" *RES* 6 (1955):12–25. The additions to Munday's original version of the play are in five hands, including those of Chettle and Shakespeare. The play was written between 1598 and 1601.

Wilson, J. Dover. "The New Way with Shakespeare's Texts: An Introduction for Lay Readers. III. In Sight of Shakespeare's Manuscripts." *ShS* 9 (1956):69–80. Wilson briefly comments on Chettle's involvement in *Sir Thomas More*.

Wright, Celeste Turner. "Munday and Chettle in Grub Street." *BUSE* 5 (1961):129–38. Munday and Chettle were both employed by printers and both were friendly with Nashe and Greene.

Bowers, Fredson T. "Established Texts and Definitive Editions." *PQ* 41 (1962):1–17. Chettle's *Tragedy of Hoffman* is used to illustrate how a printer's "corrections" can corrupt an author's text.

Nelson, Malcolm A. "*Look about You* and the Robin Hood Tradition." *N&Q* 9 (1962):141–43. H. Dugdale Sykes's attribution of *Look* to Chettle, in *Sidelights on Elizabethan Drama* (1924), is incorrect. *Look about You* borrows from Chettle and Munday's Robin Hood plays and from Shakespeare's *1 Henry IV*. There is not enough evidence for any attribution of the play.

Meagher, John C., ed. *The Downfall of Robert, Earl of Huntingdon.* 1965 for 1964. This Malone Society edition includes a brief preface and lists of variant, irregular, and doubtful readings. Munday is perhaps sole author; "the extant text was apparently printed from foul papers which at least in part, and probably altogether, antedated even Henslowe's entry for 15 February 1598, and there is no reason to suppose that Chettle's later additions are present in any form."

———, ed. *The Death of Robert, Earl of Huntingdon.* 1967 for 1965. The apparatus of this Malone Society edition is uniform with that in Meagher's edition of *The Downfall.* "It seems impossible to settle the question of authorship satisfactorily." However, two hypotheses are offered:

"A. The extant text of *The Death* is all by Munday, and the work for which Chettle was paid was either added at a later stage of composition or devoted to the representation of King Richard's funeral, which was originally intended to form part of this play . . . but subsequently became a separate play . . . .

"B. The extant text is primarily the work of Munday, and Chettle's contribution was either very small or reworked by Munday."

Austin, Warren B. "Technique of the Chettle-Greene Forgery." *ShN* 20 (1970):43. Chettle, not Greene, is the author of *Groatsworth of Wit*, including the allusion to Shakespeare.

Marder, Louis L. "Chettle's Forgery of the *Groatsworth of Wit* and the 'Shake-scene' Passage." *ShN* 20 (1970):42. Marder accepts Austin's attribution of the pamphlet to Chettle.

JOHN DAY

Three recent American Ph.D. dissertations on Day should be noticed: Raymond S. Burns, an edition of *The Ile of Guls* in 1963, William T. Cocke, III, an edition of *The Parliament of Bees* in 1968, and Elmer M. McDonald, Jr., a study of Day's coterie comedy, 1971.

Greg, W. W. "The Two Issues of Day's *Isle of Gulls*, 1606." *Library* 3 (1923):307-9. The two issues differ only in the first line of the imprint; the later deletes the publisher's name. Parody of King James evidently made the publisher nervous; the alteration was made while the first sheet was being printed.

Sykes, H. Dugdale. "The Dramatic Work of Henry Chettle." *N&Q* 144 (1923):263-65, 283-86, 303-6, 324-27, 345-47, 365-66, 386-89. On the evidence of verbal parallels, Sykes claims Chettle, not Day, is the author of the main plot of *The Blind Beggar of Bednal Green*.

————. *Sidelights on Elizabethan Drama.* 1924. Day's hand is discernible in *Timon of Athens* in the Timon-Apemantus scenes. Without offering evidence or argument, Sykes assigns Day shares in *Lust's Dominion* (with Dekker and Haughton), *Blind Beggar* (with Chettle), *Law Tricks* (with Wilkins), *Travels of the Three English Brothers* (with Rowley and Wilkins).

Golding, S. R. "The Authorship of *The Maid's Metamorphosis.*" *RES* 2 (1926):270-79. Neither Day nor Daniel (ascriptions by earlier authorities) had a hand in it; the unnamed playwright modelled the poetic scenes on Peele and the prose scenes on Lyly.

————. "Day and Wilkins as Collaborators." *N&Q* 150 (1926): 417-21, 436-38. Using verbal parallels, Golding assigns shares of *Law Tricks* to Day and Wilkins, of *Travels of the Three English Brothers* to Day, Rowley, and Wilkins, and claims—the evidence is scanty—that Wilkins had a hand in Day's *Humour Out of Breath*.

————. "*The Parliament of Bees.*" *RES* 3 (1927):280-304. Golding establishes 1633-34 as the date of the MS on evidence from dedications of Day's work and the known dates of its sources, *The Noble Soldier* and *The Wonder of a Kingdom*. He claims (on the evidence of parallel passages) that Day's literary craftsmanship is discernible in those portions of the characters which deviate from these two plays; those portions which do not deviate are Dekker's.

―――. "The Authorship of *Lust's Dominion.*" *N&Q* 155 (1928): 399-402. Golding argues against Sykes's assignments of parts to Dekker, Day, and Haughton, and against Collier that the *Spanish Moor's Tragedy* is to be identified with *Lust's Dominion*.

Sisson, C. J. *The Elizabethan Dramatists Except Shakespeare.* 1928. Briefly notices Day.

Brereton, J. Le Gay, ed. *Lust's Dominion, or The Lascivious Queen.* 1931. In this edition for Materials for the Study of the Old English Drama, Brereton discusses authorship, considers and dismisses the arguments for Marlowe and Chettle, argues for Dekker (structure and style), and assigns shares to Haughton and Day on characterization and style. (Sykes, *Sidelights,* gives the play to Dekker, Haughton, and Day, but assigns shares differently.)

Hotson, Leslie. "The Adventure of the Single Rapier." *Atlantic,* July, 1931, pp. 26-31. A lively account of the discovery in the Record Office of Henry Porter's death at the hand of John Day in 1599.

Borish, M. E. "John Day's *Humour Out of Breath.*" *Harvard Studies and Notes in Philology and Literature* 16 (1934):1-12. Dismisses Golding's evidence and argument (in "Day and Wilkins as Collaborators," above) for Wilkins's hand in *Humour.* While the ambiguous sentence in the prefatory address may refer either to Sharpham or Marston, Borish believes *Humour* was "completed by Day alone."

Harrison, G. B., ed. *The Ile of Gvls, 1606.* 1936. This Shakespeare Association Facsimile includes a brief discussion of the play's reception, its satiric aim at contemporary scandal, and its reflection of conditions in the private theaters.

Borish, M. E. "John Day's *Law Tricks* and George Wilkins." *MP* 34 (1937):249-66. A detailed examination of parallel passages in *Law Tricks* and Day's acknowledged work is used to argue that Day is sole author of the play.

Halstead, W. L. "Dekker's *Cupid and Psyche* and Thomas Heywood." *ELH* 11 (1944):182–91. Dekker, Chettle, and Day used Aldington's translations of Apuleius's *Golden Ass* as their source. Chettle or Day, as easily as Dekker, may have written the lines in *England's Parnassus* assigned to Dekker.

Peery, William. "Notes on Bang's Edition of *The Blind-Beggar of Bednal-Green.*" *ES* 27 (1946):152–55. The sixty-two readings in Bang's edition not found in the quarto "illustrate the danger of basing a textual study on too few copies."

———. "Correction at Press in *The Blind-Beggar of Bednal-Green.*" *PBSA* 41 (1947):140–44. Bang's edition indicates that inner C, outer and inner D, and outer K were corrected during impression; Peery presents evidence which shows inner C, outer E, and inner H were corrected. Bang examined too few copies.

———. "Correction at Press in the Quarto of *Law Trickes.*" *Library* 2 (1947):186–90. Variants in six American copies establish that seven formes underwent press correction.

Crow, John, ed. *Law Tricks, 1608.* 1950, for 1949. Collation of six English copies of the quarto revealed variants in addition to those recorded by Peery (above) for the six American copies he examined. This Malone Society reprint was set up from the Eton College copy, but the "readings of the variant formes have been made to conform with what appears to be the most corrected state of each." The edition supplies a list of variant readings by forme and a list of irregular and doubtful readings common to all the copies collated.

Bromberg, Murray. "The Reputation of Philip Henslowe." *SQ* 1 (1950):135–39. In claiming that Henslowe's contemporaries thought better of him than literary historians have, Bromberg presents eight points to refute Fleay's and Chambers's identification of Henslowe with the Fenerator Bee in Day's *Parliament of Bees.*

Peery, William. "*The Noble Soldier* and *The Parliament of Bees.*" *SP* 48 (1951):219–33. Takes exception to Golding's argument from parallel passages (above) that Dekker's craftsmanship is discernible in *Bees.* "Evidence from rhyme, metre, sentence structure, word order, and diction suggests that the version in *Bees* is earlier than that in

Soldier, which is a free rendition of it in blank verse." Day, not Dekker, is the originator.

Schoenbaum, Samuel. "John Day and Elizabethan Drama." *Boston Public Library Quarterly* 5 (1953):140–52. Day collaborated on twenty-two plays with Henslowe's other writers (including Haughton, S. Rowley, Dekker, and Chettle) between 1598 and 1603. Two public theater plays he had a hand in survive: *The Blind-Beggar of Bednal-Green* (1600) and *The Travailes of the Three English Brothers* (1607). The character of Tom Stowd is noteworthy in the first, as is the "Elizabethan medley" of the second. Day's remaining surviving plays were written independently for the private houses. *The Ile of Guls* (1606), with its abuse, bombast, and bawdry, is weak; *Law-Trickes* (1607) "a step in the wrong direction" of Marston, is insipid; *Humour Out of Breath* (1608) expresses Day's "slender but precious gift" for the "sunshiny" comedy of Shakespeare. *The Parliament of Bees* "contains Day's best poetry." "His most characteristic works are naive little plays, abounding in word-play, romance, extravagance, and a curious combination of satire and good spirits."

Wadsworth, Frank W. "The Relationship of *Lust's Dominion* and John Mason's *The Turke.*" *ELH* 20 (1953):194–99. *The Turke* (1606–8) was "strongly influenced by, if not deliberately modeled upon" *Lust's Dominion* (ca. 1600); the argument is made on verbal parallels and similarities in character, situation, and plot devices. Wadsworth regards *Lust's Dominion* as an anonymous play.

Cross, K. Gustav. "The Authorship of *Lust's Dominion.*" *SP* 55 (1958):39–61. Cross reviews the authorship controversy in regard to Marlowe and Dekker, discusses the validity of vocabulary tests, and accepts the identification of the play with *The Spanish Moor's Tragedy.* Likenesses and unlikenesses in vocabulary are used to argue that the finer scenes are by Marston, who "was the first to rewrite or revise the old play":- he also "outline[d] more firmiy the characters of Eleazer and the Queen Mother, and create[d] what Bullen called its 'tragic luridness' and 'iron gloom.' " The play was further revised by Dekker, Haughton, and Day.

———. "The Vocabulary of *Lust's Dominion.*" *NM* 59 (1958): 41–48. The play is mainly by Dekker with assistance from Haughton and Day; Marston's hand is also evident. Cross cites sixty-seven words in the play which antedate the *OED*'s earliest example, and twenty-two which are not recorded.

Hoeniger, F. D. "How Significant Are Textual Parallels? A New Author for *Pericles*?" *SQ* 11 (1960):27-38. Remarkable textual parallels between *Pericles*, II.i and II.iii, and Day's plays (four of which were printed in 1606-8, three years before the first quarto of *Pericles*) suggest identical authorship. Structural features of Day's plays support the evidence of textual parallels: tragicomic plots, reconciliation of enemies brought about by the love of their children, the notion of birth and re-creation, use of a chorus, and for lost plays, dramatization of a biographical action of immense size. Extant plays solely Day's are *The Ile of Guls*, *Law-Tricks*, *Humour Out of Breath*, and *The Parliament of Bees;* he wrote *The Blind-Beggar* with Chettle, and *The Travels* with Wilkins and W. Rowley.

Crow, John. "Shakespeare Echoed." *SQ* 14 (1963):185-86. Notices an echo of *1 Henry IV* in the Prologue to the *Ile of Guls*.

Hoeniger, F. D., ed. *Pericles*. 1963. The editor of this Arden edition offers the argument made in his *SQ* article (above) that Day is the author of II.i and II.iii, and possibly of I.ii. Hoeniger carefully uses as evidence "textual parallels and close similarities in idiom and syntax"; Day's career and work is not contrary to the thesis of the argument.

Jeffs, Robin. "Introduction." In *The Works of John Day*. 1963. This reprint of Bullen's 1881 edition is meant to "fill a gap" until W. Peery publishes his promised edition. Jeffs provides the few known facts of Day's life and describes Day's lost plays (in three classes: collaborations for the Admiral's Men, 1598-1603, collaborations for Worcester's Men, 1602-3, and collaborations with Dekker after 1618). For the surviving plays, Jeffs discusses composition, performance and printing dates, place of performance, printing history, collaboration, sources, historical background, and modern editions. Full footnotes provide a survey of Day materials.

Ayres, Philip J. "The Revision of *Lust's Dominion*." *N&Q* 17 (1970):212-13. Ayres argues for original authorship in 1600 by Dekker, Day, and Haughton (Henslowe records part payment to them in February) and subsequent revision. The *Diary* entry is as likely a record of payment for an original play as for a revision. Allusions in the last five lines of the play (to the expulsion of the Spanish Moors in 1609–10) suggest a post-1610 revision (as do four passages which contain imagery recalling the Gunpowder Plot).

WILLIAM HAUGHTON

Sykes, H. Dugdale. *Sidelights on Elizabethan Drama.* 1924. Assigns Haughton a share of *Lust's Dominion* and *Patient Grissil*, and all of *Grim the Collier*.

Lawrence, W. J. *"Englishmen for My Money:* A Possible Prototype." *RES* 1 (1925):216–17. The plot and a striking piece of stage business may have been inspired by a lost play, *The Three Sisters of Mantua*.

Golding, S. R. "The Authorship of *Lust's Dominion." N&Q* 155 (1928):399–402. See entry under John Day, above.

Brereton, J. Le Gay, ed. *Lust's Dominion, or The Lascivious Queen.* 1931. See entry under John Day, above.

Thompson, D. W. "Belphegor in *Grim the Collier* and Riche's *Farewell." MLN* 50 (1935):99–102. *Grim the Collier of Croyden* is a revision of Haughton's *The Devil and His Dame. Grim* "owes its main plot to Machiavelli's novella directly." (The *Annals* lists: *"The Devil and His Dame* [prob. same as *Grim the Collier of Croydon, or The Devil and His Dame*, pub. 1662].")

Cross, K. Gustav. "The Authorship of *Lust's Dominion." SP* 55 (1958):39–61. See entry under John Day, above.

———. "The Vocabulary of *Lust's Dominion." NM* 59 (1958): 41–48. See entry under John Day, above.

Ayres, Philip J. "The Revisions of *Lust's Dominion." N&Q* 17 (1970):212–13. See entry under John Day, above.

WILLIAM RANKINS

A.D. "The Genesis of Jonson's *Epicoene." N&Q* 193 (1948):

55-56. A passage about a boy actor who feigns dumbness in Rankins's "Satyrus Peregrinans" in his *Seauen Satyres Applyed to the Weeke* (1598) may have suggested the plot of *Epicoene* to Jonson.

George, J. "A Note on William Rankins." *N&Q* 194 (1949): 420-21. The allusion to a "bard" who wrote about Merlin in Hemminges's poem "Elegy on Randolph's Finger," lines 113-16, is to Rankins, who, George surmises, might have written an early form of the play *The Birth of Merlin*, published in 1662.

SAMUEL ROWLEY

Sykes, H. Dugdale. *Sidelights on Elizabethan Drama*. 1924. In addition to *When You See Me You Know Me*, the only play published under his name, Samuel Rowley wrote all or major parts of: *The Famous Victories of Henry V, Joshua, Judas, The Taming of a Shrew*, and *Wily Beguiled*; he also wrote additions to Greene's *Orlando Furioso* and Marlowe's *Faustus*.

Oliphant, E. H. C. "Marlowe's Hand in *Arden of Feversham*: A Problem for Critics." *Criterion* 4 (1926):76-93. Marlowe wrote at least part of *Arden*; the play, however, is collaborative and Kyd and Rowley may have worked closely with Marlowe. Parts of *Arden* parallel the plot and language of *When You See Me You Know Me*.

Oliver, Leslie M. "Rowley, Foxe, and the *Faustus* Additions." *MLN* 60 (1945):391-94. William Bird and Samuel Rowley are the authors of a scene added to the 1616 quarto text of *Faustus*. Foxe's *Acts and Monuments* is a source for both this added scene and for *When You See Me You Know Me*.

Parrott, T. M. "*The Taming of a Shrew*—a New Study of an Old Play." In *Elizabethan Studies and Other Essays in Honor of George F. Reynolds*, Univ. of Colorado Studies, Ser. B. Studies in the Humanities, vol. 2, no. 4 (1945), pp. 155-65. Rowley may have written large parts of *A Shrew* and the entire plot may be his. An unidentified collaborator was also involved. [For additional discussion and references see the entry under the play title in *The Predecessors of Shakespeare*.]

Houk, Raymond A. "*Doctor Faustus* and *A Shrew*." *PMLA* 62 (1947):950-57. Rowley could have revised *A Shrew* and both the

1604 and the 1616 texts of *Faustus*. A common source could explain similarities in the revisions of *A Shrew* and *Faustus*.

―――. "Shakespeare's *Shrew* and Greene's *Orlando.*" *PMLA* 62 (1947):657-71. Rowley could have been involved in a memorial reconstruction of *Orlando*. His familiarity with Greene's play could account for the parallels to it in *A Shrew*. Sykes's attribution of *A Shrew* to Rowley is accepted and additional arguments are introduced in support of the claim.

Wilson, F. P., ed. *When You See Me You Know Me*. 1952. This edition, for the Malone Society, includes a discussion of the first edition, comments on the play's use of recent historical material, and a list of variant readings.

Carpenter, Nan Cooke. "Christopher Tye and the Musical Dialogue in Samuel Rowley's *When You See Me, You Know Me.*" *Journal of Research in Music Education* 8 (1960):85-90. The character in the play is based on the real Tye who studied at Cambridge and held doctorates from both universities.

Somerset, J. A. B. "New Facts concerning Samuel Rowley." *RES* 17 (1966):293-97. Parish records, legal papers, and Rowley's will indicate that he was respectable and prosperous. His real estate holdings were large.

―――. "William Poel's First Full Platform Stage." *Theatre Notebook* 20 (1966):118-21. Poel's 1927 production of *When You See Me You Know Me* used a full platform stage and multiple stage levels.

WILLIAM ROWLEY

Lawrence, W. J. "New Facts from Sir Henry Herbert's Office Book." *TLS*, 29 Nov. 1923, p. 82. The book has been mutilated. Malone's reading notes indicate licensing date entries of May 7, 1622 for *The Changeling* and July 9, 1623 for *The Spanish Gypsy*.

Lucas, F. L. "An Unexplained Allusion in Webster and Rowley." *TLS*, 15 April 1926, p. 283. The allusion to a ballad of the flood in *A Cure for a Cuckold* can be clarified by reference to a pamphlet

Lucas discovered in the British Museum. The play was written between 1624 and 1626.

Sykes, H. Dugdale. "The Authorship of *The Witch of Edmonton.*" *N&Q* 151 (1926):435-38, 453-57. Ford wrote most of the play; Rowley's contribution was slight. Fleay's attributions of specific parts to Ford, Dekker, and Rowley are rejected and Sykes proposes his own division of writing responsibility.

Gray, Henry David. "*A Cure for a Cuckold* by Heywood, Rowley, and Webster." *MLR* 22 (1927):389-97. The play "is mainly by Rowley, with three scenes by Webster and four by Heywood." Webster may also have revised what Rowley and Heywood wrote.

Sisson, Charles J. "*Keep the Widow Waking:* A Lost Play by Dekker." *Library* 8 (1927-28):39-57, 233-59. The play, a collaborative work by Dekker, Ford, Rowley, and Webster, closely followed a contemporary scandal involving the widow Anne Elsden; records of her libel suit furnish material for a partial reconstruction of the lost play. This material is reprinted, with minor changes, in *Lost Plays of Shakespeare's Age* (1936), pp. 80-124.

Dickson, M. J. "William Rowley." *TLS*, 28 March 1929, p. 260. Rowley was buried on 11 February 1625/26. On 16 Feb. his widow appeared before a notary to petition to be relieved of the administration of his estate.

Dunkel, Wilbur D. "Did Not Rowley Merely Revise Middleton?" *PMLA* 48 (1933):799-805. Rowley's contribution to *The Changeling, The Spanish Gypsy,* and *A Fair Quarrel* has been exaggerated. Middleton did most of the main and minor plots; Rowley was merely a skilled reviser who contributed nothing original.

Empson, William. *Some Versions of Pastoral.* 1935. The comic subplot of *The Changeling* "is woven into the tragic part very thoroughly." The madhouse action makes the audience uneasy and contributes to the play's central tension.

Sackville-West, Edward. "The Significance of *The Witch of Edmonton.*" *Criterion* 17 (1937):23-32. The 1936 Old Vic production showed the play's considerable power. Its poetry is, at times, evocative of Yeats's.

Szenczi, N. I. "The Tragi-Comedies of Middleton and Rowley." In *Essays Presented . . . to Professor A. B. Yolland, Department of English, Royal Hungarian Univ. of Sciences*, Studies in English Philology, vol. 2 (Budapest, 1937). *YWES* 18 (1937): Rowley contributed "a far larger share" of *A Fair Quarrel* than is usually recognized. In some of his *Spanish Gypsy* scenes Rowley's verse is "sweet langorous music" with a tone like Fletcher's. [Not seen.]

McKeithan, D. M. "Shakespearian Echoes in the Florimel Plot of Fletcher and Rowley's *The Maid in the Mill.*" *PQ* 17 (1938):396-98. Painter's *Palace of Pleasure* is the source of the Florimel plot; some plot changes reflect the influence of the Perdita plot in *Winter's Tale*.

Mathews, Ernst G. "The Murdered Substitute Tale." *MLQ* 6 (1945):187-95. There are oriental and medieval European analogues of the substituted-bride plot in *The Changeling*. Middleton and Rowley's immediate source was probably a novella version of the common story.

Holzknecht, Karl J. *Outlines of Tudor and Stuart Plays, 1497-1642.* 1947. Holzknecht includes outlines of *The Changeling* and *The Witch of Edmonton*.

Robb, Dewar M. "The Canon of William Rowley's Plays." *MLR* 45 (1950): 129-41. Rowley did more than simply revise the work of other playwrights but it is difficult to determine his specific contributions. Stylistic analyses are used to determine the plays Rowley wrote unaided and his shares in nineteen collaborative plays.

Engelberg, Edward. "A Middleton-Rowley Dispute." *N&Q* 198 (1953):330-32. P. G. Wiggin, *An Inquiry into the Authorship of the Middleton-Rowley Plays* (1897), is essentially correct in her assignments of the shares of the two playwrights. Her ascription of *The Changeling*, III.iv, to Rowley and several smaller assignments are doubtful.

Price, George R. "The Authorship and the Manuscript of *The Old Law.*" *HLQ* 16 (1953):117-39. Middleton wrote sixty percent of the original play and Rowley the remainder. Massinger completely revised the play in 1626 for a production by the King's Men. Copy for the 1656 quarto was a promptbook with authorial changes. The play was written in 1614 or 1615.

Holzknecht, Karl J. "The Dramatic Structure of *The Changeling.*" *RenP*, 1954, pp. 177–87. The subplot carefully parallels and amplifies the main plot; critics who regard the subplot as extraneous fail to appreciate that it, too, is concerned with changelings.

Schoenbaum, Samuel. *Middleton's Tragedies: A Critical Study.* 1955. Rowley, "a third-rate dramatist who never in his independent work gave any indication of exceptional talent," had very little influence on Middleton. Of their one collaborative tragedy, *The Changeling*, one may "conclude that Middleton is responsible for the characterization of the principal figures and the general conduct of the main action, and that he wrote the following scenes: II, i–ii; III, i–ii, iv; IV, i–ii; V, i–ii. Rowley was entrusted with the composition of the first and last scenes and the minor plot—I, i–ii; III, iii; IV, iii; V, iii."

Bawcutt, N. W., ed. *The Changeling.* 1958. The introduction to this Revels Plays edition discusses the first and selected later editions, the authors' lives, the sources, and the theatrical and critical history of the play.

Price, George R. "The Quartos of *The Spanish Gypsy* and Their Relation to *The Changeling.*" *PBSA* 52 (1958):111–25. The watermarks on the 1653 quartos of these plays are identical, despite the fact that the quartos were done by different printers. This and other bibliographical evidence suggests that the texts of the plays were together before being sent off to the printers.

Wells, Stanley W. "William Rowley and *The Golden Legend.*" *N&Q* 6 (1959):129–30. Caxton's *Golden Legend* and Deloney's *The Gentle Craft* are the probable sources of Rowley's *A Shoemaker a Gentleman.*

Hoy, Cyrus. "The Shares of Fletcher and His Collaborators in the Beaumont and Fletcher Canon (V)." *SB* 13 (1960):77–108. Hoy analyzes the shares of Fletcher and Rowley in *The Maid in the Mill*, assigns *Wit at Several Weapons* to Middleton and Rowley, and questions Rowley's authorship of *A Match at Midnight.*

Ricks, Christopher. "The Moral and Poetic Structure of *The Changeling.*" *Essays in Criticism* 10 (1960):290–306. The verbal structure of the play has linguistic and critical implications; wordplay is an important element in the play's greatness.

Shapiro, I. A. " 'Tityre-tu' and the Date of William Rowley's *Woman Never Vext.*" *RES* 11 (1960):55–56. "Tityre-tu," a reference to a Catholic fraternity, was not in use before 1623. The play can be dated 1624–25.

Wells, Stanley W. "The Lady and the Stable Groom." *N&Q* 7 (1960):31. *Wit at Several Weapons* is perhaps by Middleton and Rowley. An additional previously unnoticed parallel to *A Shoemaker a Gentleman* strengthens the case for Rowley's hand in *Wit*.

———. "Some Stage Directions in *A Shoemaker, a Gentleman.*" *N&Q* 7 (1960):337–38. Wells speculates on ways to stage the ascending and descending angel called for at the end of the first act.

Lawrence, Robert G. "A Bibliographical Study of Middleton and Rowley's *The Changeling.*" *Library* 16 (1961):37–43. The printer was unusually careful; there are few typographical errors and a collation of more than thirty copies of the 1653 quarto shows close attention to detail.

Engelberg, Edward. "Tragic Blindness in *The Changeling* and *Women Beware Women.*" *MLQ* 23 (1962):20–28. In both plays blindness is used to create "a convincing and terrifying focus."

Helton, Tinsley. "Middleton and Rowley's *The Changeling* V, iii, 175–177." *Expl* 21 (1963), item 74. The "token" in De Flores's dying words to his mistress is not his wound but the dead Alonzo's ring.

Levin, Richard. "The Lady and Her Horsekeeper: Middleton or Rowley?" *N&Q* 10 (1963):303–6. *Wit at Several Weapons* has more parallels with Middleton's *A Mad World, My Masters* and *The Family of Love* than with Rowley's *A Shoemaker a Gentleman*.

———. "The Three Quarrels of *A Fair Quarrel.*" *SP* 61 (1964): 219–31. The main plot and two subplots are not closely developed. Honor is a key concept in the main plot but not in the subplots.

Thomson, Patricia, ed. *The Changeling*. 1964. This edition, for the New Mermaid series, has a critical introduction which includes a detailed analysis of how Beatrice's increasing cynicism and guilt work to increase her attachment to De Flores.

Tomlinson, T. B. "Poetic Naturalism—*The Changeling*." *JEGP* 63 (1964):648–59. The play has "a depth of focus unique in Jacobean (and probably any other) drama." Middleton is the only dramatist of his period who was capable of great tragedy.

Huddlestone, Eugene L. "*The Spanish Gypsy* and *La Gitanilla*: An Unnoticed Borrowing." *N&Q* 12 (1965):103–4. The play's sources are *La Gitanilla* and *La Fuerza de la Sangre*. An additional borrowing from *La Gitanilla* is noted.

Kazan, Elia. "Elia Kazan Ad-Libs on *The Changeling* and Its Critics." *Show*, Jan. 1965, pp. 33–41. Kazan reflects on his production of the play at Lincoln Center. The play is tough and anarchistic and "violates the unities, all of them." The plots do not blend together in production.

Black, Matthew, ed. *The Changeling*. 1966. The edition includes a brief introduction and notes; the text is set in large type.

Schoenbaum, Samuel. *Internal Evidence and Elizabethan Dramatic Authorship: An Essay in Literary History and Method*. 1966. Schoenbaum reconsiders the attribution evidence for fourteen plays associated with Rowley.

Williams, George Walton, ed. *The Changeling*. 1966. This RRDS edition includes a short but comprehensive introduction. Williams does not see the plots as unrelated; rather, they combine to establish the play's single major theme.

Brodwin, Leonora Leet. "The Domestic Tragedy of Frank Thorney in *The Witch of Edmonton*." *SEL* 7 (1967):311–28. Frank Thorney is the best domestic tragedy hero in Elizabethan and Jacobean drama. Thorney is the work of Dekker and Ford; Rowley had no hand in those sections of the play.

Farr, Dorothy M. "*The Changeling*." *MLR* 65 (1967):586–97. The play is a bold experiment in treating the tragedy of ordinary mediocre people. The authors use the methods of comedy to broaden the scope of tragedy.

Kehler, Dorothea. "Rings and Jewels in *The Changeling.*" *ELN* 5 (1967–68):15–17. A pattern of ring and other jewelry imagery is used to establish the play's very clear moral framework.

Burelbach, Frederick M., Jr. "Middleton and Rowley's *The Changeling*, I. i, 52–56." *Expl* 26 (1968), item 60. Intuitive feeling is considered the best of the three types of knowledge involved in the play.

———. "Theme and Structure in *The Spanish Gypsy.*" *HAB* 19 (1968):37–41. Much of the play is set in an ideal pastoral world. Each of the four plots is essentially a variation of the prodigal-son theme.

Kehler, Dorothea. "Middleton and Rowley's *The Changeling*, V, iii, 175-77." *Expl* 26 (1968), item 41. Tinsley Helton's note (*Expl* 21, see above) is incorrect. The "token" De Flores refers to is not a ring but an act of intercourse he has just completed with Beatrice in Alsemero's closet.

Berger, Thomas L. "The Petrarchan Fortress of *The Changeling.*" *RenP*, 1969 (1970), pp. 37–46. The play dissects the Petrarchan metaphor of the beloved as a fortress to expose the ultimate horror at its base. Beatrice is seen as a fortress but "the metaphorical and the literal begin to become mixed and they will remain so until the deaths of Beatrice-Joanna and De Flores dissolve them."

Lake, D. J. "The *Pericles* Candidates—Heywood, Rowley, Wilkins." *N&Q* 17 (1970):135–41. Wilkins is the most likely author of the small part of the play not by Shakespeare; Rowley is the "next best candidate." The contributions of Rowley and Wilkins to *The Travels of the Three English Brothers* are also discussed.

ANTONY WADESON

Greg, W. W., ed. *Look About You, 1600*. 1913. In this Malone Society edition, Greg inclines to attribute the play to Wadeson on evidence in Henslowe's *Diary* that Wadeson was advanced money to write a play which would have been the sequel to *Look About You.*

Jones, Fred L. *"Look About You* and *The Disguises." PMLA* 44 (1929):835–41. *Look About You* is by Chettle. It and *The Disguises* are the same play for reasons of date, a vogue for multi-disguise plays, relationship to other Robin Hood plays, and appropriateness of the title. (The *Annals* lists *Look About You* as anonymous, but possibly by Chettle, Dekker, or Wadeson.)

GEORGE WILKINS

The relationship of Wilkins's novel, The Painful Adventures of Pericles, *to Shakespeare's* Pericles *results in Wilkins being mentioned in studies of and introductions to* Pericles; *the fuller discussions have been included in this list. The connections of* The Miseries of Enforced Marriage *with* A Yorkshire Tragedy *also result in Wilkins being mentioned in studies of the latter play. Fuller discussions are included here; see the essay on* A Yorkshire Tragedy *in the anonymous-plays section of this volume.*

Golding, S. R. "Day and Wilkins as Collaborators." *N&Q* 150 (1926):417–21, 436–38. See the entry under John Day, above.

Allen, Percy. *Shakespeare, Jonson, and Wilkins as Borrowers: A Study in Elizabethan Dramatic Origins and Imitations.* 1928. Wilkins wrote *Pericles*, plagiarizing extensively from Shakespeare's romances.

Clark, Arthur Melville. *Thomas Heywood: Playwright and Miscellanist.* 1931. Heywood wrote *A Yorkshire Tragedy* but not *The Miseries of Enforced Marriage*; it is probably Wilkins's. Clark argues against Sykes's use of stylistic evidence and conclusions in *Sidelights.*

Spiker, Sina. "George Wilkins and the Authorship of *Pericles." SP* 30 (1933):551–70. While Wilkins's novel *The Painful Adventures of Pericles* corresponds closely to the play, he was not thoroughly familiar with the play. He wrote the novel "with a performance in mind," following the play, but the borrowings from Twine and the "fragmentary character" of the likenesses between the novel and the play suggest that Wilkins was not one of the authors of *Pericles.*

Hastings, William T. "Exit George Wilkins." *ShAB* 11 (1936):

67-83. The arguments for Wilkins's hand in *Pericles* are examined and rejected. They include the association of the play and the novel, the type of play, the manner of *Pericles*, versification, and parallel passages.

Dickson, George B. "The Identity of George Wilkins." *ShAB* 14 (1939):195-208. A survey of Wilkins's biography: cites contemporary evidence about Wilkins's publishing activities; shows he cannot be associated with any of the Wilkins families, nor with any of the persons bearing the same name in London; corrects the date of death of a "Poet" named George Wilkins to August 19, 1603, not August 9, 1613; traces Wilkins's biography in the accounts of dramatic poets; regards 1608 as a likely date for Wilkins's death; and rejects associations of Wilkins with any of the acting companies.

McManaway, James G. "Recent Studies in Shakespeare's Chronology." *ShS* 3 (1950):22-33. Scholarship 1930-1950 generally agrees that Wilkins had no hand in *Pericles*.

Edwards, Philip. "An Approach to the Problem of *Pericles*." *ShS* 5 (1952):25-46. Wilkins's novel is a "report" of the play given by the King's Men, just as the quarto of *Pericles* is also reconstructed by two reporters; neither of the two is Wilkins.

Blayney, Glenn H. "G. Wilkins and the Identity of W. Calverley's Guardian." *N&Q* 198 (1953):329-30. Contemporary records cite Richard Gargrave as Calverley's guardian "when some of the action of *The Miseries of Inforst Mariage* and *A Yorkshire Tragedy* might have taken place." A conjectural argument attempts to explain Wilkins's confusion about the correct name of the guardian.

Maxwell, Baldwin. "Walter Calverley's Guardian and *Miseries of Enforced Marriage*." *N&Q* 198 (1953):450. Cites letters which refute Blayney (above); the letters show that Lady Gargrave was Calverley's guardian, Calverley was born later than has been thought, his wife was Sir Henry Cobham's daughter, Calverley married according to his wishes, and the letters foreshadow the tragedy. Wilkins had some correct information, but he either had misinformation or he deliberately introduced changes in the story.

Muir, Kenneth, ed. *The Painfull Aduentures of Pericles Prince of*

Tyre. 1953. Sykes is wrong in claiming "that Wilkins based a play about Pericles, before it was revised by Shakespeare, on his own novel, for there are several passages in the novel which must have been based on a play." Muir summarizes arguments about the authorship of *Pericles*; he inclines to the view that both novel and play borrow from a source play, and he does not rule out Wilkins's hand in the play.

Blayney, Glenn H. "Variants in the First Quarto of *The Miseries of Inforst Mariage.*" *Library* 9 (1954):176-84. The variants in six formes of the eight extant copies provide evidence that Wilkins's handwriting was difficult, that at least one forme, B(o), was set from Wilkins's foul papers, that he might have corrected one forme, B(o), in the printing house but not later formes, and that the possibility of minor stylistic revision is strong in the early part of the play.

———. "Field's Parody of a Murder Play." *N&Q* 2 (1955):19-20. Blayney reads a scene in Field's *A Woman Is a Weather-Cocke* as a parody of a scene in a play about enforced marriage which ends in murder. Wilkins's *Miseries* comes to mind even though it does not exactly suit Field's description, which is made "at the expense of the excesses of all murder plays."

———. "Wardship in English Drama, 1600-1650." *SP* 53 (1956): 470-84. The abuses of wardship (sales of wardships and enforced marriages) in the early seventeenth century provide the unifying social theme in *The Miseries of Enforced Marriage*. Blayney also discusses the theme in other seventeenth-century plays.

Maxwell, Baldwin. *Studies in the Shakespeare Apocrypha.* 1956. While Wilkins made use of *Two Unnatural Murthers* and *A Yorkshire Tragedy*, he possessed knowledge of the Calverley incident not supplied by them. Maxwell presents evidence against Sykes's claims about the close relationship of *Miseries of Enforced Marriage* to *A Yorkshire Tragedy*, and argues that the "peculiarities" of Wilkins's style as described by Sykes are common to many writers in the period. *Miseries* is dated not later than the first five months of 1606.

Blayney, Glenn H. "Wilkins's Revisions in *The Miseries of Inforst Mariage.*" *JEGP* 56 (1957):23-41. The revisions reveal that perhaps "Wilkins did not publish his play in a form consistent with his first and best intentions." The ending of the play is not revised from *A Yorkshire Tragedy*, but from a very different earlier and superior conclusion. In likelihood, censorship accounts for the revision of the ending.

―――. *The Miseries of Enforced Marriage, 1607.* 1963. This Malone Society edition describes the play's early printing history, the quarto used as copy text, the play's relationship to *A Yorkshire Tragedy*, and summarizes useful scholarship.

Hoeniger, F. D., ed. *Pericles.* 1963. In the Introduction to this Arden edition, Hoeniger summarizes arguments for Wilkins's share, remarking that "the evidence is just about as considerable as any internal evidence can be." Yet two points make it difficult to believe that Wilkins wrote Acts I and II: in the novel he wrote based on the play, Wilkins, a habitual plagiarist, scarcely quotes from Acts I and II at all, and some scenes in those acts "are even more closely paralleled in the works of John Day."

Wood, James O. *"Pericles,* I.ii." *N&Q* 14 (1968):141-42. Wilkins's novel—which is based on playhouse performances—is used to demonstrate the "coherence and continuity" of I.ii, widely thought to be corrupt.

Lake, D. J. "Wilkins and *Pericles*: Vocabulary (1)." *N&Q* 16 (1969):288-91. The frequency of occurrence and context of the two words "yon" and "sin" in the non-Shakespearean parts of *Pericles* are in Wilkins's manner; but in "The *Pericles* Candidates" (see below), Lake no longer regards the frequency of "yon" in Acts I-II as a "serious argument for Wilkins's authorship."

―――. "The *Pericles* Candidates: Heywood, Rowley, Wilkins." *N&Q* 17 (1970):135-41. Stylistic evidence (vocabulary and rhyme) is used to argue that Wilkins is the "most likely candidate" for the "non-Shakespearean" parts of *Pericles* (Acts I-II, parts of III, and V.ii), and that William Rowley is "apparently the next best candidate"; Heywood is excluded.

―――. "Rhymes in *Pericles.*" *N&Q* 16 (1970):139-43. Lake presents new evidence about assonances in *Pericles* I-II, parts of III, and V.ii to argue that Wilkins, not Shakespeare, Day, or Rowley, is the author.

Prior, Roger. "The Life of George Wilkins." *ShS* 25 (1972): 137-52. Hitherto unpublished information about Wilkins from the Middlesex Sessions in the Greater London Record Office (with a summary of the few facts discovered about Wilkins from other sources) enable Prior to describe Wilkins's life and character. He kept an inn (perhaps a brothel) and was often in court for theft and assault (the latter for kicking women). Prior believes Wilkins was a melancholic who "destroyed his talent in riotous living" after his prolific literary output between the ages of 28 and 32. Henry Gosson, the publisher of *Pericles*, stood bail for him once. He sometimes came before magistrate Henry Fermor, to whom Wilkins dedicated his novel on Pericles.

ROBERT YARINGTON

Golding, S. R. "The Authorship of the *Two Lamentable Tragedies.*" *N&Q* 151 (1926):347-50. Allusions support a composition date of 1594. Golding rejects Day as author and finds no evidence of Chettle's craftsmanship. The characteristics of the verse indicate a "youthful dramatist," believed to be Yarington.

Law, Robert Adger. "Further Notes on *Two Lamentable Tragedies.*" *N&Q* 153 (1927):93-94. Additional internal evidence is cited to support Golding's claim (above) of single authorship and early date.

Wagner, Bernard M. "Robert Yarrington." *MLN* 45 (1930):147-48. Greg's conjecture, that Yarington was merely the scribe, not the author, of *Two Lamentable Tragedies*, is supported by the fact that a "Robt. Yarrington junr." is recorded as a scribe in the records of the Company of Scrivenors.

Schoenbaum, S. *Internal Evidence and Elizabethan Dramatic Authorship.* 1966. Schoenbaum summarizes early speculation on the attribution of *Two Lamentable Tragedies.*

LIST OF CONTRIBUTORS

JOHN B. BROOKS is Professor of English at the University of Wisconsin—Oshkosh.

JOSEPH S. M. J. CHANG is Associate Professor of English at the University of Wisconsin—Milwaukee.

ANN HAAKER is Professor of English at California State University at Fullerton.

JAMES P. HAMMERSMITH is a Teaching Assistant and NDEA Title IV Graduate Fellow in English at the University of Wisconsin—Milwaukee.

RICHARD F. HARDIN is Associate Professor of English at the University of Kansas.

ANNE LANCASHIRE is Associate Professor of English at University College, University of Toronto.

JILL LEVENSON is Assistant Professor of English at Trinity College, University of Toronto.

DON D. MOORE is Associate Professor of English at Louisiana State University.

DENZELL S. SMITH is Professor of English at Idaho State University.

M. L. WINE is Professor of English at the University of Illinois—Chicago.

INDEX

PERSONS

INDEX

PLAYS

Alphabetization and modernized spelling follow the "Index of English Plays" in Alfred Harbage, Annals of English Drama 975-1700 *(1940; rev. S. Schoenbaum, 1964).* Long titles have frequently been abbreviated.